Springer Series in Cognitive Development

Series Editor
Charles J. Brainerd

Springer Series in Cognitive Development

Series Editor: Charles J. Brainerd

Cognitive Strategy Research
Educational Applications

Edited by
Michael Pressley and Joel R. Levin

Springer-Verlag
New York   Berlin   Heidelberg   Tokyo

Michael Pressley
Department of Psychology
University of Western Ontario
London, Ontario
Canada N6A 5C2

Joel R. Levin
Department of Educational
Psychology
and Wisconsin Center for
Education Research
University of Wisconsin
Madison, Wisconsin 53706, U.S.A.

L B
1067
.C 57
1983

Series Editor
Charles J. Brainerd
Department of Psychology
University of Western Ontario
London, Ontario
Canada N6A 5C2

With 11 Figures

Library of Congress Cataloging in Publication Data
Main entry under title:
Cognitive strategy research : educational applications.
  (Springer series in cognitive development)
  Bibliography: p.
  Includes index.
  1. Cognition in children—Addresses, essays, lectures. 2. Concept learning—Addresses,
essays, lectures. 3. Moral education—Addresses, essays, lectures. 4. Language arts—
Addresses, essays, lectures. 5. Lesson planning—Addresses, essays, lectures. I. Pressley,
Michael. II. Levin, Joel R. III. Series. [DNLM: 1. Cognition. 2. Educational psychology.
3. Learning. 4. Teaching—Methods. LB 1060 C676]
LB1067.C57 1983   370.15'2   83-642

Typeset by Ms Associates, Champaign, Illinois.
Printed and bound by R. R. Donnelley & Sons, Harrisonburg, Virginia.
Printed in the United States of America.

9 8 7 6 5 4 3 2 1

ISBN 0-387-90817-X Springer-Verlag New York Berlin Heidelberg Tokyo
ISBN 3-540-90817-X Springer-Verlag Berlin Heidelberg New York Tokyo

Series Preface

For some time now, the study of cognitive development has been far and away the most active discipline within developmental psychology. Although there would be much disagreement as to the exact proportion of papers published in developmental journals that could be considered cognitive, 50% seems like a conservative estimate. Hence, a series of scholarly books devoted to work in cognitive development is especially appropriate at this time.

The *Springer Series in Cognitive Development* contains two basic types of books, namely, edited collections of original chapters by several authors, and original volumes written by one author or a small group of authors. The flagship for the Springer Series is a serial publication of the "advances" type, carrying the subtitle *Progress in Cognitive Development Research*. Each volume in the *Progress* sequence is strongly thematic, in that it is limited to some well-defined domain of cognitive-developmental research (e.g., logical and mathematical development, development of learning). All *Progress* volumes will be edited collections. Editors of such collections, upon consultation with the Series Editor, may elect to have their books published either as contributions to the *Progress* sequence or as separate volumes. All books written by one author or a small group of authors are being published as separate volumes within the series.

A fairly broad definition of cognitive development is being used in the selection of books for this series. The classic topics of concept development, children's thinking and reasoning, the development of learning, language development, and memory development will, of course, be included. So, however, will newer areas such as social-cognitive development, educational applications, formal modeling, and philosophical implications of cognitive-developmental theory. Although it is anticipated that most books in the series will be empirical in orientation, theoretical and philosophical works are also welcome. With books of the latter sort, heterogeneity of theoretical perspective is encouraged, and no attempt will be made to foster some specific theoretical perspective at the expense of others (e.g., Piagetian versus behavioral or behavioral versus information processing).

C. J. Brainerd

Preface

This is one of two companion volumes on cognitive strategy research within the *Springer Series in Cognitive Development*. These volumes were motivated by the large number of studies in recent years on cognitive strategy training, studies that have appeared in the developmental, educational, and clinical literatures. The present volumes summarize much of the most important work on the topic, juxtaposing diverse applications and theoretical perspectives. We hope that by bringing together so many different approaches, the volumes will promote general knowledge about strategies that will integrate future research and practice.

The chapters are broadly grouped into developmental, educational, and treatment-related contributions. This volume is directed specifically toward educational applications of cognitive strategy research. As editors, we have provided introductory comments for each of the three major sections of the book. Readers interested in quickly identifying the major themes developed in the volume should begin with these introductions.

The authors were not asked to provide exhaustive reviews of research. Instead, we wanted them to summarize exemplary research studies and programs of research. In doing so, authors were requested to provide a discussion of what the term *strategy* meant in their particular domain. Authors were also asked to present a brief historical account of strategy research in their area, and to suggest future research directions. We are most pleased with the result.

In order to promote continuity from chapter to chapter, and to assist readers in identifying themes that cut across chapters, we inserted cross-references in each contribution to other chapters in the two volumes. In many ways this was a difficult task for us because of the many potential interconnections that could have been built, and because we did not want to clutter the chapters with cross-references. Thus, we inserted only what we regarded as the most relevant citations across the two volumes, which appear in the authors' running text.

Michael Pressley's participation was supported in part by a grant from the Natural Sciences and Engineering Research Council of Canada. Editorial work on this book was supported partially by a grant to Joel Levin from the National Institute of Education through the Wisconsin Center for Education Research. We also wish to acknowledge the encouragement and assistance of the Series Editor, Charles Brainerd, and the staff of Springer-Verlag.

Joel R. Levin
Michael Pressley

Contents

Contributors

Diane M. Borwick Department of Psychology, University of Waterloo, Waterloo, Ontario, Canada N2L 3G1.

Charles J. Brainerd Department of Psychology, University of Western Ontario, London, Ontario, Canada N6A 5C2.

Irwin S. Butkowsky Family Court Clinic, Clarke Institute of Psychiatry, Toronto, Ontario, Canada M4W 2J4.

Linda Cook Department of Psychology, University of California, Davis, California 95616, U.S.A.

W. Patrick Dickson Department of Child and Family Studies, University of Wisconsin, Madison, Wisconsin 53706, U.S.A.

Robert D. Enright Department of Educational Psychology, University of Wisconsin, Madison, Wisconsin 53706, U.S.A.

D. L. Forrest-Pressley Psychology Department, Children's Psychiatric Research Institute, London, Ontario, Canada N6A 4G6.

Laurie A. Gillies Department of Psychology, Dalhousie University, Halifax, Nova Scotia, Canada B3H 4J1

Daniel K. Lapsley Department of Educational Psychology, University of Wisconsin, Madison, Wisconsin 53706, U.S.A.

Joel R. Levin Department of Educational Psychology and Wisconsin Center for Education Research, University of Wisconsin, Madison, Wisconsin 53706, U.S.A.

Victor M. Levy, Jr. Department of Educational Psychology, University of Wisconsin, Madison, Wisconsin 53706, U.S.A.

Richard E. Mayer Department of Psychology, University of California, Santa Barbara, California 93106, U.S.A.

Allan Paivio Department of Psychology, University of Western Ontario, London, Ontario, Canada N6A 5C2.

Penelope L. Peterson Department of Educational Psychology and Wisconsin Center for Education Research, University of Wisconsin, Madison, Wisconsin 53706, U.S.A.

Michael Pressley Department of Psychology, University of Western Ontario, London, Ontario, Canada N6A 5C2.

Susan R. Swing Department of Educational Psychology and Wisconsin Center for Education Research, University of Wisconsin, Madison, Wisconsin 53706, U.S.A.

Dale M. Willows Department of Curriculum, Ontario Institute for Studies in Education, Toronto, Ontario, Canada M5S 1V6.

Part I
Strategy Training of Piagetian Concepts

Piagetian theory revolutionized cognitive development, providing many general and specific hypotheses for education. The first three chapters in this volume are concerned with problems that were first introduced to psychology and education via the Genevan school of thought. At the same time, the chapters reveal that traditional Piagetian conceptions are not as adequate at explaining strategy effects in these domains as are contemporary information processing approaches to cognition. In fact, the Piagetians largely rejected the idea that training could positively affect children's cognitions—a position that is now untenable given the abundance of positive strategy-training effects reviewed in the present chapters.

Brainerd provides a historical review of research on training Piagetian logical concepts (most notably conservation). He identifies three phases. At first, consistent with Piagetian-theoretic notions, it was assumed that Piagetian concepts could not be trained, a position supported by early training experiments. During a second phase, a number of more soundly designed experiments appeared in which positive training effects occurred, and thus opinion shifted to a more positive evaluation of training. In the most recent phase, researchers have searched for developmental limits to training. Also, the training of many more Piagetian concepts has occurred, with strategy-training hypotheses for Piagetian concepts springing from diverse theoretical orientations (e.g., social learning theory). Brainerd reviews a number of specific strategies that have facilitated the acquisition of Piagetian logical concepts. These include perceptual, cognitive, social, and question-answering strategies. Brainerd concludes his chapter with speculations about the relevance of the work reviewed to information processing models of cognitive development, especially working-memory models.

In addition to logical concepts, Piaget offered discussion of children's social cognitions. Dickson reviews research on one aspect of this domain, namely, children's communication skills. Just as Piaget was pessimistic about training logical concepts, he also assumed that young children's egocentrism would pervade their communications with other children—a point of view that predominated in the early research on children's referential communication. Although the research literature on the topic is small, Dickson has identified several strategy-training approaches that have resulted in improving children's communication skills. He also considers the dearth of data on naturalistic referential communications and the kind of research that should be conducted to fill this void. Dickson provides a strong argument for more careful task analyses in referential communication research, offering critiques of some recent and prominent studies that have failed to produce general improvements in children's communications after specific strategy training. He also reviews critically the potential role of metacognition in referential communications. Dickson concludes with a discussion of emerging educational directions in the referential-communication field, including the potential of children interacting with "talking" microcomputers.

Enright, Lapsley, and Levy review strategy approaches to moral education. After discussing briefly the most prominent theory of moral cognition—Kohlberg's elaboration of Piaget's theory—the authors consider the five most promising strategies for moral education that have been studied to date. Three strategies appear to be effective: The *plus-one* technique was derived from traditional cognitive-development theory, and involves presenting material just beyond the child's current cognitive level; the *deliberate psychological education* approach includes teaching communication skills, counseling techniques, and role playing; the third effective approach (*information processing*) is derived from a process analysis of social and moral cognition. On the other hand, Enright and his colleagues conclude that *didactic* approaches have not been effective in promoting moral cognitive growth. That is, teaching ethics, social studies, civil rights issues, prejudice issues, and the like do not promote moral growth. A fifth approach, based on Kohlberg's theory, is termed the *just community* strategy. It is hypothesized that living in a truly democratic society should increase moral cognition. Unfortunately, the strategy has not been tested enough to evaluate its efficacy, although there exist some data suggesting that this ambitious approach to moral education may prove effective. Throughout their commentary, Enright, Lapsley, and Levy offer extensive criticism of previous work in this area, as well as an abundance of suggestions for future research.

1. Varieties of Strategy Training in Piagetian Concept Learning

Charles J. Brainerd

Occasionally, the proscriptions of a theory have more influence on the behavior of scientists than do its positive predictions (see Chapter 2 for additional comments about this phenomenon). A situation of this sort occurred some two decades ago in connection with what Piagetian theory anticipates about the laboratory learning of its stage-related concepts. At that time it was widely supposed that the theory predicts no learning effects. Although this interpretation was not entirely accurate, it was correct in spirit, and it spawned a large number of learning experiments on Piagetian concepts, especially the concrete-operational concepts of middle childhood. What began as some modest attempts to assess the trainability of conservation ultimately blossomed into a substantial literature containing multiple experiments on concepts such as perspective taking (e.g., Cox, 1977; Iannotti, 1978), seriation (e.g., Bingham-Newman & Hooper, 1974; Coxford, 1964), identity (e.g., Hamel & Riksen, 1973; Litrownik, Franzini, Livingston, & Harvey, 1978), proportionality (e.g., Brainerd, 1971; Brainerd & Allen, 1971b), isolation of variables (e.g., Case, 1974; Siegler, Liebert, & Liebert, 1973), ordinal and cardinal number (e.g., Brainerd, 1973, 1974b), subjective moral reasoning (e.g., Arbuthnot, 1975; Jensen & Larm, 1970; also Chapter 3 in this volume) and many others. In fact, I would venture to say that there is no concept that figures prominently in Piaget's summary writings on his stages (e.g., Piaget, 1970; Piaget & Inhelder, 1969) that has not been subjected to training in several experiments.

My concern in this chapter is to discuss selected aspects of this literature that are particularly relevant to the aims of this volume. As there have now been two decades of experimentation, the time seems ripe for a brief historical synopsis. This is the topic of the first section. The second section is the core of the chapter.

Research dealing with four categories of strategy training that have proved particularly effective with Piagetian concepts (perceptual strategies, cognitive strategies, social strategies, and question-answering strategies) is reviewed. In the third and final section, I attempt to straighten out a nagging conceptual problem in this literature, the problem of equivalent routes to conceptual understanding, using working-memory analysis.

Historical Prologue

Slicing a literature into historical stages is, of course, open to the criticism that any conceivable segmentation will be arbitrary in some degree. Nevertheless, there are certain landmarks in this literature that make it convenient to think in terms of an early phase, running from 1959 to 1963; a middle phase, running from 1964 to 1971; and a late phase, running from 1972 to the present. As we shall see, the issues of principal concern to experimenters have been rather different during each of these periods.

You Can't Train It: 1954-1963

Piagetian concept-learning research may be properly said to have begun with two pilot studies conducted in Geneva during the late 1950s, although the investigators were not themselves Genevans. Both studies, one by Smedslund and the other by Wohlwill, were summarized in the ninth volume of Piaget's *Etudes d'Epistémologie Génétique* (Smedslund, 1959; Wohlwill, 1959). Wohlwill subsequently replicated his study with larger numbers of subjects and more controlled procedures (Wohlwill & Lowe, 1962). Smedslund's study led to an ambitious series of experiments in which Piaget's views on learning were contrasted with the predictions of other theories (Smedslund, 1961a, 1961b, 1961c, 1961d, 1961e).

In view of the pivotal status of conservation in Piagetian theory, both lines of research were concerned with conservation learning. Wohlwill attempted to train number conservation. He studied the effects of three procedures (feedback, rule instruction, and perceptual set) on nonconservers of number. There was no evidence of learning; the posttest performance of trained children was not significantly better than that of untrained controls. Smedslund attempted to train conservation of mass and weight. In two initial experiments, he studied the effects of direct reinforcement of conserving responses and conserving rules (Smedslund, 1961b) and the effects of extinction of irrelevant cues (Smedslund, 1961c) on conservation of weight. As in Wohlwill's research, none of these treatments was effective; there were no significant posttest differences between experimentals and controls. These negative findings were widely interpreted as surprising from the standpoint of then-current learning theories.

In the first authoritative secondary source on Piagetian theory, Flavell (1963) reviewed the Smedslund and Wohlwill experiments, together with some other early studies (Churchill, 1958a, 1958b; Harker, 1960). Following the review, he commented:

> What can be concluded from all these experiments? Probably the most certain conclusion is that it can be a surprisingly difficult undertaking to manufacture Piagetian concepts in the laboratory. Almost all the training methods reported impress one as sound and reasonable and well-suited to the educative job at hand. And yet most of them have had remarkably little success in producing cognitive change. It is not easy to convey the sense of disbelief that creeps over one in reading these experiments. . . . There is more than a suspicion from present evidence that when one does succeed in inducing some behavioral change through this or that training procedure, it may not cut very deep. (p. 377)

Subsequent experiments have shown these pessimistic interpretations to have been premature—but not in the minds of Genevan authors. Despite the massive evidence of positive learning effects in later experiments, even the most recent Genevan writings on learning cite these early studies as grounds for the conclusion that Piagetian concepts can be accelerated only under very restricted conditions and within very narrow limits. For example, Sinclair (1973) has remarked that

> these experiments were undertaken . . . to see whether the providing of information from the outside—that is to say, giving the child the opportunity for verification of the predicted outcome of an action—could change the child's reasoning. . . . Strictly empirical epistemological tenets were to be applied to the learning of cognitive structures. Almost universally the results were negative. . . . Empirical methods, whereby the subject has to accept a link between events because the link is imposed on him, do not result in progress. (p. 57)

Yes You Can: 1964–1971

Workers other than Flavell were plagued by a "sense of disbelief" about the results of the early experiments, and studies published during the middle phase were motivated in large measure by this reaction. The middle phase begins with the appearance of the first successful training experiment following Flavell's (1963) review, a conservation-learning study by Wallach and Sprott (1964). It culminates with the publication, within a few months of each other, of three independent literature reviews (Beilin, 1971; Brainerd & Allen, 1971a; Goldschmid, 1971). Naturally, the authors differed on many fine points of interpretation. However, the reviews themselves seemed to leave little doubt that concrete-operational concepts—more particularly, conservation concepts—could be (a) dramatically improved by a variety of procedures that Genevans view as being based on "strictly empirical epistemological tenets" and (b) could be trained by the same procedures that proved ineffective in Smedslund's and Wohlwill's experiments.

Although the mere trainability of Piagetian concepts was, at least in retrospect, the central question of the middle phase, some interesting secondary themes soon emerged. Perhaps the most important one dealt with the breadth and generality of learning effects. Thanks to the belief engendered by early experiments that training effects "may not cut very deep," an experiment was not generally regarded as having demonstrated "true concept learning" unless experimental-control differences were observed in something more than posttest performance on items measuring the trained concept. In addition, it was thought that trained subjects should show certain types of transfer, should be able to give satisfactory explanations of their posttest answers, and should show long-term retention. Two types of transfer posttests were administered most often: near transfer (items measuring the concept that was trained but using slightly different materials than during training) and far transfer (items measuring a concept that was different than the one that was trained but was related to it in some way). If number conservation were trained, for example, far transfer items would consist of posttests for other conservation concepts (length, mass, etc.). Concerning the second index of generality of training effects, subjects were required to provide logical explanations of the sort given by children who have already acquired the concept "naturally." Concerning the third index, subjects were required to show retention across intervals of at least a few days following training.

Some of the initial experiments reported during the middle phase left some uncertainty as to whether all of these criteria could be met. With respect to transfer, for example, far transfer was obtained in a few experiments (e.g., Gelman, 1969; Sullivan, 1967) but it was absent from most studies (see Brainerd & Allen, 1971a). Insofar as explanations were concerned, a dissertation experiment by Gruen (1965) seemed to show that whereas trained children gave more accurate answers on posttest items, they could not explain these answers any better than control children. Still other experiments suggested that experimental-control differences vanish after a few days. By 1971, however, the positive evidence on all three criteria was too extensive to be dismissed. For example, Emrick (1967), Gelman (1969), and Goldschmid (1968) reported experiments in which training some specific concept produced large near and far transfer effects, produced large experimental-control differences in explanations, and produced training effects that were stable a few days to several months after training.

What Can You Train and How Can You Train It? 1972–Present

Since the early 1970s, the literature has become much more pluralistic. The evidence of pluralism is both empirical and theoretical. Empirically, learning research has been focused on a much broader range of Piagetian concepts. Although some experiments on concepts other than conservation had been reported prior to 1971 (e.g., Coxford, 1964), nearly all of the literature available at that time was on conservation learning (cf. Beilin, 1971). Consequently, almost the entire data base on the learning of other concepts has accumulated very recently. Theoretically, whereas experimentation during the early and middle phases was, with few exceptions (e.g., Bruner, Olver, & Greenfield, 1966), dominated by Piaget's ideas, other theoretical accounts of concept learning (e.g., behavior modification) have been under active study lately. (The historical progression in referential communication presented by Dickson in Chapter 2 parallels the advances outlined here.)

Despite this healthy proliferation of new themes and directions, two questions have predominated in much of the recent literature: (a) What are the developmental limits of concept training? (b) What training methods derived from theories other than Piaget's are effective (Chapter 3 offers more on this topic)? I consider these questions separately.

Limits of Trainability. The first question is significant because implicitly it asks: To what extent can the results of concept-training experiments be reconciled with orthodox Piagetian theory? Although it was originally supposed, at least in North America, that the theory predicts negligible learning effects, some clarifications by Genevan authors during the late 1960s (e.g., Inhelder & Sinclair, 1969; Inhelder, Sinclair, Bovet, & Smock, 1966) suggested that the theory's constraints on learning were less severe. Specifically, it became clear that what the theory actually predicts is, first, that children will not be able to learn a concept that is clearly above their current stage of cognitive development and, second, that children's tendency to benefit from training will increase as they approach the stage at which the to-be-trained concept "spontaneously" appears. An illustration of the first prediction is that it should not be possible to teach truly preoperational children to conserve. An illustration of the second prediction is that it should be easier to teach children to conserve if they are in the transition phase between preoperations and concrete operations than if they are still preoperational. Two lines of attack on each prediction have been developed.

1. Evidence on the First Prediction. There is a preliminary conceptual obstacle to testing either prediction. Note that the term *stage* appears in both proposals. Since stage is a hypothetical construct, it is not open to direct measurement. Hence, we are confronted with the familiar problem of finding some measurable variable that can be substituted, with the usual strategy in psychological research being to substitute a variable that presumably is monotonically related to the hypothetical construct (e.g., Krantz & Tversky, 1972). Two such variables, pretest performance on the to-be-trained concept and age, have been studied, and they delimit the two lines of attack on the first prediction.

Concerning the pretest performance variable, suppose that we sought to test the first prediction in a conservation-learning experiment. Piagetian theory explains the appearance of conservation concepts on the ground that children have attained the concrete-operational stage. Hence, pretest performance on conservation concepts qualifies as a measure of attainment of concrete operations. More particularly, according to the theory, any child who fails an extensive battery of conservation items across the board is preoperational. It follows from the first prediction that conservation learning should be poor in such subjects.

Concerning the age variable, suppose that we are still attempting to test the first prediction in a conservation-learning experiment. An even simpler approach is to consider the nominal age ranges for preoperations and concrete operations. Although Genevan authors have stressed that the 2-7 and 7-11 ranges for preoperations and concrete operations, respectively, are only averages (e.g., Inhelder, 1956), hardly anyone inside or outside Geneva would object to the notion that samples of children from the first half of the 2-7 range are truly preoperational; otherwise, the norms make no sense. Hence, preschool children, like children who fail conservation pretests across the board, should be essentially impossible to train.

The data on both the pretest performance variable and the age variable are clear and consistent: The first prediction is wrong. Concerning pretest performance, a large number of experiments, most of them on conservation, have been reported in which children who showed no evidence of the to-be-trained concept on the pretest nevertheless showed dramatic improvement on posttests. Some early examples from the post-1971 period include Murray (1972), Rosenthal and Zimmerman (1972), and Zimmerman and Rosenthal (1974a). It should also be noted that the learning effects observed in these experiments were satisfactorily general—that is, near transfer, far transfer, improved explanations, and long-term retention were all demonstrated. Concerning age, although the number of concept-learning experiments with preschoolers is still modest in comparison to those with older children, the absolute number is sufficiently large to permit prudent conclusions. These studies show that, for conservation at least, it is possible to produce durable and generalized concept learning in preschoolers. Depending on design features, the data of one or more preschool experiments provide credible evidence of near transfer (e.g., Bucher & Schneider, 1973), far transfer (e.g., Brainerd, 1974a), improved explanations (e.g., Denney, Zeytinoglu, & Selzer, 1977), and long-term retention across intervals ranging from several days (e.g., Zimmerman & Lanaro, 1974) to a few months (e.g., Field, 1981).

2. Evidence on the Second Prediction. According to the second prediction, concept learning covaries as children approach the target stage. Once again, we need to replace "stage" with a measurable variable before the prediction can be tested. The two variables that have been used in most experiments are pretest variations in performance on the to-be-trained concept and pretest variations in skills that are known to be closely related to the to-be-trained concept.

The rationale for the first variable is simple. As Piagetian theory explains the emergence of new concepts in terms of the attainment of higher stages, children who differ in pretest performance on the to-be-trained concept presumably also differ in their respective stages. Thus, there should be a monotonic-increasing relationship of some sort between level of pretest performance and level of learning. The rationale for the second variable is somewhat more complicated. In Piagetian theory, certain concepts are always prerequisites for other concepts. In the case of conservation, for example, normative data (e.g., Blanchard, 1975; Brainerd, 1976, 1977b; Curcio, Kattef, Levine, & Robbins, 1972; Siegler, 1981) indicate that there are several conservation-related rules that appear in most children's thinking before the conservation concepts themselves. The most familiar examples are qualitative identity (e.g., Papalia & Hooper, 1970), quantitative identity (e.g., Cowan, 1979), reversibility (e.g., Murray & Johnson, 1969), and compensation (e.g., Silverman & Rose, 1982). According to the theory, acquisition of these rules defines transitional steps in the acquisition of conservation. Likewise, the acquisition of prerequisite rules for other concepts (e.g., classification, seriation) defines transitional steps in the acquisition of these concepts. Therefore, we again expect a monotonic-increasing relationship between pretest performance and learning, except that here we are concerned with pretest performance on rules that are prerequisites for the to-be-trained concept rather than pretest performance on the concept itself.

Until recently, the data on these two variables appeared to be contradictory. Experiments involving the second variable appeared to argue against a stage-learning correlation. In such experiments, the strategy was to look for an Aptitude X Treatment interaction, where the Aptitude variable was pretest knowledge of certain rules. Assuming that subjects are equated for their pretest knowledge of the to-be-trained concept, the essential idea was that experimental-control differences should interact with Aptitude such that these differences should increase as Aptitude increases. By and large, such interactions have not been observed (see Brainerd, 1976, 1977b; Silverman & Rose, 1982). I shall return to these experiments later in the section on rule training. On the other hand, experiments involving the first variable seemed to confirm a stage-learning correlation. Beginning with two experiments published within a year of each other, one on seriation learning by Coxford (1964) and the other on conservation learning by Beilin (1965), several studies appeared in which the authors concluded that children with higher pretest scores on the to-be-trained concept were more likely to profit from training than children with lower pretest scores. In addition to seriation, experiments leading to similar conclusions were reported on other concrete-operational concepts (e.g., Kuhn, 1972; Youniss, 1971). In these studies, the evidence presented in favor of a stage-learning correlation usually consisted of various correlations between pretest scores and posttest scores of trained subjects. That is, children with higher pretest scores were said to be "more likely to profit from training" if they also had higher posttest scores.

Fortunately, it turns out that the data on the first and second variables are not actually inconsistent with each other. In a review of experiments on the first variable (Brainerd, 1977a), an elementary statistical artifact was noted, namely, that pretest-posttest correlations do not provide a valid test of stage-learning relationships because they are contaminated by the reliability of the tests. Regardless of the true underlying relationship between pretest knowledge and learning, a positive correlation between pre- and posttest scores is more or less guaranteed if the tests are reliable. When pretest-posttest relationships in earlier experiments were corrected for reliability, there appeared to be no correlation between pretest knowledge and susceptibility to training (see Brainerd, 1977a, Table 1). Since this reliability confound was pointed out, some further experiments have been reported that are not subject to the confound (Brainerd, 1979; May & Norton, 1981; White, 1981). The evidence from these studies is also negative. Thus, the respective literatures on both the first and second variables do not provide any consistent support for a stage-learning correlation.

Alternate Theories. In addition to sifting through Piagetian predictions, another goal of recent research has been to determine whether other theories can do as good or better a job of accounting for the acquisition of given concepts. This question has been extensively investigated, especially as regards conservation. The standard approach has been to use some well-established learning theory to formulate an acquisition scenario for some target concept. Experiments are then conducted wherein trained subjects receive experiences of the type deemed to be essential in the model. The logic of these experiments was aptly summarized in a review by Glaser and Resnick (1972): "The assumption behind such a research strategy for isolating the components of conservation is that if a hypothesized underlying process is trained and if this results in successful learning of conservation, then the trained process is crucial to the conservation concept" (p. 236).

For the most part, the training experiences that have been studied in such experiments are strategic in nature. I now consider the four categories of strategy training that account for the bulk of the literature.

Forms of Effective Strategic Experience

The specific types of training to be considered in this section are perceptual strategies, cognitive strategies, social strategies, and question-answering strategies. For each type of training, I begin by summarizing its theoretical rationale. Next, the actual mechanics of training treatments and some illustrative findings are summarized. Last, possible limitations of such treatments are reviewed.

Perceptual Strategies

Training in perceptual strategies is rooted in the attentional theories of discrimination learning that were popular during the 1960s. The original aim of such theories was to explain how simple concept identification tasks are solved by infrahumans (e.g., Lovejoy, 1966), human adults (e.g., Bower & Trabasso, 1964), and children (e.g., Zeaman & House, 1963). The hypothesis that is common to most of these theories is that a two-step process, consisting of learning to pay attention to the relevant dimension followed by acquisition of instrumental responses along that dimension, is involved. For example, suppose that subjects are administered a four-dimensional simultaneous discrimination, with the dimensions of stimulus variation being shape (circle or triangle), size (large or small), brightness (black or white), and position (left or right). Suppose that black stimuli are always winners. According to attentional theorists, the subject may or may not be paying attention to brightness at the start of the problem. (Research on "dimensional sensitivity" shows that most human subjects will be attending to shape or size at the outset.) If not, the subject must learn to attend to brightness and ignore other cues. Once this is accomplished, the subject must learn the specific instrumental responses for the two brightness cues, that is, black = winner and white = loser rather than black = loser and white = winner. Finally, attentional theorists view the initial (learning-to-attend) stage as far more important and time consuming than the second stage. In fact, the second stage is often regarded as a one-trial all-or-none event (cf. Trabasso & Bower, 1968).

Trabasso (1968) and others observed that children who fail conservation problems, like children who have not yet solved a concept identification item, may simply be attending to the wrong stimulus dimensions. The explanation protocols for nonconservers provide some anecdotal support for this interpretation. Nonconservers of number, for example, will typically refer to the irrelevant dimensions of length and density in their explanations. Similarly, nonconservers of liquid quantity typically refer to the irrelevant dimensions of height and width in their explanations. If nonconservation is simply a product of misdirected attention, then procedures that extinguish the tendency to pay attention to irrelevant dimensions should transform nonconservers into conservers.

Actually, this possibility had been explored some years earlier in an experiment by Smedslund (1961c), who attempted to extinguish the tendency of nonconservers of weight to attend to the size of an object by using prediction-outcome feedback. Although such training failed to improve conservation, the absence of a number of elementary methodological precautions (e.g., screening children for their understanding of how the experimental apparatus worked) render the data uninterpretable (Brainerd, 1978; Hatano, 1971).

The first successful attempts to improve conservation by redirecting the attention of nonconservers were twin doctoral dissertation experiments conducted in 1967 by two of Trabasso's students, J. Emrick and R. Gelman. Since only Gelman's experiment was subsequently published (Gelman, 1969), Emrick's results are not well known. Except for the subjects that were studied, the two experiments were very similar. Gelman (1969) trained kindergarten nonconservers, whereas Emrick (1967) trained preschool nonconservers. The training trials themselves focused on attentional skills that are ostensibly connected to number conservation and length conservation. On half the trials, subjects were shown triads of stimuli, with each stimulus consisting of a row of dots. The three stimuli varied along three dimensions, namely, number of dots per row, length of each row, and distance between dots (density). On each trial, the subject was asked to make a number-based response (e.g., select the two rows that have the same number) rather than a length-based or a density-based response. Correct responses were rewarded. On the other half of the trials, subjects were shown triads of stimuli in which each stimulus was a straight line. These stimuli varied in length and position, and the subjects were rewarded for making length-based responses.

Although this general procedure was very similar to an unsuccessful perceptual training method in an earlier experiment by Beilin (1965), it proved to be highly effective. In Gelman's experiment, kindergarten nonconservers of number and length showed virtually perfect performance on tests for these concepts that were administered 2-3 weeks after training. Correct number and length answers were almost always accompanied by correct explanations. Further, roughly 60% transfer to two untrained conservation concepts (liquid quantity and mass) was observed. Analogous results were obtained in Emrick's study. On posttests administered 2-3 weeks after training, correct responses occurred on approximately three quarters of the number and length tests. The amount of far transfer to untrained mass and liquid quantity concepts was about 41%. Thus, training a simple perceptual strategy (pay attention to the relevant dimension) proved to be a powerful inducer of conservation in both preschoolers and kindergartners.

Despite the size of the learning effects in these two studies, the existence of previous negative results (Beilin, 1965; Smedslund, 1961c) makes replication data desirable. Fortunately, such data are available in ample supply. The triad method has been used in several subsequent experiments, some with elementary schoolers (e.g., May & Tisshaw, 1975) and some with preschoolers (e.g., Field, 1981). Large learning effects for conservation concepts have been consistently reported.

A remaining question about this method of training is whether or not it actually affects what children pay attention to. Note that so far the evidence that nonconservers attend to the wrong things and that children who have been trained by the foregoing technique attend to the correct things is all indirect. The former assumption is based on the tendency of nonconservers' responses to correlate strongly with irrelevant aspects of the stimuli, and the latter assumption is based on the fact that this correlation disappears after nonconservers have been trained. However, we would be on safer ground if it could be shown that (a) conservers and nonconservers actually *look at* different aspects of stimuli and (b) the visual behavior of nonconservers becomes like that of conservers after training. Data of this sort were obtained in an interesting experiment by Boersma and Wilton (1974).

Boersma and Wilton used the Emrick-Gelman procedure to train conservation in nonconserving elementary schoolers. Following training, the subjects were administered posttests for number conservation, length conservation, liquid quantity conservation, and mass conservation. In addition, their eye movements were filmed during the conservation posttests. The same posttests were administered to a matched sample of nonconservers who had not received attentional training, and their eye movements were filmed. As usual, large differences favoring the experimental group were obtained on posttests for all four concepts. However, there were also differences in the eye movements of the two groups. Trained conservers tended to explore the stimuli much more thoroughly than nonconservers did. Also, there was considerably more perceptual centration in the control subjects. In short, these data suggest that attentional training does in fact affect children's visual analysis of stimuli and that there are conserver-nonconserver differences in the perceptual strategies that children apply to stimuli.

Turning to criticisms, we find that the major objection to attentional analyses of Piagetian concepts is their lack of generality. On the one hand, it is absurd to maintain, as Piagetian authors have occasionally done, that attentional training is not a powerful method of improving conservation performance. A massive amount of data argues otherwise. There are also certain other Piagetian concepts that appear susceptible to attentional interpretations, with infant object concepts (e.g., Cornell, 1981) and spatial perspective taking (e.g., Cox, 1977) being the most promising candidates. On the other hand, there is a far larger group of Piagetian concepts that does not seem to lend itself to attentional analysis. For example, there is one especially large group of concepts, which includes such things as transitive inference (e.g., Trabasso, 1977) and probability judgment (e.g., Brainerd, 1981), where failures in children's short-term memory hardware appear to be the critical variables. There is another large group of concepts, which includes such things as class inclusion and causal inference, where the most important factor seems to be the absence of certain rules. It appears quite improbable that the assumptions of attentional theories of discrimination learning can be stretched to cover such phenomena.

Cognitive Strategies

The second category of strategic manipulations is the one that is most closely related to Piagetian theory. The key idea is that performance on concept tests is an instance of rule-governed behavior, and for that reason, poor performance on such tests means that incorrect rules are being applied. It follows that one should be able to improve performance by training children on the appropriate rules. Although Piaget's co-workers have occasionally objected to rule inculcation on the ground that it is tantamount to "coercion" (Inhelder, Sinclair, & Bovet, 1974), all of the training experiments that have come out of Geneva to date have involved procedures designed to transmit rules (cf. Inhelder et al., 1966).

As the bulk of literature is concerned with training concrete- and formal-operational concepts, it is important to note at the outset that the evidence that performance on tests for these concepts is, in some sense, rule governed is overwhelming. For one thing, the pattern of responses by children who perform poorly is almost never random. However, the most direct findings come from two sources, explanations and nonverbal rule assessment. Concerning explanations, three general results are of interest. First, children normally describe very simple rules when they are asked to explain their answers on Piagetian concept tests. For example, a child who says automobiles are alive on an animism test may simply reply, "It moves," when asked to explain. This rule, though incorrect, is nevertheless an algorithm for classifying objects as animate or inanimate. Second, children who give different answers on the same test describe different rules. For example, a child who says that automobiles are *not* alive may explain this response on the ground that "it does not move by itself," but not on the ground that "it moves." Last, children rarely describe multiple rules in their explanations; they tend to focus on one. For example, a conserver of number who explains his or her answer by saying "They had the same number to begin with" (reversibility rule) will probably not also say "Nothing was added or taken away" (addition/subtraction rule).

The other source of direct evidence on rules comes from the nonverbal rule assessment technique that has been extensively used by Siegler and his associates (e.g., Siegler, 1981; Siegler & Richards, 1979). Here, patterns of choice responses on a sequence of items are used to infer rules. The same three findings observed with explanations are also obtained: Stable patterns are observed for virtually all subjects; the patterns are different for children who perform differently on the target concept test; and only one pattern is typically observed for individual children.

The first successful concept-learning experiments published in North America were rule-training studies concerned with conservation. Generally speaking, one of two methods has been used to transmit relevant rules: visual demonstration, a technique pioneered by Wallach (Wallach & Sprott, 1964; Wallach, Wall, & Anderson, 1967); and verbal description, a technique pioneered by Beilin (1965, 1969). In Wallach's original study (Wallach & Sprott, 1964), the objective was to induce nonconservers of number to conserve by exposing them to the reversibility rule. During the training trials, the materials consisted of rows of objects for which there was a close functional connection between the objects in different rows (e.g., a row of dolls and a row of doll beds). Perceptual transformations of these rows were carried out with a view toward encouraging children to notice that the original element-by-element correspondence between the two rows (e.g., one doll sleeping in each bed) could always be reinstated after the transformations.

The verbal-rule method typically involves giving instruction in more than one rule simultaneously. For example, in Beilin's (1965) original study, nonconservers received a series of training trials on which tests for conservation of number and length were administered. Following the subject's response to a given item, the experimenter gave a detailed statement of reversibility and identity rules. A verbal-rule treatment in a later study by Smith (1968) contained three rules. During the training trials, nonconservers of weight were administered tests of weight conservation. Whenever an answer was incorrect, the experimenter delivered the following statement: "If we start with an object like this one [indicating the stimulus that had not been transformed] and we don't put any pieces of plasticine on it or take any pieces away from it [addition/subtraction rule], then it still weighs the same even though it looks different [quantitative identity rule]. See, I can make it back into a . . . so it hasn't really changed [reversibility rule]" (p. 520).

There are a total of five rules that conservers most frequently cite to justify their answers: (a) reversibility (what can be done can be undone); (b) compensation (perceptual transformations in one dimension are compensated by perceptual transformations in some other dimension); (c) qualitative identity (the transformed stimulus is the "same object" as before); (d) quantitative identity (the transformed stimulus is the "same amount" as before); (e) addition/subtraction (only the addition or subtraction of matter affects quantitative relationships between objects). Successful learning experiments using visual demonstration or verbal statement, or both, have been reported for each of the rules. For example: Most successful experiments published up to 1971 had trained reversibility in some way (Brainerd & Allen, 1971a; Glaser & Resnick, 1972); Sheppard (1974) and Halford and Fullerton (1970) used compensation instruction to train liquid quantity conservation and number conservation, respectively; Hamel and Riksen (1973) used qualitative identity instruction to train liquid quantity conservation; Litrownik et al. (1978) used quantitative identity instruction to train liquid quantity conservation; and Hatano and Suga (1969) used addition/subtraction instruction to train number conservation.

In sum, rule instruction, whether via visual demonstration or verbal description, is known to produce robust learning of Piagetian concepts—that is, learning in the sense of near transfer, far transfer, improved explanations, and long-term retention. For many years, these findings were confined to children within the elementary school age range. Lately, however, a substantial number of successful rule-training studies has accumulated for preschool children. In one of the earliest of these studies, Denney and Zeytinoglu (reported as Experiment 1 in Denney et al., 1977) trained 20 nonconserving 4-year-olds using verbal-rule instruction. During the training trials, the subjects were administered tests of number and length conservation accompanied by a rule statement that was similar to the one in Smith's (1968) experiment. On posttests administered 1 week after training, the children showed near transfer plus improved explanations on number and length items. However, far transfer (to mass conservation) was not obtained. In another study reported in the same paper (Denney et al., 1977, Experiment 2), the same procedure was used to train 16 4-year-olds on conservation of mass and length. When posttests were administered 1 week after training, the children in this study showed far transfer (to number and weight conservation), in addition to near transfer and improved explanations. More recently, Field (1981) has reported analogous results for 3- and 4-year-olds. Field studied the effects of instruction in three rules (quantitative identity, reversibility, and compensation) in a 2 (Identity Rule vs. No Identity Rule) × 2 (Reversibility Rule vs. No Reversibility Rule) × 2 (Compensation Rule vs. No Compensation Rule) factorial design. There were main effects for both Identity and Reversibility, with identity training being somewhat more effective than reversibility training, a result that agrees with an earlier experiment involving elementary schoolers by Hamel and Riksen (1973). On posttests administered 1 week after training and 2½–5 months after training, subjects who were exposed to the identity rule and/or the reversibility rule showed near transfer, far transfer, and improved explanations. However, training on the compensation rule appeared to have no effect.

Thus, rule instruction, like the training of perceptual strategies, is known to produce substantial learning effects in preschoolers as well as elementary schoolers. But whereas perceptual training has been largely confined to the study of conservation learning, rule instruction has been used with many concrete- and formal-operational concepts. Some of the more familiar concepts that have been trained in this manner are classification, class inclusion, seriation, perspective taking, the "other things being equal" strategy, proportionality, and subjective morality. As an illustration of such research, consider an experiment on classification by Denney and Actio (1974). Denney and Actio administered to 2- and 3-year-olds pretests that measured children's ability to classify objects exhaustively in terms of their form (circle, square, triangle), their color (red, blue, orange), and their size (large and small). During the training trials, one third of the subjects observed the experimenter classify the objects exhaustively in terms of the three dimensions. The experimenter described rules for sorting the objects (e.g., "I'll get all the ones that look alike") during the training trials. On posttests administered immediately after training, subjects who had been trained in this manner were much better at classifying objects in terms of their similarities than untrained control children were.

Finally, although rule instruction clearly enhances performance on an impressive array of Piagetian concepts, this research is subject to the criticism that very few experiments have managed to address the central question in this area: Is knowledge of a certain rule or rules necessary to a given concept? As mentioned earlier, the general hypothesis that has motivated rule-training experiments is the view that Piagetian concepts are cases of rule-governed behavior, and consequently, successful performance presupposes knowledge of the appropriate rules. But in an experiment where a certain rule is trained and improvement on tests for some target concept results, the most that we can conclude is that knowledge of the trained rule is *sufficient* for the concept. There are no grounds for supposing that it is also necessary.

To answer the necessity question, of course, we require Aptitude X Treatment designs in which the degree of covariation between pretest knowledge of rules and learning of the target concept is studied. If the rule-governed hypothesis about Piagetian concepts is correct, strong covariation should be observed. Unfortunately, experimentation has as yet failed to confirm this prediction. There are two main difficulties. First and most important, the literature contains very few Aptitude X Treatment experiments. So it is impossible to construct a general picture of the relationship between rule knowledge and trainability for a variety of concepts. Second, with the only concept for which reasonably extensive Aptitude X Treatment data are available—conservation—the picture is predominantly negative. The relationship between rule knowledge and trainability has been studied for four conservation rules: reversibility, compensation, quantitative identity, and qualitative identity. In the earliest of these experiments, Curcio, Kattef, Levine, and Robbins (1972) reported a virtually perfect relationship between compensation knowledge and conservation learning; the only children who appeared to benefit from conservation training were those who performed well on compensation pretests. However, this finding could not be replicated in three subsequent experiments conducted in other laboratories (Blanchard, 1975; Brainerd, 1976, 1977b). Other negative evidence of this sort is discussed in Silverman and Rose's (1982) review of research on the relationship between compensation and conservation.

Insofar as the other three rules are concerned, no evidence of a conservation-learning/qualitative-identity interaction was obtained in two experiments (Blanchard, 1975; Brainerd, 1977b), and no evidence of a conservation-learning-quantitative-identity interaction was obtained in the same two experiments. On the other hand, there *was* a conservation-learning-reversibility interaction in both experiments. Thus, the evidence that rule knowledge is a necessary precondition for conservation is mixed at best, and it is essentially nonexistent for other Piagetian concepts.

Training Social Strategies

Another line of very successful research, one that is nearly as old as rule training, involves exposing children who perform poorly on pretests to skilled models who perform well. Conceptually, of course, these experiments are inspired by social learning theory. As Zimmerman has pointed out in several papers, chapters, and books (e.g., Zimmerman, 1983; Zimmerman & Rosenthal, 1974b; Rosenthal & Zimmerman, 1978), social learning theorists also treat performance on Piagetian tests as rule-governed behavior. However, they emphasize the preeminence of the socializing agents in children's environments, especially parents and peers, in transmitting the relevant rules: "The model performs a double role as both a device to transmit correct response instances and as a representative of society, who presumably is demonstrating the response sanctioned within, at least, the micro-culture of the experimental situation" (Zimmerman & Rosenthal, 1974a, p. 39).

The standard experiment in which such claims have been evaluated involves training children to acquire some concrete-operational or formal-operational concept by having them observe a skilled model (live or filmed, adult or peer). To my knowledge, the first successful attempt to train a Piagetian concept via modeling was a study by Sullivan (1967) that was conducted at the Ontario Institute for Studies in Education (cf. also Waghorn & Sullivan, 1970). However, the largest single group of experiments has been reported by Ted Rosenthal, Barry Zimmerman, and their associates. The bulk of this work has been reviewed in a recent book (Rosenthal & Zimmerman, 1978).

In what is perhaps the most influential article in this series, Rosenthal and Zimmerman (1972) reported four experiments concerned with conservation learning in first graders (Experiments 1, 2, and 3) and preschoolers (Experiment 4). During the pre- and posttest phases of the experiments, Goldschmid and Bentler's (1968) standardized test of six conservation concepts was administered. Experiment 1 was a 2 X 2 design in which the factors were Feedback versus No Feedback and Rules versus No Rules. The children in all four conditions observed an adult model give correct answers to six conservation problems. The experimenter verbally praised the model in the two feedback conditions, and the model was asked to explain each of her answers in the two rule conditions. The amounts of pre- to posttest improvement in children's answers on the six trained problems were 880% (both the no-feedback-no-rules condition and the feedback-no-rules condition), 740% (no feedback-rules), and 394% (feedback-rules). The amounts of near transfer observed for these same subjects were 800% (no feedback-no rules), 760% (feedback-no rules), 680% (no feedback-rules), and 382% (feedback-rules). A no-model control condition was also included. The amounts of pre- to posttest improvement for these children were 39% (trained problems) and 85% (transfer problems).

Rosenthal and Zimmerman (1972, Experiment 4) used a modified version of the no-feedback-no-rules treatment to train preschoolers. The only significant modification was that conservation posttests were interspersed between the model's answers to training problems rather than being administered in a single lengthy battery at the end of training. Preschoolers, like first graders, showed large improvements in the accuracy of their answers on both the trained problems and on near transfer problems. In absolute terms, however, these improvements were only half as large as those observed in first graders. Further, there were no pre- to posttest improvements in preschoolers' explanations of their answers, whereas first graders did show improved explanations.

Despite the consistent and large modeling effects in the Rosenthal and Zimmerman (1972) article, there are some weaknesses in the data, particularly from the Genevan point of view. The major ones are that far transfer to untrained conservation concepts was not demonstrated, that long-term retention was not dem-onstrated, and that preschoolers' explanations did not change. Two of these deficiencies have been corrected in subsequent experiments. Concerning far trans-fer, such tests have now been administered in several observational-learning experi-ments with Piagetian concepts, and the results have been consistently positive (e.g., Charbonneau, Robert, Bourassa, & Gladu-Bissonette, 1976; Zimmerman & Rosenthal, 1974b). Concerning long-term retention, Charbonneau et al. (1976), Siegler and Liebert (1972), Zimmerman and Rosenthal (1974b), and others have found that modeling effects for Piagetian concepts are stable for intervals of 1 week to 3 months. Finally, there does not yet appear to be clear evidence that pre-schoolers' explanations improve as a consequence of observing skilled models. But as improved explanations have been observed for preschoolers with other methods (e.g., Emrick, 1967), it seems likely that this is merely a consequence of the fact that preschoolers have not been frequently studied in Piagetian modeling experiments.

As was the case for rule training, observational learning has been investigated with concepts other than conservation. Although the range of concepts is not nearly as broad as for rule training, successful experiments have been reported for such concepts as subjective morality (Arbuthnot, 1975), probability (Rosenthal, White, & Rosenthal, 1975), and classification (Zimmerman, 1974). Readers who are interested in a detailed treatment of such experiments are referred to Rosenthal and Zimmerman's (1978) excellent review.

Finally, observational-learning studies of Piagetian concepts seem to share the same conceptual difficulty as rule-learning studies. At most, these experiments establish *sufficient* conditions for concept acquisition; they show that it is possible for children to learn to conserve, to classify, to make probabilistic inferences, and so forth by observing models who can do these things. But they do not establish that children must learn these concepts through observation, nor even that this is how children usually learn such concepts. In view of the fact that students of cognitive development tend to be more interested in questions of necessity than in questions of sufficiency, the theoretical payoff of observational-learning experi-ments is not entirely clear, at least not from the perspective of traditional cognitive-developmental theory. However, the technological payoff, in terms of ideas about cheap and efficient methods for conveying important concepts to children, is considerable.

Question-Answering Strategies

The last category of manipulations is by far the least complicated of the four. It is based on a common sense observation about performance differences on Piagetian tests: From a purely *behavioral* standpoint, the key datum on such tests is that younger subjects answer the experimenter's questions differently than older subjects do. To some investigators, this has suggested that younger subjects' per-formance could be improved merely by training them to give the same answers as older subjects. That is, training could consist of telling children who perform poorly on the target test something like "Yes, that is the right answer" whenever they respond correctly, and of telling them something like "No, that is the wrong answer. The right answer is . . ." whenever they respond incorrectly. Following terminology introduced by Smedslund (1961a), manipulations of this sort were called "external reinforcement" in the early literature, although they are usually called "corrective feedback" nowadays. Corrective feedback has been consistently criticized in Genevan writings on learning as being incapable of producing "true concept learning" (e.g., Inhelder et al., 1974).

Feedback of some type (positive and/or negative) was often incorporated in early experiments involving attentional training, rule training, and observational learning. In Rosenthal and Zimmerman's (1972) research, for example, we have already seen that the model was verbally reinforced for conserving answers in some conditions. Similarly, in rule-training experiments a verbal statement of a rule was often introduced upon correction of a wrong answer ("No, the right answer is . . . because . . .") or as confirmation of a correct answer (e.g., Hamel & Riksen, 1973; Overbeck & Schwartz, 1970). Concerning attentional training, corrective feedback, sometimes accompanied by tangible rewards, was invariably used to teach children which aspects of the stimuli should be attended to. In all these experiments, the role played by feedback is primarily that of a confounding variable; we cannot tell whether it was the particular training method or the feedback (or both) that was responsible for learning. We also cannot tell whether feedback is capable of producing learning by itself.

The first experiment to provide evidence on the latter question was reported by Smedslund (1961b), who used a pan balance to deliver both positive and negative feedback to a group of nonconservers of weight. During the training phase, the children were administered a sequence of standard weight conservation problems. Each time a subject answered a question, he or she was allowed to determine the accuracy of the answer by weighing the objects on the balance. Smedslund reported that this procedure did not produce significant improvements in posttest conservation performance. These are the data that Genevan authors typically cite in connection with their arguments about the ineffectiveness of feedback training.

Subsequent experiments conducted in my own laboratories have shown that Smedslund's results were not definitive. The same basic design has been used in all these studies. Children who have failed several pretest items for concepts such as transitivity and conservation receive a readministration of these items during training. On each training item the subjects are told, "No, you're wrong. The right answer is . . . ," following errors. They are told, "Yes, you're right. The right answer is . . . ," following correct responses. To date, substantial learning effects have been observed for concrete-operational concepts such as conservation (e.g., Brainerd, 1972b), transitivity (e.g., Brainerd, 1974a), and class inclusion (e.g., Brainerd, 1982), and for formal-operational concepts such as density (e.g., Brainerd & Allen, 1971b). Further, it has been found that feedback training produces (a) learning effects that are durable a week or more after training (Brainerd, 1974a), (b) far transfer to untrained concepts (Brainerd, 1977b), and (c) improved explanations of correct answers (e.g., Brainerd, 1972a).

For some years an important criticism of such training was that children might simply be learning question-answering sets, not concepts. The plausibility of this criticism can be seen to best advantage in the case of conservation learning. The children who are trained in such experiments have failed to conserve the initial quantitative equivalence between pairs of objects after one of them has been deformed; that is, they say no when asked whether the objects are still equal and yes when asked whether the objects are unequal. Corrective feedback training consists of teaching them to give the opposite answers. Hence, it is possible that they simply acquire a set to say no to difference questions and yes to equivalence questions. Blanchard (1975) and I (Brainerd, 1977b) have both reported experiments that focus on this criticism, neither of which generated supportive findings. In both experiments, children were administered tests for three types of conservation (quantity, weight, length); but there were two versions of each test, namely, equivalence and difference. As usual, on the equivalence tests initially equal objects remained equal following perceptual transformations that made them look different. But on the difference tests, initially unequal objects remained unequal following perceptual transformations that made them look the same. During training, children were given standard feedback training on equivalence items. On the posttests, both equivalence and difference problems were readministered. If the children were only acquiring equivalence question-answering sets during training, then one obviously would expect that, relative to the pretests, equivalence performance should be better and difference performance should be worse. But if the children were acquiring conservation concepts during training, then one would expect that both equivalence and difference performance should be better than they were on the pretests. In the event, both Blanchard and I obtained the latter result.

The most important empirical limitation of the feedback-training literature centers on the ages of the subjects. We have seen that there is substantial evidence of Piagetian concept learning in preschoolers using attentional training (Emrick, 1967), rule training (Field, 1981) and observation of skilled models (Zimmerman & Lanaro, 1974). However, the corresponding evidence for feedback is very thin. I have reported a single experiment in which, depending on their treatment condition, older preschoolers (mean age = 5 years, 2 months) were given feedback training on class inclusion or conservation or transitivity. For all three concepts, significant differences were obtained between the performance of trained children and untrained controls; but with two of the concepts, class inclusion and conservation, the learning effects were small in absolute terms. For trained children who had scored 0% on pretests for these concepts, the level of accuracy was only 38% (class inclusion training) and 46% (conservation training) on posttests administered immediately after training. These effects are far smaller than those that have been obtained with kindergarten and first-grade children. Worse, there are doubts as to their replicability. Denney et al. (1977, Experiment 1) have reported an experiment in which no improvements in preschoolers' conservation performance were observed following feedback. A possible explanation of the discrepancy between the two studies is that Denney's subjects were 6 months younger. The only defensible conclusion, however, is that there is no credible proof that feedback manipulations enhance Piagetian concepts in preschoolers.

Conceptually, the key weakness of feedback training is that it is not what one could call a theoretically motivated manipulation. Whereas attentional training, rule training, and observational learning are all rooted in sets of theoretical assumptions about the nature of concept acquisition, feedback is not. It is merely a technology for getting younger subjects to perform like older subjects. This is not to say that it is impossible to give a theoretical rationale for why feedback training works. For example, an explanation in terms of working-memory concepts has been offered recently (Brainerd, 1983). According to this explanation, feedback improves performance on concept tests by causing children to rely on more appropriate retrieval cues. This explanation assumes that many children who fail such tests do so because they use the wrong cues from short-term memory to guide their attempts to retrieve processing operations from long-term memory. However, the possibility of formulating such explanations does not alter the fact that training children to answer questions by providing them with feedback is not a theory-based methodology. By itself, then, it does not lead to advances in theoretical understanding.

Concluding Remarks

Above, I summarized what I take to be the principal interpretative difficulties associated with each of the four categories of strategy training. In closing, however, it must be added that there is another conceptual problem that afflicts all Piagetian learning research. The problem, which was first alluded to in Beilin's (1971) review, is sometimes called the "all roads lead to Rome" dilemma. Briefly stated, it runs as follows.

As we have seen, the training regimens imposed in these experiments have traditionally been motivated by theoretical hypotheses to the effect that some experience (observation of models, conflict resolution, etc.) or some prerequisite skill (e.g., knowledge of a rule) is the royal road to acquisition of the target concept. But as Beilin (1971) pointed out, just about any training procedure, including many that fall outside the scope of this review, seems to work for Piagetian logical concepts (e.g., transitivity, class inclusion, conservation). (Strategy interventions are not so consistently effective, however, for Piagetian social-cognitive concepts, as is documented in Chapters 2 and 3 of this book.) So it seems that theories that emphasize *specific* experiences and/or *specific* prerequisite items are incapable, in principle, of accounting for the available data. Unfortunately, theories of this sort are the only ones that have been extensively investigated (Brainerd, 1982).

Although there may be many ways to resolve this dilemma, a solution that has been suggested very recently is to rely on modern working-memory models of children's performance on complex cognitive tasks (e.g., Brainerd, 1981). In such models, it is assumed that children activate a basic working-memory system on tasks such as conservation, transitivity, and perspective taking. The fine-grain structure of the system depends on task considerations. However, the system always has certain fundamental features. Regardless of the concept being assessed, it is assumed that children's first task is to encode some crucial background facts (e.g., the initial equivalence of the stimuli in conservation, the premises in transitive inference, the cardinal numbers of the various sets in class inclusion) *and* to hold the encoded traces in short-term memory for however long it takes to complete the task. When the experimenter poses a question, children are assumed to respond by sampling some traces from short-term memory and then using these traces as retrieval cues to guide their search through long-term memory for processing operations that will generate responses from the information in short-term memory. Once an appropriate package of processing operations has been located, children are assumed to retrieve the operations to consciousness and apply them to the contents of short-term memory, thereby producing answers to the experimenter's questions.

Returning to Piagetian learning research, working-memory analysis explains the multiplicity of effective training treatments by noting that since a working-memory system consists of several components, all of which are necessary to correct performance, it is possible to have treatments that enhance different components of the system. Thus, for example, it has already been mentioned that the effects of simple feedback have been explained on the ground that they increase the chances that children will use the correct cues from short-term memory when retrieving processing operations from long-term memory. The beneficial effects of attentional training, on the other hand, might be explained on the ground that such training encourages children to encode the correct background facts into short-term memory in the first place. Finally, the enhanced performance that results from rule training might be explained on the ground that such experiences deliver processing algorithms directly to children's short-term memories, thereby circumventing performance errors attributable to failures to retrieve processing operations from long-term memory.

These proposals are obviously speculative and have not as yet been subjected to experimentation. I mention them only to illustrate that from the perspective of modern information processing analyses of memory, the "all roads lead to Rome" problem is not insuperable.

References

Arbuthnot, J. Modification of moral judgment through role playing. *Developmental Psychology*, 1975, *11*, 319–324.

Beilin, H. Learning and operational convergence in logical thought development. *Journal of Experimental Child Psychology*, 1965, *2*, 317–339.

Beilin, H. Stimulus and cognitive transformation in conservation. In D. Elkind & J. H. Flavell (Eds.), *Studies in cognitive development*. New York: Oxford, 1969.

Beilin, H. The training and acquisition of logical operations. In M. F. Rosskopf, L. P. Steffe, & S. Taback (Eds.), *Piagetian cognitive-developmental research and mathematics education*. Washington, DC: National Council of Teachers of Mathematics, 1971.

Bingham-Newman, A. M., & Hooper, F. H. Classification and seriation instruction and logical task performance in the preschool. *American Educational Research Journal*, 1974, *11*, 379–393.

Blanchard, J. *Identity and reversibility rules in conservation*. Unpublished bachelor's thesis, University of Alberta, 1975.

Boersma, F. J., & Wilton, K. M. Eye movements and conservation acceleration. *Journal of Experimental Child Psychology*, 1974, *17*, 49–60.

Bower, G. H., & Trabasso, T. Concept identification. In R. C. Atkinson (Ed.), *Studies in mathematical psychology*. Stanford, CA: Stanford University Press, 1974.

Brainerd, C. J. The development of the proportionality scheme in children and adolescents. *Developmental Psychology*, 1971, *5*, 469–476.

Brainerd, C. J. Reinforcement and reversibility in quantity conservation acquisition. *Psychonomic Science*, 1972, *27*, 114–116. (a)

Brainerd, C. J. The age-stage issue in conservation acquisition. *Psychonomic Science*, 1972, *9*, 115–117. (b)

Brainerd, C. J. The origins of number concepts. *Scientific American*, 1973, *228*(3), 101–109.

Brainerd, C. J. Training and transfer of transitivity, conservation, and class inclusion. *Child Development*, 1974, *45*, 324–344. (a)

Brainerd, C. J. Inducing ordinal and cardinal representations of the first five natural numbers. *Journal of Experimental Child Psychology*, 1974, *18*, 524–534. (b)

Brainerd, C. J. Does prior knowledge of compensation increase susceptibility to conservation training? *Developmental Psychology*, 1976, *12*, 1–5.

Brainerd, C. J. Cognitive development and concept learning: An interpretative review. *Psychological Bulletin*, 1977, *84*, 919–939. (a)

Brainerd, C. J. Feedback, rule knowledge, and conservation learning. *Child Development*, 1977, *48*, 404–411. (b)

Brainerd, C. J. Learning research and Piagetian theory. In L. S. Siegel & C. J. Brainerd (Eds.), *Alternatives to Piaget: Critical essays on the theory*. New York: Academic Press, 1978.

Brainerd, C. J. Concept learning and developmental stage. In H. J. Klausmeier et al. (Eds.), *Cognitive learning and development: Piagetian and information-processing perspectives*. Cambridge, MA: Ballinger, 1979.

Brainerd, C. J. Working memory and the developmental analysis of probability judgment. *Psychological Review*, 1981, *88*, 463–502.

Brainerd, C. J. Children's concept learning as rule-sampling systems with Markovian properties. In C. J. Brainerd (Ed.), *Children's logical and mathematical cognition*. New York: Springer-Verlag, 1982.

Brainerd, C. J. Working-memory systems in cognitive development. In C. J. Brainerd (Ed.), *Recent advances in cognitive-developmental theory*. New York: Springer-Verlag, 1983.

Brainerd, C. J., & Allen, T. W. Experimental inductions of the conservation of "first-order" quantitative invariants. *Psychological Bulletin,* 1971, *75,* 128–144. (a)

Brainerd, C. J., & Allen, T. W. Training and transfer of density conservation. *Child Development,* 1971, *42,* 693–704. (b)

Bruner, J. S., Olver, R. R., & Greenfield, P. M. *Studies in cognitive growth.* New York: Wiley, 1966.

Bucher, B., & Schneider, R. E. Acquisition and generalization of conservation by pre-schoolers, using operant training. *Journal of Experimental Child Psychology,* 1973, *16,* 187–204.

Case, R. Structures and strictures: Some functional limitations on the course of cognitive growth. *Cognitive Psychology,* 1974, *6,* 544–573.

Charbonneau, C., Robert, M., Bourassa, G., & Gladu-Bissonette, S. Observational learning of quantity conservation and Piagetian generalization tasks. *Developmental Psychology,* 1976, *12,* 211–217.

Churchill, E. The number concepts of the young child: Part 1. *Researches and Studies,* Leeds University, 1958, *17,* 34–39. (a)

Churchill, E. The number concepts of the young child: Part 2. *Researches and Studies,* Leeds University, 1958, *18,* 28–46. (b)

Cornell, E. H. The effects of cue distinctiveness on infants' manual search. *Journal of Experimental Child Psychology,* 1981, *32,* 330–342.

Cowan, R. A. Reappraisal of the relation between performances of quantitative identity and quantitative equivalence conservation tasks. *Journal of Experimental Child Psychology,* 1979, *28,* 68–80.

Cox, M. V. Perspective ability: The conditions of change. *Child Development,* 1977, *48,* 1717–1724.

Coxford, A. F. The effects of instruction on the age placement of children in Piaget's seriation experiments. *Arithmetic Teacher,* 1964, *10,* 4–9.

Curcio, R., Kattef, E., Levine, D., & Robbins, O. Compensation and susceptibility to conservation training. *Developmental Psychology,* 1972, *7,* 259–265.

Denney, N. W., & Actio, M. A. Classification training in two- and three-year-old children. *Journal of Experimental Child Psychology,* 1974, *17,* 37–48.

Denney, N. W., Zeytinoglu, S., & Selzer, S. C. Conservation training in four-year-olds. *Journal of Experimental Child Psychology,* 1977, *24,* 129–146.

Emrick, J. A. *The acquisition and transfer of conservation skills by four-year-old children.* Unpublished doctoral dissertation, University of California, Los Angeles, 1967.

Field, D. Can preschool children really learn to conserve? *Child Development,* 1981, *52,* 326–334.

Flavell, J. H. *The developmental psychology of Jean Piaget.* Princeton, NJ: Van Nostrand, 1963.

Gelman, R. Conservation acquisition: A problem of learning to attend to relevant attributes. *Journal of Experimental Child Psychology,* 1969, *7,* 167–187.

Glaser, R. W., & Resnick, L. B. Instructional psychology. *Annual Review of Psychology,* 1972, *23,* 207–276.

Goldschmid, M. L. Role of experience in the acquisition of conservation. *Proceedings of the American Psychological Association,* 1968, *76,* 361–362.

Goldschmid, M. L. Role of experience in the rate and sequence of cognitive development. In D. R. Green, M. P. Ford, & G. B. Flamer (Eds.), *Measurement and Piaget.* New York: McGraw-Hill, 1971.

Goldschmid, M. L., & Bentler, P. M. Dimensions and measurement of conservation. *Child Development,* 1968, *39,* 787–802.

Gruen, G. E. Experiences affecting the development of number concepts in children. *Child Development,* 1965, *36,* 963–979.

Halford, G. S., & Fullerton, T. J. A discrimination task which induces conservation of number. *Child Development,* 1970, *41,* 205–213.

Hamel, B. R., & Riksen, B. O. M. Identity, reversibility, verbal rule instruction, and conservation. *Developmental Psychology,* 1973, *9,* 66–72.

Harker, W. H. *Children's number concepts: Ordination and cardination.* Unpublished master's thesis, Queen's University, 1960.

Hatano, G. A developmental approach to concept formation: A review of neo-Piagetian learning experiments. *Dokkyo University Bulletin of Liberal Arts and Education,* 1971, *5,* 66–72.

Hatano, G., & Suga, Y. Equilibration and external reinforcement in the acquisition of number conservation. *Japanese Psychological Research,* 1969, *11,* 17–31.

Iannotti, R. J. Effects of role-taking experiences on role taking, empathy, altruism and aggression. *Developmental Psychology,* 1978, *14,* 119–124.

Inhelder, B. Criteria of the stages of mental development. In J. M. Tanner & B. Inhelder (Eds.), *Discussions on child development* (Vol. 1). London: Tavistock, 1956.

Inhelder, B., & Sinclair, H. Learning cognitive structures. In P. H. Mussen, J. Langer, & M. Covington (Eds.), *Trends and issues in developmental psychology.* New York: Holt, Rinehart & Winston, 1969.

Inhelder, B., Sinclair, H., & Bovet, M. *Learning and the development of cognition.* Cambridge, MA: Harvard University Press, 1974.

Inhelder, B., Sinclair, H., Bovet, M., & Smock, C. On cognitive development. *American Psychologist,* 1966, *21,* 160–164.

Jensen, L. C., & Larm, C. Effects of two training procedures on intentionality in moral judgment among children. *Developmental Psychology,* 1970, *2,* 310.

Krantz, D. H., & Tversky, A. Conjoint-measurement analysis of composition rules in psychology. *Psychological Review,* 1972, *78,* 151–169.

Kuhn, D. Mechanisms of change in the development of cognitive structures. *Child Development,* 1972, *43,* 833–844.

Litrownik, A. J., Franzini, L. R., Livingston, M. K., & Harvey, S. Developmental priority of identity conservation: Acceleration of identity and equivalence in normal and moderately retarded children. *Child Development,* 1978, *49,* 201–208.

Lovejoy, E. Analysis of the overlearning reversal effect. *Psychological Review,* 1966, *73,* 87–103.

May, R. V., & Norton, J. M. Training-task orders and transfer in conservation. *Child Development,* 1981, *52,* 904–913.

May, R. B., & Tisshaw, S. K. Variations of learning-set training and quantity conservation. *Child Development,* 1977, *48,* 661–667.

Murray, F. B. Acquisition of conservation through social interaction. *Developmental Psychology,* 1972, *6,* 1–6.

Murray, F. B., & Johnson, P. E. Reversibility in nonconservation of weight. *Psychonomic Science,* 1969, *16,* 285–286.

Overbeck, C., & Schwartz, M. Training in conservation of weight. *Journal of Experimental Child Psychology,* 1970, *9,* 253–264.

Papalia, D. E., & Hooper, F. H. A developmental comparison of identity and equivalence conservations. *Journal of Experimental Child Psychology*, 1970, *12*, 347-361.

Piaget, J. Piaget's theory. In P. H. Mussen (Ed.), *Carmichael's manual of child psychology* (Vol. 1). New York: Wiley, 1970.

Piaget, J., & Inhelder, B. *The psychology of the child*. New York: Basic Books, 1969.

Rosenthal, R. H., White, G. M., & Rosenthal, T. L. Probability matching through direct and vicarious experience. *Psychological Reports*, 1975, *36*, 883-889.

Rosenthal, T. L., & Zimmerman, B. J. Modeling by exemplification and instruction in training conservation. *Developmental Psychology*, 1972, *6*, 392-401.

Rosenthal, T. L., & Zimmerman, B. J. *Social learning and cognition*. New York: Academic Press, 1978.

Sheppard, J. L. Compensation and combinatorial systems in the acquisition and generalization of conservation. *Child Development*, 1974, *45*, 717-730.

Siegler, R. S. Developmental sequences within and between concepts. *Monographs of the Society for Research in Child Development*, 1981, *46*(2, Whole No. 189).

Siegler, R. S., & Liebert, R. M. Effects of presenting relevant rules and complete feedback on the conservation of liquid quantity. *Developmental Psychology*, 1972, *7*, 133-138.

Siegler, R. S., Liebert, D. E., & Liebert, R. M. Inhelder and Piaget's pendulum problem: Teaching preadolescents to act as scientists. *Developmental Psychology*, 1973, *9*, 97-101.

Siegler, R. S., & Richards, D. D. The development of time, speed, and distance concepts. *Developmental Psychology*, 1979, *15*, 288-298.

Silverman, I. W., & Rose, A. P. Compensation and conservation. *Psychological Bulletin*, 1982, *91*, 80-101.

Sinclair, H. Recent Piagetian research in learning studies. In M. Schwebel & J. Raph (Eds.), *Piaget in the classroom*. New York: Basic Books, 1973.

Smedslund, J. Apprentissage des notions de la conservation et de la transitivité du poids. *Etudes d'Epistémologie Génétique*, 1959, *9*, 3-13.

Smedslund, J. The acquisition of conservation of substance and weight in children, I: Introduction. *Scandinavian Journal of Psychology*, 1961, *2*, 11-20. (a)

Smedslund, J. The acquisition of conservation of substance and weight in children, II: External reinforcement of conservation of weight and of the operations of addition and subtraction. *Scandinavian Journal of Psychology*, 1961, *2*, 71-84. (b)

Smedslund, J. The acquisition of conservation of substance and weight in children, IV: An attempt at extinction of the visual components of the weight concept. *Scandinavian Journal of Psychology*, 1961, *2*, 153-155. (c)

Smedslund, J. The acquisition of conservation of substance and weight in children, V: Practice in conflict situations without external reinforcement. *Scandinavian Journal of Psychology*, 1961, *2*, 156-160. (d)

Smedslund, J. The acquisition of conservation of substance and weight in children, VI: Practice on continuous versus discontinuous material in conflict situations without external reinforcement. *Scandinavian Journal of Psychology*, 1961, *2*, 203-210. (e)

Smith, I. D. The effects of training procedures on the acquisition of conservation of weight. *Child Development*, 1968, *39*, 515-526.

Sullivan, E. Acquisition of conservation of substance through film modeling technique. In D. W. Brison & E. Sullivan (Eds.), *Recent research on the acquisition of substance*. Toronto, Ontario: Ontario Institute for Studies in Education, 1967.

Trabasso, T. Pay attention. *Psychology Today*, 1968, *2*(5), 30–36.

Trabasso, T. The role of memory as a system in making transitive inferences. In R. V. Kail, Jr., & J. W. Hagen (Eds.), *Perspectives on the development of memory and cognition*. Hillsdale, NJ: Erlbaum, 1977.

Trabasso, T., & Bower, G. H. *Attention in learning*. New York: Wiley, 1968.

Waghorn, L., & Sullivan, E. V. The exploration of transition rules in conservation of quantity (substance) using film mediated modeling. *Acta Psychologica*, 1970, *32*, 65–80.

Wallach, L., & Sprott, R. L. Inducing number conservation in children. *Child Development*, 1964, *35*, 1057–1071.

Wallach, L., Wall, A. J., & Anderson, L. Number conservation: The role of reversibility, addition/subtraction and misleading perceptual cues. *Child Development*, 1967, *38*, 425–442.

White, G. V. *Feedback training of number and length conservation*. Unpublished master's thesis, University of Western Ontario, 1981.

Wohlwill, J. F. Un essai d'apprentissage dans le domaine de la conservation du nombre. *Etudes d'Epistémologie Génétique*, 1959, *9*, 125–135.

Wohlwill, J. F., & Lowe, R. C. An experimental analysis of the conservation of number. *Child Development*, 1962, *33*, 153–167.

Youniss, J. Classificatory schemes in relation to class inclusion before and after training. *Human Development*, 1971, *14*, 171–183.

Zeaman, D., & House, B. J. The role of attention in retardate discrimination learning. In N. R. Ellis (Ed.), *Handbook of mental deficiency*. New York: McGraw-Hill, 1963.

Zimmerman, B. J. Modification of young children's grouping strategies: The effects of modeling, verbalization, incentives, and praise. *Child Development*, 1974, *45*, 1032–1041.

Zimmerman, B. J. Contextualism, social learning, and cognitive development. In C. J. Brainerd (Ed.), *Recent advances in cognitive-developmental theory*. New York: Springer-Verlag, 1983.

Zimmerman, B. J., & Lanaro, P. Acquiring and retaining conservation of length through modeling and reversibility cues. *Merrill-Palmer Quarterly*, 1974, *20*, 145–161.

Zimmerman, B. J., & Rosenthal, T. L. Conserving and retaining equalities and inequalities through observation and correction. *Developmental Psychology*, 1974, *10*, 260–268. (a)

Zimmerman, B. J., & Rosenthal, T. L. Observational learning of rule-governed behavior by children. *Psychological Bulletin*, 1974, *81*, 29–42. (b)

2. Training Cognitive Strategies for Oral Communication

W. Patrick Dickson

Theory imposes expectations on practice, and where theory leads us to expect training to be of limited success, initial training studies frequently seem to support theory (see Chapters 1 and 3 in this volume). Such has been the case in research on training communication skills.

Piaget's (1926) theory has been the preeminent theoretical framework for studying the development of communication skills in children. It should be kept in mind that Piaget's primary interest was in cognition and the cognitive limitations of young children as compared to adults. Consistent with his position that children's communication was tied to their cognitive competence, he brought over into his research on communication skills the concept of egocentrism, which was derived largely from the inabilities of young children to rotate mentally three objects in space. Also, because he presumed little cognitive competence in children, he was led to structure the communicative tasks he used in ways likely to highlight deficiencies. In his early work Piaget concluded that before the age of 7 or 8 understanding between children "occurs only in so far as there is contact between two identical mental schemes already existing in each child" (Piaget, 1926, p. 120). Piaget based this conclusion in part on observations of young children's communication failures when they were asked to explain the operation of laboratory apparatus to other children. These early experimental situations evolved into what are now called "referential communication tasks."

Much of the experimental research on children's oral communication skills, especially research that includes a training component, has been conducted using these tasks. A brief description of them provides a context for the discussion that follows. The problems posed to children in these standardized situations involve giving directions to another person, either an adult experimenter or another child. Typically, one child is designated the speaker and another child the listener, with the children separated by a visual barrier. The speaker attempts to describe one of a set of objects or pictures so that the listener can select the item described. For example, the speaker may be asked to describe a large red triangle in an array of triangles that differ in color and size. Other commonly used referential tasks include giving directions on a map or describing how to assemble a model from separate parts. The primary dependent meaure in such research has been the accuracy of the listener's choices. Often an adult experimenter has played the role of either the speaker or the listener in this research, especially in the training studies described below. A detailed review of referential communication research with an emphasis on research designs and experimental tasks is available elsewhere (Dickson, 1982b).

Referential communication tasks are useful in research because they provide experimental control over communicative intent and yield unambiguous measures of communication accuracy. Communicative intent is controlled because the task is defined for the speaker and the target referent is specified. In addition, because the listener is required to make an overt response, questions about the listener's understanding are circumvented. The major criticism of the use of such tasks centers on their artificiality and apparent lack of ecological validity, although a case can be made that such tasks are representative of a wide range of naturally occurring communication situations (Dickson, 1982a).

Piaget's pessimistic view of children's communication skills was brought forward into research in the United States. From the mid-1960s to the mid-1970s research on the development of communication skills focused primarily on the link between role taking and communication hypothesized by Piaget, a link that could not be found, despite repeated efforts by researchers (Shantz, 1981). A few studies were conducted in which attempts were made at training referential communication skills, but the training was quite weak at best (Flavell, Botkin, Fry, Wright, & Jarvis, 1968; Fry, 1966). Glucksberg, Krauss, and Higgins (1975) correctly concluded, in their review of research on the topic, that "there have been few studies that have attempted to train or improve communicative behaviors in normal children. Those that have made an attempt have not had outstanding success" (p. 336). These early training failures seemed to lend support to Piaget's view that young children had limited communication competence.

During the mid- to late 1970s, however, opposition to this view arose from two directions. Observational studies of young children in more natural contexts provided ample evidence of quite sophisticated communication skills in young children, well exemplified by Shatz and Gelman (1973) who showed that 4-year-old children adapt the form of their messages to the age of their listeners. Concurrently, researchers in the more experimental referential communication tradition began to analyze the component skills required for communication. This was a departure from the position that communication skills were a kind of global ability analogous to general intelligence (see Asher, 1979, for an excellent review).

In contrast to the earlier studies, which were attempts to train skills globally (e.g., Fry, 1966), during the late 1970s attention shifted to training specific sub-skills, with a major distinction being made at that time between speaking and listening skills. In addition, the training was carried out with greater intensity. For example, Whitehurst (1976) studied the effects of adult modeling on children's speaking skills, and Cosgrove and Patterson (1977) studied the effects of training children to ask questions when performing the role of listener. The combined effects of more intense training and training of specific component skills began to yield success. Flavell's (1977, pp. 172–179) observations on the striking differences in conclusions from the earlier referential studies and the naturalistic studies convey the strong feelings of dissonance induced in the field by the sharply contrasting views of children's communicative competence. Indicative of the shift away from Piagetian perspectives in research on communication skills is the fact that Piaget is not mentioned once in a recent monograph on the development of communication (Flavell, Speer, Green, & August, 1981).

Of the various interventions attempted, two types seem to have been ineffective. First, training role-taking skills does not seem to result in improved communication performance (Asher, 1979, pp. 182–183; Shantz, 1981). Second, simple practice seems not to lead to rapid improvement (see Dickson, 1974, as well as the control groups in many of the training studies cited later).

On the other hand, evidence has accumulated demonstrating that referential communication skills can be improved by training cognitive strategies that are directed at either listening or speaking skills. Although the evidence is encouraging, the reader should keep in mind that cognitive strategy training is not as well developed in the area of oral communication skills as it is in many other domains discussed in this volume. After discussing the relevant studies in detail, I will take up their implications for education and future research.

Cognitive Strategies for Listening Skills

In a referential communication task, the listener receives a message, holds it in memory, compares it with the set of alternatives, ensures that it refers to only one of the alternatives, and then chooses that alternative. If the message refers to more than one alternative, the listener must ask for more information before choosing. Further, the more skillful listener asks specific questions that elicit from the speaker the essential information. Compared to the skillful listener, young children often fail to request more information spontaneously when given inadequate descriptions and proceed to choose alternatives not explicitly excluded by the description.

One of the most successful applications of cognitive strategy training in oral communication research was concerned with children's failure to ask questions. Cosgrove and Patterson (1977) verbally instructed children to ask questions by telling them, "Whenever you are not sure what the right answer is, you can ask questions to help yourself to figure it out" (p. 559). Control subjects were told to remember that "the only rule in this game is that you can't look on the other side of the table" (p. 560). This brief verbal training was conducted between a pre- and posttest consisting of eight trials on which inadequate descriptions of four-picture arrays were given. The results were dramatic. For children given instructions to ask questions, the number of questions asked increased significantly, from about 4 to about 12 for fourth graders, from about 1 to about 9 for second graders and kindergartners, and from about 1 to about 3 for preschoolers. These increases were statistically significant for all except the preschool group. Children in the control condition showed only slight increases from pretest to posttest.

The same cognitive strategy training was used in a second study with first-grade children (Cosgrove & Patterson, 1978) with similar success. (In this study, a video-taped modeling condition in which children were shown four instances of a child's asking for more information was also found to be effective.) The benefits accruing to children who ask questions was established in a study by Patterson and Massad (1980). In that research, when children asked more questions, they were usually given useful answers by child speakers, and consequently the listeners' choices were more accurate.

The strong effect of such a relatively short intervention raises the issue of why children, even fourth graders, fail to ask questions spontaneously. One possible explanation is that young children as listeners fail to compare the message to all possible referents and consequently do not realize the need to ask questions. This possibility was tested by Patterson, Massad, and Cosgrove (1978), who contrasted the effects of instructions highlighting the importance of comparing the message to all referents in the set with instructions to ask questions. The results were again clear. Simply reminding the 6- to 10-year-olds in the study to compare the message with all referents had no effect on their tendency to ask questions when given an inadequate message, whereas instructing them in the question-asking strategy did result in increased questioning.

The type of question a child asks is also important. Questions can be either general ("Which one is it?") or specific ("Is it red or blue?"). Asking a specific question is more likely to elicit an informative response from a speaker. Asking specific questions also gives evidence that children in the role of listener are in fact engaging in comparisons between messages and referents. A careful examination of the analyses of children's questions in three studies reveals an interesting pattern (Dickson, 1974, pp. 77-83; Cosgrove & Patterson, 1977, p. 562; Ironsmith & Whitehurst, 1978, pp. 549-551). First, following instructions to ask questions, children ranging in age from 4 to 10 ask predominantly specific questions. For example, in Dickson (1974) the percentage of specific questions over specific and general questions combined was 62, 72, and 80, for preschool, kindergarten, and second-grade children, respectively. In Cosgrove and Patterson (1977) over 90% of the questions were specific questions at all grade levels studied, from preschool through Grade 4. Ironsmith and Whitehurst (1978) provided instruction that explicitly encouraged asking specific questions (in contrast to the strategy provided by Cosgrove and Patterson, which simply encouraged asking questions). They found that about 63% of the questions asked by kindergartners and 95% of the questions asked by second graders were specific questions. Thus, children do ask appropriately specific questions, which means that they probably engage in comparison between the message and the referent display.

The study by Ironsmith and Whitehurst (1978), however, provided a puzzling result in terms of cognitive strategies. In that experiment three instructional conditions were compared with a control condition. The instructional conditions all involved an adult model. In one condition the model asked general questions, in the second condition the model asked specific questions, and in the third condition the adult modeled a cognitive strategy of comparing the message to all of the referents and then asking a specific question. For example, in the third condition the model might say (pointing to a pair), "It must be one of these two. They're both girls and they both have their arms down at their sides. The only difference is that one's short and one's tall. Is she short or tall?"

All three of the instructional groups asked more questions than the control group. In addition, the types of question asked were highly related to type of instruction. Children who saw a model ask specific questions asked predominantly specific questions, and children who saw a model ask general questions asked predominantly general questions. The children who saw a model verbalize the cognitive strategy leading to a specific question did tend to ask predominantly specific questions, but the percentage of specific questions asked by these children was less than that of the children who saw the model who asked only specific questions (about 55% vs. 68%). Although not statistically significant, the direction suggested that the provision of a cognitive strategy for the more complex behavior of specific questioning may have confused the children, perhaps exceeding what they could process in this task situation. With more complex strategies, more time might be required for children to acquire the strategy.

In summary, these studies show that many children in the early elementary grades do not spontaneously request more information when given inadequate descriptions. The failure to request more information does not seem to result entirely from a failure on the part of the children to compare the message with all referents, although young children often fail to make such comparisons spontaneously. When instructed in the cognitive strategy of asking questions when uncertain, children greatly increase the number of questions they ask, and consequently obtain more information from speakers. Finally, the majority of questions asked by children in this age range tend to be the more effective specific questions rather than general questions. However, modeling of specific questioning has been shown to increase the number of specific questions.

Cognitive Strategies for Speaking Skills

A speaker in a referential communication situation must compare the assigned target referent with the array of other potential referents and identify features that differentiate the target from the other referents. Next, the speaker must formulate a description that includes these differentiating features. Finally, the speaker must respond to requests from the listener for more information.

Cognitive strategies for these component speaking skills have been trained, with encouraging results. The two most prominent lines of research on cognitive strategies for comparison across referents have differed in the explicitness of the strategy in terms of the behavior expected of the speaker. Asher and Wigfield (1981a; 1981b) describe a series of comparison-training studies, following the modeling plus self-guidance statement procedure used by Meichenbaum and Goodman (1971). Children in these studies saw a videotape of a model giving clues for 10 word pairs. The videotaped model verbalized a cognitive strategy. For example, the model's script for the first pair (child–baby, where baby is the target referent) was as follows: "Let's see, there's 'child' and 'baby' and 'baby' has a line under it. How about 'play' as a clue? A baby plays. No, that's no good, because a child plays too, and the person won't know which word has the line under it. How about 'mother,' because a baby has a mother. No, a child has a mother too. Oh, I've got one. 'Rattle.' Because a baby plays with a rattle and a child doesn't. Rattle." Following exposure to the model, the children were given a practice item and asked to generate a clue: "Think out loud just like the person on TV." When the child gave a poor clue, the experimenter said, "No, that might not be a good clue because . . . . Try again." When the child gave a good clue, the experimenter said, "Yes, that's a good clue because . . . ." The sequence of mode, practice, and feedback was repeated for a total of 10 trials. A control group was given practice on the same 10 word pairs without the comparison training. Following training the children were given a list of 10 word pairs unrelated to those used in training.

Three separate experiments were conducted using this basic design with third- and fourth-grade children. The results were consistent across these studies. The children given the comparison training were consistently better than children in the control group in terms of the adequacy of the clues they gave (about 5 vs. 2, as scored by adult judges). The scores of the trained children did not, however, reach adult levels on the posttest, falling between the control groups' scores and the scores of untrained college students (who averaged only about 6 out of the possible maximum of 10). The performance of the college students suggests that this word pair task is a fairly difficult one.

In their second experiment Asher and Wigfield (1981b, p. 119) conducted a second training session aimed at providing the children with more specific cognitive strategies for generating clues. The children who had been given the comparison training were divided into two groups; one was given only a reminder of the comparison instruction and the other was given the reminder plus training in two specific cognitive strategies for generating messages. The two strategies were to "think of a word that goes with the referent in a sentence" and to "think of an example of the referent." The addition of these strategies had only a slight effect, with girls (but not boys) given the strategies performing better than those in the comparison reminder group. I would interpret these results as I interpreted the results of the Ironsmith and Whitehurst study discussed earlier. More complex cognitive strategies probably require more extensive training and practice if they are to be effective.

One further qualification on claims of effectiveness of the cognitive strategy training as employed in the Asher and Wigfield study comes from the failure to find transfer from the word pair task to a task involving photographs of snowflakes (Experiment 2) or a task involving line drawings with fixed features (Experiment 3). Failure to obtain generalization is a common problem in communication-training research, as it is in other domains (e.g., Borkowski & Büchel, 1983; Pressley, Levin, & Bryant, 1983; Pressley, Reynolds, Stark, & Gettinger, 1983).

A second major line of research was aimed at training children as speakers to compare the target with other referents (Whitehurst & Sonnenschein, 1981). In Whitehurst and Sonnenschein's first experiment, they contrasted instructions to "tell me about it so that I will know which one you are talking about" with instructions to "tell me how [the referent] looks different from the other one." The task involved pairs of triangles that differed in color, size, or pattern. The 5-year-olds in the experiment gave much more informative messages when instructed to tell how the target referent differed from the other referent than did the children in the other condition (73% vs. 50%). Robinson (1981, pp. 180–182) also reports success in comparison training. The success of this cognitive strategy training is all the more impressive in view of a number of studies suggesting that children of this age are unable to compare stimuli in referential communication tasks (e.g., Asher & Parke, 1975; Whitehurst & Merkur, 1977; as well as others cited by Whitehurst & Sonnenschein, 1981, p. 132).

Whitehurst and Sonnenschein (1981) conducted additional experiments using the same basic format but varying the instruction and feedback combinations. The most effective training procedure that they studied was one in which children were given instructions highlighting the communicative purpose of the task ("Tell me about it so that I will know which one you are talking about"), supplemented by feedback following each trial that reminded the children of the cognitive strategy. The reminder was "That's wrong. You did not tell me how it was different from the other," with comparable feedback given for correct responses. This combination of communication instructions with the feedback reminder resulted in 85% informative responding by the kindergarten children. Although the training did not transfer to a more complex form of the training task (Experiment 2), transfer was obtained when a somewhat simpler speaking task was used (Experiment 3). No transfer was obtained to a listening task, where the children were asked to report whether descriptions uniquely specified a referent. Indeed, in a follow-up study, Whitehurst and Sonnenschein (1981, pp. 137–138) found that children who were given the speaker training described above were much worse than control group children at identifying ambiguous messages in a listening transfer task (20% vs. 71%). We will return to this puzzling case of negative transfer shortly.

In summary, training of two types of cognitive strategies has been successful in improving children's speaking skills. Children have been taught to compare word pairs when choosing a clue that discriminates between the two words as well as to describe differences when formulating a message to differentiate a target picture from other pictures. In both of these approaches the effects of training seem to be maintained for a week or more, but the training does not appear to generalize to tasks that differ much from the training task. Also, training of speaking skills does not appear to transfer to listening skills, though successful cross-modal transfer is reported in a recent unpublished study (Sonnenschein & Whitehurst, Note 1).

Generalization of Training

The optimism accompanying the training successes described above must be tempered by the concomitant generalization failures. Detailed discussions of factors influencing transfer are available elsewhere and will not be repeated here (Borkowski, in press; Pressley, 1982, pp. 300-302; Pressley et al., 1983). With respect to training communication skills, however, several general principles seem to apply to the issue of achieving generalization. First, transfer decreases the greater the difference between the training task and the transfer task. Second, the more complex the strategy trained, the more difficult it is to obtain transfer. Third, children may need to be explicitly trained to generalize the strategies. Fourth, extensive practice is needed in order to obtain transfer.

Consider the failure to transfer reported in Asher and Wigfield (1981a, 1981b) discussed earlier. Recall that children observed a model verbalizing a strategy for generating a one-word discriminating clue for word pairs, where the reasoning for the child–baby pair went as follows: "How about 'play' as a clue? A baby plays. No, that's no good, because a child plays too. . . ." Asher and Wigfield first sought transfer to a task using pictures of snowflakes and encouraged the children to create a message of any length that would enable the listener to choose the designated snowflake. No generalization of training was found. But notice how many ways the transfer task differed from the training task. The training task required the selection of only one word; the transfer task allowed long descriptions. The training task required the child to repress the word itself (baby) and give only a "clue" (an artificial communication strategy in and of itself), whereas the transfer task could hardly be accomplished with wholistic words and required analytic, descriptive language such as "It has three sharp points and broad leaves," to give an imaginary example. Although Asher and Wigfield emphasize the commonalities in saying, "Like the word pair task, the snowflake description task requires speakers to engage in comparison activity; speakers must ensure that their messages are more highly related to the referent than to the similar nonreferent" (1981b, p. 120), the cognitive strategy modeled for the word pair task hardly equips the child to generate long descriptive messages and to compare their application to two snowflakes. In a second test of generalization, Asher and Wigfield used a transfer task in which the target referent was a picture surrounded by six similar pictures that differed on discrete features. Again the messages could be of any length, and again no generalization was found. But surely a careful task analysis would suggest that the strategies involved in scanning an array of pictures for discrete features are quite different from looking at one of a pair of words, so the failure to generalize can hardly be surprising.

Troublesome as this failure to generalize across communication tasks may seem for those who would like to believe in some global communication skill analogous to general intelligence, it suggests to me that a wide variety of quite discrete skills are required for different communicative settings. Given such a wide variety of skills, much more careful thought needs to be given to underlying processes when designing transfer tasks. In short, I think that we need to look for near transfer before seeking far transfer, and we should seek far transfer only to the extent that the cognitive strategies trained actually apply to the far transfer task.

Just as researchers attempting to find transfer of speaking training to quite different speaking tasks seem not to have analyzed the task demands of the transfer tasks, attempts at finding transfer from speaking training to listening tasks also seem to me to be logically flawed. The most fundamental division in any analysis of the component skills involved in communication is between those skills required for speaking and those required for listening. Higgins, Fondacaro, and McCann (1981) discuss some of those differences and cite research indicating little evidence of correlations between speaking and listening skills. The essential conclusion of their analysis is that there are many important differences in the cognitive processes underlying performance in the speaker and listener roles. On the basis of task demands alone, there is little reason to expect that training a cognitive strategy for effective speaking, such as that trained by Whitehurst and Sonnenschein (1981), would automatically result in improved performance on a listening task.

In a recent study Sonnenschein and Whitehurst (in press) showed that both speaking and listening skills could be trained, but that neither form of training transferred to the other skill. One explanation for the failure to generalize that was considered by Sonnenschein and Whitehurst is the possible existence of a general metacognitive deficit, raising the question whether children's communicative limitations are best attributed to inadequate cognitive strategies or to inadequate metacognitive knowledge. This is a question of both theoretical and practical importance that will be examined next. See also Borkowski and Büchel's (1983) comments on generalization of strategies.

Metacognitive Knowledge Versus Cognitive Strategies

Metacognition (sometimes referred to as "thinking about thinking") has received increasing attention and the concept has been brought over into research on oral communication. Flavell (1981) provides a thorough review of work on metacognition and its application to oral communication. Many people have argued that metacognition plays an important role in oral communication of information, oral persuasion, oral comprehension, and a number of other domains (Flavell, 1981, p. 37). Despite the intuitive appeal of the notion that self-reflection will contribute to improved performance, the evidence for such a relationship is in short supply. Flavell (1981, pp. 43–55) draws a distinction between metacognitive knowledge and cognitive strategies (which he calls "cognitive actions"). He suggests that cognitive strategies can contribute to performance as well as to monitoring that performance. Monitoring performance is more heavily metacognitive in nature.

This perspective was applied in two experiments concerned with comprehension monitoring and knowledge about communication (Flavell et al., 1981). In these studies kindergarten and second-grade children were given incomplete messages describing how to build a tower of blocks. The verbal and nonverbal behaviors of the children in response to these inadequate messages were analyzed. The verbal and nonverbal indications of awareness of message ambiguities increased from kindergarten to second grade, but even the second graders were far from perfect in their detection and criticism of inadequate messages. Flavell et al. (1981) attribute at least part of the children's communicative inadequacies to "insufficient metacognitive development" (p. 52).

Unfortunately, this interpretation is circular, as pointed out by Whitehurst (1981) in his commentary on the Flavell et al. monograph. The linkage between thinking about what would make for successful communication and the set of well-rehearsed cognitive strategies necessary for successful communication should not be assumed to be direct. The cognitive strategy training that has been successful in improving communication performance cited above consisted of instructions to use appropriate actions rather than self-reflection: If unsure, ask questions; if a speaker, describe differences.

Metacognitive knowledge about communication may yet prove to be an important contributor to generalized communication skill. But if it is to affect performance, such knowledge must include strategies for action. In many ways metacognitive knowledge bears the same relationship to cognitive strategies that subsidiary awareness bears to focal awareness: "Subsidiary awareness and focal awareness are mutually exclusive. If a pianist shifts his attention from the piece he is playing to the observation of what he is doing with his fingers while playing it, he may get confused and stop" (Polanyi, 1964, p. 56; discussed by Cazden, 1972, p. 237). There is a risk that future researchers, influenced by the current interest in metacognition, may try short interventions aimed at metacognition, expecting to find improvements in communicative performance. Such expectations are not likely to be fulfilled. Indeed, unless clearer formulations of metacognition and its potential role in strategy transfer are developed, metacognitive deficit may simply become as much of a tautology for communicative deficit as egocentrism was a decade earlier.

On the other hand, metacognitions about communication, if developed over a long period of time, may play an important role in communicative performance. For example, Robinson (1981, pp. 175–177) has found that young children get remarkably little explicit feedback from adults in the home or school about the causes of communicative failures. Robinson and her co-workers found that less than 4% of preschool children's inadequate messages were followed by explicit instructions about appropriate forms of requests (e.g., "You should tell me whether you want the blue or the red one, otherwise I can't tell what you mean"). Explicit feedback was almost never observed in homes or elementary schools. These observations are all the more interesting because Robinson has shown that many children who are well into their school years remain ignorant of the fact that when they are unable to understand a speaker, the latter may be to blame. Being aware of this research, my wife and I have taken considerable time to point out ambiguities to our son in his messages. Recently, we were standing in our driveway and he asked, "Daddy, which car are we going to take?" When I absentmindedly replied, "The red one," he looked and said, "But Daddy, there are two red ones!" The work of Robinson (1981) and Flavell et al. (1981) suggests that such comments are rare among children just turned 3 years old. Similarly, the work of Bearison and Cassel (1975) suggests that different home environments may affect children's development of communicative effectiveness.

There are large individual differences among children in their metacommunicative knowledge, and these differences come from somewhere. At present we know little about their origins, although the home environment is a likely influence. We also know little about the relationships between metacommunicative knowledge and communicative performance. Given the primitive state of our understanding of these two issues, we should not be too optimistic that brief training of metacommunicative knowledge will lead directly to observable improvements in children's communication skills.

Future Directions

All of the successful interventions using cognitive strategy training cited above have involved direct training on an individual basis by an adult. Recent advances in microcomputer technology may open up ways to apply the fruits of this research in classrooms. I would like to describe briefly research of my own that is currently in progress. The domain of interest is oral communication skills, but the basic technique may be applicable to other areas.

Over the past 2 years my colleagues and I have developed a referential communication game that runs on an Apple II microcomputer. The game displays arrays of figures on the screen. One child is designated as the speaker and another as a listener. The number of the target referent is displayed in such a way that only the speaker sees the number. The speaker then describes the target referent and the listener (who may ask questions if he is uncertain which one his partner means) chooses one of the pictures by pressing its number on the keyboard. The computer program then indicates whether the choice is correct or incorrect. If incorrect, the children get two more tries; if correct, the next array of pictures is presented. The game is highly motivating for children and brings about oral communication that is rich in its social and linguistic properties (Dickson & Bilow, Note 2).

As pointed out in the present review, cognitive strategy training has recently been applied to oral communication, and the initial results seem promising. One obstacle to implementing the training described here in schools is that virtually all of the training has been done with the adult experimenter giving one-to-one training. With the rapid advances in microcomputer technology it is now possible at a cost of about $300 to make the microcomputer "talk." We are now adding this feature to our microcomputer game, and the first words the microcomputer will speak to children will be cognitive strategies. Specifically, the children will be told that they are going to learn how to play a communication game and the computer will teach them how to play it well. The microcomputer will serve as the speaker and will both think out loud, along the lines of the work by Asher and Wigfield discussed earlier, and will verbalize the strategy of telling how the target differs from other pictures in the array, along the lines of the work of Whitehurst and Sonnenschein also cited earlier. The children will initially listen to the microcomputer and then act as speakers to other children. We will tell the child to "think like the computer" and seek evidence of the child's using cognitive strategies modeled by the computer. Should this technique for training cognitive strategies prove to be as successful as the use of an adult trainer, it would have important applications for training other cognitive strategies as well.

Acknowledgments. This chapter is based in part upon work supported by the U.S. National Institute of Education under Grant No. NIE-G-0009. Any opinions, findings, and conclusions or recommendations expressed in this chapter are those of the author and do not necessarily reflect the views of the Institute or the Department of Education. S. Sonnenschein and G. J. Whitehurst provided helpful comments on this paper.

Reference Notes

1. Sonnenschein, S., & Whitehurst, G. J. *Developing referential communication skills: The interaction of role-switching and difference rule training.* Manuscript submitted for publication, 1982.
2. Dickson, W. P., & Bilow, C. *The microcomputer communication game* (Release 5.0. Tech. Manual). Madison: Wisconsin Center for Education Research, 1982.

References

Asher, S. R. Referential communication. In G. J. Whitehurst & B. J. Zimmerman (Eds.), *The functions of language and cognition.* New York: Academic Press, 1979.

Asher, S. R., & Parke, R. D. Influence of sampling and comparison processes on the development of communication effectiveness. *Journal of Educational Psychology,* 1975, *67,* 64–75.

Asher, S. R., & Wigfield, A. Influence of comparison training on children's referential communication. *Journal of Educational Psychology,* 1981, *73,* 232–241. (a)

Asher, S. R., & Wigfield, A. Training referential communication skills. In W. P. Dickson (Ed.), *Children's oral communication skills.* New York: Academic Press, 1981. (b)

Bearison, D. L., & Cassel, T. Z. Cognitive decentration and social codes: Communicative effectiveness in young children from differing family contexts. *Developmental Psychology,* 1975, *11,* 29–36.

Borkowski, J. G. Signs of intelligence: Strategy generalization and metacognition. In S. R. Yussen (Ed.), *The development of reflection.* New York: Academic Press, in press.

Borkowski, J. G., & Büchel, F. P. Learning and memory strategies in the mentally retarded. In M. Pressley & J. R. Levin (Eds.), *Cognitive strategy research: Psychological foundations.* New York: Springer-Verlag, 1983.

Cazden, C. B. *Child language and education.* New York: Holt, Rinehart & Winston, 1972.

Cosgrove, J. M., & Patterson, C. J. Plans and the development of listener skills. *Developmental Psychology,* 1977, *13,* 557–564.

Cosgrove, J. M., & Patterson, C. J. Generalization of training for children's listener skills. *Child Development,* 1978, *19,* 513–516.

Dickson, W. P. The development of interpersonal referential communication skills in young children using an interactional game device (Doctoral dissertation, Stanford University, 1974). *Dissertation Abstracts International,* 1974, *35,* 3511A. (University Microfilms No. 74–27, 008)

Dickson, W. P. Creating communication-rich classrooms: Insights from the sociolinguistic and referential traditions. In L. C. Wilkinson (Ed.), *Communicating in the classroom.* New York: Academic Press, 1982. (a)

Dickson, W. P. Two decades of referential communication research: A review and meta-analysis. In C. J. Brainerd & M. Pressley (Eds.), *Verbal processes in children.* New York: Springer-Verlag, 1982. (b)

Flavell, J. H. *Cognitive development.* Englewood Cliffs, NJ: Prentice-Hall, 1977.

Flavell, J. H. Cognitive monitoring. In W. P. Dickson (Ed.), *Children's oral communication skills.* New York: Academic Press, 1981.

Flavell, J. H., Botkin, P. T., Fry, C. L., Jr., Wright, J. W., & Jarvis, P. E. *The development of role-taking and communication skills in children.* New York: Wiley, 1968.

Flavell, J. H., Speer, J. R., Green, F. L., & August, D. L. The development of comprehension monitoring and knowledge about communication. *Monographs of the Society for Research in Child Development,* 1981, *46*(5, Serial No. 192).

Fry, C. L. Training children to communicate to listeners. *Child Development,* 1966, *37,* 675–685.

Glucksberg, S., Krauss, R. M., & Higgins, E. T. The development of referential communication skills. In F. D. Horowitz (Ed.), *Review of child development research* (Vol. 4). Chicago: University of Chicago Press, 1975.

Higgins, E. T., Fondacaro, R., & McCann, C. D. Rules and roles: The "communication game" and speaker-listener processes. In W. P. Dickson (Ed.), *Children's oral communication skills.* New York: Academic Press, 1981.

Ironsmith, M., & Whitehurst, G. J. How children learn to listen: The effects of modeling feedback styles on children's performance in referential communication. *Developmental Psychology,* 1978, *14,* 546–554(a).

Meichenbaum, D. H., & Goodman, J. Training impulsive children to talk to themselves: A means of developing self-control. *Journal of Abnormal Psychology,* 1971, *77,* 115–126.

Patterson, C. J., & Massad, C. M. Facilitating referential communication among children: The listener as teacher. *Journal of Experimental Child Psychology,* 1980, *29,* 357–370.

Patterson, C. J., Massad, C. M., & Cosgrove, J. M. Children's referential communication: Components of plans for effective listening. *Developmental Psychology,* 1978, *14,* 401–406.

Piaget, J. *Language and thought of the child.* New York: Harcourt, Brace, 1926.

Polyani, M. *Personal knowledge: Towards a post-critical philosophy.* New York: Harper & Row, 1964.

Pressley, M. Elaboration and memory development. *Child Development,* 1982, *53,* 296–309.

Pressley, M., Levin, J. R., & Bryant, S. L. Memory strategy instruction during adolescence: When is explicit instruction needed? In M. Pressley & J. R. Levin (Eds.), *Cognitive strategy research: Psychological foundations.* New York: Springer-Verlag, 1983.

Pressley, M., Reynolds, W. M., Stark, K. D., & Gettinger, M. Cognitive strategy training and children's self-control. In M. Pressley & J. R. Levin (Eds.), *Cognitive strategy research: Psychological foundations.* New York: Springer-Verlag, 1983.

Robinson, E. J. The child's understanding of inadequate messages and communication failure. In W. P. Dickson (Ed.), *Children's oral communication skills.* New York: Academic Press, 1981.

Shantz, C. U. The role of role-taking in children's referential communication. In W. P. Dickson (Ed.), *Children's oral communication skills.* New York: Academic Press, 1981.

Shatz, M., & Gelman, R. The development of communication skills: Modification in the speech of young children as a function of listener. *Monographs of the Society for Research in Child Development,* 1973, *38*(5, Serial No. 152).

Sonnenschein, S., & Whitehurst, G. R. Training referential communication skills: The limits of success. *Journal of Experimental Child Psychology,* in press.

Whitehurst, G. J. The development of communication: Changes with age and modeling. *Child Development,* 1976, *47,* 473–482.

Whitehurst, G. J. Commentary. In J. H. Flavell, J. R. Speer, F. L. Green, & D. L. August, The development of comprehension monitoring and knowledge about communication. *Monographs of the Society for Research in Child Development,* 1981, *46*(5, Serial No. 192).

Whitehurst, G. J., & Merkur, A. E. The development of communication: Modeling and contrast failure. *Child Development,* 1977, *48,* 993–1001.

Whitehurst, G. J., & Sonnenschein, S. The development of informative messages in referential communication: Knowing when versus knowing how. In W. P. Dickson (Ed.), *Children's oral communication skills.* New York: Academic Press, 1981.

3. Moral Education Strategies

Robert D. Enright, Daniel K. Lapsley, and Victor M. Levy, Jr.

Moral education has recently become a popular force in social education. There are now two journals, the *Journal of Moral Education* and the *Moral Education Forum,* devoted to the topic. Reviews of the literature and "how to" books are now abundant (Arbuthnot & Faust, 1981; Damon, 1978; Hersh, Paolitto, & Reimer, 1979; Lawrence, 1980; Leming, 1981; Lickona, 1978; Lockwood, 1978; Purpel & Ryan, 1976; Rest, 1974a; Scharf, 1978). Although there are numerous moral education paradigms, Kohlberg's (1969) cognitive-developmental model seems, on the basis of sheer volume of publications, to be one of the most popular. This chapter will concentrate exclusively on the Kohlbergian model.

The basic theoretical principles of Kohlbergian moral education are the following:

1. Morality is confined to the cognitive realm.
2. As people mature, they increase the complexity of their moral thinking by progressing through a series of stages.
3. Moral thinking is considered to be internally consistent, consisting of a structured whole of reasoning.
4. The progression is one stage at a time.
5. Regression is theoretically impossible.
6. The corresponding Piagetian logical reasoning and role-taking stages are necessary for the emergence of a given moral stage. For example, if a person cannot hold in memory the perspectives of self and other (Level 2 role taking), he or she will not be able to understand sharing between two people (Level 2 moral development). See Kohlberg (1976) for an elaboration of this principle.
7. The stages at least up to Stage 3 are considered universal (see Simpson, 1974, and Kurtines and Greif, 1974, for a refutation of universality on the higher levels).

The stage progression is as follows:

Stage 1. The child takes one perspective, that of the authority, and believes it is best to submit to that authority to avoid punishment.

Stage 2. The child takes a self-and-other perspective and believes that in any social interaction, both self and other should benefit. Reciprocity is the key to fairness.

Stage 3. The child takes a group perspective and believes it is best to conform to group norms, which may lead to approval from the group.

Stage 4. The adolescent takes a systems, or societal, perspective and believes that he or she should follow the law for its own sake in order to maintain an orderly society.

Stage 5. The person formulates his or her own moral principles, or abstract rules, that guide moral behavior. The principles usually concern a social contract in which the majority must agree on a given moral sanction.

Although a Stage 6 exists, it is considered so rare that it has not been included in Kohlberg's recent scoring manuals. Assessment is usually in the form of a lengthy Moral Judgment Interview (MJI) of up to nine dilemmas followed by questions (Kohlberg, Note 1) or by a standardized paper-and-pencil Defining Issues Test (DIT; see Rest, Note 2). The latter does not give a stage score but instead gives a percentage of time the subject uses Stage 5 and Stage 6 reasoning in solving the dilemmas. Although some moral education programs use a paper-and-pencil form of the Kohlberg interview, this measurement form has not been examined psychometrically. The moral development construct is considered valid by some (Rest, 1974b) and open to question by others (Kurtines & Greif, 1974; Phillips & Nicolayev, 1978). Suffice it to say that 20 years of intensive work has not damaged the core of Kohlberg's theory (see Colby, 1978, for a sensitive discussion of the evolution of Kohlbergian theory).

Moral education is far more recent than the 1958 origins of basic research in moral development (Kohlberg, 1958). Despite the existence of three reviews of the literature dating from 1978, there is no comprehensive review of existing moral education strategies. For instance, Lockwood's (1978) highly regarded review examined only 11 studies, which represented virtually all available literature at the time. Leming (1981) restricted himself to classroom interventions using pre- and posttest and control group designs; as we will see, this procedure omits a great deal of the literature. Finally, Lawrence (1980) restricted herself to interventions involving the DIT only.

This chapter will review in the chronological order of their emergence the five major strategies in moral education. The first strategy to emerge (in 1963 and 1966) and the least complex, although possibly the most difficult to implement, is the *plus-one exchange*. Here, the educator, through modeling of ideas one level above the student's current level, attempts to induce cognitive disequilibrium and eventually to stimulate growth to the next higher moral level. The second strategy to emerge is *deliberate psychological education,* in which counseling communication techniques are introduced to students. The communication exercises are seen as role-taking experiences that may stimulate moral growth (see Principle 6 regarding moral development).

Next is a series of didactic courses in ethics, social studies, and logic. These are more like traditional high school courses in which moral development becomes a dependent variable in assessing outcome. The fourth strategy is an information processing approach to the plus-one exchange in which both thought and behavior are part of the program. Finally, we will discuss the *just community* strategy, which focuses on changing the structure of the environment rather than focusing exclusively on individual moral growth. The attempt here is to make social institutions more democratic, thus stimulating growth in individuals to Stage 5 moral development, in which democratic principles are understood and valued. For each strategy we will evaluate the existing programs from an empirical perspective so that the reader can choose strategies that not only seem appropriate, but also seem to work.

Plus-One Exchange Strategy

The earliest and most frequently employed moral education strategy is based on the plus-one model (Arbuthnot & Faust, 1981). As noted previously, this model assumes that development is facilitated when a child is exposed to reasoning at the next higher stage in the developmental sequence. The first group of studies to be discussed will be the pioneering work. Subsequent research will be reviewed with all of the variations and refinements that have been developed.

The Early Work

The plus-one methodology is concerned with the invariant sequence assumption of cognitive development. The first study to examine the invariance assumption was conducted by Bandura and McDonald (1963; see also LeFurgy & Woloshin, 1969). They attempted to influence children's moral intentionality judgments (objective vs. subjective responsibility; see Piaget, 1932/1965) through the use of modeling and social reinforcement. By reinforcing adult models who expressed judgments that were contrary to the child's current stage orientations, Bandura and McDonald (1963, p. 275) hoped to demonstrate that "moral judgment responses are less age-specific than implied by Piaget, and that children's moral orientation can be altered and even reversed by the manipulation of response reinforcement contingencies and by the provision of appropriate social models." From their results the authors concluded that children at all age levels have available to them both objective and subjective response tendencies. Whether one or the other is actually elicited is largely dependent on the potency of reinforced modeling cues.

If left unchallenged, the interpretation of the Bandura and McDonald (1963) study would have grave implications for any stage theory positing an invariant sequence. In a later study Turiel (1966) questioned whether Bandura and McDonald (1963) adequately tested Piaget's theory. Turiel pointed out that Piaget's stage theory of intentionality does not satisfy the criterion that "stage" must be representative of mental structures, as opposed to mere verbal responses. The implication is that whereas verbal responses can be manipulated by a reinforcement contingency, mental structures cannot. Turiel (1966) further maintained that Bandura and McDonald (1963) misidentified Piaget's two stages. The objectivity-subjectivity dimension is only a surface feature of the more general heteronomous-autonomous orientation. Thus, the induced changes, in Turiel's (1966) view, did not represent underlying structure, but only subjects' guesses as to what the expected answer was.

In his now classic study Turiel examined Kohlberg's (1963a) moral development theory of the invariant sequence in the following hypotheses: (a) More learning results from exposure to the stage directly above one's own than from exposure to the stage two above one's own; and (b) more learning results from exposure to the next higher stage than to the preceding one.

Turiel distributed subjects, determined by a pretest to be in Kohlberg's Stages 2, 3, or 4, into three experimental groups and one control group. Experimental subjects were exposed to moral reasoning in role-playing situations with an adult. The experimental groups corresponded to whether subjects were exposed to reasoning one or two stages higher than or one stage lower than their current stage of reasoning. For each of three dilemmas (from the Kohlberg interview) the subject played the role of the main character. As such, the subject was required to seek advice from two "friends," each role played by the experimenter. The "friends" gave conflicting advice on how to resolve the dilemma (e.g., pro vs. con), but always at the treatment-appropriate stage of reasoning. There is some controversy as to whether Turiel actually found support for his hypotheses because when experimental and control groups were compared, it was found that the latter actually regressed to a greater extent than the experimentals improved, indicating that differences between groups were not due exclusively to experimental gain (see Broughton, 1978; Kurtines & Greif, 1974). In any event, Turiel concluded that exposure to the stage directly above one's dominant stage (i.e., "plus-one") is the most effective strategy for inducing new modes of thought (see also Turiel & Rothman, 1972).

How well have Turiel's findings been corroborated in subsequent moral development intervention research? Table 3-1 summarizes, in a chronologically ordered list, the details of each study using the plus-one strategy. The "weaknesses" column that appears in all the subsequent tables is omitted here because the methodologies used here are for the most part sound. As can be seen in the table, although Turiel's general approach for inducing moral development is surely prototypic, design features are not. The plus-one methodology can vary in a number of ways. For example, the intervention can be either structured or unstructured, adult directed or peer directed. Treatments may consist of discussion or role-play episodes, or a combination of discussion and role playing. The length of the intervention can also vary from a single session, as in the Turiel (1966) study, to multiple sessions over the course of many weeks. Whereas all studies employ pretest-posttest designs, only some of them test for long-term effects of the treatment. Not all studies employ the same dependent measure. While Kohlberg's MJI is probably the most popular measure, his paper-and-pencil measure is also used, as are Piagetian moral judgment tasks and Rest's (Note 2) DIT.

Subsequent Educational Applications

In two studies Blatt and Kohlberg (1975) explored the effects of guided peer discussions of moral conflicts (plus-one) on junior and senior high school children's reasoning. In the first study with 11- to 12-year-olds, 13 of 30 subjects were randomly selected for pretesting. Of these 13, 11 were available for posttesting and 10 were available for a 1-year follow-up test. Three comparison groups were used from the Turiel (1966) experiment. The first group served as the basic pretest control. The second group served as the control for the 1-year follow-up test. The third control group was added to determine whether the intervention produced a larger change than that obtained by mere exposure to higher level thinking. The experimental condition consisted of asking children to resolve moral conflict situations. Spontaneous peer arguments were said to arise because of the wide range of moral judgment levels exhibited by the children. The examiner would then "take the 'solution' proposed by a child who was one stage above the majority of the children discussing the dilemma and clarify and support that child's argument" (Blatt & Kohlberg, 1975, p. 133). The role of the examiner throughout was to summarize and clarify arguments, and to encourage higher level thinking by demonstrating the inadequacy of lower level reasoning. The major finding of this study was that the plus-one intervention experience led to significant increases in moral maturity scores. These gains were still evident a year after the first posttest. The average gain from pre- to posttest in the treatment group was over one-half stage, whereas change in the control group was negligible. This pattern of change was replicated in a more extensive investigation using randomized groups in Study 2, and in a recent study by Hayden and Pickar (1981). In the latter study classroom moral discussion based on the plus-one method increased one quarter of a stage on the average.

The plus-one methodology was also successful in stimulating progressive moral development in college students (Justice, 1978), though it was generally unsuccessful for 7- to 9-year-olds (Williams, 1974). Wright (1978) also found no effect of a plus-one treatment for elementary school age delinquents and nondelinquents. Biskin and Hoskisson (1977), employing moral dilemmas found in children's literature in discussions with 9- to 10-year-olds, found no support for the plus-one approach (authors' claims notwithstanding) in the first experiment, although more positive results were forthcoming in the second. Keasey found that exposure to a model using higher stage reasoning induced immediate change, but was no more successful than any other approach (e.g., same stage, opinion) in inducing longer term (2 weeks) changes. Keasey (1973) concluded that children seek to resolve conflict induced by any intervention method, but whether this resolution results in a more equilibrated state is dependent on whether the child is in transition and ready to develop (see Brainerd, 1977, for a critique of this position).

In one of the briefest plus-one interventions on record, Arbuthnot (1975) required college subjects to role-play Kohlbergian dilemmas against an opponent whose level of reasoning may have been higher, equal to, or lower than the subjects' own. Subjects were given the general set to convince the other person that one's own view was more justifiable and to do so with most convincing arguments. The role-playing episode lasted 15–20 minutes.

Table 3-1 Plus-One Exchange Studies

Author	Age and N	Measure
Turiel (1966)	44 seventh-grade boys between 12 and 13.7 years	MJI
Crowley (1968)	First graders, N not specified	Intentionality paradigm
Jensen & Larm (1970)	35 kindergartners randomly assigned to two experimental groups and one control group	Intentionality paradigm
Turiel & Rothman (1972)	43 seventh and eighth graders randomly assigned to two experimental groups and one control group	MJI
Colby (1973)	42 11- to 13-year-olds assigned to two experimental groups and a control group	MJI
Jensen & Hafen (1973)	36 4-year-olds assigned to two experimental conditions and one control condition	Intentionality paradigm
Search (1973)	46 20-year-old college women assigned to three experimental groups and a comparison group	MJI
Keasey (1973)	42 10- to 11-year-olds assigned to one of six experimental groups (stages) and a control group	MJI
Williams (1974)	48 7- to 9-year-olds factorially assigned to treatment (experimental-control) and moral judgment stage (3 levels)	Modified MJI
Dozier (1974)	112 sixth graders randomly assigned to two experimental groups and one control group	MJI
Blatt & Kohlberg (1975)	Experiment 1 30 11- to 12-year-olds; three control groups from Turiel (1966) used for comparison	MJI
	Experiment 2 132 12- to 16-year-olds from four schools randomly assigned to two experimental conditions; one comparison group	MJI

Length of Treatment	Treatment	Results
One session (length unspecified)	Subject role-plays both sides of an issue for three dilemmas	+
Unspecified, probably one brief session	Reinforced labeling of verbal responses vs. discussion of intentionality	+[a]
One brief session	Discussion about intentionality vs. verbal discrimination vs. control	+[b]
One session (length unspecified)	Exposure to reasoning plus-one and minus-one stage	0
16 sessions over 10 weeks	Moral discussions for both experimental groups	++[c]
Five 18- to 23-minute sessions	Discussion of intentionality vs. reinforced verbal discrimination vs. control	+[d]
1 hour a week for 7 weeks	Role playing vs. "challenging discussion" vs. didactic instruction vs. a comparison group	+[d]
One-session	Exposure to three reasoning conditions through role play; plus-one, dominant stage, and unsupported opinion	+ 0[e]
24 discussion sessions over 8 weeks	Discussion of value conflicts	0[f]
12 55-minute sessions	Discussion of dilemmas vs. self-examination of value vs. control	+[d]
12 hours of discussion over 12 weeks	Discussion of open moral dilemmas	++[g] (two-thirds stage gain)
18 sessions held twice a week, 45 minutes each	Discussion of moral dilemmas	++[g] (one-third stage gain)

Table 3-1 (Continued)

Author	Age and N	Measure
Tracy & Cross (1973)	76 seventh-grade boys assigned to treatment or control condition	Kohlberg's scoring used on three sets of moral dilemmas
Arbuthnot (1975)	96 female introductory psychology students, three treatments	Written MJI
Keefe (1975)	70 eighth graders randomly assigned to four treatment groups and a control	MJI
Selman & Lieberman (1975)	68 second graders divided equally by sex and social class randomly assigned to two experimental groups and a control	Intentionality paradigm
Bono (1975)	45 sixth graders divided into two experimental groups and a control	MJI
Fleetwood & Parish (1976)	29 juvenile delinquents assigned to experimental or control	DIT
Plymale (1977)	152 third and sixth graders assigned to two levels of teacher training, two levels of group leadership techniques, and a control group	Unspecified
Biskin & Hoskisson (1977)	Experiment 1 10 fourth graders and 10 fifth graders randomly assigned to experimental or control group	MJI
	Experiment 2 34 fifth graders assigned to experimental or control group	MJI
Kavanagh (1977)	96 high school students assigned to three treatments and a control condition	MJI
Harris (1977)	45 11th graders randomly assigned to two treatments and a control group	MJI

Length of Treatment	Treatment	Results
1 session	Exposure to plus-one reasoning through role playing	+[h]
One 20-minute session	Role-playing dilemmas +1, +2, and −1	++[i]
10 sessions over 10 weeks	Write answers to and discuss two types of dilemmas; discussions led by a "biased" or "neutral" teacher	+
One semester, twice per week, 20–30 minutes per session	Discussion of film-strip dilemmas led by either an expert or an informed adult vs. a control group	+[d]
Three half-hour sessions a week for 10 weeks	Adult-stimulated discussion of moral issues vs. direct inculcation vs. control	+[j]
6.5 sessions over 4 weeks	Stimulated moral discussion	+
10 hours of discussion twice weekly for 5 weeks	Developmentally trained or informed teachers conducted either peer- or teacher-led discussions	+[k]
7 weeks	Analysis of moral dilemmas found in children's literature vs. control	0
18 weeks	Same as above	+
18 50-minute sessions over 9 weeks	Peer group vs. adult-led discussion vs. writing vs. control; 18 films generated moral issues	+[l]
18-week course	Moral discussion vs. deliberate psychological education and/or moral discussion vs. control	+

Table 3-1 (Continued)

Author	Age and N	Measure
Justice (1978)	College students; N unspecified; experimental vs. control	DIT
Wright (1978)	38 sixth-grade "delinquents," or "nondelinquents," assigned to experimental, "placebo," and control condition	MJI
Walker & Richards (1979)	44 female adolescents aged 14–16; assigned to experimental or control group on basis of logical reasoning tasks vs. control	MJI
Walker (1980)	146 fourth to seventh graders classified by cognitive and perspective-taking stage vs. control	MJI
Hayden & Pickar (1981)	36 seventh-grade girls assigned to experimental or control group	MJI

Note. In the last column, "+" means "reported significant treatment effects"; 0 means "no significant results.

[a] All training groups made more subjective responses than a control group, but discussion provided no advantage over labeling.

[b] Discussion-type training was superior to reinforced discrimination.

[c] Moral development was found to be constrained by logical operational limitations. The second posttest was 3 months after the first posttest.

[d] All treatments were equally effective.

[e] Plus-one exposure was more effective only on the first posttest.

[f] Few differences in favor of treatment groups were significant. Descriptive analysis supports the efficiency of adult-led discussions.

[g] Follow-up was approximately 1 year after intervention.

Length of Treatment	Treatment	Results
Course	Moral dilemma solving, analysis, vs. control	+
Six half-hour discussions over 6 weeks	Stimulated moral discussion vs. social studies vs. control	0
One 25 to 40-minute session	Role playing of moral dilemmas with two adults	$+^m$
One session	Role playing (Stage 3) of moral dilemmas with two adults	$+^n$
6½ hours over 10 weeks	Discussion of moral dilemmas	+ (ca. one-quarter stage change)

[h] Subjects at the preconventional level showed more development than conventional subjects. Social desirability, but not role taking, was an effective antecedent of shift.

[i] The combined plus-one and plus-two treatments were more effective than the minus-one.

[j] Discussion group was more successful than inculcation and control. Inculcation group did not differ from control.

[k] Sixth-grade students in expert-teacher-led discussions showed more moral development than other conditions.

[l] Both the peer group and the writing group, but not the adult-led discussion group, differed from control.

[m] Attempts to stimulate moral development to Stage 4 were successful only for subjects in "early basic" formal operations.

[n] Development to Stage 3 was constrained by cognitive and perspective-taking stages.

Immediately following the session subjects were posttested on the MJI. Arbuthnot found that where subjects were paired with more mature opponents (+1, +2) moral maturity scores increased 49 points on average, whereas those with equally or less mature opponents had an average increase of only 2 points. The increase by subjects having more mature opponents was significantly different from that by control groups. This pattern of change was also observed on a second posttest 1 week later. Arbuthnot, however, did not test whether the greatest shift in moral judgment scores was from subjects exposed to reasoning one stage or two stages higher than the subject's own. Arbuthnot claimed that structural change had occurred for those exposed to arguments at levels higher rather than lower than the subjects' current reasoning levels.

Teacher Effects with Plus-One

A number of studies have attempted to assess the effects of teacher-led discussions in classroom interventions. Selman and Lieberman (1975), for example, compared an "expert-led" group of second graders to an "informed lay-led" group and a control group. The dependent variable was change from pretest to two posttests in the subjects' usage of the intentionality concept. The authors found no difference between these treatments. Both groups of second graders showed progressive development in moral judgment. Thus, according to Selman and Lieberman (1975), "The lack of difference between expert and lay teachers . . . implies that the process of group discussion, and not the knowledge of cognitive-developmental theory, is of greater importance" (p. 716). A similar conclusion was reached by Keefe (1975), who found no difference between groups led by teachers who actively directed the discussion and those led by neutral teachers who went along with student leadership in the direction of the discussion. Both groups significantly improved their level of moral reasoning when compared to a control group. These findings are puzzling because they are in direct contrast to Blatt and Kohlberg's findings (Study 2). Teacher-led groups with no deliberate plus-one strategy had no influence on moral growth; deliberate plus-one strategies worked best.

To further complicate matters, we have a series of studies comparing adults with peer leaders that yielded equivocal results. Kavanagh (1977) varied three different treatment conditions for changing freshman and senior high school students' moral judgments. One treatment featured peer group discussion, another adult-guided peer discussion, a third group used writing "as a procedure to gain insights about perspectives on life," and a fourth group served as a control. Eighteen films were used to generate cognitive conflict. Only the adult-guided discussion seemed to explicitly involve a plus-one approach. Kavanagh found that both the writing and peer group conditions differed from the control, but the (Kohlbergian-inspired) adult-directed peer discussion group did not. It is not clear, however, whether the plus-one strategy was consciously and deliberately employed in any of Kavanagh's conditions.

Plymale (1977) found results contrary to the foregoing. As in the Selman and Lieberman (1975) study, Plymale (1977) varied two levels of teacher training—

"developmentally trained" and "informed." She also varied two kinds of group-leadership techniques: peer and teacher. Her analyses of the posttest results indicated that sixth-grade students who participated in an "expert" teacher-led discussion group showed greater forward movement in moral reasoning than (sixth-grade) students with informed or control teachers. Further, students who engaged in discussions employing a teacher-leadership technique showed more advancement in moral reasoning than those subjects in peer-led and control groups. Thus, in this study, teacher leadership was more effective than peer leadership, and expert teachers more effective than merely informed teachers.

The findings in this section may be contradictory because the methods employed were not standard across studies. For instance, it is unclear in all studies here whether the plus-one exchange was ever deliberately used, or whether mere discussion (whether peer or adult, expert or informed) was used. We do not know, therefore, if cognitive conflict one level above the subject's current level was being introduced into the program.

Studies of Antecedents to Growth

An advance over general classroom applications is the attempt by some researchers to specify clearly the prerequisites for moral growth as discussed in Principle 6 in the introduction here. All studies examining antecedents employ teacher-led plus-one strategies. Tracy and Cross (1973) were interested in the antecedents of moral development shifts induced by the Turiel (1966) plus-one method. After completing pretests on moral judgment (Kohlberg interview), role taking (Hogan, 1969 empathy scale), Feffer's (1959) communicative role-taking task, intelligence (Culture Fair Intelligence Test), and social desirability (Children's Social Desirability Questionnaire), subjects were matched in pairs and assigned to a control or plus-one experimental group. As in Turiel (1966), the boys were asked to imagine that they were the main characters depicted in the three moral dilemmas. They were then asked to seek advice from their "friends" (two experimenters), who argued both sides of the question using reasoning one stage higher than the subjects. The authors found that although both preconventional and conventional reasoners showed significant changes on the posttest as a result of the intervention, preconventional subjects benefited more. However, they also found that role taking and intelligence (as pretest measures) were not related to change, but that social desirability was. Subjects lower on social desirability tended to have higher morality scores. The role-taking finding, though, might be attributed to the fact that inappropriate measures of role taking were employed. Empathy need not require role taking (Higgins, 1981), while the Feffer task has consistently demonstrated poor psychometric properties (Enright & Lapsley, 1980).

In her dissertation, Colby (1973) attempted to determine whether interventions designed to stimulate principled moral reasoning would be constrained by an individual's lack of formal operational reasoning. After assessing children for moral stage, moral comprehension, and logical reasoning, the experimenter randomly assigned the subjects to either one of two experimental groups or to a control group. The only apparent difference between the experimental groups was that one group had three subjects who already evidenced principled reasoning on the pretest. The experimental groups both participated in a 10-week 16-session moral discussion series designed by Blatt (1970). The control group was not exposed to any treatment.

Colby found that subjects in both experimental groups showed more progressive moral development than control subjects. These differences were maintained 3 months later on a subsequent posttest. Further, only subjects who exhibited formal operations benefited from the intervention. Subjects at the concrete operational stage on the pretest showed no advancement to Stage 5 reasoning. Thus, this study demonstrates that a relatively long-term intervention (10 weeks) can effect long-term stable changes in one's structure of moral reasoning. An important proviso of interest to educational planners, however, is that one should not expect to effect a change in children's moral reasoning that would outpace their current stage of logical reasoning.

Following Colby, Walker and Richards (1979) and Walker (1980) have also attempted to demonstrate the "necessary but not sufficient" relationships between moral development and cognitive and perspective-taking development. In the first study Walker and Richards (1979) attempted to stimulate subjects at the "early basic" and "beginning" formal operations stage to reason at Kohlberg's moral stage 4. Since the beginning formal operations substage is theoretically linked with moral stage 3, it was hypothesized that the intervention would not be successful for subjects at this stage, since that would require reasoning at a higher moral stage (Stage 4) than was possible in the cognitive domain (beginning formal). On the other hand, subjects in the early basic formal substage were expected to benefit from the intervention, since moral stage 4 is associated, in theory, with reasoning at that cognitive substage. The treatment, as in the Tracy and Cross (1973) study, consisted of brief role-playing situations where the subject was asked to imagine that he or she was the main character in the dilemma. Consistent with the plus-one methodology, subjects were also exposed to reasoning one stage above (Stage 4) their current mode of reasoning (Stage 3) by role-playing the dilemma with two adults. Using the Kohlberg interview in a pretest-posttest design, Walker and Richards did indeed find that the induced perspective taking generated by the intervention had the greatest effects on experimental subjects in the early basic formal substage, as opposed to subjects in the beginning formal substage or control group(s). In a subsequent study Walker (1980) found that not only were subjects constrained in their moral development by their concomitant stage of cognitive development, but they were also constrained by their stage of perspective taking, contrary to the findings of Tracy and Cross (1975). Taken together, then, these studies (Colby, 1973; Walker & Richards, 1979; Walker, 1980) indicate that moral education programs should not expect to advance moral reasoning beyond the cognitive and perspective-taking capacities of children. The success of an intervention may very well depend on how well logical reasoning and perspective-taking exercises are incorporated into the moral education curriculum (Walker, 1980).

Plus-One Versus Other Interventions

A number of studies have attempted to compare the efficacy of the plus-one approach with that of other intervention methodologies. Search (1973) compared three methods for stimulating moral judgment, namely, role playing, discussion, and didactic instruction. The author made the rather daring predictions that role playing will advance subjects two stages in moral reasoning, discussion one stage, and didactic instruction not at all. No reason, as far as we know, exists to weigh one method over the other to this extravagant a degree. Nevertheless, after a pretest on Form A of Kohlberg's interview, subjects were assigned to the treatment conditions. The method of assignment, however, is somewhat unclear. There is a distinct impression that these subjects were randomly assigned to the three treatment groups, whereas the controls were volunteers not part of the original subject pool. Form B of the Kohlberg interview was administered as the posttest measure 3 weeks after the end of treatment. Although the overall one-way ANOVA on the four groups was significant, post hoc Scheffes could not locate any differences among the three treatment means, although all these means were significantly different from the control. Hence, the author was unable to claim that the three training methods are *differentially* effective in stimulating moral development.

Bono (1975) compared a plus-one technique with direct inculcation to determine which would be the more efficacious stimulant to development. In one group the teacher stimulated discussion by asking probing questions about moral dilemmas. The teacher was said to have ensured that each subject was exposed to moral judgments one stage above her dominant stage. The second group of subjects was presented with the same dilemmas, but here the teacher resolved the issues by using the range of rationales that emanated from the first group. A control group participated in free reading sessions. Bono found that the plus-one discussion method was significantly better in advancing the subject's progression through the moral stages than were the inculcation approach or the control condition.

The plus-one technique did not fare as well in a study by Dozier (1974). Here a directed discussion group was compared with an "experiental" condition and a control group. The experiental condition required subjects to participate in activities designed to encourage self-reflection and examination of parent beliefs and attitudes. No significant differences emerged between the experimental treatments, although both treatments differed significantly from the control condition.

Harris (1977) devised a series of curricular sequences in order to compare a plus-one discussion approach with deliberate psychological education (e.g., training in counseling skills). Two treatment groups and a control group were employed. The moral discourse (MD) group participated in an 18-week values course that consisted of discussion and resolution of open-ended moral dilemmas. Classes were arranged so that students encountered modes of moral thought one stage above their own. The second group, labeled psychological awareness (PA), was exposed to 9 weeks of deliberate psychological education, then 9 weeks of MD. Students were randomly assigned to these treatment groups and to a control group that participated in no values discussion. Each subject was pretested and posttested on Form A of the Kohlberg interview. Form B was used to generate a midterm score (9 weeks). We reanalyzed the midterm data (9 weeks) with the t statistic, comparing the MD group with the PA portion of the PA-MD group (this analysis was not done in Harris, 1977). Although the MD group appeared higher at midterm, the t value of 1.58 was nonsignificant. The two conditions, then, were statistically equivalent at midterm. Although the experimental groups differed at posttest from the control, they were not statistically different from each other. Despite the absence of post hoc tests, this conclusion is obvious on inspection of the MD ($\overline{X}$ = 323.6) and PA-MD ($\overline{X}$ = 320.8) MJI posttest scores. The two experimental conditions, then, are equivalent after 9 and after 18 weeks. Even if differences were found, however, one could not draw direct conclusions about the relative effectiveness of the plus-one and the deliberate psychological education strategies after 18 weeks because the latter confounded 9 weeks of MD and 9 of PA. It should also be noted that 40% of the subjects in the treatment groups failed to advance in moral reasoning, indicating that curricular interventions are not universally effective. In addition, a future study should include another control group that also experiences a change in curriculum at the 9-week mark, in order to assure that the rapid advancement evident in the PA-MD condition was not the result of a mere change in the classroom routine.

What Changes with Plus-One?

Although most studies in Table 3-1 involve multiple training sessions over many weeks, seven studies using the Kohlbergian paradigm found significant results after only one session (Arbuthnot, 1975; Keasey, 1973; Tracy & Cross, 1975; Turiel, 1966; Turiel & Rothman, 1972; Walker, 1980; Walker & Richards, 1979). Crowley (1968), using Piaget's intentionality paradigm, also produced change in one session, while Jensen and Larm (1970) produced similar development in kindergartners over a 5-day period. Perhaps the specific nature of intentionality makes it amenable to quick change, as Crowley (1968) suggests.

Given the complexity of the Kohlbergian stages, however, one would not expect such rapid change in this domain. Because it does occur, one must ask, *What* changes in these interventions? If structuralism (Piaget, 1970) is a valid model, then one must infer that performance is being accessed where competence has already existed (see Flavell & Wohlwill, 1969). In other words, it is quite possible that a person already understands sharing prior to intervention, but if he or she is not asked to do so, if others do not encourage it, the person may not think often about it. Once this thought pattern is needed, reinforced, or encouraged in a given environment, such as an intervention, one quickly accesses the already established skill or structure. Interventions, then, especially the brief ones, may be successful in awakening dormant cognitive structures (at least dormant on a pretest); they may not actually be changing existing thought patterns to more complex ones.

There is also evidence that not even performance is accessed—that instead there is short-term memorization of higher level responses that is quickly lost. This is suggested in Keasey's (1973) follow-up study in which a washout of brief treatment effects was observed.

Summary and Discussion of Plus-One

Despite the variety of techniques (discussion, role playing), teacher variations (adult, peer), and treatment lengths, one pattern is clear: The plus-one approach works. Only 4 of the 28 studies in Table 3-1 show no effect. This strategy, then, does advance posttest scores over pretest; but as previously suggested, the change may be in performance rather than in competence, whereas improved competence is what most educators hope for and claim.

It also appears that this strategy is ineffective in the elementary school years and only begins to be consistently effective in junior high. All three studies accepting the null hypothesis were done with elementary school children (Biskin & Hoskisson, 1977; Williams, 1974; Wright, 1978). Even though Selman and Lieberman (1975) and Jensen and Larm (1970) show significance in the elementary grades, they used Piaget's intentionality paradigm, not the more complex Kohlbergian model.

Although the data suggest that the plus-one strategy is effective, it should be realized that every study except that of Williams (1974) has failed to acknowledge the inordinate difficulty of actually conducting plus-one discussion groups. According to Williams (1974), although reasoned disagreement is easy for moderators to provoke, "the techniques of instantaneous stage diagnosis of responses and support of responses one stage higher as suggested by the theory [is], for all practical purposes, impossible to accomplish during the discussion" (p. 803A). Since this strategy no doubt proves difficult even for experienced or expert discussion leaders, it would be quite impossible to expect a plus-one methodology to be always in effect when peers are responsible for leading discussions.

Deliberate Psychological Education

Virtually all deliberate psychological education (DPE) studies rely on the theoretical and practical work of Mosher and Sprinthall (1971). Although the studies range in content from high school classes in English (Erickson, Colby, Libby, & Lohman, 1976) and the psychology of counseling (Bernier & Rustad, 1977) to a college course in Black studies (Tucker, 1977), most include a seminar and practicum format designed to improve students' counseling communication skills. The basic idea is to first learn communication techniques and to then try them out by counseling, role playing, or teaching.

Consider Sprinthall's (Note 3) program, which is prototypical. The core of the curriculum is Carkhuff's (1971) Active Listening Scale, which ranges from 1 (no awareness or communication of the other's feelings) to 5 (providing the other with a major new view of the emotions expressed). The goal is to achieve Level 3 communication (expressing an accurate understanding of the other's feelings, expressed in the listener's own words). The students first practice Level 3 listening and responding skills through role playing. As the course progresses, the students shift from role playing to "reciprocal helping," in which actual counseling among the students occurs. The weekly training was conducted with a seminar and practicum format. The seminar includes didactic instruction on effective counseling skills, watching films of the "masters" such as Carl Rogers, Fritz Perls, and Albert Ellis, and reading and/or writing assignments. The seminar also includes a discussion of the counseling experience. The practicum is where the skills are applied in role playing and helping. All studies described in Table 3-2 share a major strength of clearly explaining the intervention content. Although all include multiple components, what these are (and the sequence of events) is clear.

Of the 22 studies reviewed (see Table 3-2), 12 claim significant results whereas 9 show none (one did not provide statistical analyses). When only those studies that have used comparison (no randomization) or control groups are inspected, we see a stronger picture, with 10 claiming significant differences and only 4 not. It should be noted, however, that of the 10 claiming significance, 7 were statistically analyzed

Table 3-2 Deliberate Psychological Education Studies

Author	N and Ages	Measure	Length of Treatment
Dowell (1971)	Grades 10–12 ($N = 20$)	Written MJI	16 weeks (3½ hours once a week)
Sprinthall (Note 3)	30 high school students (no specifics)	Written MJI	10-week course, two periods per week
Erickson (1978, Note 4)	23 sophomore (high school) females; follow-up included 21 only	Written MJI	10-week course (number of days per week not reported)
Mackie (1974)	12 juniors, low achieving (comparison groups were included, but not analyzed)	MJI	Two class periods per week for one semester
Schaffer (1974)	10 juniors 20 seniors	Written MJI	12 weeks, 5 days per week, 1 hour per time

inappropriately (see Table 3-2). The majority of the studies that used the MJI, from which a stage score can be obtained, showed approximately one third of a stage change. This was the case regardless of the statistical significance of the results. It seems, then, that approximately one semester of deliberate psychological education leads to a one-third stage upward shift in moral development. The studies that employed long-term follow-ups of a year or more (Bernier & Rustad, 1977; Erickson, 1978; Wong, 1977) reported either a significant upward shift or maintenance of posttest levels. Maturation, not the program's effectiveness, may be the cause of the change or maintenance. Even so, it should be noted that the change seems to be stable because the students did not regress to pretest levels subsequent to intervention. Possibly the most provocative finding is that moral growth was apparent for people from junior high school through adulthood. Despite a basic research finding (Rest, Davison, & Robbins, 1978) that a moral asymptote is reached in the college years, four studies here demonstrated that moral intervention can promote significant upward change in the adult years.

Kind of Treatment	Results	Weaknesses
Counseling, empathy training	0	No interrater reliability of measure
Counseling, empathy training	0 (one-third stage change was not significant)[b]	No control group
Counseling, empathy training; discussion of women's issues; interviewing females in the community	0 pre- to posttest; + posttest to follow-up (one-third stage change at posttest, one-third stage change at follow-up)[a]	No control group; selective attrition
Counseling, empathy training	4 of 8 subjects gained one-third stage	Comparison groups not randomized; reported "antagonism" of subjects to testing; no statistical tests
Moral discussions; interviewing of a young child; acquisition of "personal skills" and role taking in a group format	0	No control group

Table 3-2 (Continued)

Author	N and Ages	Measure	Length of Treatment
Sullivan (1975)	14 high school juniors and seniors in experimental group, 14 in each of two comparison groups	Written MJI	1 academic year; 2½ hours once a week
Paolitto (1976)	17 eighth graders in experimental group; N not reported in control	MJI	Two 40-minute sessions per week for 23 weeks
Sprinthall (1976)	27 high school students	Written MJI	10-week course, 2 periods per week
Bernier (1977)	26 teachers (18 in experimental and 8 in control group)	DIT	1. one summer session, 3 or 4 days per week; 2. 2 months during school year, twice per month for 3 hours a session
Stanley (1976)	10 parents, 7 ninth and tenth graders in group A; 6 parents only in group B; 10 parents and 7 adolescents in comparison group	MJI	10 weeks
Erickson et al. (1976)	19 junior high school students	DIT	English elective class (no other information given; presumed to have been one semester)
Schepps (1977)	12 high school juniors in experimental; N not reported for comparison group	MJI	One semester of 12 weeks (no other information reported)
DiStefano (1978)	11 high school juniors and seniors in experimental; 11 in comparison group	MJI	One semester, 3 hours per week
Hurt & Sprinthall (1977)	Curriculum 1 = 28 teachers; curriculum 2 = 20 teachers; comparison group = 23	DIT	11 weeks for 2 days per week, 2 hours a day

Kind of Treatment	Results	Weaknesses
Moral discussions; counseling, empathy training; leading moral discussions with elementary school students	+ (between one-third and one-half stage change)	No randomization to condition; experimentals higher at pretest
Moral discussion; role playing; interviewing people in community	+ (about one-third stage change)	No major weaknesses
Counseling, empathy training	0 (one-third stage change was not significant)[b]	No control group
Deliberate instruction in developmental theory; counseling, empathy training	+[b]	Nonrandomized comparison group; inappropriate statistics
Empathy training; family conflict resolution	0	Nonrandomized comparison group
Moral discussion; peer teaching; discussion of laws	+[b]	No control group
Moral discussions; counseling, empathy training; interviews with school personnel	0	Nonrandomized comparison groups
Students' discussion of their own interpersonal relationships	0	Nonrandomized comparison group, although they did volunteer for the study.
Counseling, empathy training	+[c]	Nonrandomized comparison group; inappropriate statistics

Table 3-2 (Continued)

Author	N and Ages	Measure	Length of Treatment
Nichols, Isham, & Austad (1977), Study 1	48 seventh graders in experimental; 48 in control	DIT	9 weeks, 5 days a week, 50-minute periods
Nichols et al. (1977), Study 2	46 eighth graders in experimental; 46 in control	DIT	Same as above
Nichols et al. (1977), Study 3	41 ninth graders in experimental; 41 in control	DIT	Same as above
Tucker (1977)	31 college students in experimental group; 14 in control	DIT	12 weeks (no other information available)
Wong (1977)	29 adult women in 3 experimental classes; 25 in comparison classes	DIT	32 hours over 8 weeks (exp. groups 1 and 3); 32 hours over 4 weeks (exp. group 2)
Bernier & Rustad (1977)	13 high school students	Written MJI	Psychology of counseling class (no other information given; presumed to have been one semester)
Cognetta & Sprinthall (1978)	15 tenth–twelfth graders in experimental group; 16 in comparison group	DIT	Social studies class (no other information given; presumed to have been one semester)
Oja & Sprinthall (1978)	27 teachers in experimental group; 21 in comparison group	DIT	5 weeks, 4 days per week, 3½ hours per day

[a] Pre- to posttest result with the 23 subjects was nonsignificant ($p < .07$). With only 21 subjects the pre- to posttest and the posttest to follow-up results were both significant. Selective attrition was probably operating here.

[b] The statistical test was from pre- to posttest within the experimental condition.

[c] The statistics were not between groups but were a series of correlated t tests within groups.

Kind of Treatment	Results	Weaknesses
Moral discussions; examination of one's own values; didactic instruction in psychological needs and motives	$+^c$	Inappropriate statistics
Moral discussion; empathy training; didactic instruction in ethics	$+^c$	Same
Moral discussions; examination of relations between the individual and sociopolitical institutions	$+^c$	Same
Empathy training; discussions of racism, sexism	$+^c$	Nonrandomized comparison group; inappropriate statistics
Empathy training; discussion of sex-role stereotypes; interviewing females in the community	$+^d$	Nonrandomized comparison group; slight variations in treatment across the three experimental groups
Counseling, empathy training	0^e (about one-third stage change was not significant)	No comparison group
Empathy training; cross-age teaching	$+^c$	Nonrandomized comparison group; inappropriate statistics
Counseling, empathy training	$+$	Nonrandomized comparison group

[d] Statistics were correlated t tests within groups; only the experimental groups 1 and 3 showed growth, suggesting that the 8-week program was more effective than the 4-week one. A 15-month follow-up showed gain between posttest and follow-up for experimental groups 1 and 3.
[e] From pre- to posttest there was a nonsignificant gain of 30 points (from 371 to 401). At the 1-year follow-up the score was 402.

In surveying the large number of deliberate psychological education studies, one is struck by three patterns. First, with the exception of Dowell's (1971) and Paolitto's (1976) well-designed studies, all have serious methodological and/or statistical flaws. The majority use comparison rather than control groups; there is no randomization to group (see Cognetta & Sprinthall, 1978; DiStefano, 1978; Hurt & Sprinthall, 1977; Mackie, 1974; Oja & Sprinthall, 1978; Schepps, 1977; Stanley, 1976; Sullivan, 1975; Tucker, 1977; Wong, 1977). A large number of others have only an experimental group (see Bernier, 1977; Bernier & Rustad, 1977; Erickson, 1978; Erickson, Colby, Libby, & Lohman, 1976; Schaffer, 1974). These studies confound maturation and the independent variable, which makes conclusions about the program's effectiveness difficult. Even some that have comparison or control groups use inappropriate statistics by examining within-group change without a concomitant between-groups analysis (see Cognetta & Sprinthall, 1978; Hurt & Sprinthall, 1977; the three studies in Nichols, Isham, & Austad, 1977; Tucker, 1977; Wong, 1977).

Second, almost a decade of work has not produced revision or refinement in either the substantive strategies employed or the methodology. Moral discussion and/or counseling training are the basis of virtually all programs. There are few attempts to extend the pioneering work beyond a generalization to different groups (e.g., teachers). For instance, what components of the counseling experience are the powerful inducements to change? Could these components be learned in, for instance, 5 weeks rather than a semester, which has become the modal length of the programs? Why should one expect moral growth from exposure to Carkhuff's communication model? What seems to have happened is that modeling of past programs has supplanted innovation and refinement. Refinements are so slight as to suggest copious replications of the original work in the area. We are left, therefore, with bold, creative initial ideas but no growth in conceptualization of the strategies.

Third, and finally, despite the serious methodological flaws and lack of conceptual growth, one gets a sense that the programs really may be making a difference in the lives of the students. There is a refreshing sense of competence that pervades the informal clinical evaluations of the students. For example, Sprinthall (Note 3) cites the following as prototypes:

Table 3-3 Didactic Strategies in Moral Education

Author	Age/N	Measure	Length of Treatment
Ethics courses			
Lorimer (1971)	130 16½ to 19½ year-olds in three groups	Written MJI	3 weeks, once a week for 1 hour
Beck et al. (1972)	17 eleventh graders in experimental group; 17 in comparison group	Written MJI	4 months, two 40-minute periods a week

It was easy to listen to and learn from others in the class, teachers and students. My group seemed together and powerful working toward a common goal, we achieved a lot.

A weird class but I think I learned a lot without the usual books, and just from other people. Also, it's useful outside of school too and in the future.

In criticizing the programs we must realize that the "real world" is not the laboratory; comparison groups may be the only recourse in a given high school or college. We also must realize, however, that expediency does not build a viable research program that would lead to valuable refinements. It is hoped that future deliberate psychological education programs will keep both of these perspectives in mind.

Didactic Instruction Strategies

The series of studies in Table 3-3 do not represent a homogeneous set of strategies. The only commonality among them is that all are didactic courses centering for the most part on one theme, although that theme differs across studies. For instance, several concern ethics instruction (Beck, Sullivan, & Taylor, 1972; Boyd, 1980; Lorimer, 1971; Panowitsch, 1976). Others center on social studies, such as police issues (Rest, Ahlgren, & Mackey, Note 5); civil rights (Morrison, Toews, & Rest, Note 6); prejudice issues (Alexander, 1977); and political, economic, and history themes (Colby, Kohlberg, Fenton, Speicher-Dubin, & Lieberman, 1977). One was an acculturation course for United States immigrants (Arredondo-Dowd, 1981). The strategies here differ substantially from deliberate psychological education in not emphasizing empathy communication skills and in the exclusion of a seminar-practicum format (Alexander, 1977, is an exception to the seminar-practicum).

Given the heterogeneity of strategies, it is impossible to draw general conclusions. Most of the studies are long-term interventions of a semester or longer, and therefore effects due to differential training lengths cannot be assessed. The shortest intervention (Lorimer, 1971), however, did have a washout of effects on follow-up.

Kind of Treatment	Results	Weaknesses
Exposition (ethics class); film class ("Fail Safe" and discussion)	+, 0[a]	Unconventional scoring of MJI
Ethics class	0, +[b]	Nonrandomized comparison group

Table 3-3 (Continued)

Author	Age/N	Measure	Length of Treatment
Panowitsch (1976)	152 college students (age range: 17–44) in an unspecified number of courses	DIT	College quarter (no specifics given)
Boyd (1980)	16 college students in experimental and 10 in comparison group	MJI	Unspecified
Social studies courses			
Rest et al. (Note 5, in Lawrence, 1980)	61 junior high school students	DIT	12 weeks (no specifics given)
Morrison et al. (Note 6, in Lawrence, 1980)	103 junior high school students	DIT	4 months (no specifics given)
Alexander (1977)	14 high school juniors and seniors in each group, experimental and control	MJI	16 weeks (no specifics given)
Colby et al. (1977)	358 13- to 17-year-olds in 39 classrooms (controls not specified)	Some oral and some written MJI	1 school year (no specifics given)
Acculturation course			
Arredondo-Dowd (1981)	17 adolescents, 15–19 years old in experimental, 36 in three control groups	MJI	One semester, 3 hours a week

[a] There were no differences between control and experimental conditions at a 2-month follow-up. There was a significant upward change from posttest to follow-up within the exposition condition only. The score used was the number of Level 5 and *double* the number of Level 6 judgments of each subject. This is a highly unusual procedure and no validation evidence is reported.

[b] Significance was achieved only at a 1-year follow-up between experimental and control groups.

[c] Pre- to posttest was significant for only the younger (17- to 20- vs. 21- to 44-year-olds) of the two ethics groups. Only within-group change (rather than between-group differences) was analyzed. The

Kind of Treatment	Results	Weaknesses
Ethics class	+, +[c]	Nonrandomized comparison groups
Ethics course	+, 0[d] (one-third stage change)	Nonrandomized comparison group
Social studies unit to change attitudes toward police	0	No control group
Social studies, civics unit (about civil rights)	0	Nonrandomized comparison group
Course to decrease feelings of prejudice	+ (one-quarter stage change)	Nonrandomized comparison group
Social studies class that stressed moral dilemma discussion	+ (mixed results; ca. one-third stage change)	Although nonrandomization occurred, the large sample allowed for replications
Acculturation course for immigrants	0[e]	Unclear intervention and statistical methods; nonrandomized comparison groups; possible confound with language development

5-month follow-up was only on a subsample from the ethics and logic courses. Pretest to follow-up was the level of analysis.

[d] The one-third stage change at posttest for the experimentals was no longer statistically different from the comparison group at the 9-month follow-up.

[e] The kind of one-way ANOVA used is unspecified, but it appears to have been a comparison of the pre- to posttest gains across the four groups. Significance was reported for the overall main effect ($p < .053$), but no post hoc analyses were done.

It should also be noted that the only studies to claim no significance at all (at a posttest or follow-up) used junior high school students (Rest et al., Note 5: Morrison et al., Note 6). It may be that didactic instruction works best in middle adolescence and later. Those showing significance at posttest on the MJI (Alexander, 1977; Boyd, 1980; Colby et al., 1977) report changes of about one quarter to one third of a stage, although there were large classroom variations in the Colby et al. study. These magnitudes of change compare favorably with deliberate psychological education studies that are of approximately the same treatment length.

The one clear pattern across all ethics courses is that most do not work, regardless of the age group chosen. Of the four surveyed, two found differences at posttest but these washed out at follow-up (Lorimer, 1971; Boyd, 1980); another (Beck et al., 1972) found no differences at posttest but did find differences between groups at a 1-year follow-up. Intervening variables within the year interval, however, may be responsible for this result. Only Panowitsch (1976) claims success, but as is seen in Table 3-3, the analyses were fraught with difficulties.

The social studies courses fare little better. Two find no significance in moral development (Rest et al., Note 5; Morrison et al., Note 6), whereas two claim significance (Alexander, 1977; Colby et al., 1977). When it is realized that the Alexander study was the rare exception here with a seminar-practicum format (as in DPE) and the Colby et al. curriculum directly concerns Kohlbergian moral dilemmas in politics, economics, and history, the results begin to make sense. Both use techniques that have been shown previously to work. Most curricula here, in ethics or social studies, are only remotely related to the Kohlbergian model. Changing attitudes toward police (Rest et al., Note 5), for instance, is not a cognitive as much as it is an affective and/or attitudinal intervention. In other words, moral development does not seem to be influenced by general social curricula.

Finally, the acculturation study (Arredondo-Dowd, 1981) is a glaring example of how inappropriate methodology can lead to inappropriate conclusions in moral education. The author makes a claim for significance from a one-way ANOVA comparing four groups: an experimental group of Vietnamese immigrants, a control of immigrants who wanted to get into the program, and two control groups of white Americans. It is clear that the first control group is the most crucial comparison with the experimental. The main-effect ANOVA was significant, but no post hoc analyses were done to see which group(s) differed from which others. Our reanalysis of the data with a post hoc Scheffe test revealed no significant differences between the experimental and control immigrant groups; both improved to a statistically equivalent degree. English-language improvement may be the mediator here.

Information Processing Strategy

The next strategy to emerge is the information processing approach (Enright, 1980, 1981). It is a complex synthesis of Flavell's information processing model and developmental stage theory. The assumptions behind the strategy are as follows:

1. The content of the social curriculum should come from the child's own social behavior and interactions. Hypothetical dilemmas, then, should be used only as a supplement to the "real-world" content.
2. If the child is encouraged to think about his or her own social experiences, then he or she should be challenged to think more complexly about the newly formed thought. In other words, once the child reflects on an actual experience, the educator should model a statement one level above the child's own.
3. Once a child demonstrates understanding of a social concept, he or she should be encouraged to try that concept out in social action so that the new experience can become the basis of new thoughts. For example, if a child has recently demonstrated the understanding of sharing, the child should be encouraged to act on the conception. If the child then shares with someone, this new social experience could become used in social thinking curricula.

These three points are illustrated in Figure 3-1. Dashed line 1 describes the process of the child reflecting on his or her own behavior. Dashed line 2 describes the process of the thought being reconsidered in a different way. This can be brought about, as stated above, by an educator's challenging the initial thought. Pathway 3 from thought to behavior shows a link between what is thought and what is done in the child's environment. The educator, in other words, can encourage sharing once the child understands it. This sets up the possibility of again reflecting on the new behavior, and the cycle is repeated. The needs, defined by Flavell (1974) as an awareness that one must think or act in a given situation, are included only to suggest that the educator does not try to control the child's thought or behavior, but instead tries, through questioning, to motivate social thought, behavior based on the thought, and again, social thought based on the behavior. See Enright (1980) for other details of this model.

Two studies were done to test the model's effectiveness in stimulating growth. In the first (Enright, 1980) 24 sixth graders were randomly assigned to experimental

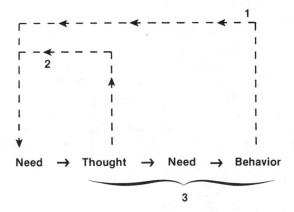

Figure 3-1. Information processing approach to moral education.

or control conditions. The experimentals met twice a week (35–45 minutes per time) for 22 weeks. The intervention consisted of the subjects' learning a social-cognitive stage sequence (Selman's, 1976, interpersonal conceptions) and then leading dilemma discussion groups with first graders. The context of the discussions was always hypothetical interpersonal situations. Sixth graders taught in pairs with about five first graders per group. Session 1 each week was the cross-age experience (Behavior in Figure 3-1); Session 2 concerned a discussion of the experience with two knowledgeable adults. Here the processing components illustrated in lines 1 and 2 and pathway 3 of Figure 3-1 were employed. For example, reflection on an actual interpersonal behavior from Session 1 was an attempt to put into practice the process illustrated by dashed line 1 in Figure 3-1; the adults' challenge of the subject's subsequent thought was an attempt to put into practice the process of dashed line 2; the adults' pointing out any discrepancies between the subject's thought and action was an attempt to put into practice the process illustrated by line 3. In other words, Session 2 always found the adults asking the subjects to reflect on their Session 1 teaching experiences, consider them in more depth than the initial thought, and to consider discrepancies between what was said in Session 2 (e.g., "I was trying to be nice to the first graders") and what actually happened in Session 1.

Between-groups statistical analyses showed no significant differences at pretest, but significance favoring the experimentals at posttest on Carroll's (1974) moral development scale. There was a full stage increase from approximately Level 2 to Level 3 in interpersonal conceptions for the experimental group.

A subsequent study (Enright, 1981) was done within the actual classrooms of two first grades ($N = 19$ in Class 1, 21 in Class 2). The teachers, trained in the use of the model, disciplined the children individually during experimental periods by (a) spontaneously asking the child to reflect on the behavior whenever an altercation occurred (dashed line 1 in Figure 3-1); (b) then asking the child to consider a more complex perspective on the matter (similar to plus-one exchange, as illustrated in dashed line 2 of Figure 3-1); and (c) then pointing out discrepancies between what the child is now saying and what he or she usually does (line 3 in Figure 3-1).

The program lasted 22 weeks. For the first semester Class 1 was the experimental and Class 2 was the control group (the teacher's usual disciplinary procedures). For the second semester, Class 1 continued the intervention; Class 2 began it.

No statistical differences emerged at pretest between the classes. The first posttest occurred after the first semester. As expected, Class 1 (the experimental group) was significantly higher in Damon's (1975) moral development interview than the control class. There was an approximate one-quarter stage increase for the experimentals. At the second posttest following the second semester both classes were equivalent and were significantly higher than their original pretest scores. In other words, Class 1 gained in moral development following the first intervention. The gains were maintained. Class 2, as with Class 1, gained after its intervention with the model.

Because both studies (sixth-grade and first-grade studies) showed growth not only in interpersonal conceptions but also in moral development, it appears that actual structural change occurred. In other words, both studies consciously eliminated moral discussion from the interpersonal conceptions interventions. Yet, at posttest in both studies the children showed generalized gain (interpersonal and moral development). In all likelihood, memorization of "correct" responses would not have led to this generalization.

This series of studies demonstrated the usefulness of moral education within an ecologically valid setting. As with deliberate psychological education, the method's strategies were rather straightforward. Given Arbuthnot's (1975) and Turiel's (1966) results in the plus-one exchange, however, prospective users of this method should keep in mind that a 22-week program may not be at all necessary if the goal is simply a change on dependent measures of moral development. The method should be tried in shorter time spans.

The Just Community Strategy

The just community is an anomaly. It is the most ambitious and possibly the most promising of all moral strategies, yet is the least empirically studied, despite its existence since the early 1970s. The focus of this strategy is no longer on the individual exclusively, but on the structure of the environment. Hersh et al. (1979) best summarize the method as follows: "Democratic governance stands at the heart of the just-community approach. For students and teachers to overcome their reliance on traditional authority patterns, they have to learn to share democratically the responsibility for decision making" (p. 235).

The origin of the just community is in the prisons. Hickey's (1972) plus-one strategy was extended to an entire section or cottage of the Niantic, Connecticut, women's prison. Details of the strategy can be found in Kohlberg, Kauffman, Scharf, & Hickey (1974). A summary of the democratic strategy is as follows: (a) Regular "town meetings" are held; (b) an inmate or staff member can call a meeting at any time; (c) the community (staff and inmates) are the jury for anyone in violation of the rules; (d) discipline is referred to a board of two inmates and one staff member chosen at random; (e) cottage rules are redefined every 12 weeks by the community.

Results of this experiment are reported by Scharf (1975). Assessing 17 females from the experimental cottage and 10 from a traditional one, Scharf reports a significant gain of approximately one third of a stage by the experimentals. It is unclear what statistic was used. An examination of his Table IV (1975, p. 31) suggests, however, a within-experimental and within-control comparison, similar to the statistical errors made in deliberate psychological education programs. Given that the subjects in the traditional cottages were not placed there at random, and given a possible social desirability bias by those in the experiment, the conclusion must be viewed cautiously.

A just community high school in Cambridge, Massachusetts, is described by

Wasserman (1976) and Powers (1979a, 1979b). This is a school within a larger Boston area high school. As in the prison setting, there are community meetings and discipline boards. In addition, there are advisor groups in which each faculty member meets weekly with a small group of students to discuss personal and academic problems; there is also a once-a-week evening meeting to discuss the function and/or process of all the foregoing groups. The only existing evidence for this ambitious effort is anecdotal observations of teachers in the school, who, it must be assumed, have a vested interest in the outcomes.

Two empirical investigations similar to the foregoing, however, do suggest that school type may influence the students' moral development. McCann and Bell (1975) report on 20 children between the ages of 6 and 11 matched on various characteristics and assessed in two different schools, one stressing adherence to authority and the other stressing democratic decision making (a Freiret school of Montreal). The children in the latter environment showed significantly higher levels of moral development than the other group. The dependent measure, however, involved stories adopted from Piaget (1932/1965) using Kohlberg's (1963b) scoring criteria. No reliability or validity of the measure is reported.

The other study concerns what the author calls "intensive education"; in this case the student takes one course at a time for concentrated periods (Maul, 1980). The purpose, in theory, is to promote a small independent community in each class. The results with 75 students between grades 10 and 12 indicated that moral development (as measured by the DIT) was highest for those who had been exposed the longest to this form of education, independent of grade level. One has to wonder whether intelligence or verbal ability is a mediator in the observed results. Could it be that intensive education makes one smarter, and that this is seen in the DIT, which does share variance with IQ? No such controls on IQ or verbal ability are apparent in the study. It should be noted that the two studies here do not measure *change* as it is directly influenced by an intervention. Instead, both show differences that exist across school types or within-school differences in types of courses. A priori subject characteristics, then, may be responsible for the differences. The just community approach must await carefully planned intervention analyses before its effectiveness can be explored.

Conclusions and Recommendations

Moral education does not represent a homogeneous approach. The five approaches reviewed here show marked differences in treatment strategy. They also show marked differences in results. The plus-one, deliberate psychological education, and information processing strategies all have claimed success.

Within the plus-one strategy, it is difficult to know which variants work best. As previously pointed out, many studies did not clearly distinguish in their methods sections the plus-one from a general discussion strategy, attenuating any possible conclusions about the variants. In general, all of the following have claimed success in at least one study: expert adult leader of plus-one, informed adult leader of plus-one, peer-run plus-one, and general moral discussion without plus-one. Deliberate psychological education has less consistent positive results, but it too has had many replicated successes. The methodological problems, however, do attenuate the positive conclusions here. The two information processing studies speak well to this model's validity with elementary school students.

There is evidence to suggest that in plus-one and deliberate psychological education the youngest subjects have the least probability of showing gains. This was seen in the elementary school samples in plus-one interventions and the junior high school samples in the other. The information processing approach, on the other hand, is appropriate for children as young as 6.

No definite conclusion can be reached regarding the most parsimonious length of treatment because this has not been systematically examined. One is struck by the pattern, however, that regardless of training length the subjects gain approximately one quarter to one half a stage (see Tables 3-1 to 3-3). This is the case whether the intervention is 15 minutes (Arbuthnot, 1975) or 1 academic year (Sullivan, 1975); this is the case regardless of the strategy used. The evidence, however, suggests that programs of 10 weeks or longer maintain posttest gains (Bernier & Rustad, 1977; Blatt & Kohlberg, 1975; Colby, 1973; Erickson, 1978; Wong, 1977). Keasey's (1973) one-session treatment, on the other hand, showed a washout of posttest effects, as did Lorimer's (1971) 3-week study. Given these patterns, we recommend that moral educators give much more attention to the issues of structural competence, performance, and memorization. At present, *any* change at posttest is hailed as a success. Achieving an actual structural change, however, may be a different matter.

Because the different strategies entail different problems, we will consider separate recommendations. For the plus-one strategy we recommend the following:

1. Researchers should be explicit as to whether they are using a general discussion strategy or an actual plus-one approach. It is not always clear which is used.
2. If plus-one is used, independent assessment of the taped discussions should be done to verify the extent of plus-one usage in the program. As of now, given Williams's (1974) observations, it is unclear how well this strategy is implemented. Two observers blind to the hypotheses could be used.
3. Researchers should begin to chart the average length of time needed for a change in competence rather than in performance. This could be done with Walker's (1980) model. He already has shown that if $X + 1$ has been attained in role taking, those with X in moral development will reach $X + 1$ in one session. This, we claim, taps performance. We suggest working with those assessed as X in both domains. Chart the number of sessions necessary for attainment of $X + 1$ in moral reasoning (Walker has shown that one session is insufficient here). Once a subject reaches $X + 1$ in moral development, he or she on posttest should also show $X + 1$ in role taking if valid *structural* change has occurred. We suspect that such valid generalized structural change will take weeks to achieve.

For deliberate psychological education we recommend the following:

1. More careful attention to design and analyses seems like the easiest of changes suggested here. Even if comparison groups only are available, one can still strengthen this design, as seen in the information processing approach.
2. Because of the multiple instructional procedures, it would be worthwhile to begin testing subsets of them. For example, one could eliminate films, writing assignments, and interviews of community members. Only a counseling practicum and seminar could be tried. Although this would still tell us the sufficient and not the necessary conditions of growth, it may reduce the number of sufficient conditions now being used.
3. It would be of major theoretical import to know why moral growth results from such programs. If counseling is equated with role taking that stimulates moral thinking, this could be tested by examining individual differences in counseling. For instance, two independent raters could judge each counselor's communication for accuracy in judging others' feelings. In theory, the more accurate communicators may be having the more high-level role-taking experiences. One would then expect that the more accurate communicators would show the most gain, not only in moral development but also in role taking.

For the information processing model, the following are recommended:

1. As in the plus-one strategy, one needs independent corroboration that the procedures outlined are actually occurring.
2. As in deliberate psychological education, individual differences could be analyzed to see if those with the most exposure to the model (in the spontaneous use of it in the classroom) show the greatest gains.
3. Because this strategy has been used only in long-term programs, it could be tried over a few weeks. This trial, however, should involve assessments in more than one social-cognitive domain to be sure that structural competence has changed.

For the didactic instruction approach, we recommend an abandonment of this strategy *if the aim is moral growth.* This is not to say that these courses do not have benefits; moral growth is just not one of them. If moral growth is the goal, this is the least efficient way to bring it about. As was seen, the only ones to work used components of the plus-one strategy or deliberate psychological education. Finally, the just community could benefit from empirical tests. From these may come proposed refinements in the programs. It would be premature to suggest such refinements when no tests have yet been made.

As a final recommendation across all strategies, it is imperative that moral educators begin to show benefits in ways other than higher scores at posttest. Relation of treatment outcomes to behavior (however defined) is conspicuously absent in *all* studies. In fact, one gets the impression after reviewing this literature that this entire educational movement may be misdirected. It is not unlike a situation where experts have concluded that standing on one's head is a viable educational goal. We might then see dozens of studies testing various strategies for promoting headstanding. Some work better than others, but the major question remains: Why have we put so much effort into headstanding? After all, students are very cooperative. They usually conform to the demand characteristics of the curriculum regardless of its utility.

What is now needed is careful attention to the utility and the benefits of these moral programs for the students studied. Changing one's responses on a posttest relative to a pretest must be challenged as worthwhile. Increased complexity of moral thought, for its own sake, may only make the blood rush to one's head without direct behavioral benefits. It is time to treat Kohlbergian theory as a *theory* to be tested, not as a law that we as educators accept on faith as true.

Reference Notes

1. Kohlberg, L. *Moral stage scoring manual.* Unpublished manuscript, Laboratory of Human Development, School of Education, Harvard University, 1976.
2. Rest, J. *Manual for the Defining Issue Test.* Unpublished manuscript, Department of Social and Psychological Foundations of Education, University of Minnesota, 1974.
3. Sprinthall, N. *A high school curriculum in the psychology of counseling* (Rep. 1). Unpublished report, Minneapolis Public Schools, 1973.
4. Erickson, V. L. *Psychological growth for women: A high school curriculum intervention* (Rep. 2). Unpublished report, Minneapolis Public Schools, 1973.
5. Rest, J. R., Ahlgren, C., & Mackey, J. *Minneapolis Police report.* Unpublished manuscript, University of Minnesota, 1972. (In Lawrence, 1980.)
6. Morrison, T. R., Toews, B., & Rest, J. R. *Youth, law, and morality.* Unpublished manuscript, Winnipeg, 1975. (In Lawrence, 1980.)

References

Alexander, R. A moral education curriculum on prejudice (Doctoral dissertation, Boston University, 1977). *Dissertation Abstracts International,* 1977, *37,* 7497A–7498A. (University Microfilms No. 77-11, 349)

Arbuthnot, J. Modification of moral judgment through role playing. *Developmental Psychology,* 1975, *11,* 319–323.

Arbuthnot, J., & Faust, D. *Teaching moral reasoning: Theory and practice.* New York: Harper & Row, 1981.

Arredondo-Dowd, P. The psychological development and education of immigrant adolescents: A baseline study. *Adolescence,* 1981, *16,* 175–186.

Bandura, A., & McDonald, F. Influence of social reinforcement and the behavior of models in shaping children's moral judgments. *Journal of Abnormal and Social Psychology,* 1963, *67,* 274–281.

Beck, C., Sullivan, E., & Taylor, N. Stimulating transition to postconventional morality: The Pickering High School study. *Interchange,* 1972, *3,* 28–37.

Bernier, J. A psychological education intervention for teacher development (Doctoral dissertation, University of Minnesota, 1976). *Dissertation Abstracts International*, 1977, *37*, 6266A–6267A. (University Microfilms No. 77-6932)

Bernier, J., & Rustad, K. Psychology of counseling curriculum: A follow-up study. *The Counseling Psychologist*, 1977, *6*, 18–22.

Biskin, D., & Hoskisson, K. An experimental test of the effects of structured discussions of moral dilemmas found in children's literature on moral reasoning. *Elementary School Journal*, 1977, *77*, 407–415.

Blatt, M. *Studies on the effects of classroom discussion upon children's moral development.* Unpublished doctoral dissertation, University of Chicago, 1970.

Blatt, M., & Kohlberg, L. The effects of classroom moral discussion upon children's level of moral judgment. *Journal of Moral Education*, 1975, *4*, 129–161.

Bono, F. The effects of two teaching approaches on the moral judgment of sixth-grade children (Doctoral dissertation, Ohio University, 1975). *Dissertation Abstracts International*, 1975, *36*, 6436A. (University Microfilms No. 76-8846)

Boyd, D. The condition of sophomoritis and its educational cure. *Journal of Moral Education*, 1980, *10*, 24–39.

Brainerd, C. Cognitive development and concept learning: An interpretive review. *Psychological Bulletin*, 1977, *84*, 919–939.

Broughton, J. The cognitive-developmental approach to morality: A reply to Kurtines and Greif. *Journal of Moral Education*, 1978, *7*, 81–96.

Carroll, J. *Children's judgments of statements exemplifying different moral stages.* Unpublished doctoral dissertation, University of Minnesota, 1974.

Carkhuff, R. *The development of human resources.* New York: Holt, Rinehart & Winston, 1971.

Cognetta, P., & Sprinthall, N. Students as teachers: Role taking as a means of promoting psychological and ethical development during adolescence. *Character Potential: A Record of Research*, 1978, *8*, 188–195.

Colby, A. Logical operational limitations on the development of moral judgment (Doctoral dissertation, Columbia University, 1973). *Dissertation Abstracts International*, 1973, *34*, 2331B. (University Microfilms No. 73-28, 193)

Colby, A. Evolution of a moral-developmental theory. In W. Damon (Ed.), *Moral development.* San Francisco: Jossey-Bass, 1978.

Colby, A., Kohlberg, L., Fenton, E., Speicher-Dubin, B., & Lieberman, M. Secondary school moral discussion programmes led by social studies teachers. *Journal of Moral Education*, 1977, *6*, 90–111.

Crowley, P. Effect of training upon objectivity of moral judgment in grade-school children. *Journal of Personality and Social Psychology*, 1968, *8*, 228–232.

Damon, W. Early conceptions of positive justice as related to the development of logical operations. *Child Development*, 1975, *46*, 301–312.

Damon, W. (Ed.). *Moral development.* San Francisco: Jossey-Bass, 1978.

DiStefano, A. Adolescent moral reasoning after a curriculum in sexual and interpersonal dilemmas (Doctoral dissertation, Boston University, 1977). *Dissertation Abstracts International*, 1978, *38*, 5348A. (University Microfilms No. 77-32, 762)

Dowell, R. *Adolescents as peer counselors: A program for psychological growth.* Unpublished doctoral dissertation, Harvard University, 1971.

Dozier, M. The relative effectiveness of vicarious and experiential techniques on the development of moral judgment with groups of desegregated sixth grade pupils

(Doctoral dissertation, University of Miami, 1974). *Dissertation Abstracts International,* 1974, *35,* 2045A. (University Microfilms No. 74-23, 391)

Enright, R. An integration of social cognitive development and cognitive processing: Educational applications. *American Educational Research Journal,* 1980, *17,* 21–41.

Enright, R. A classroom discipline model for promoting social cognitive development in early childhood. *Journal of Moral Education,* 1981, *11,* 47–60.

Enright, R., & Lapsley, D. Social role-taking: A review of the constructs, measures, and measurement properties. *Review of Educational Research,* 1980, *50,* 647–674.

Erickson, V. L. The development of women: An issue of justice. In P. Scharf (Ed.), *Readings in moral education.* Minneapolis: Winston, 1978.

Erickson, V. L., Colby, S., Libbey, P., & Lohman, G. The young adolescent: A curriculum to promote psychological growth. In G. D. Miller (Ed.), *Developmental education and other emerging alternatives in secondary guidance programs.* St. Paul, MN: Minnesota Department of Education, 1976.

Feffer, M. The cognitive implications of role-taking behavior. *Journal of Personality,* 1959, *27,* 152–168.

Fenton, E., Penna, A., & Schultz, M. *Comparative political systems.* New York: Holt, Rinehart & Winston, 1973.

Flavell, J. The development of inferences about others. In T. Mischel (Ed.), *Understanding other persons.* Totowa, New Jersey: Rowan and Littlefield, 1974.

Flavell, J., & Wohlwill, J. Formal and functional aspects of cognitive development. In D. Elkind & J. Flavell (Eds.), *Studies in cognitive development.* New York: Oxford, 1969.

Fleetwood, R., & Parish, T. Relationship between moral development test scores of juvenile delinquents and their inclusion in a moral dilemma discussion group. *Psychological Reports,* 1976, *39,* 1075–1080.

Harris, D. A curriculum sequence for moral development. *Theory and Research in Social Education,* 1977, *5,* 1–21.

Hayden, B., & Pickar, D. The impact of moral discussions on children's level of moral reasoning. *Journal of Moral Education,* 1981, *10,* 131–134.

Hersh, R., Paolitto, D., & Reimer, J. *Promoting moral growth from Piaget to Kohlberg.* New York: Longman, 1979.

Hickey, J. The effects of guided moral discussion upon youthful offenders' level of moral judgment (Doctoral dissertation, Boston University, 1972). *Dissertation Abstracts International,* 1972, *33,* 1551A. (University Microfilms No. 72-25, 438)

Higgins, E. Role-taking and social judgment: Alternative developmental perspectives and processes. In J. Flavell and L. Ross (Eds.), *Social cognitive development: Frontiers and possible futures.* New York & London: Cambridge University Press, 1981.

Hogan, R. Development of an empathy scale. *Journal of Consulting and Clinical Psychology,* 1969, *33,* 307–316.

Hurt, B. L., & Sprinthall, N. Psychological and moral development for teacher education. *Journal of Moral Education,* 1977, *6,* 112–119.

Jensen, L., & Hafen, G. The effect of training children to consider intentions when making moral judgments. *Journal of Genetic Psychology,* 1973, *122,* 223–233.

Jensen, L., & Larm, C. Effects of two training procedures on intentionality in moral judgments among children. *Developmental Psychology,* 1970, *2,* 310.

Justice, G. Facilitating principled moral reasoning in college students. A cognitive-developmental approach (Doctoral dissertation, St. Louis University, 1977). *Dissertation Abstracts International,* 1978, *39,* 1406A–1407A. (University Microfilms No. 7814587)

Kavanagh, H. Moral education: Relevance, goals and strategies. *Journal of Moral Education,* 1977, *6,* 121–130.

Keasey, C. Experimentally induced changes in moral opinions and reasoning. *Journal of Personality and Social Psychology,* 1973, *26,* 30–38.

Keefe, D. A comparison of the effect of teachers and student led discussions of short stories and case accounts on the moral reasoning of adolescents using the Kohlberg model (Doctoral dissertation, University of Illinois, 1975). *Dissertation Abstracts International,* 1975, *36,* 2734A. (University Microfilms No. 75-24, 335)

Kohlberg, L. *The development of modes of moral thinking and choice in the years ten to sixteen.* Unpublished doctoral dissertation, University of Chicago, 1958.

Kohlberg, L. Moral development and identification. In H. Stevenson (Ed.), *Child psychology (62 Yearbook of the National Society for the Study of Education).* Chicago: University of Chicago Press, 1963. (a)

Kohlberg, L. The development of children's orientation towards a moral order: Sequence in the development of moral thought. *Vita Humana,* 1963, *6,* 11–33. (b)

Kohlberg, L. Stage and sequence: The cognitive-developmental approach to socialization. In D. Goslin (Ed.), *Handbook of socialization theory and research.* New York: Rand McNally, 1969.

Kohlberg, L. Moral stages and moralization: The cognitive-developmental approach. In T. Lickona (Ed.), *Moral development and behavior.* New York: Holt, Rinehart & Winston, 1976.

Kohlberg, L., Kauffman, K., Scharf, P., & Hickey, J. *The just community approach to corrections: A manual* (Parts I and II). Cambridge, MA: The Moral Education Research Foundation, 1974.

Kurtines, W., & Greif, E. The development of moral thought: Review and evaluation of Kohlberg's approach. *Psychological Bulletin,* 1974, *81,* 453–470.

Lawrence, J. Moral judgment intervention studies using the Defining Issues Test. *Journal of Moral Education,* 1980, *9,* 178–191.

LeFurgy, W., & Woloshin, G. Immediate and long-term effects of experimentally induced social influence in the modification of adolescents' moral judgments. *Journal of Personality and Social Psychology,* 1969, *12,* 104–110.

Leming, J. Curricular effectiveness in moral/values education: A review of research. *Journal of Moral Education,* 1981, *10,* 147–164.

Lickona, T. Moral development and moral education. In J. Gallagher and J. Easley (Eds.), *Knowledge and development* (Vol. 2). New York: Plenum Press, 1978.

Lockwood, A. The effects of values clarification and moral development curricula on school-age subjects: A critical review of recent research. *Review of Educational Research,* 1978, *48,* 325–364.

Lorimer, R. Change in the development of moral judgements in adolescence: The effect of a structured exposition vs. a film and discussion. *Canadian Journal of Behavioral Science,* 1971, *3,* 1–10.

Mackie, P. Teaching counseling skills to low achieving high school students (Doctoral dissertation, Boston University, 1974). *Dissertation Abstracts International*, 1974, *35*, 3427A. (University Microfilms No. 74-26, 444)

Maul, J. A high school with intensive education: Moral atmosphere and moral reasoning. *Journal of Moral Education*, 1980, *10*, 9–17.

McCann, J., & Bell, P. Educational environment and the development of moral concepts. *Journal of Moral Education*, 1975, *5*, 63–70.

Mosher, R., & Sprinthall, N. Psychological education: A means to promote personal development during adolescence. *The Counseling Psychologist*, 1971, *2*, 3–82.

Nichols, K., Isham, M., & Austad, C. A junior high school curriculum to promote psychological growth and moral reasoning. In G. D. Miller (Ed.), *Developmental theory and its application in guidance programs*. St. Paul, MN: Minnesota Department of Education, 1977.

Oja, S., & Sprinthall, N. Psychological and moral development for teachers: Can you teach old dogs? *Character Potential: A Record of Research*, 1978, *8*, 218–225.

Panowitsch, H. Change and stability in the Defining Issues Test: An objective measure of moral development (Doctoral dissertation, University of Minnesota, 1975). *Dissertation Abstracts International*, 1976, *37*, 201A. (University Microfilms No. 76-14, 948)

Paolitto, D. Role-taking opportunities for early adolescents: A program in moral education (Doctoral dissertation, Boston University, 1976). *Dissertation Abstracts International*, 1976, *36*, 7214A. (University Microfilms No. 76-11, 829)

Phillips, D., & Nicolayev, J. Kohlbergian moral development: A progressing or degenerating research program? *Educational Theory*, 1978, *28*, 286–301.

Piaget, J. *The moral judgment of the child*. London: Routledge & Kegan Paul, 1965. (Originally published, 1932.)

Piaget, J. *Structuralism*. New York: Harper & Row, 1970.

Plymale, S. The effects of a developmental teacher training program on the moral reasoning ability of third and sixth grade students (Doctoral dissertation, West Virginia University, 1977). *Dissertation Abstracts International*, 1977, *38*, 2062A. (University Microfilms No. 77-22, 725)

Powers, C. The moral atmosphere of the school-part I. *Moral Education Forum*, 1979, *4*(1), 9–14. (a)

Powers, C. The moral atmosphere of the school-part II. *Moral Education Forum*, 1979, *4*(2), 20-27. (b)

Purpel, D., & Ryan, K. *Moral education . . . it comes with the territory*. Berkeley, CA: McCutchan, 1976.

Rest, J. Developmental psychology as a guide to value education: A review of "Kohlbergian" programs. *Review of Educational Research*, 1974, *44*, 241–259. (a)

Rest, J. The cognitive developmental approach to morality: The state of the art. *Counseling and Values*, 1974, *18*, 64–78. (b)

Rest, J., Davison, M., & Robbins, S. Age trends in judging moral issues: A review of cross-sectional, longitudinal, and sequential studies of the Defining Issues Test. *Child Development*, 1978, *49*, 263–279.

Schaffer, P. Moral judgment: A cognitive-developmental project in psychological education (Doctoral dissertation, University of Minnesota, 1974). *Dissertation Abstracts International*, 1974, *35*, 808A. (University Microfilms No. 74-17, 279)

Scharf, P. Democracy and prison reform: A theory of democratic participation in prison. *The Prison Journal*, 1975, *55*, 21–33.

Scharf, P. (Ed.). *Readings in moral education*. Minneapolis: Winston, 1978.

Schepps, C. An examination of the high school as a just institution: A program in moral education for adolescents (Doctoral dissertation, Boston University, 1977). *Dissertation Abstracts International*, 1977, *37*, 7549A. (University Microfilms No. 77-11, 375)

Search, P. An experimental study in developing moral judgment through the comparative effectiveness of three methods: Role-playing, discussion, and didactic instruction (Doctoral dissertation, Catholic University of America, 1973). *Dissertation Abstracts International* 1973, *34*, 1139A. (University Microfilms No. 73-19, 772)

Selman, R. A structural approach to the study of developing interpersonal relationship concepts: Research with normal and disturbed preadolescent boys. In A. Pick (Ed.), *Tenth Annual Minnesota Symposium on Child Psychology*. Minneapolis: University of Minnesota Press, 1976.

Selman, R., & Lieberman, M. Moral education in the primary grades: An evaluation of a developmental curriculum. *Journal of Educational Psychology*, 1975, *67*, 712-716.

Simpson, E. Moral development research: A case study of scientific cultural bias. *Human Development*, 1974, *17*, 81-106.

Sprinthall, N. Learning psychology by doing psychology: A high school curriculum in the psychology of counseling. In G. D. Miller (Ed.), *Developmental education and other emerging alternatives in secondary guidance programs*. St. Paul: Minnesota Department of Education, 1976.

Stanley, S. A curriculum to affect the moral atmosphere of the family and the moral development of adolescents (Doctoral dissertation, Boston University, 1976). *Dissertation Abstracts International*, 1976, *36*, 7221A. (University Microfilms No. 76-11, 830)

Sullivan, P. A curriculum for stimulating moral reasoning and ego development in adolescents (Doctoral dissertation, Boston University, 1975). *Dissertation Abstracts International*, 1975, *36*, 1320A. (University Microfilms No. 75-20, 971)

Tracy, J., & Cross, H. Antecedants of shift in moral judgment. *Journal of Personality and Social Psychology*, 1973, *26*, 238-244.

Tucker, A. Psychological growth in a liberal arts course: A cross-cultural experience. In G. D. Miller (Ed.), *Developmental theory and its application in guidance programs*. St. Paul: Minnesota Department of Education, 1977.

Turiel, E. An experimental test of the sequentiality of developmental stages in the child's moral judgments. *Journal of Personality and Social Psychology*, 1966, *3*, 611-618.

Turiel, E., & Rothman, G. The influence of reasoning on behavioral choices at different stages of moral development. *Child Development*, 1972, *43*, 741-756.

Walker, L. Cognitive and perspective-taking prerequisites for moral development. *Child Development*, 1980, *51*, 131-139.

Walker, L., & Richards, B. Stimulating transitions in moral reasoning as a function of stage of cognitive development. *Developmental Psychology*, 1979, *15*, 95-103.

Wasserman, E. Implementing Kohlberg's "Just Community Concept" in an alternative high school. *Social Education*, 1976, *40*, 203-207.

Williams, M. The effects of the discussion of moral dilemmas on the moral judgment of children, age seven to nine years (Doctoral dissertation, University of

Wisconsin-Milwaukee, 1974). *Dissertation Abstracts International,* 1974, *36,* 803A. (University Microfilms No. 75-17, 815)

Wong, J. Psychological growth for adult women: An in-service curriculum intervention for teachers. In G. D. Miller (Ed.), *Developmental theory and its application in guidance programs.* St. Paul: Minnesota Department of Education, 1977.

Wright, I. Moral reasoning and conduct of selected elementary school students. *Journal of Moral Education,* 1978, *1,* 199–205.

Part II
Cognitive Strategies in Reading and Language

There is a long history to strategy intervention work in the fields of reading and language. The research and writing of David Ausubel, Lawrence Frase, Ernst Roth-kopf, John Carroll, Wilga Rivers, and many others come to mind immediately as historically prominent in these fields. With every passing year since the late 1960s, there has been a notable expansion of the empirical literature on the use of cognitive strategies while reading text and learning language. The four chapters in this section focus on contemporary concerns in these domains, presenting some of the most recent theory and providing trenchant commentary on the significant research of the late 1970s and early 1980s.

Cook and Mayer review instructional techniques that influence readers' strategies for processing expository prose. The authors first analyze what they call the *reading strategy problem* into four components—reading strategies, encoding processes, learning outcomes, and performance measures. A number of reading strategies are reviewed with reference to this framework. These include strategies developed in laboratory studies, such as note taking, summarizing, underlining, and answering adjunct questions, and strategies developed in the field, such as SQ3R, REAP, DRTA, and ReQuest. (For readers unfamiliar with these abbreviations, we thought that our not decoding them here might provide additional motivation for reading the chapter!) Cook and Mayer close with a discussion of potential future research. The possibility of investigations of specific content rather than general strategies is raised, and the authors develop the case that cognitive-theoretical ideas should be merged more explicitly with behavioral and pedagogic notions in the creation of new reading strategies.

Forrest-Pressley and Gillies present a discussion of children's flexible use of strategies during reading. The specific concern in the chapter is with the selection, monitoring, and modification of cognitive processes during reading. These executive processes are conceptualized within a metacognitive framework proposed by the authors, a framework that is largely consistent with the model of cognitive processing proposed by Miller, Galanter, and Pribram two decades ago. In developing their model, the authors specifically contrast the use of strategies, knowledge of strategies, and monitoring of strategies in older and/or better readers and younger and/or poorer readers, as well as how strategy use, knowledge, and monitoring may be articulated during mature reading.

Willows, Borwick, and Butkowsky explicitly address the interface between theory and practice in reading by posing the question, "Why has reading theory and research not led to improvements in reading instruction?" In order to answer this question, the authors reviewed the 267 studies on reading published in the *Journal of Educational Psychology* and the *Reading Research Quarterly* during the last 15 years, with the focus of their analysis on the methodologies of the papers reviewed. Willows and her colleagues conclude that simple comparisons between good and poor readers (which pervade reading research) are inadequate in that they do not allow separation of the effects of children's attitudes, strategies, and facility at reading subskills from more basic differences in ability. In the language of artificial intelligence, the software cannot be separated from the hardware in these designs. In light of this problem, the authors do not find it surprising that the strategies spontaneously used by good readers often are not easily adaptable for poor readers who do not spontaneously use the strategies, inasmuch as these poor readers probably also differ from good readers in more fundamental ways.

Paivio's concern is with strategies for language learning. He first distinguishes between language learning in informal (naturalistic) and formal (school) settings, between mnemonic and nonmnemonic strategies for learning languages, and between comprehension and production goals. He then offers a variety of commentary on issues surrounding these aspects of language learning. For instance, he cites the paucity of data on the language-teaching techniques that parents and others use in informal settings. Paivio reviews recent research on vocabulary learning in formal settings, including work on the effects of semantic contexts on vocabulary acquisition. He then reviews several potent mnemonic strategies for language learning and suggests that some nonmnemonic strategies that are intuitively appealing are not in fact effective, at least given data to date. He also discusses in detail some relatively new strategies that have been proposed as aids to language learning. Paivio concludes with a discussion of the relevance of language strategy results to his own dual-coding theory, and with the observation that there is a great deal left to be researched relative to what is already known about language-learning strategies.

4. Reading Strategies Training for Meaningful Learning from Prose

Linda K. Cook and Richard E. Mayer

Theoretical Framework

The Reading Strategy Problem

Consider the passage in Table 4-1, selected from a standard science textbook (Slesnick, Balzer, McCormack, Newton, & Rasmussen, 1980, p. 651-652). If you were reading this passage, what would you do in order to ensure that you would understand the material? How would you choose to process the information? What recommendations would you make to help a reader who does not understand what the passage is saying? What happens when you ask a reader to take notes or reread or underline the passage? These questions form the basis for what could be called the *reading strategy problem*—the question of how reading strategies affect the learning process and whether reading strategies can be taught.

The purpose of this chapter is to explore answers to the reading strategy problem by examining the current state of theory, research, and practice in the area of reading strategies. In particular, this chapter focuses on techniques for influencing how adults process prose such as the passage on the nitrogen cycle in Table 4-1. This chapter is intended to provide a representative overview of how reading strategies may influence the encoding process and what is learned.

It seems that an appropriate place to begin to solve the reading strategy problem might be to try to delineate the major characteristics that underlie the adult reading task. One avenue is to examine the reading process within a developmental perspective. Chall (1979) has provided an excellent stage analysis of the acquisition of reading skills, which is briefly reviewed here.

Table 4-1 A Passage About the Nitrogen Cycle

The Nitrogen Cycle

Molecular nitrogen (N_2) makes up about 78% of the earth's atmosphere. It is the fourth major element found in living tissues after carbon, oxygen, and hydrogen. It is an essential part of amino acids.

The complex nitrogen cycle differs from the oxygen and carbon cycles in several ways. First, atmospheric nitrogen cannot be used directly by most green plants. It must be changed into a usable form—either ammonia or nitrate—before green plants use it. Second, once nitrogen has been incorporated into nucleic acids and proteins, it can only be returned to inorganic forms through several steps, some of which require specialized types of bacteria. Third, most of these reactions occur in the soil, where availability of nitrogen is influenced by the solubility of inorganic nitrogen compounds.

The process by which atmospheric nitrogen is changed to ammonia is called nitrogen fixation. Only certain species of bacteria are capable of nitrogen fixation. For example, Rhizobium, which lives in symbiosis with legumes such as beans, is a bacterium of plant root nodules. Some blue-green bacteria are important for nitrogen fixation in acquatic systems.

Molecular nitrogen may also be converted to usable forms by nonbiological processes. Atmospheric nitrogen can be converted to nitrate (NO_3) through energy provided by lightening. It may also be fixed industrially to produce the chemical fertilizer ammonium nitrate.

Remember, biological fixation produces ammonia. Notice that ammonia also comes from the decay of dead organisms and wastes. This process is called ammonification.

The conversion of ammonia to nitrate is called nitrification. This process occurs during decomposition. For example, some soil bacteria convert the nitrogen of the proteins in the manure to ammonia (ammonification). Other soil bacteria may then convert the ammonia, first to nitrite (NO_2), and finally to nitrate (NO_3).

Nitrogen Assimilation

Nitrogen is taken up by plants and incorporated into amino acid molecules, which are eventually linked to become protein molecules. The process by which nitrogen is incorporated into organic molecules is called nitrogen assimilation. Nitrogen assimilation is the opposite of ammonification.

We still have not explained how molecular nitrogen is returned to the atmosphere. If nitrogen were fixed only from the atmosphere and cycled through living communities, the atmosphere would eventually run out of atmospheric nitrogen. The process that returns molecular nitrogen to the atmosphere is called denitrification. This is done by a variety of bacteria. The job these bacterial populations do is very important because it completes the nitrogen cycle.

Note. From Slesnick, I. L., Balzer, L., McCormack, A. J., Newton, D. E., and Rasmussen, F. A., *Biology*, Glenview, IL: Scott, Foresman, 1980, p. 651–652. Reprinted by permission.

During the early stages of formal reading instruction, the reading task is largely that of symbol decoding and bringing meaning to the printed page. This has frequently been referred to as the "learning to read" stage. The materials young readers are exposed to are actually structured in ways that promote immediate understanding. The texts are highly stereotypical stories filled with actions, objects, and characters with which the average child should be familiar. Pictures may even detail the sequence of events introduced in the text, making comprehension that much more inevitable. Chall describes the goal of reading at this point as being to "confirm what is already known." Readers are seldom asked to retain the materials they read for an information value in their own right. Instead, they serve as a familiar practice ground in which to improve growing reading skills.

At some point there is a large but subtle shift in the reading process. According to Chall, readers begin to read to gain new knowledge and information, or more simply, they "read to learn." This may begin in the fourth grade when readers are introduced to new and unfamiliar content areas such as geography, science, social science, or history, and it continues on through junior and senior high school, college, and beyond. Prose with highly familiar concepts is now replaced by text information that is largely unfamiliar to the reader. The implication, too, is that the materials read are now to be retained for an information value in their own right, as evidenced by the use of tests as a measure of retention. This is much different from the earlier stage of reading, in which readers are asked only to demonstrate overall comprehension of already highly familiar concepts. As Chall stresses, the function of prior knowledge changes dramatically in "reading to learn." Instead of relying on everyday common knowledge to bring meaning to print, readers must build upon increasingly complex layers of previously acquired concepts inherent in a particular subject area. She points also to the necessity of developing a reading process, or the ability to execute efficiently specific strategies designed to meet particular goals.

Analyzing the Reading Strategy Problem

The framework proposed in this chapter consists of four major parts: reading strategies, encoding processes, learning outcomes, and performance measures. These four parts are summarized in Table 4-2. It should be pointed out that reading strategies and performance measures refer to external observable events, whereas encoding processes and learning outcomes refer to internal cognitive events that cannot

Table 4-2 A Framework for Analyzing the Reading Strategy Problem

Reading Strategies	Encoding Processes	Learning Outcomes	Performance Measures
Note taking	Selection	Number and type	Retention tests
Underlining	Acquisition	Internal connections	Recall tests
Summarizing	Construction	External connections	Recognition tests
Elaborating	Integration		Inference tests
Question answering			Problem-solving tests

be directly observed. The incorporation of internal cognitive processes and states into the framework may help to explain the relationship between the behaviors exhibited during learning and performance exhibited during test performance.

Reading Strategy. The first component in Table 4-2 is the learner's reading strategy. A *reading strategy* is a behavior that a reader engages in at the time of reading and that is related to some goal. Thus, a reading strategy refers to something the learner *does* (i.e., observable behaviors during learning). Examples of reading strategies for the nitrogen cycle passage include underlining key words, answering questions, or making a summary of the material. Reading strategies are tied to how one defines the reading goal. In this chapter, we define several different goals in terms of the basic encoding process that a reader is trying to use, as discussed next.

Encoding Processes. The second component in Table 4-2 is the encoding process. An encoding process is an internal cognitive event that involves manipulation of incoming information. These encoding processes may serve as the goals of various reading strategies. For example, the reading strategy of underlining may serve the goal of selection of key ideas to be stored in memory.

Table 4-2 lists four general types of encoding processes that may be most relevant for the reading strategy problem: selection, acquisition, construction, and integration.

Selection refers to the process of selective attention, in which the learner pays attention to certain pieces of information in the passage. For example, in the nitrogen cycle passage, selection involves focusing on specific aspects of the text, such as each fact involving a number or the word *nitrogen.*

Acquisition refers to the process of transferring information from active consciousness (i.e., attention) to long-term memory. For example, in the nitrogen cycle passage, acquisition involves storing specific pieces of information, such as "nitrogen accounts for 78% of the earth's atmosphere."

Together, the processes of selection and acquisition involve the transfer of information from the printed page to active consciousness and finally to long-term memory. If these were the only two processes that were affected by reading strategies, we would need to be concerned only with which information is learned (due to selective attention) and how much is learned (due to acquisition). However, the framework includes two more processes, which influence the structure of the learned information as well as the amount.

Construction refers to building internal connections among ideas acquired from the passage. This process involves reorganization of the ideas that have been selected into a coherent structure. For example, in the nitrogen cycle passage, construction involves seeing how each of the five major steps in the cycle fit in with one another. One step is a precondition for the next, and so on.

Integration invovles locating relevant existing knowledge and building external connections between that knowledge and ideas acquired from the passage. This process involves both accessing existing knowledge and mapping new ideas onto that knowledge. For example, in the nitrogen cycle passage, integration might consist of thinking of the cycle as a factory with each step having a definite input and output.

As can be seen, selection and acquisition involve transfer of information units from outside into memory, whereas construction and integration involve actively building internal and external connections involving those information units.

Each of these four encoding processes may be seen as the goal of reading, with each particular reading strategy aimed at influencing one or more of these encoding processes. For example, a reader's attention may be focused (i.e., selection) by using adjunct questions about verbatim facts in the nitrogen cycle passage. A reader's amount of acquisition may be increased by asking the reader to repeat each sentence aloud. A reader's building of internal connections (i.e., construction) may be enhanced by asking the reader to outline the passage. A reader's building of external connections (i.e., integration) may be enhanced by asking the reader to paraphrase the passage in terms of a factory. Thus, each of the reading strategies listed in the first column of Table 4-2 may affect one or more of the encoding processes listed in the second column of the table.

Learning Outcomes. The third component in Table 4-2 is the learning outcome. A learning outcome refers to the internal cognitive knowledge that a reader acquires as a result of reading. A learning outcome may be represented as a network consisting of nodes and connections among nodes. In this chapter, we will investigate three basic dimensions along which learning outcomes may differ.

1. *Number and type of nodes.* Learning outcomes may differ with respect to how many nodes are acquired, which particular kinds of nodes are acquired, and the degree of "verbatim-ness" of the nodes. For example, in reading the nitrogen cycle passage, some readers will be able to recall more propositions than other readers; or some readers may recall technical facts well, whereas other readers recall conceptual principles well; or some may recall each idea in verbatim form, while others recall each idea in paraphrased form.
2. *Internal connections.* Learning outcomes may also differ with respect to the degree to which the reader has reorganized the information. Reorganization involves building new internal connections among the nodes. For example, in the nitrogen cycle passage, some readers may remember the ideas exactly in the order presented, whereas others may reorganize the passage around the five major steps in the nitrogen cycle.
3. *External connections.* Learning outcomes may also differ with respect to the degree to which the reader has connected the presented information with a meaningful body of existing knowledge. For example, in the nitrogen cycle passage, some readers may see the connection between the cycle and the idea of an industrial system, whereas other readers may not make external connections.

For purposes of this chapter, we can distinguish between two general types of learning outcomes—rote and meaningful. However, the distinction should be viewed as a description of two poles on a continuum rather than as an either-or dichotomy.

A rote learning outcome is based on only the first two encoding processes of selection and acquisition, and involves a list of ideas from the passage. In particular, rote outcomes may be characterized as limited and verbatim—due to focusing of attention on certain types of nodes—and as lacking internal and external connections. For example, in the nitrogen cycle passage, rote learning outcomes involve retaining some of the ideas in approximately the same order and form as presented, without any intrusions.

A meaningful learning outcome is based on all four encoding processes, including selection of conceptual nodes and building a new internal and external organization for the material. For example, in the nitrogen cycle passage, meaningful learning involves remembering the essential conceptual information organized into a logical structure and integrated with existing knowledge.

Performance Measures. Performance measures relate to the readers' behavior on tests of reading comprehension or related measures. Some measures focus on amount of target information learned, such as amount recalled, amount recognized, or score on a retention test. Some measures focus on the format of what is learned, such as tests of verbatim recognition or verbatim recall.

Strong selection and acquisition processes in rote learning should exert influence on the foregoing performance measures. In particular, processes leading to rote outcomes should be related to measures showing that retention is limited to target information, retention of target information is high, and retention of target information is verbatim.

Some measures focus on whether learners remember details as well as main ideas. If learners build coherent structures during the construction process, they may be more efficient at storing details that fit into the structure.

Some measures focus on whether learners produce intrusions in their recall or can make inferences in tests of recognition and on short-answer tests. If learners build coherent structures during the construction process, they may be more likely to produce intrusions and inferences.

Some measures focus on whether learners can apply what they have learned in tests of creative problem solving. If learners build useful external connections during the integration process, they may be more likely to excel in creative problem solving.

Some measures of retention focus on which information is retained, as noted above. If learners build useful internal and external connections, their retention should be high for the conceptual information that is needed for understanding the material.

In summary, when the dependent measure is intended to evaluate the influence of construction and integration processes, performance measures should focus on learners' memory for details and conceptual information in nonverbatim form, as well as on inferences and creative problem solving.

Two Approaches to the Reading Strategy Problem

There are two general approaches to the reading strategy problem, each of which tends to pose different sorts of research questions. The S-R approach to learning is a traditional approach that searches for behavioral laws describing the relationship between stimuli and responses. Thus, a traditional approach to the reading strategy problem is to focus solely on observable behavior—that is, reading strategies and performance measures. In this case, learning from prose is viewed within the simple dichotomy of input and output. Reading strategies function at input, whereas performance measures are taken at output in order to assess the adequacy of the strategies. For example, one topic might be, "Does note taking during reading increase recall?" In this case, the focus of research is on describing the relationship between an observable independent variable (i.e., presence or absence of note taking) and an observable dependent variable (i.e., amount of words recalled). A major shortcoming of this approach is that it does not provide information concerning the learning mechanisms that underlie behavioral findings.

The cognitive approach to learning and memory is a more recent approach that searches for the underlying mechanisms that intervene between stimuli and responses. When applied to the reading strategy problem, this approach adds internal cognitive processes and states to the theoretical framework (i.e., encoding processes and learning outcomes). For example, one topic might be, "How does note taking influence the encoding process and the structure of the resultant learning outcome?" In this case, the focus of research is on cognitive processes and structures that help explain the relation between stimuli and responses. The cognitive approach may be useful because it allows the instructional psychologist to predict conditions under which various methods should be successful, and to determine which dependent measures would be most sensitive to various methods. This is the approach summarized in Table 4-2 and followed throughout this chapter.

In the remainder of this chapter, we use the framework in Table 4-2 to explore the reading strategy problem. The next section treats the processes of construction and integration, with special focus on the role of prior knowledge. Then, subsequent sections look into the relation between various reading strategies and the processes, learning outcomes, and performance they elicit.

Meaningful Learning from Prose

Cognitive Theory

In order to develop an adequate theory of instruction for reading strategies, there must also be an adequate theory of learning from prose. In particular, a theory of meaningful learning from prose provides information concerning how readers process and store presented information.

A cognitive theory of learning from prose assumes that a reader comes to the reading task with a vast storehouse of existing knowledge. The storehouse includes content, structural, and process knowledge.

Content knowledge is specific factual knowledge concerning the world, such as knowing that "the atmosphere of earth is made up of gases" or that "living things must eat."

Structural knowledge is general schematic knowledge of how various elements
are related to one another, such as the organization of a passage that provides
a "list of attributes for a term" or of the organization of a passage that "compares and contrasts two ideas."

Process knowledge is procedural knowledge of how to operate on new incoming
information, such as rehearsing or reciting or elaborating.

This section provides a brief overview of cognitive research related to these types of
prior knowledge.

Content Knowledge

One kind of knowledge that influences learning of prose is the content knowledge that a reader brings to the learning situation. It is hypothesized that prior
content knowledge is instrumental in allowing readers both to "construct" and
"integrate" passage information. These processes succeed in transforming a list of
facts into a conceptually relevant whole. Constructing a meaningful representation
of a passage necessitates that the text elements (words, phrases, and sentences) be
related to each other in some manner. This might also be called intratext cohesion,
in which the reader attempts to build bridges of passage information. On the other
hand, a learner assumes that a particular passage is connected to or anchored to
relevant concepts already extant in the learner's knowledge system. For instance,
readers use their prior knowledge states to make plausible inferences from or draw
conclusions about text input that may be only suggested or implied in the passage
itself. This process of extratext cohesion augments a particular passage by additional
relevant but unstated concepts.

Some of the prose processing research during the early 1970s demonstrates what
happens to a reader's understanding and representation of passage information
when relevant prior content knowledge is not activated. For example, read the
following passage.

The procedure is actually quite simple. First you arrange items into different
groups. Of course one pile may be sufficient depending on how much there is
to do. If you have to go somewhere else due to a lack of facilities that is the next
step; otherwise, you are pretty well set. It is important not to overdo things.
That is, it is better to do too few things at once than too many. In the short run
this may not seem important but complications can easily arise. A mistake can
be expensive as well. At first, the whole procedure will seem complicated. Soon,
however, it will become just another facet of life. It is difficult to foresee any
end to the necessity for this task in the immediate future, but then, one can
never tell. After the procedure is completed one arranges the materials into
different groups again. Then they can be put into their appropriate places. Eventually, they will be used once more and the whole cycle will then have to be
repeated. However, that is part of life.

Bransford and Johnson (1973) had three groups of subjects read this passage,
rate its comprehensibility, and then recall it. One group read just the passage, while

another group was given the topic "Washing Clothes" before reading. The researchers reasoned that the topic would allow this group to activate relevant knowledge prior to reading, making the passage more understandable. Not surprisingly, this group rated the passage as more comprehensible and were also able to recall more idea units than the group that was given no topic. A third group in this study was given the topic after reading the passage. Neither comprehensibility ratings nor recall of topic-after subjects was improved relative to the no-topic group. The authors concluded that just having the prior knowledge is not sufficient for understanding, but what is important is that the prior knowledge be active during the acquisition of information.

A similar study by Dooling and Lachman (1971) also demonstrates how content knowledge can assist comprehension during reading. Assume for the following passage that the sentence fragments divided by the slash marks appear individually on index cards:

> with hocked gems financing him/our hero bravely defied all scornful laughter/ that tried to prevent his scheme/your eyes deceive/he had said/an egg/not a table /correctly typifies this unexplored planet/now three sturdy sisters sought proof/ forging along sometimes through calm vastness/yet more often over turbulent peaks and valleys/days became weeks/as many doubters spread fearful rumors about the edge/at last/from nowhere/welcome winged creatures appeared/signifying momentous success

When subjects received this passage with the title "Christopher Columbus Discovers America" they recalled more from the passage than those receiving no title. This was true whether the passage appeared one word on each card, in phrases such as are shown here, or in complete sentences.

Both of these studies demonstrate that when prior content knowledge is absent, the text appears to be nothing more than a series of unrelated facts. When the organizing title is present, however, readers can actively construct a relationship between the text elements and the passage takes on a more conceptually related meaning.

Other studies have shown that activating *different* types of content knowledge can alter the manner in which a text is understood and retained. Pichert and Anderson (1977) gave two groups of subjects a passage that described two boys playing in a home. Both groups were given different perspectives within which to interpret the passage. One group assumed the role of a home buyer and the other that of a burglar. From their recall protocols, it was evident that they retained much different types of information. The home buyers were more likely to recall a leaky roof than the color TV, but for those taking a burglar's perspective the recall probabilities were reversed.

In the Pichert and Anderson study, the different perspectives for understanding the passage were supplied by the experimenter. However, readers themselves bring different perspectives to texts based on different kinds of content knowledge developed from special experiences. Anderson, Reynolds, Schallert, and Goetz (1977) gave the following passage to two groups of students, one enrolled in an educational psychology class and another enrolled in a weight-lifting course.

> Rocky slowly got up from the mat, planning his escape. He hesitated a moment and thought. Things were not going well. What bothered him the most was being held, especially since the charge against him had been weak. He considered his present situation. The lock that held him was strong but he thought he could break it. He knew, however, that his timing would have to be perfect. Rocky was aware that it was because of his early roughness that he had been penalized so severely—much too severely from his point of view. The situation was becoming frustrating; the pressure had been grinding on him for too long. He was being ridden unmercifully. Rocky was getting angry now. He felt he was ready to make his move. He knew that his success or failure would depend on what he did in the next few seconds.

Subjects in the weight-lifting class were more likely to answer multiple-choice questions as though the passage were about a wrestler, whereas those in the education course perceived the passage as being about a convict planning a prison escape. These studies again demonstrate the importance of content knowledge in developing text coherence, but they also indicate that specialized interests can lead to qualitatively different ways of interpreting text events.

In all of the studies cited above, there was a good deal of overlap between what the subjects already knew about the passage and the information within the passage itself. In other words, most of the information in the washing clothes passage could be easily matched for both its content and sequence based on a subject's expectations about what the clothes-washing procedure actually entails. Prior content knowledge can also be beneficial when this match is missing or when the text contains novel information. Consider the following passage and assume that a test event will follow:

> If the balloons popped, the sound would not be able to carry since everything would be too far away from the second floor. A closed window would also prevent the sound from carrying since most buildings tend to be well insulated. Since the whole operation depends on a steady flow of electricity, a break in the middle of the wire would also cause problems. Of course the fellow could shout, but the human voice is not loud enough to carry that far. An additional problem is that a string could break on the instrument. Then there could be no accompaniment to the message. It is clear that the best solution would involve less distance. Then there would be fewer potential problems. With face to face contact, the least number of things could go wrong.

In this instance, there is nothing within people's prior knowledge that can be immediately and easily activated to help promote comprehension. A simple title or theme such as was available in the previous studies does not exist. How can comprehension and learning be enhanced for passages of this type?

Bransford and Johnson (1972) had subjects listen to this passage and were asked to rate its comprehensibility and also recall it. One group of subjects (no context) heard the passage and then rated and recalled it. Another group (context before) viewed the picture shown in Figure 4-1 for 30 seconds prior to hearing the passage. This group recalled more than twice the number of idea units recalled by the no-context group. Another condition (no context 2) in this experiment had subjects listen to the passage twice before making their rating and recall. Both of these dependent measures were almost undistinguishable from those in the no-context-1

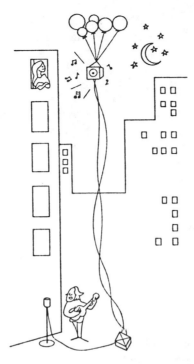

Figure 4-1. A context for the balloons passage. From "Contextual Prerequisites for Understanding: Some Investigations of Comprehension and Recall" by J. D. Bransford and M. K. Johnson, *Journal of Verbal Learning and Verbal Behavior*, 1972, *11*, 717–726. Reprinted by permission.

group. This seems to indicate that repetition on input has negligible impact on comprehension and retention. One other interesting condition included in this study was a partial-context group. These subjects saw a picture with the same objects as in Figure 4-1 but with the items inappropriately arranged relative to the passage. The performance of the partial-context group was not much improved relative to the no-context group. This seems to suggest that what was important in understanding and retaining this passage was not an understanding of the parts alone but also of the relationship of those parts. In this example, there is no existing knowledge that can be tapped in order to assist comprehension, and so the appropriate content knowledge was built prior to the introduction of the passage. This allowed for a structure within which to interpret the incoming information.

The role or prior knowledge in comprehension is not restricted to just making incoming information meaningful, or what has been described as construction or developing intratext cohesion. Numerous research articles have also demonstrated that people do not store short passages like those described above in a veridical manner. They distort, augment, generalize, and make inferences that go beyond the original text. This vast amount of information available in the memory system allows for the addition of "extratextual" information. Thus, what gets reproduced in the subject's recall, for instance, may be logically accurate but not necessarily a part of the intended input. For example, suppose a reader encounters these two sentences (Anderson & Ortony, 1975):

The container held the apples.
The container held the cola.

People's interpretation of the word *container* in these two sentences is likely to be quite different based on their prior knowledge about apples and colas. People make a number of different assumptions about incoming information that are supplied by their general knowledge of the world and how it operates. In the example just presented, the sentences are ambiguous, and in order to make them more sensible, readers are likely to supply their own information to fill in the gaps (e.g., *carton* or *bushel basket* for the first, vs. *can* or *bottle* for the second).

Other studies have indicated that the process of adding information to input is more subtle. Johnson, Bransford, and Solomon (1973) had one group of subjects listen to the following input:

John was trying to fix the bird house. He was pounding the nail when his father came out to watch him and help him do the work.

while another heard this:

John was trying to fix the bird house. He was looking for the nail when his father came out to watch him and help him do the work.

Who would be the most likely to mistake the following for what they had just heard?

John was using the hammer to fix the bird house when his father came out to watch him and help him do the work.

Their explanation of why the subjects in the first group were more likely to be taken in by the above distractor is attributed to inferential reasoning during comprehension. "Pounding a nail" usually implies the presence of a hammer but "looking for a nail" does not. The first group may have thought they remembered the boy using a hammer, but in reality it was only inferred by them.

Taken together, these results suggest that reading involves far more than decoding each word. Instead, a reader uses existing content knowledge to interpret the meaning of each incoming sentence, to decide its relevance, to add more information, and so on. (See Collins & Wiens, 1983, for a discussion of similar processes in the interpretation of TV content.) One implication of this work is that readers who lack domain-specific knowledge will have a very difficult time comprehending a passage, much as Chall has suggested might happen to readers as early as the fourth grade. Readers need to be able to acquire relevant content knowledge and to assess when they lack sufficient content knowledge.

Structure Knowledge

The previous section dealt with how people employ their prior knowledge in making sense of incoming input. That prior knowledge was labeled "content" because it dealt largely with specific information concerning the passage and its general theme. Structural knowledge is another form of knowledge that people rely heavily on during their processing of text information. Structural knowledge deals with the organization or arrangement of text elements and the rules that prescribe these arrangements. Reading is a domain that relies heavily on mandatory arrangements in its structure. For example, certain sequential letter combinations (such as *ch*) are acceptable, whereas others (such as *hc*) are not. Sequences of words also follow a prescribed structure—for example, nouns follow articles *(the hat)* but articles do not follow nouns *(hat the)*. There are also higher order structural relationships in text, which deal with intersentential relationships as well as interparagraph relationships. Investigations pertaining to these types of structures form the basis for the rest of this section.

Story Grammar Theory. Theorists who have worked primarily with narrative passages have attempted to develop a syntax, or story "grammar," that represents the underlying structure found in most stories. The general hypothesis underlying story grammars is that, after years of exposure to simple stories, readers have extracted a general structure for the way stories are written, and they rely on these structures to guide their reading (See Chapter 9 in this volume, as well as Worden, 1983.). Story grammars have tried to capture this abstract structure and test whether or not the structure is employed during story comprehension. Rumelhart (1975, 1977) is usually credited with the first formal grammar capable of representing a large number of stories. Other researchers (Mandler & Johnson, 1977; Stein & Glenn, 1979) have developed similar story grammars, but this chapter will focus on that developed from Rumelhart's original work by Thorndyke (1977; see also Bower, 1976).

Thorndyke's grammar is based on a series of rewrite rules that can be applied to a number of different stories, even though the contents of each story may differ. The rewrite rules have a number of empty slots that can be filled by input from any particular story. For example, the first rewrite rule is the following:

RULE 1   STORY → SETTING + THEME + PLOT + RESOLUTION

The first rule indicates that a story is made up of a setting, theme, plot, and resolution. (The arrow can be interpreted as meaning "consists of.") Subsequent rewrite rules break this rule down into smaller and smaller rule units. For example, the setting consists of characters, location, and time. A story that begins "Once upon a time in the land of Not there lived an old king with three lovely daughters . . ." can fill these three slots. Similarly, theme can be broken down into an event and a goal. For the story just begun, a dragon might capture the daughters (event), setting up the goal of their safe return. The plot details the various attempts to achieve the stated goal, and the resolution is the outcome that satisfies the intended goal (the daughters are saved).

Research has generally been supportive of the notions of story grammars. Thorndyke (1977) constructed a series of story structures with identical content but that ranged from a normal narrative structure to a text that was void of this causal sequencing. Results indicated that as the amount of story structure decreased across conditions, so did subjects' recall and comprehensibility ratings. Thorndyke concluded that stories with intact structures were more easily understood because they could match a subject's prior expectations. The further the story structure was removed from a subject's internal representation, the more difficult the processing became.

An interesting by-product of the story grammar rewrite rule is that it allows for a hierarchical arrangement of story information. Each rewrite rule succeeds in adding finer and finer details to the story structure itself. Thorndyke (1977) hypothesized that the higher up the information was in the structure, the more salient it became both to the story comprehension and to subjects' recall. In other words, successful retelling of a story would necessitate knowing at least the setting, theme, plot and resolution. When subjects were exposed to the range of structures described above, they tended to recall units higher in the hierarchy if the story was normal. Recall for the other story forms decreased as they deviated from the normal structure. It appears that subjects are quite sensitive to and rely on the structure of story content in both their understanding and recall of passage information. Because of this initial success, other researchers have begun to look for structures of prose that are not limited to stories.

Structural Analysis of Expository Prose. Meyer's (1975) work, unlike the narrative analysis described above, has focused largely on expository text. Whereas narratives usually deal with texts that contain sequential events over time, expository text attempts to convey new explanatory information. Meyer's earliest work attempted to explain why some information in a text is almost always recalled and other information only infrequently appears in subjects' reproductions. She developed a prose-analysis technique that attempted to define and classify intersentential and interparagraph relations. (A more in-depth discussion of this technique can be found in Meyer, 1975.) It is easiest to think of this system as the decomposing of a particular passage into a treelike structure with nodes (called lexical predicates) connected by a series of labeled lines (called rhetorical predicates). Its appearance is somewhat like an outline showing a particular structure containing the passage content. The top-level structures appear to the left, with subordinate information appearing to the right and downward. This system of prose analysis yields an abstract representation of a passage content that can eventually be compared to an individual subject's recall of that passage.

In examining why some information is better remembered than others, Meyer identified three possible aspects of passages that might bear some relationship to this recall pattern. These three were structure of a passage, serial position of information (beginning, middle, and end), and the individual rating of idea units from most to least important. Her findings indicated that structure alone was the single most important variable in predicting the hierarchical recall found for subjects.

Meyer (1977) continued investigating the structure of prose and its effect on subjects' representation and recall of passage information. In one study, subjects were exposed to either one, two, or three presentations prior to recall. For all three conditions, subjects recalled information higher in the passage structure significantly more often than information lower in the structure. She concluded that passage structure is effective during the first exposure, indicating that subjects acquire main ideas first and then add details after subsequent presentations. She has also found that information in the same format but placed either higher or lower in the structure of a passage produced a predictable outcome. If the information was high in the structure, it was recalled significantly more often than if it was low in the structure.

More recent work by Meyer (Meyer, 1981) has identified five different categories of these top-level structures. These include comparison (points out the similarities and differences between two or more topics), covariance (relation of an antecedent to a consequence), response (problem plus solution), collection (how ideas are related together on the basis of commonalities), and attribution (the listing of attributes). The first four are termed "conceptual hierarchies" because the idea units are organized around one general topic and also relate to each other. The last, attribution, lists attributes that relate back to the general topic but not necessarily to each other.

Meyer, Brandt, and Bluth (1980) investigated the effects of two of these text structures (problem/solution and comparison) on ninth-grade students' recall of passage information. Their findings indicated that students who tended to express their recall by using the author's intended structure recalled more information than those who did not employ that structure. In addition, those students rated as good comprehenders were more likely to use the author's structure during recall, but those rated as poor comprehenders did not. Thus, there may be a relationship between the awareness of top-level structure and overall comprehension. Promising research by Bartlett (1978) has found that ninth graders can be taught to use top-level structures in organizing free recall, and this instruction does facilitate recall. Improved comprehension, therefore, may be enhanced by increasing the students skill in identifying top-level structures and using that structure to efficiently store and retrieve information.

Common Prose Structures. One interesting implication of recent work on structural analysis of narrative and expository prose is that there may be certain structures that are characteristic of various content domains. For example, Robinson (1975) has identified five structures commonly found in science textbooks: generalization, sequence, cause/effect, enumeration, and classification. Eisenberg (1978) has suggested the following basic prose structures: examples, classification and listing, compare and contrast, cause and effect. Mallery (1967) has suggested three basic expository structures: exposition by definition, exposition by comparison, and exposition by division or enumeration. Kirszner and Mandell (1980) suggest the following structures for expository prose: description, exemplification, process, cause and effect, comparison and contrast, division and classification, definition, argumentation. Numerous "writing guides" have offered tips on how to write these kinds of passages.

Cook (1982) has investigated the role of text structure and the comprehension of scientific prose such as chemistry and physics. Based on earlier work by Robinson (1975), she identified five different text types: generalization, sequence, enumeration, cause and effect, and compare and contrast. Initial research with the text structures indicated that subjects were capable of matching prototypical passages with their respective structural category. Subsequent work focused on developing reading and study strategies specific to each type of text structure and using these within an instructional setting. For example, a generalization structure is defined by its root word, *to generalize,* which means to represent the whole. A passage of this type seeks to convey one main idea, and uses most of the passage to explain and extend this one idea. Often structures of this type deal with principles, definitions, or scientific laws as the basis for the main idea. For example, a passage may begin with "Elements can combine in several ratios or what is defined as *multiple proportions.*" The rest of the passage attempts to justify and explain this main idea. This subsequent information is called the supporting evidence. One type of supporting evidence is the use of an example. Thus, the passage begun above goes on to explain that CO and CO_2 both contain carbon and oxygen, but they differ in their element proportions, leading to very different types of substances. CO is carbon monoxide, a poisonous gas, and CO_2 is carbon dioxide. The suggested reading strategy for this structure is a two-step procedure in which the reader is first asked to locate the main idea, define each of its terms (elements, combine, ratios, multiple proportions), and then reexplain it in their own words. In the second step, the readers are asked to explain how the supporting evidence relates back to the main idea (i.e., CO and CO_2 differ on the basis of the ratio of oxygen present: 1 to 2).

Students in a beginning chemistry class were trained to identify three of these structures (generalization, enumeration, and sequence), and to use the appropriate reading strategies with their course-assigned textbook. On unfamiliar biology passages for each type of structure as pre- and posttest measures, the instructed students outperformed a noninstructed control group on both recall and problem-solving tests.

Conclusion. These results suggest that text structure may play a substantial role in developing conceptual relationships between text elements. In light of Chall's (1979) comment that prior knowledge becomes increasingly important for readers beyond primary school, the lack of appropriate knowledge may be overcome somewhat by relying on the manner in which the text is structured (see Chapter 9). This is particularly true if common text structures, as well as appropriate reading strategies for each, are further developed.

Process Knowledge

Knowledge about how to process information is the third kind of knowledge that a reader brings to the reading situation. In particular, different encoding processes may be applied to incoming information and may result in different learning outcomes. An encoding process refers to the mental operations that are applied to the incoming information to prepare it for storage in memory.

Levels of Processing. One straightforward idea, introduced by Craik and Lockhart (1972), is the levels-of-processing hypothesis, which proposes that (1) prose may be processed at a shallow level (such as a "sensory analysis") or at a deep level (such as a "semantic analysis"), and (2) the more deeply prose is processed, the better it will be remembered.

Support for this idea comes from a series of studies in which subjects perform various "orienting tasks" while learning a word list. Subjects who were required to perform semantic analyses—such as categorizing each word—performed better on a recall test than subjects who were required to perform lower level analyses—such as crossing out each vowel (Jenkins, 1974; Hyde & Jenkins, 1969, 1973; Till & Jenkins, 1973; Tresselt & Mayzner, 1960; Walsh & Jenkins, 1973).

Complementary results have been obtained in studies using prose passages. For example, Arkes, Schumacher, and Gardner (1976) found that subjects who were asked to outline a passage (i.e., deeper analysis) performed better on recall than subjects who were asked to circle every letter *e* in a passage (i.e., lower level analysis).

An implication for reading strategy training seems to be that readers must learn how to process deeply. However, a major omission in the levels-of-processing theory concerns the idea that "what is learned" may vary qualitatively as well as quantitatively as a result of processing style. Different types of processing may lead not to "more learning" but rather to a "different kind of learning." The next section explores this idea in more detail.

Transfer Appropriate Processing. A more recent theory of encoding processes is the transfer-appropriate-processing hypothesis (Morris, Bransford, & Franks, 1977). This hypothesis asserts that one type of processing might enhance performance for one type of test, whereas another type of processing might enhance performance on another type of test.

For example, Stein (1978) presented a word list containing items like *raDio*. Some subjects were asked questions that required only a sensory analysis of the stimuli, such as "Does this word have a capital D?" Other subjects were asked questions that required a semantic analysis of the stimuli, such as "Does this word use electricity?" One subsequent test measured memory for the sensory details of the stimuli, such as asking the subject to indicate which of the following had been on the list: raDio, Radio, rAdio, radiO, radIo. Another test measured memory for the words themselves by asking the subject to indicate which of the following had been on the list: ceDar, raDio, caDdy, tiDbit. Results indicated that subjects who had engaged in semantic processing during learning performed better than the sensory processing group on the word recognition test, as predicted by the levels-of-processing hypothesis. However, in contrast to the levels-of-processing hypothesis, the sensory processing group outperformed the semantic processing group on memory for sensory details. Morris et al., (1977) reported complementary results in another series of studies.

Several researchers have made distinctions between two kinds of encoding processes: for example, Santa, Abrams, and Santa (1979) have distinguished between "storage encoding" (i.e., getting information into memory) and "retrieval encoding" (i.e., elaborating on information so that it will be accessible later on). Similarly, Mayer (1979) has distinguished between "addition" of new information to memory and "assimilation" of new information to existing knowledge. Kintsch and van Dijk (1978) have provided a model of reading processes that involves a "leading edge" strategy—connecting each new proposition with preceding ones that share arguments. This strategy can be modified so that it operates like storage encoding or so that it operates at a higher level like retrieval encoding.

The implications of this work are that some types of reading strategies might enhance meaningful learning of the material, while others might enhance retention of specific factual details. Thus, it seems unproductive to ask which reading strategy results in more learning; rather, the appropriate approach is to ask how each reading strategy influences "what is learned."

Studies on Manipulation of Reading Strategies

This section explores research on the role of reading strategies in learning from prose. First, this section explores "reader-initiated" strategies, such as note taking, as well as "text-initiated" strategies, such as answering adjunct questions. Levin and Pressley (1981) have made a similar distinction between "processor-dependent" and "prose-dependent" learning strategies. The goal of this section is to explain how manipulations such as these influence the reader's cognitive processing and structuring of prose material.

Note Taking, Summarizing, and Underlining

Definition. Note taking refers to writing information about the text in one's own words at the time of reading. Summarizing refers to writing information about the text in one's own words after reading a portion of text, with the text no longer present. Underlining refers to placing lines under information in the text, or highlighting portions of the text, during reading. The quality and quantity of notes or summaries, or even of underlining, may vary greatly from person to person, ranging from exhaustive outlines to a random list of facts. In addition, as Levin (in press) points out, prose-learning strategies may serve to "enhance the students' *understanding*" or to "enhance the text's *memorability.*"

Functions of Note Taking. How does note taking (or summarizing or underlining) influence learning? There are several possible answers, including the following.

1. *Directing attention.* Note taking might serve to direct the reader's attention toward certain information in the text and away from other information. This could be called the selective attention hypothesis. If the selective attention hy-

pothesis is correct, then note taking should improve performance only in retention of the noted information but not on incidental information.

2. *Limiting attention.* Note taking might serve to limit the amount of attention that a reader can pay to the information in the passage. In other words, the act of note taking requires time and attentional resources, and thus may diminish the amount of time and attention available for encoding the passage. This could be called the limited attention hypothesis. If the limited attention hypothesis is correct, then note taking may decrease performance overall on tests of retention.

3. *Encouraging verbatim encoding.* In addition to limiting and directing attention, note taking may encourage the reader to add information to memory in verbatim form. This could be called the verbatim encoding hypothesis. If this idea is correct, note taking should improve performance in tests of verbatim recognition or verbatim recall but not on tests of inference or problem solving.

For example, note taking may involve verbatim copying of key definitions from a passage, as shown in the top of Table 4-3. This activity could also direct the reader's attention, and limit the reader's attention, as well as encourage the reader to use verbatim encoding. This view sees note taking as mainly influencing the processes of acquisition and selection, as discussed earlier.

4. *Building internal connections.* Note-taking activities may force the learner to build a coherent outline or organization for the material. This could be called the reorganization encoding hypothesis. If this idea is correct, then note-taking activities should increase performance on tests of inference—since relations among ideas will be better specified—and should increase recall of information related to the main ideas—since there is an efficient structure for holding infor-

Table 4-3 Three Note-Taking Activities for the Nitrogen Cycle Passage

---

Verbatim List of Facts (Selection and Acquisition Processes)
N_2 makes up 78% of the earth's atmosphere.
It is the fourth major element found in living tissues.
Rhizobium lives in symbiosis with legumes.
Nitrogen assimilation is the opposite of ammonification.

Reorganized Outline (Construction Process)
Nitrogen Cycle
  1. Nitrogen fixation: Atmospheric nitrogen is changed to ammonia.
  2. Ammonification: Organic decay is changed into ammonia.
  3. Nitrification: Ammonia is changed to nitrate.
  4. Nitrogen assimilation: Nitrate is changed to protein.
  5. Denitrification: Nitrate is changed into atmospheric nitrogen.

Elaborated Comments (Integration Process)
Nitrogen fixation is like a factory in which soil microorganisms are the workers. They take atmospheric nitrogen and oxygen as raw materials and put them together to form nitrates (NO_3).

---

mation. For example, note taking may involve outlining the material, or making comparisons and contrasts among ideas in the material, or locating the main theme, as shown in the middle of Table 4-3. In this view of note taking, the process of construction is affected.

5. *Building external connections.* Note-taking activities may force the learner to add his or her own comments or reactions to the material. For example, note taking may involve writing about a related example that fits in with the ideas presented in the passage. This could be called the integration encoding hypothesis. If this idea is correct, then note-taking activities should increase performance on tests of creative problem solving and transfer, since the reader has encoded material as broad learning outcomes. The bottom of Table 4-3 provides an example of how note taking might encourage the building of external connections. This view of note taking focuses mainly on the process of integration as discussed above.

Some Exemplary Note-Taking Studies. The foregoing list summarizes five possible effects of note-taking activities on the processing of incoming prose. The following sections present examples of research concerning how note-taking activities influence prose processing.

Selective Attention Strategies. Note-taking activities can serve to focus the learner's attention on certain aspects of the passage and away from others. For example, Aiken, Thomas, and Shennum (1975) found that material that was in a learner's notes was twice as likely to be recalled as material that was not in a learner's notes. Similar results have been reported by Howe (1970), Carrier and Titus (1981), and Barnett, DiVesta, and Rogozinski (1981). These findings hold even when students are not allowed to review their notes.

When the rate of presentation and information density place strain on the learner's allocation of attentional resources, note taking can serve to shift attention. In these circumstances measures of overall amount recalled or overall amount retained on a multiple-choice test may not be sensitive to the selective attention effects of note taking. In these cases, we would not predict note taking to increase overall retention; rather, note-takers should perform relatively well on recall or retention of noted information only. This effect should be diminished or eliminated when the strain on attentional resources is eliminated, as by allowing learners to read at their own rates. With unlimited time, readers can pay attention to "low-priority" information. Unfortunately, these predictions cannot be clearly evaluated because most studies do not examine "what information" is remembered.

Limited Attention Strategies. Some note-taking activities may serve not only to focus attention, but also to limit the amount of attention available during learning. For example, Aiken et al. (1975) and Faw and Waller (1976) suggested that concurrent note taking is most likely to limit the overall amount learned under the following conditions: when the material is difficult or technical or high density;

when the presentation rate is relatively fast; when the learner does not have a chance to review the notes; or when the learner lacks efficient encoding skills. Under these conditions, the processing capacity needed to take even brief notes detracts from the available attentional resources for reading the entire passage.

Reviews of note-taking studies often yield lists of experiments in which concurrent note taking resulted in poorer performance than no note taking (e.g., Peters, 1972) or in which note taking did not result in better performance than no note taking (e.g., see Weener, 1974; Faw & Waller, 1976). As predicted, these studies generally involve experimenter-paced presentation and no pauses for review of notes. For example, Peters (1972) asked students to listen to a 1600-word passage about steel as an alloy. Subjects who were told to take notes during the lecture performed worse on a subsequent multiple-choice test than subjects who were not allowed to take notes. This pattern was particularly strong for less efficient learners.

If concurrent note taking reduces the amount of attention available for processing the incoming information, then this detriment should be eliminated by allowing review. For example, Carter and Van Matre (1975) asked subjects to listen to a 17-minute recorded lecture on survival among sharks. As in many lecture presentation studies, taking notes did not result in better retention performance than not taking notes. However, when subjects were allowed to review their notes for 5 minutes after the lecture, performance on retention tests was greatly enhanced. DiVesta and Gray (1972, 1973), Fisher and Harris (1973), and Crawford (1925) also found that students who took notes and reviewed them recalled more information than subjects who listened only; however, in the DiVesta and Gray (1973) and Fisher and Harris (1973) studies, note taking without review also enhanced recall. One major difference among the studies is that Carter and Van Matre used much longer passages (i.e., 17 minutes) than DiVesta and Gray (i.e., 5 minutes), and the presentation rate was much faster in the Carter and Van Matre study than in the Fisher and Harris study.

Most of the foregoing studies have involved lectures that are presented at a rate determined by the experimenter (e.g., usually between 150 and 200 words per minute). If concurrent note taking reduces the amount of attention available for processing the incoming information, then this detriment should be eliminated by allowing self-paced presentation rates. For example, Kulhavy, Dyer, and Silver (1975) asked students to read an 845-word passage at their own rates. Bretzing and Kulhavy (1981) allowed 15 minutes for students to read a 1000-word passage. For both studies, subjects who were told to take notes studied longer and retained more information than subjects who read without taking notes.

Another way to eliminate the limiting affects of note-taking activities on attentional resources is to take summary notes (i.e., summarizing). While the passage is being presented, the learner can pay full attention. During a break after presentation, the learner can take notes. One effect of summary notes may be to increase the attentional resources available as compared to concurrent note taking. Thus, one prediction is that in cases where concurrent note taking decreases overall retention, summary note taking should not decrease overall retention. For example,

Aiken, Thomas, and Shennum (1975) found that although concurrent note taking tended to reduce performance as compared to a control group, summary note taking did not.

Verbatim Processing Strategies. Note-taking activities can elicit verbatim processing strategies in some cases. For example, Mayer and Cook (1980) asked students to listen to a 650-word tape-recorded passage on how radar works. The passage contained pauses after each phrase. Some students were asked to shadow the passage, that is, to repeat each phrase during the pause. Other students were asked only to listen.

On a subsequent series of tests, the shadowers performed better than the non-shadowers on test of verbatim recognition, but the nonshadowers outperformed the shadowers on tests of problem-solving transfer. In addition, the groups did not differ in the amount of recall for the factual information in the passage, but the nonshadowers recalled more than twice as much of the conceptual information in the passage than the shadowers.

Apparently, having to repeat every word encouraged verbatim processing for the shadowers. This treatment decreased the tendency to restructure or elaborate on the material. Thus, when a student is encouraged to repeat every word carefully, the outcome can be a loss of construction and integration processes.

The previous study suggested that shadowing an ongoing lecture can eliminate time needed for constructive and integrative processing. In similar situations, concurrent note taking may lead to verbatim processing. For example, when the presentation rate is fast and the learner must copy each word—as in dictation—time for constructive and integrative processing is diminished. In these circumstances, we would predict that note taking would lead to superior verbatim retention but poor performance on tests of understanding, such as creative problem solving. Unfortunately, this prediction remains to be tested because most note-taking studies have failed to measure verbatim retention or transfer performance.

DiVesta and Gray (1972) have distinguished between the "storage" function of notes and the "encoding" function of notes. The storage function refers to the role notes play in providing an external memory store, whereas the encoding function refers to the role notes play in influencing the way that information is learned. The foregoing review has explored note-taking activities that may have adverse affects on the encoding process. In these situations, the main advantage of notes is in the storage function. However, note taking can also enhance the encoding process; the next sections explore conditions under which note taking encourages construction and integration processes.

Reorganization Strategies. Under appropriate conditions, note-taking activities can serve to help the learner organize the material into a coherent structure. In these cases, the increased construction processes should lead to superior retention of details that fit into the structure and superior performance on tests of inference and transfer.

For example, Shimmerlik and Nolan (1976) presented a 1220-word anthopology lesson to subjects for 9 minutes. One version of the passage was organized by society (i.e., giving the attributes of one society and then the next society, etc.). Another version of the passage was organized by attribute (i.e., telling how each of four societies dealt with one aspect of life, and then how they all dealt with the next aspect of life, etc.). Some subjects were asked to take sequential notes (i.e., to follow the order of ideas given in the passage). Other subjects were asked to take notes that reorganized the material; for example, if the subject read the society version of the passage, the notes should use the attributes as the main topics.

Subjects in the reorganize group took notes that encouraged active construction of a coherent structure for the passage. These subjects recalled substantially more than the subjects who took sequential notes. This difference was particularly strong for students of average verbal ability (rather than higher ability), suggesting that reorganized note taking elicited constructive processes that would not otherwise be used by average readers. DiVesta, Schultz, and Dangel (1973) reported similar findings in a study where subjects were trained and instructed to engage in reorganization or sequential organization of material.

Barnett et al. (1981) asked subjects to listen to an 1800-word passage on the history of roads in America. The passage was presented at a moderately slow rate of 120 words per minute to college students. Note-takers were asked to identify the main ideas and to outline them. Thus, in this experiment subjects were encouraged to actively organize the material and were given sufficient time to do so. Results indicated that the note-takers performed more than twice as well as a listen-only group on cued recall of facts in the passage. In addition, if subjects were encouraged to outline the material or elaborate on the material during a subsequent review period, these activities increased the performance of the listen-only group but not of the note-taking group. Apparently, the note-takers had already formed a coherent outline of the material during presentation.

Santa et al. (1979) provide another example of a note-taking study that attempts to examine cognitive processes in learning. Subjects were allowed 40 minutes to read a 2400-word passage about the science of thirst or the history of the 1920s. Subjects were either asked to take notes while reading (under several subconditions) or not take notes. In this experiment, subjects had plenty of time to organize and think about their notes.

If note taking facilitates the "first level of encoding" (i.e., getting information into memory), then we would expect better recall of the main information. If note taking facilitates the "second level of encoding" (i.e., elaborating on the material so that it fits within a structure), then we would expect better recall of details. The results of a subsequent recall test indicated that note taking aided recall of details, but not of main ideas. These findings are most consistent with the idea that note taking creates a "retrieval cue structure" (i.e., an organization of the main ideas) so that details can easily be connected and fit into the structure.

Reorganization allows the learner to build a coherent structure of the main ideas in the passage. This coherent structure provides a better scaffolding for details that are related to the main ideas in the passage. Thus, recall may be improved because more details can be remembered. Santa et al. (1981) provided a direct test of this idea. Apparently, when subjects are given adequate time and encouragement to produce organized outlines, note taking affects the structure of what is learned.

Integration Strategies. Under some conditions, note taking may help the learner to relate the presented information to existing knowledge. For example, in mathematics or computer science, note taking may encourage the learner to relate presented information to a "mental model" of the system (Mayer, 1981). This integration process should enhance recall of conceptual information and problem-solving performance, but may hurt verbatim retention.

These predictions were recently tested by Peper and Mayer (1978). In a series of experiments, subjects viewed a 15-minute videotaped lecture on computer programming or statistics. Some subjects were asked to take unrestricted notes during the lecture and others were not allowed to take notes.

If note taking served mainly to focus the learner's attention, we would expect superior performance on problems like those given in the lesson. If note taking served mainly to elicit integrative processing (i.e., building connections with one's existing knowledge), then we would expect superior performance on tests of creative transfer. Subsequent problem-solving tests revealed that the note-takers outperformed the control group on solving far transfer problems, which went beyond those given in the lesson, but not on near transfer problems, which were very similar to those given during instruction.

If note taking serves mainly to focus attention on the main facts in the lesson, we would expect better recall of specific facts. If note taking helps the learner to construct conceptual understanding of the lesson, we would expect better recall of the subtle "conceptual" information in the lesson. Subsequent recall tests revealed that note-takers excelled mainly on recall of conceptual information but not on recall of specific facts, and that note-takers produced more "instructions" about information that was not in the lesson.

These results are consistent with the idea that note taking helps the reader to generate connections among ideas in the lesson and ideas already in memory. When appropriate dependent measures are used—such as far transfer and recall of concepts or intrusions—evidence for integrative processes emerges. Studies that fail to use these measures may not be sensitive to the encoding processes involved. It should also be pointed out that some more restricted forms of note taking may not elicit constructive encoding processes. For example, verbatim copying of "definitions" is unlikely to lead to constructive encoding processes.

Mixed Strategies for Summarizing and Underlining. Taking "summary notes" may be considered a modification of conventional note taking. In summary note taking, the learner reads (or listens to) a portion of the passage, and then pauses to take notes to summarize that portion. Thus, note taking occurs *after* reading or listening to the material.

Like conventional note taking, summary note taking may lead to a variety of encoding processes. Wittrock (1974) has argued that one possible outcome of summary note taking is that the learner will "generate" relations between the presented material and existing knowledge. Because the process of "generative learning" is idiosyncratic, summarizing activities should free the learner to summarize in a way that is best for each individual.

In an exemplary study, Doctorow, Wittrock, and Marks (1978) asked elementary school children to read passages with either note-taking or no-note-taking instructions. The subjects in the summary notes condition were asked to write a sentence to summarize the meaning of each paragraph. The summary notes group retained more than 50% more information than the control groups, and this advantage was enhanced when one- or two-word titles were provided for each paragraph.

In this study, the note-taking treatment was designed to encourage learners to generate connections rather than to memorize specific facts. Wittrock (1974) has distinguished between "generative processing" (e.g., reorganizing the material so that it "makes sense") and "reproductive processing" (e.g., copying all or part of the material). When note taking elicits generative processing we can expect superior performance on measures of retention and transfer. When note taking elicits reproductive processing we can expect better verbatim retention of the target material only.

Reviews of the role of subject-generated underlining offer mixed results. For example, Hartley, Bartlett, and Branthwaite (1980) found 6 studies that produced "positive effects," 13 studies that produced "neutral effects," and 0 that produced "negative effects." This box-score approach, however, fails to adequately examine or evaluate the cognitive processes that may be influenced by underlining.

Some types of underlining treatments might serve mainly to direct attention away from some material and toward other material in the passage; thus, measures of overall amount remembered would be insensitive to the role of underlining. Other types of underlining treatments might encourage the learner to construct a coherent representation or to integrate the passage with existing knowledge; thus, measures of amount remembered and transfer would be influenced. As can be seen, it is important to distinguish among the various cognitive processes that may be influenced by underlining.

A study by Rickards and August (1975) provides a nice example of how to study the cognitive processes related to underlining. Subjects read an 80-sentence passage on the evolution of the brain. Subjects were asked either to underline any sentence in each paragraph, to underline the most important sentence in each paragraph, to underline the least important sentence in each paragraph, or to read without underlining. In addition, some subjects read the passage with either the most important sentence or the least important sentence already underlined.

The group that is free to underline any sentence in each paragraph is most able to fit the passage in with his or her own particular existing knowledge. This group is most free to engage in what Rickards and August (1975) call the "idiosyncratic nature of the assimilation process." Results of a subsequent recall test show that this group performed better than all others on overall recall, including recall of incidental information (i.e., nonunderlined information). Apparently, being able to generate one's own idiosyncratic underlining allowed the reader to build an efficient cognitive structure. Learning in this condition may have been more of a "constructive act" or a "generative act" (Wittrock, 1974).

In contrast, subjects who were constrained—either by having experimenter-generated underlining or by having to underline a certain type of sentence—may have had their attention directed away from the "incidental" material. These subjects performed particularly poorly on recall of incidental information, so that total amount recalled was not significantly different from the control group.

In conclusion, the Rickards and August study (1975) exemplifies the point that all underlining treatments do not elicit the same encoding processes. To the extent that underlining constrains the learner to focus on certain types of information in the text, measures of overall amount recalled are unlikely to reveal positive effects, but measures specific to the target information are likely to reveal positive effects. To the extent that underlining encourages the reader to build his or her own idiosyncratic representation, measures of overall recall and even transfer may reveal positive effects.

Conclusion. Concurrent note taking, summary note taking, and underlining can influence the learner's encoding processes. Under some conditions, these activities may serve to focus or limit the learner's attention. Under other conditions, these activities may serve to encourage construction and integration of knowledge. There is no need for any more studies aimed at determining whether note taking (or summarizing or underlining) increases learning. Instead, research should focus on the conditions under which these activities elicit cognitive processes such as construction and integration, and research should focus on dependent measures that are sensitive to these processes, such as transfer tests.

Answering Adjunct Questions

Definition. Question answering refers to writing down (or verbalizing) answers to questions that are presented during the course of learning. Adjunct questions are questions that are placed within the body of prose, such as before or after each major section. Incidental information refers to information in the passage that is not queried by the adjunct questions.

McGraw and Groteleuschen (1972) have suggested that question answering may exert both "forward" and "backward" effects. Forward effects refer to how previous questions influence the encoding of the new material, and backward effects refer to reviewing the material after the initial encoding of the material. Since many fine reviews of the adjunct question literature are available elsewhere (Anderson & Biddle, 1975; Andre, 1979; Faw & Waller, 1976), this section will focus specifically on how the question answering influences the learner's encoding process. (See Chapter 5 in this volume for additional commentary on questions in text.) Thus, this section examines the forward effects of question answering, with special focus on the conditions under which various encoding processes are elicited.

Functions of Question Answering. Question answering, like note taking, may have several different influences on learning, including the following.

1. *Directing attention, limiting attention, encouraging verbatim encoding.* Answering questions may focus attention on just certain information in the passage or may reduce the amount of attention paid to material in the passage. For example, factual or verbatim questions placed before each section of the passage may encourage learners to search only for information that is relevant to the question and to ignore incidental information. Examples are given in Table 4-4. In this case, question answering may enhance performance on retention of the information in the particular question answers, but may not enhance (or may reduce) retention of incidental information.

2. *Building internal connections.* Alternatively, question answering could encourage the learner to build a coherent structure for the passage. For example, structural questions about the logical or sequential relations among events or elements in the passage may encourage the reader to look for internal relations. Examples are given in Table 4-4. If question answering elicits structural reorganization, then we would expect better performance on tests or retention of details and inferences but not on verbatim retention.

3. *Building external connections.* Some question-answering activities may elicit integration processing, in which the learner connects presented material with existing knowledge. For example, questions about the relationship between text material and concrete analogies may encourage the learner to "map" onto existing knowledge. Examples are given in Table 4-4. If question answering leads to integration processing, then we would expect increased performance on tests of creative problem solving, but not on tests of verbatim retention of facts.

Some Exemplary Question-Answering Studies. Some question-answering activities may affect mainly the attentional processes, whereas other types of question-answering activities may influence the building of internal or external connections. Below, several exemplary studies are reviewed, with special focus on how question answering influences selective attention, construction, and integration processes.

Table 4-4 Three Types of Questions for the Nitrogen Cycle Passage

---

Verbatim Fact Questions (Selection and Acquisition Processes)
What percentage of the atmosphere is made up of nitrogen?
What organisms are important for nitrogen fixation in aquatic systems?

Organization Questions (Construction Process)
How does atmospheric nitrogen becomes part of organic protein?
How does nitrogen in the soil return to the atmosphere?

Integration Questions (Integration Process)
What would happen to the nitrogen cycle if all the world's bacteria disappeared?
How can we use our knowledge of the nitrogen cycle to improve crop yields?

Limiting or Directing Attention. There are two major findings that suggest that question answering can serve to limit or focus attention. One major finding concerns the placement of questions: In general, when questions are placed before each section of the passage, posttest performance is enhanced only for information that is specific to the questions, as compared to a control group (Anderson & Biddle, 1975; Rothkopf & Bisbicos, 1967). In some cases, placing questions before has no effect on retention of incidental information, but in other cases placing questions before tends to decrease performance on retention of incidental material as compared to a control group (Boker, 1974; Frase, 1970; Frase, Patrick, & Schumer, 1970). Apparently, prequestions may focus the reader's attention only on material that is relevant to answering the question. The attention-directing effects of prequestions tend to be stronger when the questions are very specific or verbatim (Anderson & Biddle, 1975).

A second major finding concerns the type of question. In general, verbatim questions, such as filling in a specific word in a sentence, tend to enhance posttest performance only for information that is specific to the question, as compared to a control group (Mayer, 1975; Rickards & DiVesta, 1974; Watts & Anderson, 1971). In some cases, verbatim questions have no effect on posttest retention of incidental material or on posttest performance of problem solving; in other cases, verbatim questions decrease performance on incidental retention and problem solving as compared to a control group (Felker & Dapra, 1975; Mayer, 1975). Apparently, verbatim questions may focus attention only on specific details called for in the question.

The forward effects of directing attention by verbatim questions can occur even when questions are placed after each section of the text. For example, McConkie, Rayner, and Wison (1973) asked students to read six passages. For the first five passages, the same questions were asked after each, such as fact questions (i.e., fill in a phrase from a sentence) or number questions (i.e., fill in a number from a sentence). On the sixth passage, several kinds of questions were asked. The subjects who expected fact questions performed well on fact questions but poorly on all other types; the subjects who expected number questions performed well on number questions but not on other types.

Restructuring and Integration Strategies. In the previous section we suggested that answering questions can elicit a forward reading strategy of focusing attention on just certain information in the passage. This directing of attention seems most pronounced when questions are narrow and placed before the passage, but may also occur over a long series of passages with the same type of question after each.

In contrast, question answering can serve to elicit forward reading strategies involving restructuring and integrating the material. One major source of evidence involves placement of questions. In general, when questions are placed after the passage, overall retention of information from the passage is enhanced as compared to a control group, and retention of incidental information is often enhanced as compared to a prequestion group (Anderson & Biddle, 1975). Apparently, placing questions after a passage may serve to motivate the reader to process the information carefully, without limiting attention. Thus, postquestions may affect the process of transferring information into memory. However, when the same type of question is asked after many portions of the text, subjects may build up a "set" that limits attention.

A second source of evidence concerns the type of question that is presented. Some questions may require restructuring or elaborating on the material. For example, Dansereau, Collins, McDonald, Holley, Garland, Diekhoff, and Evans (1979) provided learning strategy training such as "paraphrasing," "networking," and "analysis of key ideas." The paraphrase strategy involved putting information into one's own words. The networking strategy involved building a network or map of the key ideas and relations among them. The key idea strategy involved providing definitions and interrelations among key terms. Thus, each activity involved restructuring the information into a coherent representation. These techniques tended to increase students' performance on multiple-choice and short-answer tests for material in 3000-word passages. One explanation is that the new structures (as in networking and key ideas analysis) enabled learners to hold information more efficiently.

In another study, Mayer (1975) asked students to read six lessons on set theory in mathematics. After each lesson, subjects received either questions about definitions (definition group) or computational problems involving a formula from the passage (computation group), or they were given model questions, which asked the learner to relate the material to a specific concrete situation (model group). On the seventh and eighth lessons, subjects were given all three kinds of problems. The students in the definition group performed best on definition questions in Lessons 7 and 8, but not on the other types. However, the model group performed very well on model questions and moderately well on other types of questions. Apparently, questions that ask the learner to map material onto a concrete model foster a broader encoding that may include many kinds of information.

Similarly, Mayer (1981) asked subjects to read a manual on computer programming. After each lesson, subjects were asked to relate the material to a concrete model or to relate the material to the previous lesson, or they were given no questions. The model-question group performed particularly well on a problem-solving tests as compared to the no-question group, suggesting that the treatment was successful in encouraging the learners to build external connections. When adjunct questions are successful in building external connections, such as mapping onto a model, learners should be better able to engage in creative problem solving. Further tests of this idea are required.

Conclusion. The foregoing review suggests that different types of question-answering strategies tend to affect different encoding processes. Under some conditions, question answering seems to direct attention, whereas under others it seems to elicit integration and construction processes. We do not need any more studies that ask, "Do adjunct questions increase learning?" Instead, future research should focus on the question of how various adjunct question manipulations influence the encoding process. In addition, future research needs to use dependent measures that are appropriate for measuring the effects of integration and construction processes—such as tests of inference, problem-solving transfer, paraphrased recall, and others.

Instructional Methods for Reading Strategies

Instructional methodologists are concerned with developing instructional techniques that can be used in applied settings, such as the classroom, to improve reading skills. The instructional methods described in this section attempt to address two common problems in teaching reading and comprehension skills. First, teachers need a systematic procedure within which to present class material, methods to induce students to perform certain reading behaviors, and a means of assessing how well these methods are used and learned. Second, adequate reading skills cannot be assumed to be in the students' repertoire of reading behaviors. They need to be overtly modeled. Students need a chance to practice them individually and to modify their reading skills on the basis of corrective feedback.

SQ3R (Survey, Question, Read, Recite, and Review)

Description. SQ3R (Robinson, 1961) represents five steps a reader is encouraged to employ during independent reading, namely, survey, question, read, recite, and review. During the survey step, readers skim through the chapter title, subheadings, and summaries to get a general idea of what the chapter is about before beginning their reading. During the subsequent question stage, the reader restates each bold-face subheading in question form. For example, the heading "Causes of the Revolutionary War" may be restated as "What were the causes of the Revolutionary War?" In the third step, read, students are expected to read each subheading and formulate an answer to the previously posed question. In the recite stage, readers are encouraged to answer the question in their own words, using information obtained from the reading material, and then to check the adequacy of their response. These two steps are repeated until the end of the chapter. In the last step, review, students review the chapter in its entirety, pausing at each subheading and attempting to recall as much of the information as possible.

Theoretical Rationale. Robinson has developed this procedure on the basis of the students' need for an effective, independent reading strategy that can be systematically applied to a wide range of reading materials. Since students' retention of text material will be assessed at some point, the method encourages students to engage in practice testing to evaluate their learning outcomes.

The SQ3R strategy focuses largely on the encoding processes of selection and acquisition. The question stage helps the reader select relevant information from the text and the read-recite stage provides a means of testing the adequacy of information acquisition. Formulating and answering questions in one's own words could affect the integration process; surveying the passage in order to see its general outline could affect constructive processes.

Evaluation. One recent study has shown support for the use of recitation in improving comprehension of passage information. Orlando and Hayward (1978) compared three types of study techniques on students' comprehension of an 800-word passage containing 10 paragraphs. A read-reread group was instructed to read through the passage without stopping. After the initial reading, they were instructed to reread the passage in the same manner. Subjects in a read-mental-review condition were told to read the passage one paragraph at a time. After reading each paragraph, they were instructed to look away from the paragraph, recall as much information as they could, and then reexamine the paragraph to see what information they had missed. In a last condition, read-note take, subjects followed the same procedure as in read-mental review, but were asked to write as much information as they could after each paragraph. Reading time was unlimited, but documented for each student. One 40-item short-answer test was administered immediately after reading, and a second 40-item test was given after 1 week.

Results indicated that both the read-note-take and read-mental-review conditions yielded significantly higher performance than the read-reread condition on immediate testing. Read-note take and read-mental review did not differ significantly. For the delayed testing the same basic trends were found, but there was no significant difference among the conditions. Reading times proved longest for the read-note-take condition (26.9 minutes), followed by the read-mental-review (17.4 minutes) and the read-reread conditions (8.9 minutes). Each of these was significantly different from the others. It would appear that both read-mental review and read-note take yield similar, positive results, at least for immediate testing. Mental review, however, may be more efficient in terms of overall time investment.

Although the SQ3R method appears to have a good deal of intuitive appeal, there is not a great deal of empirical support for it. Shepherd (1978) has indicated that one problem is convincing students of the value of the SQ3R procedure. Some students generally see the procedure as too time consuming. (In Chapter 5, Forrest-Pressley and Gillies also discuss the lack of data-based support for SQ3R.)

REAP (Read, Encode, Annotate, and Ponder)

Description. REAP (Eanet & Manzo, 1976) is an instructional procedure in which students must demonstrate comprehension of text materials by translating the author's idea units into their own words. During the read step, the author's ideas are interpreted; in the encode step, the author's ideas are converted into the reader's own language. In the third step, annotate, the reader formalizes the ideas generated during encoding into a written form, such as a summary. The annotation step yields an external record of the reader's understanding of a passage, which may serve a number of purposes during the ponder stage. For example, it can be a form of review for the student or a comprehension check for the teacher.

The strength of REAP as an instructional technique lies in the annotate step. The authors provide a number of techniques students can use to formulate annotations. The most obvious type of annotation, summary, is only one of seven the authors offer. Some of these are (1) intention, which asks the student to specify why the author wrote as (s)he did; (2) thesis, which asks for a statement of the passage theme and the author's perspective; and (3) critical annotation, which necessitates an accurate statement of the author's point of view, the students' reaction to that point of view, and reasons for their reactions. Other types of annotation include heuristic, question, and motivation.

Theoretical Rationale. Eanet and Manzo (1976) and Eanet (1978) maintain that readers are often not aware of what has been retained and understood from a text until they have to communicate what they have read. Forcing students to annotate their reading supposedly sensitizes readers to more systematic and frequent evaluations of their reading outcomes. Drawing from Anderson and Biddle's (1975) summary review of adjunct questions, the REAP procedure necessitates that readers process the materials at higher inferential levels. Most of their annotation questions require that readers go beyond a verbatim level of a text. In generating their own interpretative records of the author's ideas, readers must manipulate text information, reorganize it, make additions or deletions, and so on.

The REAP procedure affects both encoding and learning outcomes in a number of ways. When the assignment of annotation type appears before the passage (as is suggested by the authors), it would probably serve as a selective encoding function. Readers will process the text by focusing on information that relates to the particular type of suggested annotation. Annotating will probably affect acquisition only if the text is removed before writing the annotation. When it is present, readers could develop their annotations without necessarily acquiring any text information.

The picture of what happens to both constructive and integrative encoding processes is less clear. Construction should be facilitated because readers are required to combine and interpret text information in novel ways. For integration to occur, however, readers must be capable of drawing connections between what they know and the new input, a skill some readers may lack.

Evaluation. The REAP procedure seems to have reasonable support from other empirical research, particularly that of adjunct questions. However, only one study directly tested this procedure within an instructional setting. Eanet (1978) conducted a 4-week training program using three experimental conditions. The REAP experimental group received practice using the REAP procedure, another experimental control condition was trained to use SQ3R, and a control group received instruction on affective readiness for reading and study skills. Several performance measures were assessed: pre- and posttest measures on the REAP group's ability to learn the annotation system; immediate and delayed recall (48 hours) of an informative article at the end of training, and a recognition test on the article following delayed recall. Reading time for the article was limited to 15 minutes for each group.

The results indicated a significant increase in the REAP group's ability to write annotations, with the most improvement being shown by subjects with cognitive styles classified as impulsive. Only one other measure was associated with significant treatment differences, namely, immediate recall. The control group recalled the most, followed next by the REAP condition and then the SQ3R group. The author offered two explanations for the lack of improved performance. First, that the control group obtained the highest score might indicate that REAP and SQ3R subjects had not integrated the new processing styles well enough to compete with those allowed to pursue their usual processing strategy. Second, the value of the REAP procedure may lie not in an increase in the quality of study, but in an increase in inspection and reflection time. If this were true, the 15-minute time restriction may have adversely penalized the REAP as well as the SQ3R group.

Structured Overview

Description. Structured overview (Earle, 1969) involves three steps: preparation, presentation, and follow-up. The most crucial step in this procedure is the initial preparation of the overview, which is done by the instructor. This involves selecting the appropriate key words or concepts in a unit and then trying different structural relationships until one succeeds in best representing the overall meaning intended by the unit. An example of structured overview appears in Figure 4-2. During the second step, presentation, the overview is discussed with the class prior to reading. The instructor provides an explanation of the organization and the class is encouraged to add other relevant information. During the last stage, follow-up, the over-

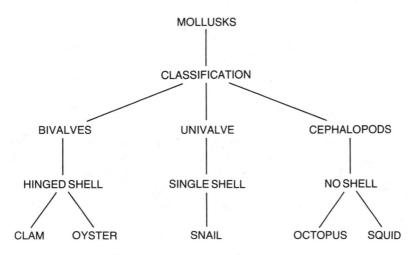

Figure 4-2. A structured overview.

view is referred to for both confirmation of what has been read and as a guide for what remains to be read.

The function of a structured overview is twofold. It first attempts to introduce the technical vocabulary or key concepts of a particular unit. Second, it tries to develop meaningful connections between these concepts such that they correspond to the interrelationship being developed in the unit. The latter function is achieved by displaying the structured overview as a visible framework illustrating how the concepts relate to each other.

Theoretical Rationale. The rationale for this procedure is based on the assumption that proficient understanding of content information requires knowing not only key concepts, or "nodes," of information, but also how those nodes are hooked together in a meaningful manner. Thus, the concern is not only with lower level information, but also with developing higher order networks that exemplify an overall passage meaning. Using the structured overview prior to reading provides readers with a meaningful context in which to fit the new information. Having access to it during reading provides a means for checking their own understanding in terms of the important concepts, as well as for identifying the conceptual relationships being developed in the text.

This procedure has the potential to positively affect all four types of encoding discussed earlier, and research generally indicates that its use does lead to more meaningful learning outcomes. The procedure strongly affects the selection and acquisition of information, since relevant information is identified for the learner and focused on during the discussion. It would seem particularly beneficial for constructive encoding, since the interrelationship of idea units is equally well stressed. How well the information is integrated depends on how much prior knowledge is generated and connected to the new input during the discussion.

Evaluation. There have been several empirical investigations of this procedure. Earle (1969) found that seventh- and eighth-grade mathematics students using structured overviews performed significantly better than a comparable control group receiving no advance instruction. Other studies have indicated that structural overviews may be more beneficial to some content areas than others. Snouffer and Thistlewaite (Note 1) had adult college students read a 2000-word passage drawn from either a history or a science text. One group of subjects received a 10-minute discussion using a structured overview of the passage. Another group received 10 minutes of instruction on the meaning of words drawn from the passages (vocabulary instruction), and a last group received no prereading instruction. All groups had 15 minutes in which to read the passages. Overall learning was assessed by a set of 10 literal and 10 inferential questions. Results indicated that the structural overview group significantly outperformed both the vocabulary and no-instruction group on both question types. The vocabulary and no-instruction groups did not significantly differ from each other. However, there were some interactions with passage types. Having the structured overview enhanced inferential question performance on the science passage but not on the historical passage. Additional research by Estes, Mills, and Barron (1969) also found structured overviews beneficial for biology but not English.

Because the goal of any reading strategy is to produce better independent reading, one suggestion for this procedure is that the learners themselves begin to take more responsibility for developing the interrelationship between key concepts. The procedure can be initially introduced much as it has been discussed, to serve as a model of comprehension, and later students can gradually assume more of this responsibility.

DRTA (Directed Reading and Thinking Activity)

Description. The directed reading and thinking activity is based on the premise that reading is a thinking process (Stauffer, 1975), and that both reading and thinking have to occur simultaneously for comprehension to take place. There are three basic steps in the DRTA process: predict, read, and prove.

During the first step, predict, students are given the title of a passage, the first paragraph, or pictures from the passage, and are asked to predict what they think the passage is about. For example, assume a class is being introduced to the nitrogen passage in Table 4-1. They are given the first subheading, "The Nitrogen Cycle," and asked to predict what they think this passage might be about. Since this is a content-area strategy, the focus during the prediction stage will be on eliciting from the students what they already know about the topic suggested by the title and what the passage might have to say about it. Students may be able to provide such facts as that nitrogen is a gas or that nitrogen is used by plants as a source of food. They might suggest that a cycle is something that has a beginning, middle, and end and repeats itself; that a cycle is circular like a bicycle tire; and so on. The predictions made during this stage are always written down for later referral.

In the read stage, students are given a segment of the text and asked to read in order to find "proof" for their predictions. At this point reading is silent and independent.

In the proving stage, readers are asked to indicate what information in the text supports or negates each of their predictions. Readers are expected to use evidence drawn directly from their reading to support or eliminate each prediction. They must reason logically and be able to point directly to evidence in the text when making decisions about the validity of each prediction.

At this point, the procedure is repeated. For the second subheading, "Nitrogen Assimilation," students are asked to predict what information will be encountered in this portion of the text. Predictions would now be based on what was learned from the initial portion of the text and any other information they may be able to call upon. These are listed, and students read to provide support for them.

Theoretical Rationale. The DRTA serves a number of different functions in promoting comprehension. First, it forces a reader to search for (and activate) a number of different types of prior knowledge. In addition, the students (and not the instructor) are responsible for eliciting relevant prior knowledge, a characteristic unique to this reading strategy. Thus, during instruction the system more closely models what the reader is encouraged to do in the independent reading situation.

Second, this system makes reading similar to an active problem-solving effort. Readers hypothesize on the basis of their best knowledge in generating predictions. They test these predictions during their reading search by looking for confirmation or negation of their ideas. Feedback from the text is used to generate new predictions. This component of forward prediction begins at a very general level and becomes more specific with the addition of new information derived from the passage.

Last, readers are always asked to justify their conclusions, using both their own knowledge and what they discover within the text. This forces them to reason logically and systematically. Because this process occurs externally, they have immediate feedback on the adequacy of both their reading and reasoning.

With respect to the model outlined earlier in this chapter, DRTA can serve a selective encoding function. When readers set up a series of predictions, they read to either confirm or negate them. This makes the reading process "search" oriented. Readers must locate and then select appropriate text information in deciding the validity of each prediction.

The DRTA may be beneficial to constructive encoding in two ways. First, predictions are not always fact oriented, as in the sample prediction that a cycle has a beginning, middle, and end and repeats itself. The validity of this prediction can be judged only by drawing inferential connections between passage facts. The second constructive encoding function DRTA may provide relates to the fact that DRTA is structured so that separate portions of the text are used one at a time. As the process moves through the text segments, the predictions begin to be based not only on the readers' own prior knowledge, but also on the information that they have derived from the text read to that point. Thus, the process ensures that each segment of the text becomes connected to the others.

Probably the most prominent concern of DRTA is that readers make as much use of their prior knowledge as is possible during their reading. Thus, integrative encoding processes are probably the most heavily affected by this procedure. Students are encouraged to search their prior knowledge and generate as much information as they can in trying to bring meaning to the passage. Its ultimate goal is to get readers to make sense of the information, based largely on what their prior knowledge dictates.

Evaluation. Most of the research conducted on the overall effects of DRTA has been done by Stauffer and his students (Stauffer, 1975) with elementary school children. Most of the studies cited in his work have focused on comparing the DRTA and the directed reading activity (DRA). The latter system (Betts, 1946) differs from the DRTA in that the teacher alone sets the purpose for reading by posing specific questions prior to reading, and students are not asked to prove question answers.

A brief summary of some of the research findings indicates that DRTA encourages not only more responses by students, but also responses of higher quality and more variety. Compared to DRA, DRTA produces more critical thinking and is effective for use with students at all levels of reading ability. Teacher questioning behavior in DRTA focuses more on interpretation and inference, whereas in the DRA it frequently focuses only on factual information. Students responses in a DRTA session are more likely to go beyond the literal level of a text, whereas DRA produces lower level verbatim responses tied more directly to the text.

ReQuest

Description. The ReQuest procedure (Manzo, 1969) is an excercise in which the student and teacher read sections of a passage silently and then take turns asking each other questions about the material they have just read. The text may be used when asking a question, but may not be used when answering. Prior to reading, the teacher reviews the types of questions that might be asked. Questions may require factual information, ask for paraphrases, examine cause-and-effect relationships, determine vocabulary knowledge, require inferential reasoning or forward predictions, and so on. Since students generally begin ReQuest sessions with questioning behaviors that focus on passage details, teacher modeling of in-depth questions is particularly important. With experience, student-generated questions become increasingly varied.

Theoretical Rationale. It is easiest to describe the rationale underlying this procedure by describing the reader as one who both generates and answers questions. Because readers are ultimately responsible for all aspects of the text, they must attend to multiple levels of text information, which can vary from directly stated information to answers that can only be inferred from information presented in the text. In addition, the text is absent during question answering, so readers must store passage information in a manner that allows for optimal retrieval.

As a question generator, readers gain experience in setting purposes and standards for their own reading. In order to assess the adequacy of others' responses, as well as to answer any question put to them, readers must attend to the written material on a variety of information levels.

Pearson and Johnson (1978) have developed a taxonomy of question-answer relations that may explain how ReQuest can affect all four types of encoding. Textually explicit questions or factual questions have obvious and definite answers that can be found directly in the text. When readers are held responsible for textually explicit questions, they must selectively attend to all the information within a text, hypothesizing which information is likely to appear in a question. In addition, they do not have access to the text while answering, so they must acquire as much information as is possible during their reading. Thus, these types of questions are likely to have an overall facilitative effect on selective encoding, as well as on acquisition.

Textually implicit questions have answers that can be obtained only by inferential reasoning, thus affecting constructive encoding. Readers must take the textually explicit information as a base and manipulate it in the manner required by the question. Scriptally implicit questions require readers to make use of the general knowledge and experience they bring to the text, but that is not a part of the text itself. These types of questions force students to activate relevant prior knowledge and map text information onto old knowledge, compelling them to link what is new to what is known.

Thus far, the discussion has focused on the reader as a receiver of text information as he or she attempts to prepare for various types of questions. During reading, students are responsible not only for generating good questions, but also for making value judgments about the adequacy of question responses. Ultimately, this allows readers to participate in designing tests of reading outcomes, a function they are seldom permitted with most reading strategies.

Evaluation. There is little empirical support for this procedure outside of Manzo's (1968) preliminary work. However, the procedure takes advantage of several significant findings from laboratory studies. First, research with adjunct questions indicates that performance is better if the questions appear after the text is read as opposed to before (Anderson & Biddle, 1975), which is inherent in the ReQuest procedure. Second, the "levels-of-questions" approach advocated by this procedure fits nicely with the research indicating that higher order questions lead to better overall understanding of the text.

General Conclusion

Future Research Topics

This chapter has explored the reading strategy problem (i.e., the question whether people can be taught or guided to process prose more effectively). The reviews of laboratory studies and instructional applications yield some reason for optimism. The laboratory studies suggest that reading strategies affect the encoding process, resulting in learning outcomes that can be measured. Analyses of instructional applications reveal that many strategies can be related to specific cognitive processes.

This chapter was not intended to provide an exhaustive review of research on reading strategies for adult prose processing. Instead, we have focused on exemplary studies that demonstrate how reading strategies can affect the reader's cognitive processes and learning outcomes. Further research is required in order to determine how each of the following processes is influenced by both reader-initiated and text-initiated reading strategies.

1. *Techniques for influencing the selection process.* In particular, further research is needed to determine how a reader decides what to pay attention to in a passage. Reader-initiated strategies that may affect the selection process include underlining, verbatim note taking, and shadowing. Text-initiated strategies that

affect the selection process include statements of instructional objectives, pre-questions, italicization of key terms, format, and spacing of sentences.

2. *Techniques for influencing acquisition.* In addition, research is needed to determine how a reader decides how much information will be encoded into long-term memory. Reader-initiated strategies that may affect how much is encoded include the level of attention and reader activity. Text-generated strategies that affect the acquisition process include postquestions, writing style, and interest.

3. *Techniques for influencing the construction process.* Further research is needed to determine how a reader comes to construct the elements in the passage into a coherent structure. Reader-initiated strategies that may affect the construction process include outlining and making comparisons among ideas in the passage. Text-initiated strategies include inference questions; providing an outline preview; providing signals such as "first, . . . second, . . . third"; and providing headings that indicate the passage outline.

4. *Techniques for influencing the integration process.* Finally, research is needed to determine how a reader comes to integrate the presented information with existing knowledge. Reader-initiated strategies that may affect the integration process include elaboration questions and elaborative note taking. Text-initiated strategies that may affect the integration process include advance organizers and concrete models.

Future Research Trends

In trying to foresee the nature of future research on the reading strategy problem, we encourage the following trends:

1. *Training of domain-specific strategies rather than general strategies.* Much of the previous work has been directed at the teaching of general strategies for processing all kinds of prose. However, one shortcoming of this approach is that it ignores the role of domain-specific knowledge in prose processing. Future research may do well to focus on reading strategies that are related to a specific domain, such as a statistics text or a physics text or a computer-programming text. Recent research on teaching of problem-solving strategies has suggested that it is not fruitful to separate "general strategies" from "specific knowledge domains" (Tuma & Reif, 1980). Similarly, in teaching of reading strategies, we foresee future research that focuses on techniques that are specific to the subject domains. (However, see Chapter 5 for a contrasting point of view.)

2. *Strategy training based on a theory of the mechanisms of learning rather than on S-R laws.* Much of the previous research has examined the behavioral effects of various manipulations, as in the question, "Does variable X increase or decrease retention?" One shortcoming of this approach is that research results may lack generalizability. Future research would do well to focus on the development of a theory of learning and instruction that includes a description of the encoding process for various manipulation. In this chapter, we have suggested four processes that deserve special attention, namely, selection, acquisition, construction, and integration.

3. *Strategy training based on a merger of psychological theory and pedagogic application.* Much of the previous research has involved either well-controlled laboratory studies that lack real-world validity or field applications that lack tight experimental control. There are some promising signs, however, that these approaches may be converging. Norman (1980) has called for the development of a "discipline of cognitive engineering." In particular, Norman suggests, "We need to develop the general principles of how to learn, how to remember, how to solve problems, and then to develop applied courses, and then to establish the place of these methods in an academic curriculum" (p. 97). The teaching of reading strategies should be a prime component of this emerging discipline of cognitive engineering.

Acknowledgments. Preparation of this chapter was partially supported by Grant SED-80-14950 from the National Science Foundation, Program of Research in Science Education. The authors appreciate the helpful comments by Patricia Masonheimer on an earlier version of this chapter.

Reference Note

1. Snouffer, N. K., & Thistlethwaite, L. The effects of the structured overview and vocabulary pre-teaching upon comprehension levels of college freshmen. Paper presented at the annual meeting of the National Reading Conference, San Antonio, November, 1979.

References

Aiken, E. G., Thomas, G. S., & Shennum, W. Memory for a lecture: Effects of notes, lecture rate, and information density. *Journal of Educational Psychology*, 1975, *67*, 439–444.

Anderson, R. C., & Biddle, W. B. On asking people questions about what they are reading. In G. H. Bower (Ed.), *Psychology of learning and motivation* (Vol. 9). New York: Academic Press, 1975.

Anderson, R. C., & Ortony, A. On putting apples into bottles—a problem of polysemy. *Cognitive Psychology*, 1975, *7*, 167–180.

Anderson, R. C., Reynolds, R. E., Schallert, D. L., & Goetz, E. T. Frameworks for comprehending discourse. *American Educational Research Journal*, 1977, *14*, 367–381.

Andre, T. Does answering higher level questions while reading facilitate productive learning? *Review of Educational Research*, 1979, *49*, 280–318.

Arkes, H. R., Schumacher, G. M., & Gardner, E. T. Effects of orienting tasks on the retention of prose material. *Journal of Educational Psychology*, 1976, *68*, 536–545.

Barnett, J. E., DiVesta, F. J., & Rogozinski, J. T. What is learned in note taking? *Journal of Educational Psychology*, 1981, *73*, 181–192.

Bartlett, B. J. *Top-level structure as an organizational strategy for recall of classroom text*. Unpublished doctoral dissertation, Arizona State University, 1978.

Betts, E. A. *Foundations of reading instruction*. New York: American Book, 1946.

Boker, J. R. Immediate and delayed retention effects of interspersing questions in written instructional passages. *Journal of Educational Psychology*, 1974, *66*, 96–98.

Bower, G. H. Experiments on story understanding and recall. *Quarterly Journal of Experimental Psychology*, 1976, *28*, 511–534.

Bransford, J. D., & Johnson, M. K. Contextual prerequisites for understanding: Some investigations of comprehension and recall. *Journal of Verbal Learning and Verbal Behavior*, 1972, *11*, 717–726.

Bransford, J. D., & Johnson, M. K. Considerations of some problems of comprehension. In W. G. Chase (Ed.), *Visual information processing*. New York: Academic Press, 1973.

Bretzing, B. H., & Kulhavy, R. W. Note-taking and passage style. *Journal of Educational Psychology*, 1981, *73*, 242–250.

Carrier, C. A., & Titus, A. Effects of notetaking pretraining and test mode expectations on learning from lecture. *American Educational Research Journal*, 1981, *18*, 385–397.

Carter, J. F., & Van Matre, N. H. Notetaking versus not having. *Journal of Educational Psychology*, 1975, *67*, 900–904.

Chall, J. S. The great debate: Ten years later, with a modest proposal for reading stages. In L. B. Resnick & P. A. Weaver (Eds.), *Theory and practice of early reading* (Vol. 1). Hillsdale, NJ: Erlbaum, 1979.

Collins, W. A., & Wiens, M. Cognitive processes in television viewing: Description and strategic implications. In M. Pressley & J. R. Levin (Eds.), *Cognitive strategy research: Psychological foundations*. New York: Springer-Verlag, 1983.

Cook, L. K. *The effects of text structure on the comprehension of scientific prose*. Unpublished doctoral dissertation, University of California, Santa Barbara, 1982.

Craik, F. I. M., & Lockhart, R. S. Levels of processing: A framework for memory research. *Journal of Verbal Learning and Verbal Behavior*, 1972, *11*, 671–684.

Crawford, C. C. Some experimental studies on the results of college notetaking. *Journal of Educational Research*, 1925, *12*, 379–386.

Dansereau, D. F., Collins, K. W., McDonald, B. A., Holley, C. D., Garland, J., Diekhoff, G. M., & Evans, S. H. Evaluation of a learning strategy system. In H. F. O'Neill & C. D. Spielberger (Eds.), *Cognitive and affective learning strategies*. New York: Academic Press, 1979.

DiVesta, F. J., & Gray, G. S. Listening and note taking. *Journal of Educational Psychology*, 1972, *63*, 8–14.

DiVesta, F. J., & Gray, G. S. Listening and note taking: II. Immediate and delayed recall as functions of variations in thematic continuity, note taking, and length of listening review intervals. *Journal of Educational Psychology*, 1973, *64*, 278–287.

DiVesta, F. J., Schultz, C. B., & Dangel, T. R. Passage organization and imposed learning strategies in comprehension and recall of connected discourse. *Memory & Cognition*, 1973, *1*, 471–476.

Doctorow, M., Wittrock, M. C., & Marks, C. Generative processes in reading comprehension. *Journal of Educational Psychology,* 1978, *70,* 109–118.

Dooling, D. J., & Lachman, R. Effects of comprehension on retention of prose. *Journal of Experimental Psychology,* 1971, *88,* 216–222.

Eanet, M. An investigation of the REAP reading/study procedure: Its rationale and efficacy. In P. E. Pearson & J. Hansen (Eds.), *Reading: Disciplined inquiry in process and practice.* Clemson, SC: National Reading Conference, 1978.

Eanet, M., & Manzo, A. V. REAP-A strategy for improving reading/writing/study skills. *Journal of reading,* 1976, *19,* 647–652.

Earle, R. A. Use of the structured overview in mathematics classes. In H. L. Herber & P. L. Sanders (Eds.), *Research in reading in the content areas: First year report.* Syracuse: Reading and Language Arts Center, Syracuse University, 1969.

Eisenberg, A. *Reading technical books.* Englewood Cliffs, NJ: Prentice-Hall, 1978.

Estes, T. H., Mills, D. C., & Barron, R. F. Three methods of introducing students to a reading-learning task in two content areas. In H. L. Herber & P. L. Sanders (Eds.), *Research in reading in the content areas: First year report.* Syracuse: Reading and Language Arts Center, Syracuse University, 1969.

Faw, H. W., & Waller, T. G. Mathemagenic behaviors and efficiency in learning from prose. *Review of Educational Research,* 1976, *46,* 691–720.

Felker, D. B., & Dapra, T. A. Effects of question type and question placement on problem-solving ability from prose material. *Journal of Educational Psychology,* 1975, *67,* 380–384.

Fisher, J. L., & Harris, M. B. Effect of notetaking and review on recall. *Journal of Educational Psychology,* 1973, *65,* 321–325.

Frase, L. T. Boundary conditions for mathemagenic behaviors. *Review of Educational Research,* 1970, *40,* 337–347.

Frase, L. T., Patrick, E. F., & Schumer, H. Effect of question position and frequency upon learning from text under different levels of incentive. *Journal of Educational Psychology,* 1970, *61,* 52–56.

Hartley, J., Bartlett, S., & Branthwaite, A. Underlining can make a difference— sometimes. *Journal of Educational Research,* 1980, *73,* 218–224.

Howe, M. J. A. Using student's notes to examine the role of the individual learner in acquiring meaningful subject matter. *Journal of Educational Research,* 1970, *64,* 61.

Hyde, T. S., & Jenkins, J. J. Differential effects of incidental tasks on the organization of recall of a list of highly associated words. *Journal of Experimental Psychology,* 1969, *82,* 472–481.

Hyde, T. S., & Jenkins, J. J. Recall of words as a function of semantic, graphic, and syntactic orienting tasks. *Journal of Verbal Learning and Verbal Behavior,* 1973, *12,* 471–480.

Jenkins, J. J. Can we have a theory meaningful memory? In R. L. Solso (Ed.), *Theories in cognitive psychology: The Loyola symposium.* Potomac, MD: Erlbaum, 1974.

Johnson, M. K., Bransford, J. D., & Solomon, S. Memory for tacit implications of sentences. *Journal of Experimental Psychology,* 1973, *98,* 203–205.

Kintsch, W., & Van Dijk, T. A. Toward a model of text comprehension and production. *Psychological Review,* 1978, *85,* 363–394.

Kirszner, L. G., & Mandell, S. R. *Patterns for college writing.* New York: St. Martin's Press, 1980.

Kulhavy, R. W., Dyer, J. W., & Silver, L. The effects of notetaking and text expectations on the learning of text material. *Journal of Educational Research,* 1975, *68,* 363–365.

Levin, J. R. Pictures as prose-learning devices. In A. Flammer & W. Kintsch (Eds.), *Discourse processing.* Amsterdam: North-Holland, in press.

Levin, J. R., & Pressley, M. Improving children's prose comprehension: Selected strategies that seem to succeed. In C. M. Santa & B. L. Hayes (Eds.), *Children's prose comprehension: Research and practice.* Newark, DE: International Reading Association, 1981.

Mallery, R. D. *Grammar rhetoric and composition.* New York: Barnes & Noble, 1967.

Mandler, J. M., & Johnson, N. S. Remembrance of things passed: Story structure and recall. *Cognitive Psychology,* 1977, *9,* 111–191.

Manzo, A. V. *Improving reading comprehension through reciprocal questioning.* Unpublished doctoral dissertation, Syracuse University, 1968.

Manzo, A. V. The ReQuest procedure. *Journal of Reading,* 1969, *13,* 123–126, 163.

Mayer, R. E. Forward transfer of different reading strategies evoked by test-like events in mathematics text. *Journal of Educational Psychology,* 1975, *67,* 165–169.

Mayer, R. E. Can advance organizers influence meaningful learning? *Review of Educational Research,* 1979, *49,* 371–383.

Mayer, R. E. The psychology of how novices learn computer programming. *Computing Surveys,* 1981, *13,* 121–141.

Mayer, R. E., & Cook, L. K. Effects of shadowing on prose comprehension and problem solving. *Memory & Cognition,* 1980, *8,* 101–109.

McConkie, G. W., Rayner, K., & Wilson, S. J. Experimental manipulation of reading strategies. *Journal of Educational Psychology,* 1973, *65,* 1–8.

McGraw, B., & Groteleuschen, A. Direction of the effect of questions in prose material. *Journal of Educational Psychology,* 1972, *63,* 586–588.

Meyer, B. J. F. *The organization of prose and its effects on memory.* Amsterdam: North-Holland, 1975.

Meyer, B. J. F. The structure of prose: Effects on learning and memory and implications for educational practice. In R. C. Anderson, R. J. Spiro, & W. E. Montague (Eds.), *Schooling and the acquisition of knowledge.* Hillsdale, NJ: Erlbaum, 1977.

Meyer, B. J. F. A selected review and discussion of basic research on prose comprehension. In D. F. Fisher & C. W. Peters (Eds.), *Comprehension and the competent reader.* New York: Praeger, 1981.

Meyer, B. J. F., Brandt, D. M., & Bluth, G. J. Use of top-level structure in text: Key for reading comprehension of ninth-grade students. *Reading Research Quarterly,* 1980, *16*(1), 72–103.

Morris, C. D., Bransford, J. D., & Franks, J. J. Levels of processing versus transfer appropriate processing. *Journal of Verbal Learning and Verbal Behavior,* 1977, *16,* 519–533.

Norman, D. A. Cognitive engineering and education. In D. T. Tuma & F. Reif (Eds.), *Problem solving and education.* Hillsdale, NJ: Erlbaum, 1980.

Orlando, V. P., & Hayward, K. G. A comparison of the effectiveness of three study techniques for college students. In P. D. Pearson & J. Hansen (Eds.), *Reading: Disciplined inquiry in process and practice.* Clemson, SC: National Reading Conference, 1978.

Pearson, P. D., & Johnson, D. D. *Teaching reading comprehension.* New York: Holt, Rinehart & Winston, 1978.

Peper, R. J., & Mayer, R. E. Notetaking as a generative activity. *Journal of Educational Psychology,* 1978, *70,* 514–522.

Peters, D. L. Effects of notetaking and rate of presentation on short-term objective test performance. *Journal of Educational Psychology,* 1972, *63,* 276–280.

Pichert, J. W., & Anderson, R. C. Taking different perspectives on a story. *Journal of Educational Psychology,* 1977, *69,* 309–315.

Rickards, J. P., & August, G. J. Generative underlining strategies in prose recall. *Journal of Educational Psychology,* 1975, *67,* 860–865.

Rickards, J. P., & DiVesta, F. J. Type and frequency of questions in processing textual material. *Journal of Educational Psychology,* 1974, *66,* 354–362.

Robinson, F. P. *Effective study.* New York: Harper & Row, 1961.

Robinson, H. A. *Teaching reading and study strategies.* Boston: Allyn & Bacon, 1975.

Rothkopf, E. Z., & Bisbicos, E. E. Selective facilitative effects of interspersed questions on learning from written prose. *Journal of Educational Psychology,* 1967, *58,* 56–61.

Rumelhart, D. Notes on a schema for stories. In D. Bobrow & A. Collins (Eds.), *Representation and understanding: Studies in cognitive science.* New York: Academic Press, 1975.

Rumelhart, D. Understanding and summarizing brief stories. In D. LaBerge & S. J. Samuels (Eds.), *Basic processes in reading.* Hillsdale, NJ: Erlbaum, 1977.

Santa, C. M., Abrams, L., & Santa, J. L. Effects of notetaking and studying on the retention of prose. *Journal of Reading Behavior,* 1979, *11,* 247–260.

Shepherd, D. L. *Comprehensive high school reading methods.* Columbus, OH: Merrill, 1978.

Shimmerlik, S. M., & Nolan, J. D. Reorganization and the recall of prose. *Journal of Educational Psychology,* 1976, *68,* 779–786.

Slesnick, I. L., Balzer, L., McCormack, A. J., Newton, D. E., & Rasmussen, F. A. *Biology.* Glenview, IL: Scott, Foresman, 1980.

Stauffer, R. G. *Directing the reading-thinking process.* New York: Harper & Row, 1975.

Stein, B. S. Depth of processing re-examined: The effects of precision of encoding and test appropriateness. *Journal of Verbal Learning and Verbal Behavior,* 1978, *17,* 165–174.

Stein, N. L., & Glenn, C. G. An analysis of story comprehension in elementary school children. In R. Freedle (Ed.), *New directions in discourse processing.* Norwood, NJ: Ablex, 1979.

Thorndyke, P. W. Cognitive structures in comprehension and memory of narrative discourse. *Cognitive Psychology,* 1977, *9,* 77–110.

Till, R. E., & Jenkins, J. J. The effects of cued orienting tasks on the free recall of words. *Journal of Verbal Learning and Verbal Behavior,* 1973, *12,* 489–498.

Tresselt, M. E., & Mayzner, M. S. A study of incidental learning. *Journal of Psychology,* 1960, *50,* 339–347.

Tuma, D. T., and Reif, F. (Eds.). *Problem solving and education.* Hillsdale, NJ: Erlbaum, 1980.

Walsh, D. A., & Jenkins, J. J. Effects of orienting tasks on free recall in incidental learning: Difficulty, effort, and process explanations. *Journal of Verbal Learning and Verbal Behavior,* 1973, *12,* 481–488.

Watts, G. H., & Anderson, R. C. Effects of three types of inserted questions on learning from prose. *Journal of Educational Psychology,* 1971, *62,* 387–394.

Weener, P. Notetaking and student verbalization as instructional learning activities. *Instructional Science,* 1974, *3,* 51–74.

Wittrock, M. C. Learning as a generative activity. *Educational Psychologist,* 1974, *11,* 87–95.

Worden, P. E. Memory strategy instruction with the learning disabled. In M. Pressley & J. R. Levin (Eds.), *Cognitive strategy research: Psychological foundations.* New York: Springer-Verlag, 1983.

5. Children's Flexible Use of Strategies During Reading

D. L. Forrest-Pressley and Laurie A. Gillies

Certainly one of the most awesome tasks facing the young reader is that of becoming sufficiently proficient in specific reading skills to be able to use these skills in a flexible manner to learn from written material (i.e., to study). However, it is virtually impossible to conceptualize study skills within a traditional cognitive model of reading. See, for example, Gibson and Levin's comments on this point (1975, p. 438). In this chapter, we suggest a conceptualization of reading within a metacognitive framework that allows us to talk about the flexible use of reading strategies, as well as the role of knowledge and comprehension monitoring in the learning situation. (For more on metacognition, see Borkowski & Büchel, 1983, and Worden, 1983.)

Mature reading has been characterized as the flexible use of various types of skills in order to meet the purpose of the situation at hand (Gibson, 1972; Gibson & Levin, 1975). Unfortunately, even though the complexity of reading is acknowledged, most research efforts have focused on more limited aspects of the task (e.g., decoding skills, comprehension skills). In so doing, the flexible way in which a mature reader uses different skills has been largely ignored. For example, a person can read for entertainment or to find an answer to a problem. The reader might need to know only a specific piece of information or, in contrast, might need to understand a set of concepts presented by a writer. The mature reader has available a number of strategies, such as rereading, skim reading, and paraphrasing, that can be used to help achieve the desired goal. In effect, the skilled reader can read in different ways to meet different purposes. However, in order to accomplish different reading purposes, the child must be cognizant of the goal of reading, the amount and type of information in the text that is important to the goal, and whether or not comprehension is sufficient to meet the goal demands—a formidable task, considering children's difficulty in recognizing and overcoming difficulties during reading (e.g., Adams, 1980).

As alluded to above, the traditional view of reading has not explicitly addressed the various types of reading strategies. A second unfortunate consequence of focusing research on cognitive subcomponents of reading is that there has been little concern for the "executive control" that is managed by a skilled reader (e.g., the selection, monitoring, and modification of cognitive processes and strategies). One way to conceptualize and study these executive processes is the framework of "metacognition." Whereas cognition refers to the actual skills and strategies that are used by the reader (e.g., decoding skills), metacognition refers to (1) what a person *knows* about his or her cognitions (in the sense that the child is able to talk about specific skills, how and when to execute them, and what they accomplish), and (2) the ability to *control* (monitor) these cognitions (in the sense of planning cognitive activities, choosing among alternative activities, monitoring the performance of activities, and changing activities). One obvious advantage of the use of knowledge and monitoring to the mature reader is that the deliberate use of reading strategies should result in an increase in reading efficiency. In this framework, a mature reader is one who knows that he or she can read in different ways for different purposes and uses available skills to do it appropriately.

In this chapter we will argue that efficient use of reading strategies cannot be achieved without the metacognitive components of knowledge and monitoring. An overview of relevant literature on reading strategies, knowledge and monitoring follows the initial outline of our conception of reading. This overview is not meant to be a comprehensive review of the literature; rather, we have tried to highlight papers that are representative of the field. Training procedures and instructional practices will be covered in the same manner. Finally, future research directions and applications will be discussed. At this point, we should note that not all of the studies discussed are as methodologically sound as we might hope. However, we do feel that the studies that are reviewed will orient the reader of this chapter to the field in general.

Conceptions of reading as involving knowledge, monitoring, and strategy use are not entirely new. In fact, many early reading theorists, including Huey (1908/1968) and Thorndike (1917), acknowledged the importance of monitoring and other study skills to aid in reading comprehension. For example, Huey (1908/1968) includes note taking, referencing, and index usage as aids to comprehension. In more recent years, reading has been considered as a complex problem-solving situation (e.g., Bransford, Stein, Shelton, & Owings, 1980; Kachuck & Marcus, 1976; Kavale & Schreiner, 1979; Olshavsky, 1976/77; Reid, 1966). Also, there are excellent review and position papers on the metacognitive research that has been conducted (e.g., Baker & Brown, in press; Brown, 1978, 1980; Brown & DeLoache, 1978; Flavell & Wellman, 1977; Yussen, Matthews, & Hiebert, 1982; Paris, Note 1).

Much of the conception proposed here is based on the results of a study conducted by Forrest-Pressley and Waller (in press). In this study, 144 children (equal groups of poor, average, and good readers from Grades 3 and 6) were assessed by means of an extensive series of tasks that included cognitive and metacognitive tests of language, memory for and use of important information, and the reading skills of decoding, comprehension, and strategies. We will refer to this study (or parts of it) repeatedly for examples of the types of skills that children have and do not have. Of course, one of our rationales for citing this study is our familiarity with the work. More important, however, is the fact that this is one of the few investigations directly relating metacognition to cognitive skills outside the area of memory (e.g., Borkowski, Reid, & Kurtz, in press; Cavanaugh & Borkowski, 1980; Flavell, 1979, 1981a, 1981b, Note 2; Schneider, Note 3), despite a growing number of hypotheses that a metacognition-reading linkage should exist (e.g., Baker & Brown, in press; Yussen et al., 1982). Moreover, it is the only work that we know of that has examined a number of different skills and processes in the same children in a very extensive manner. With this in mind, it is interesting to note that the patterns of results across skills and processes were very consistent. In general, both cognitive performance and the ability to make appropriate verbalizations about all skills increased with grade and with reading ability. Because of these consistencies in the results across processes and because of supporting evidence in the field, we have a great deal of confidence in the conception of reading that is proposed. However, it should be noted that this model is in its early stages of development and we would expect that it will change and grow as new data accumulate. Readers interested in a more detailed discussion of the specific issues involved and a closer view of the data being cited are referred to the original source (Forrest-Pressley & Waller, in press).

The proposed conception of reading can be viewed within much the same framework as the model of cognitive processing proposed by Miller, Galanter, and Pribram (1960). According to these authors, behavior is guided by the formation of *plans* (i.e., a hierarchy of instructions that controls the order in which a sequence of operations is performed). The mature individual has available in storage many more plans than the one being executed and is capable of rapid alternation between plans. The individual also has images (i.e., accumulated, organized knowledge about self and world) that are used to select an appropriate plan. Miller et al. suggest that learning occurs only when the person has some kind of a plan. Furthermore, a plan will not be achieved "without intent to learn, that is to say, without executing a *metaplan* for constructing a plan that will guide recall" (p. 129). It is these metaplans then that generate alternative plans. Once a plan is available, a control process, refered to as a TOTE unit, (test-operate-test-exit unit) guides behavior. This TOTE unit continually monitors the progress of the plan that presently is activated. We believe that TOTE units and metaplans roughly correspond to the mechanisms of cognitive knowledge and control that mature readers use, and that plans correspond to specific strategies that can be activated by the higher order cognitive control processes. It also should be noted that the Miller et al. model has influenced research in domains other than reading in much the same way as will be proposed here—areas such as language (e.g., Bloom & Lahey, 1978), memory (e.g., Pressley, Heisel, McCormick, & Nakamura, 1982), and intelligence theory (e.g., Sternberg, 1981, Note 4).

Conception of Reading

When beginning to read, the child first must learn some means of rapidly recognizing single words. There are, of course, several cognitive strategies ("plans" in the above-discussed vernacular) that can be used in order to decode words, such as recognition of features of the whole word, or "sounding out" the word (e.g., Chall, 1979); asking someone what the word says; guessing the word from context or from a single feature, such as an initial letter; or skipping the word completely. Knowledge about each of these strategies might affect the way in which the child approaches a reading task. Indeed, most third-grade readers know about different decoding strategies for single words (Forrest-Pressley & Waller, in press). Moreover, while decoding, the child must monitor progress. This process involves realizing whether or not comprehension of any particular word has occurred. If the reader realizes that decoding has failed (i.e., he or she is unable to pronounce the word), then knowledge about various decoding strategies should affect subsequent action. If a child knows about several possible strategies of decoding, the likelihood that he or she will decode the word is greater. When more is known about each particular decoding strategy, the probability of choosing the most efficient strategy, given the situation, increases. Indeed, older and/or better readers are more likely both to know about decoding skills and to use them effectively (Forrest-Pressley & Waller, in press). That is, they possess both plans and metaplans that younger readers do not.

Even when words are decoded to sound, it is possible that appropriate meanings will not be constructed or accessed. Once again, the reader must be able to monitor performance by deciding whether or not what has been read has been understood (e.g., Adams, 1980). Only older and/or better readers know that there is a difference between what a word "says" and what a word "means" (Forrest-Pressley & Waller, in press). If decoding has failed at this stage, then the reader could ask someone what the word means or could look the word up in a dictionary. Knowledge of these strategies and of the effectiveness of each should affect subsequent action.

Reading, in a decoding sense, includes not only single words but also larger units such as sentences. Certainly, the reader must be able to monitor comprehension of these larger units. If comprehension fails at this level, the reader could figure out what the sentence means by using the contextual cues, asking someone else what it means, looking up each word in a dictionary, or skipping the sentence completely. Knowledge of each of these strategies, and of the efficiency of each, should affect subsequent action. Only older and/or better readers can provide sophisticated information about how to decode sentences (Forrest-Pressley & Waller, in press). Consistent with the earlier general comments, reading in a decoding sense involves not only the use of cognitive strategies, but also knowledge of these strategies and the active monitoring of performance.

In addition to decoding strategies, the mature reader has available a number of different reading strategies to meet the demands of various situations. For example, he or she may reread, skim read, paraphrase, or concentrate on important units. Only the older and/or better reader can express knowledge of many of these strategies (Forrest-Pressley & Waller, in press; Kobasigawa, Ransom, & Holland, 1980; Myers & Paris, 1978). The knowledge that the reader has about these cognitive strategies may affect how he or she approaches the reading task. For example, the reader should be able to evaluate the task demands and choose the most efficient method of reading for that particular situation. While reading, the child must be able to identify the important units of text in order to carry out the appropriate reading strategy (e.g., Brown & Smiley, 1977). In addition, while reading, the child needs to monitor progress. The reader must realize when important information is read, decide whether or not the purpose of reading is being achieved, and determine if a change in strategy is needed. Once again, research indicates that older and/or better readers are more proficient at monitoring comprehension (e.g., Flavell, Speer, Green, & August, 1981; Forrest-Pressley & Waller, in press; Markman & Gorin, 1981; Baker, Note 5; Forrest-Pressley, Note 6; Winograd & Johnston, Note 7). If the reader realizes comprehension failure, it follows that the reader's knowledge about various reading strategies and the efficiency of each should affect subsequent behavior. The reader might realize that the problem is a matter of decoding and thus decide to use decoding strategies. It also is possible, however, that the reader might realize that important information is not being retained, and might thus decide that a change in advanced reading strategy is necessary.

The above-cited data provide some validation for three major components of flexible strategy usage by the mature reader. More mature readers do have knowledge of possible alternative strategies (metaplans), do spontaneously use reading strategies (plans), and do actively monitor and adjust strategies (TOTE units). In the discussion of the literature on these three components that follows, we intend to guide the reader to recent studies that are typical in the field.

Use of Strategies

Before considering the broader perspective of the reader choosing the most effective strategy and monitoring its efficiency during use, the question of what strategies children actually use while reading must be addressed. Although we assume that different reading strategies, such as skimming, reviewing, paraphrasing, summarizing, and identifying important ideas, are important in a learning situation, we know relatively little about how *children* learn to use these skills in a study situation; that is, most of our information about the effectiveness of the various study strategies comes from research with adults. However, it seems reasonable to argue that some "strategy" of reading must be used in silent reading if comprehension is to be maintained, particularly in speeded situations (e.g., Hausfeld, 1981), and that these skills develop during the middle elementary school years. It also seems likely that children are able to use various strategies that are not used spontaneously—that is, they exhibit a "production deficiency" (e.g., Flavell, 1977)—and that these strategies can be induced with minimal cuing (e.g., the teacher asks questions to direct reading, or suggests that the child study for a test). (Cook & Mayer, in Chapter 4 of this volume, offer extensive commentary on the strategies used by adults.)

Three observations illustrate that children do use strategies during reading, and that older children are more apt to engage in such activities. (1) Older and/or better readers adjust their rate of reading based on the type of information that is to be retained (e.g., DiStefano, Noe, & Valencia, 1981; Grabe & Doeling, Note 8), which suggests differential strategy use in different situations. (2) Brown and Smiley (1977, 1978) reported that older children were better than younger children at identifying units of prose that are thematically important, and that some children (fifth graders and older) spontaneously adopted strategies of underlining and note taking. This subset of students tended to concentrate on important elements, and their subsequent recall approximated the pattern found in adults. Since our discussion will eventually turn to the training of reading strategies, it is important to note that when underlining and note taking are not manifested spontaneously, they may not be easy to induce. In the Brown and Smiley (1978) study, they suggested the use of underlining and note taking to nonusers. Nonetheless, the students who had not shown spontaneous use of these strategies continued to show the more immature pattern of recall (see Pressley, Levin, & Bryant, 1983, for further discussion of these data). (3) Children also adjust their reading strategy when asked to read for a specific purpose. We will concretize this third point by considering two experiments that were done by the first author in collaboration with others.

Forrest and Barron (Note 9) were interested in how children in Grades 2, 4, and 6 (24 children from each grade of average reading ability and intelligence) would respond to instructions to read stories silently for three different kinds of information. Children were asked to read a story for one of three purposes: (1) to remember all of the names of people, places, and things, the *names* instructional condition; (2) to remember all of the things that happened, the *events* instructional condition; and (3) to remember both name *and* event information, the *combined* instructional condition. (The passages were excerpts, 500 or 1000 words in length, from grade-appropriate stories.) The combined instructional condition provided a baseline of the children's intentional reading performance for assessing changes in learning due to the names and the events instructions.

Based on a measure of reading efficiency (level of comprehension per unit of time, i.e., number of comprehension questions correct divided by length of time spent reading the passage), Forrest and Barron concluded the following about intentional reading: (1) Telling second and fourth graders to read for events that took place in the story produced efficiency scores that were not greater than those produced by the instruction to read for both names and events (i.e., all of the information in the story). The sixth-grade readers, however, appeared to be able to respond to the instructions in the events condition and to read intentionally for information about the events that took place in the story (i.e., the sixth-grade readers received higher efficiency scores in the events condition than in the combined events condition). These results were used in support of the argument that there is a developmental change in the ability of children to take advantage of instructions that reduce the memory demands involved in comprehending printed text. (2) Asking children to read for names is not a very effective way of finding out about the development of intentional reading, primarily because the ability to read for this type of information in this situation increased very little across grades. (See Faw & Waller, 1977, for a complete discussion of the relative value of using efficiency scores rather than comprehension scores in this type of experimental situation.)

With respect to intentional versus incidental learning, Forrest and Barron (Note 9) reported that the ratio of intentional to incidental comprehension scores increased across grades in the events instructional condition (events/names), suggesting that children were becoming progressively more selective in their intentional extraction of event information across grades and were better able to ignore information about names. In the names instructional condition, however, the ratio of the intentional to incidental comprehension scores (names/events) *decreased* across age, suggesting that it was increasingly difficult to extract name information without also extracting information about events. Finally, consistent with the theme of metacognition-reading behavior connections raised here, there was a positive correlation between the scores on some Kreutzer, Leonard, and Flavell (1975) metamemory tasks and the children's ability to read intentionally (i.e., ratio scores of events/names, events condition). The main point, however, is that Forrest and Barron (Note 9) made observations consistent with the position that selective reading abilities change with age.

The second study we will consider is a "reading for different purposes" study reported by Forrest-Pressley and Waller (in press). In that research, poor, average, and good readers in each of Grades 3 and 6 were asked to read eight stories, two under each of four different instructional conditions: "read for *fun*," "read to make up a *title*," "read as quickly as possible to find one specific piece of information" (*skim*), and "read to *study*." (Order of presentation of stories and instructional conditions were counterbalanced across subjects.) After each story, each child was given a comprehension test with 14 multiple-choice items, 7 of which were based on thematically important material and 7 of which were based on material that was thematically less important. After each item, each child was asked if he or she was sure or not sure of the answer. This judgment of accuracy was used as a metacomprehension measure.

Overall, the comprehension scores increased with grade and with reading ability. Further analyses of the pattern of comprehension scores over the four instructional conditions showed that they were consistent with the position that the ability to adjust one's reading strategy does change with grade and with reading ability. The first change occurred with third-grade good readers, whose comprehension scores dropped when they were asked to find one specific piece of information as quickly as possible (i.e., to skim). At the sixth-grade level, retention in the study condition increased compared to the skim condition. However, it was only with sixth-grade good readers that retention was significantly higher in all other conditions than in the skim condition. The analyses of metacomprehension scores showed that success at prediction also increased with grade and with reading ability. Analyses of covariance, controlling for nonverbal IQ, confirmed that both patterns of results did not result simply from differences in IQ. In addition, as will be discussed in the next section, these same children showed increases with grade and with reading ability in their ability to make appropriate verbalizations about their reading skills.

The main question that follows from the results highlighted here is why children, particularly younger, poorer readers, tend not to use appropriate strategies when reading. Possibilities consistent with the model of reading outlined earlier, and one that has been proposed by some reading investigators (e.g., Yussen et al., 1982), are that children may not know different possible strategies, they may not know enough about the strategies and reading situations to be able to choose the most appropriate strategy for the particular situation, or they may not monitor their strategy usage and effectiveness. With these hypotheses in mind, we now turn to a discussion of what the child actually does know about reading skills and reading for different purposes (i.e., possible deficiencies in the knowledge subcomponent).

Knowledge

As previously discussed, Miller et al. (1960) proposed a relation between plans and metaplans that is not dissimilar to current cognitive-metacognitive theories. In this framework, knowledge of reading situations and reading strategies is necessary for successful strategy deployment, an increasingly common theme in discussions of reading (e.g., Baker & Brown, in press; Reid, 1966; Yussen et al., 1982). However, even though knowledge is recognized as an important factor in cognitive development (e.g., Flavell, 1978), there have been relatively few empirical investigations of knowledge of reading skills.

The relation between knowledge of reading strategies and actual reading ability was examined by Forrest-Pressley and Waller (in press). In the part of the study relevant to this discussion, poor, average, and good readers in Grades 3 and 6 were asked questions about different ways of reading in different situations (i.e., reading strategies). The results of the reading portion of the interview indicated that knowledge of decoding, comprehension, and advanced strategies increased with grade and with reading ability. With regard to decoding skills, most children could think of at least one strategy for figuring out what a word says (i.e., they knew at least a little about decoding), but the number of strategies that were mentioned by any particular child increased with grade. The best decoding item was the one that asked if knowing what a word "says" is equivalent to knowing what a word "means." The tendency to recognize the difference and give an adequate explanation increased dramatically with grade and with reading ability.

In addition to differences in knowledge of decoding, younger and/or poorer readers gave little indication that they had knowledge about how to monitor comprehension. It was common for this type of reader to say that he or she would be ready to write a test after reading a story once, and that there was no way to predict accuracy until the teacher finished marking the test. On the other hand, older and/or better readers often suggested that they would know when they would be ready to write a test by using repetition along with a self-test or other-test strategy. The older and/or better readers also were able to indicate cues that would give them an idea of how well they had done before getting the test back. Some cues suggested were difficult level of the questions, length of time spent answering questions, and a number of answers that the child was sure were correct.

Younger and/or poorer readers also did not know what to do to correct comprehension problems. For example, many younger and/or poorer readers said that they would practice for a test but that there was nothing more they could do to make the information easier to remember. In addition, many indicated that they read the same way for fun as they did when preparing for a test. In contrast, the older and/or better readers indicated more knowledge of study skills, and they reported this knowledge as a general "plan of attack" rather than as isolated strategies. For example, one Grade 6 good reader, when asked what she would do when reading for a test, replied, "Well, first I'd read it once and then read it over again and I'll try to remember the important parts, and I'll read it a few times and then I'll get some people to ask me questions on it. . . I could go over it again to underline the important parts; then I could go over it again trying to remember the parts I underlined." Most younger and/or poorer readers also made some of these suggestions, but only after repeated probing by the interviewer. On the whole, their answers were both quantitatively and qualitatively different from the answers given by older and/or better readers.

In addition to the studies dealing specifically with knowledge of reading skills, researchers have begun to investigate other aspects of knowledge that may be important to reading or to teaching reading. Illustrative studies were conducted by Wellman and Johnson (1979; Johnson & Wellman, 1980), who studied children's knowledge of mental verbs such as *remember, know, guess,* and *forget* and found that young children tend to judge mental verbs mistakenly on the basis of external states or overt features of behavior. For example, even when no information was given either about the location of the hidden object or the present performance in guessing its location, preschoolers still claimed that their designation of the object's location was a matter of remembering and knowing as well as of guessing. In addition, there is a growing body of literature that suggests that the young child may not have complete knowledge of concepts used in the teaching of reading (i.e., word and sentence) when he or she enters the first grade (e.g., Forrest-Pressley & Waller, in press; Hiebert, 1981; Johns, 1980; Papandropoulou & Sinclair, 1974).

In closing this section on knowledge, we must acknowledge that knowledge alone may not always be a crucial factor in successful strategy usage. For example, Whaley (1981) asked children in Grades 3, 6, and 11 what "should or could come next" in an incomplete story (prediction task) and what "should or could fit in" a passage with one story grammar element missing (macrocloze task). Readers of all ages appeared to have similar structural expectations for stories, but younger children (Grade 3) tended to use these expectations less frequently than older children. Also, Forrest-Pressley & Waller (in press) noted that it would be quite possible for children to "mimic" what they had been told about a particular situation, but not use the knowledge to improve performance. This type of behavior was noted in poor readers, particularly when decoding skills were involved.

Based on the types of data discussed in this subsection, it is appropriate to conclude that younger and/or poorer readers are deficient in knowledge. However, metacognition involves more than just knowledge (e.g., Flavell, 1979, 1981a, 1981b, Note 2). It is the other part of metacognition, the monitoring or control processes, that we now will examine. We note in closing that Borkowski and Büchel (1983) and Worden (1983) also deal specifically with the metacognitions of poor learners.

Monitoring

It has only been within the last several years that comprehension monitoring has been identified as a key component of mature reading skills (e.g., Baker & Brown, in press; Brown, 1980; Forrest-Pressley & Waller, in press). The ability to monitor comprehension has received considerable attention in listening and reading tasks with both children and college students (e.g., Markman, 1977, 1979; Baker, Note 5; Winograd & Johnston, Note 7; Revelle, Karabenick, & Wellman, Note 10). On the whole, the findings have suggested that young children (Markman, 1979) and even college students (Baker, Note 5) fail to report logical inconsistencies in textual material. (Pressley, in Chapter 9 of this volume, outlines the paradigms involved in this type of research.) However, young children are not totally devoid of monitoring skills, as substantiated in a recent study by Revelle et al. (Note 10). In their study, even very young children (2½-4½ years old) could monitor comprehension of conversations to a certain extent. The younger children used more appropriate monitoring activities (e.g., asking for the message to be repeated) when the message was distorted ("yawn condition") than in an adequate-message control condition. In addition, Revelle et al. (Note 10) suggested that young children tended to use some monitoring activities in most conditions, but that they were not as selective as adults with respect to when they deployed them, (i.e., younger children actually overmonitored rather than undermonitored). Other indications that young children are able to monitor come from studies reported by Pace (Note 11, Note 12). After a standard listening comprehension task, Pace allowed children to listen to the stimulus story for a second time. Kindergarten children corrected previous responses on more than 33% of the trials, but second graders corrected previous responses 50% of the time. Also, older children in comparison to younger children had better comprehension of unfamiliar stories and were better able to recognize their own abilities.

Fortunately, there probably are ways in which we can encourage use of monitoring in children. For example, Markman and Gorin (1981) asked children of ages 8 and 10 to listen to stories containing one of two types of errors—inconsistencies (i.e., statements that contradicted previous text information) or falsehoods (i.e., statements that would be recognized as wrong if evaluated against common knowledge of the world). Telling children what type of error to look for increased the probability that that particular type of error would be detected, although inconsistencies were easier to detect than falsehoods. A second possible way to increase monitoring is to provide children with models of appropriate monitoring. For example, children's estimates of their ability in a nonverbal task have improved after watching a model perform such estimates (Zimmerman & Ringle, 1981). Also, preliminary data from our own laboratory document the effectiveness of behavioral modeling in a reading context (Forrest-Pressley, Note 13).

Before ending this discussion of monitoring, however, a shortcoming of the predominant paradigm (error detection) for monitoring should be acknowledged. If an error goes undetected in Markman-type situations, we have no idea why it was not identified (e.g., Winograd & Johnson, Note 7). There exist alternatives to the error-detection paradigm that are more sensitive to the underlying processing of readers during comprehension. For example, in a study by DiVesta, Hayward, and Orlando (1979), only good readers showed evidence of *using* subsequent as well as prior text in a cloze procedure task. Also, Garner and Reis's (1981) use of spontaneous "lookbacks" (turning back a page) as a measure of what one does when comprehension fails is noteworthy in this context. These investigators found that older and/or better readers produced more correct responses to questions that require a lookback than did younger and/or poorer readers. One can also examine self-corrections. Clay (1974) documented that good readers made more self-corrections in oral reading than poor readers. Finally, Just and Carpenter (1980) have shown that readers make longer pauses at points where processing loads are greater (i.e., when accessing infrequent words, integrating information from important clauses, and making inferences at the ends of sentences), and it may be possible to exploit these pauses as measures of metacognitive processing. The important point is that there are any number of comprehension measures potentially more sensitive than the Markman procedures.

Returning to the main theme of this subsection, we see that even mature readers are not always equally proficient at monitoring comprehension. For example, in a study by Baker and Anderson (1982) college students were asked to read passages with main-point inconsistencies, detail inconsistencies, or no inconsistencies. No matter what the type of inconsistency, all students spent more time on sentences containing information that conflicted with information presented elsewhere, indicating that they were monitoring while reading. In addition, more time was spent on the passages containing main-point inconsistencies than on those containing a detail inconsistency or none, yet there was no significant difference in the identification of the various types of consistencies. However, Baker and Anderson (1982) also reported, on the basis of analyses of individual data records, the presence of intraindividual differences as well as individual differences. For example, subjects who spent more time on the inconsistent target sentences during reading were no more likely to identify the consistency later than those who did not. Also, only 16% of the subjects spent more time reading both the passages with the main-point inconsistencies and those with detail inconsistencies relative to the amount of time spent on the passages containing consistent information. It would appear that even mature readers are not uniformly good monitors, nor do mature readers monitor consistently. More research is needed on the parameters of the activation of monitoring activities. Perhaps even mature readers could benefit from some training or cuing.

General Discussion: Evidence of Reading Strategy Use, Knowledge, and Monitoring Connections

Unfortunately, very little is known about the nature of the connections between strategy use, knowledge, and monitoring. The little information that we do have is concerned chiefly with knowledge and strategy usage, usually in the area of memory (e.g., Borkowski et al., in press; Borkowski & Büchel, 1983; Yussen & Berman, 1981). Moreover, the results are not always encouraging. For example, Cavanaugh and Borkowski (1980) assessed metamemory (through interview items development by Kreutzer et al., 1975) and memory performance in children in kindergarten and in Grades 1, 3, and 5. They reported significant correlations between interview and performance items when data were combined across grades, but within-grade correlations were not significant and did not generalize across memory tasks. The amount of knowledge about strategies failed to distinguish individuals who used relevant knowledge from those who did not. On the whole, the contention that successful metamemory is a necessary prerequisite for successful memory was not supported. However, it is axiomatic in the world of test construction that individual items typically are less reliable and have less predictive validity than a composite score based on a set of related items. It is probable that a similar phenomenon is affecting the data presented by Cavanaugh and Borkowski. If a composite score of memory performance was correlated with a composite score of memory knowledge, then the possibility of finding cognitive-metacognitive relations might improve. (See Rushton, Brainerd, & Pressley, Note 15, for an especially indicting commentary on the use of individual items in research on children's behaviors.) In fact, analyses based on composite scores of performance and verbalization were conducted by Forrest-Pressley & Waller (in press). The correlations between performance and verbalization composite scores within each grade were significant for all the skills assessed, with the exception of decoding. The mean correlation between performance and verbalization scores for all of the processes involved (e.g., language performance and language verbalization; decoding performance and decoding verbalization) was .41 for the third-grade children and .46 for the sixth-grade children. Also, composite scores were much better predictors than item scores of the relationships between the different processes and reading ability. The mean correlations between reading ability and the performance items was .40 for the third-grade children and .38 for the sixth-grade children. When the composite scores were used, however, the mean correlations for reading ability and performance jumped to .62 and .66 for third- and sixth-grade children, respectively. This difference between item and composite scores was even more important for the verbalization measures. The mean correlations between reading ability and verbalization items were .15 and .18 for third- and sixth-grade children, respectively. Both correlations are nonsignificant. When composite scores were used, however, the mean correlations between reading ability and verbalization jumped to a respectable (and statistically significant) level—.37 and .42 for third- and sixth-grade children, respectively. In addition to the correlational analyses, Forrest-Pressley & Waller (in press) used the composite scores to classify children as mature metacognizers (high on both performance and verbalization), in transition (high performance, low verbalization), mimickers (low performance, high verbalization), and low or immature metacognizers (low on both performance and verbalization). In all cases (use of important information, language, memory, decoding, comprehension, and strategies), only the older and/or better readers tended to be classified as mature metacognizers. Younger and/or poorer readers usually were classified as low or immature metacognizers. On the whole, very few children ever were classified as in transition or as mimickers (with the exception of in the use of decoding skills). It appears, then, that a relation between knowledge and strategy use is present in reading, and that more optimism about cognitive-metacognitive connections is warranted than has been expressed in some summaries (Cavanaugh & Perlmutter, 1982; Cavanaugh, Note 15)—see Schneider (Note 3) for a comprehensive and optimistic documentation of cognitive-metacognitive linkages.

The relation of monitoring to strategy use has received even less attention than the knowledge-use issue, and the knowledge-monitoring-use issue has been virtually ignored. However, Forrest-Pressley & Waller (in press) reported data that suggested that older and/or better readers not only are more apt to adjust their reading to meet the demands of various purposes (to skim, to study, etc.), but they also are more apt to monitor comprehension. In addition, older and/or better readers tended to know more about different strategies that can be used if comprehension breaks down.

Much more research is needed on the nature of the interconnections between knowledge, monitoring, and strategy use, but initial indications are encouraging (see Chi, in press, for additional commentary on these issues). If successful strategy usage during reading depends not only on the child's ability to use a particular strategy but also on the child's knowledge of and ability to monitor strategy usage, then the problem of training mature study skills becomes very complex. This issue will be examined in depth in the following section.

An Introduction to Metacognition and Training Study Skills

It would be unfair to suggest that educators have not been concerned with teaching advanced thinking skills in connection with reading (e.g., Kachuck & Marcus, 1976). Yet it would be fair to suggest that there have been very few attempts to validate ways of teaching these advanced strategies, and when attempts to do so have been made, they have suffered from methodological flaws. Thus, we are faced with several major problems in our discussion of training study skills. First, the tremendous gap between "experimental" training studies and the study skills training techniques that actually are used in the classroom necessitates that we deal with these two areas separately (see Chapter 4 of this volume for more information). Second, most of the studies and techniques that will be discussed concern use of strategies by adults. There is very little information about how the particular skills discussed here can be employed by children. Third, most studies have ignored the metacognitive aspects of mature reading skills, leaving us with little evidence to support our claims that metacognition is a necessary component of study skills.

Experimental Training Studies

Even without considering metacognitive factors involved in study skills situations, it is possible to attempt to improve reading with prereading, during reading, or postreading interventions. *Prereading* activities include strategies such as reviewing goals of reading and doing sample test questions. One important variable here appears to be the explicitness of prereading instructions, that is, is the child given clear and concise instructions regarding the purpose of reading? (See Anderson and Armbruster, Note 16, for a complete discussion of these activities.) *During reading* strategies include inducing imagery (e.g., Levin & Pressley, 1981; Pressley, 1976, 1977), inserting questions, and prompting self-questioning (e.g., Friedman & Rickards, 1981; Glover, Plake, Roberts, & Palmer, 1981; Tierney & Cunningham, Note 17). The most frequently researched *postreading strategy* is that of review (e.g., Petros & Hoving, 1980), a strategy often incorporated into more complex learning strategy training programs (e.g., Dansereau, Collins, McDonald, Holley, Garland, Dickhoff, & Evans, 1979). Thus, we have an abundance of strategies, all of which at least appear to force the reader's attention to the deeper semantic properties of text rather than to its superficial properties (e.g., Frase, 1977). We will not devote additional attention to most of the above-cited strategies except to note that extensive reviews exist for all of them (e.g., Anderson & Biddle, 1975; Anderson, 1980; Ausubel, 1978; Barnes & Clawson, 1975; Ford, 1981; Frase, 1972, 1975, 1977; Levin & Pressley, 1981; Rothkopf, 1972; Rothkopf & Billington, 1975; Walker & Meyer, 1980; Anderson & Armbruster, Note 16; Tierney & Cunningham, Note 17).

Substantiating a point we made earlier, Anderson and Armbruster (Note 16) argue that although deep-level processing (outlining, mapping, networking) is a costly way to improve learning in terms of time and effort, mature students know when such effort is necessary given the criterion tasks, and they use their knowledge to deploy appropriate strategies. If Anderson and Armbruster's assumptions are true, then teaching students to use study strategies in an efficient manner becomes a problem of metacognition, a problem that needs a great deal of additional exploration. The strategy that at least on the surface appears to be most closely related to metacognitive concerns is self-questioning.

In order to use the self-questioning strategy effectively, the reader must be able to focus on important information in the text, generate questions appropriate to the purpose of reading, monitor the adequacy of their answers, and judge when the required material has been learned. In fact, it appears that children retain more information when questions are self-generated rather than provided by a peer (Ross & Killey, 1977) or asked by a teacher (Singer, 1978). Unfortunately, however, much of what we know about self-questioning behaviors in the context of reading comes from the adult literature. One study on self-questioning, in particular, illustrates the self-questioning approach and how it can be studied.

Singer and Donlan (1982) attempted to train self-questioning in 11th-grade students. In that study, one group of students was taught to derive story-specific questions from schema-general questions as they read complex short stories. Schema-general questions included the following: Who is the leading character? What is the leading character trying to accomplish in the story? What stands in the way of the leading character's reaching the desired goal? Using these schema-general questions, students were required to generate story-specific questions such as the following: Is this story going to be more about the officer or the barber? Will the barber kill the officer with the razor? Will the officer be a willing victim? A control group read to answer questions posed beforehand by the teacher. Each group read the stories in six sessions over a period of 3 weeks. Significant differences between the groups on criterion-referenced posttests appeared by the third session and were maintained until the last session. Thus, this type of instruction did appear to help students improve their processing of text.

In general, we need a great deal of work like Singer and Donlan's (1982) on teaching higher order strategies, the very heart of self-regulation. This teaching very likely will depend on the development of the types of skills discussed earlier (strategy use, knowledge, and monitoring). Indeed, awareness of (1) basic strategies for reading and remembering, (2) simple rules of text construction, (3) different demands of a variety of tests to which information may be put, and (4) the importance of activating background knowledge have been suggested as prerequisites for monitoring activities and the effective use of strategies (Baker & Brown, in press; Brown, Campione, & Day, 1981). Also, many researchers (e.g., Meichenbaum & Asarnow, 1979; Ferrara, Brown, & Campione, Note 18) have suggested that a fine-grained analysis of the problems of individual reading-disabled children may be necessary in order to engineer learning experiences to meet specific needs. Thus, the obstacles to metacognitive instruction appear great, but it is our fervent hope that investigators will surmount the formidable challenges posed by metacognitive training and produce interventions that can be used in the real world of practical reading problems. It is to the real world of practical reading problems that we now turn our attention.

Classroom Methods of Teaching Study Skills

We should first note that it appears that the real world of the school does not place primary emphasis on our ideal strategy (i.e., training a number of useful strategies along with "executive" functions that would guarantee appropriate and efficient use of strategies). Even more dismaying is the fact that very few of the basic strategy skills have been objectively evaluated for effectiveness. A brief overview of the "real-world" study skills will concretize this point.

Most elementary reading programs are primarily concerned with beginning reading skills (such as phonics and word recognition), and as a result, less attention has been paid to later developing reading strategies. After surveying the reading programs presented by Ackerman (1971), we noted that most of the research evidence on these reading programs is inconclusive, particularly when considering mature reading skills. Because of the lack of emphasis placed on advanced reading skills, supplementary study programs often are added to the curriculum in later elementary grades or beyond. Although many of these programs are based primarily on intuition, some programs are evaluated (e.g., Dansereau et al., 1979). Unfortunately, however, these evaluations often are not as rigorous as they could be (see Pressley et al., 1982, for a discussion of this point). In view of the importance of study skills programs to future learning, it is appropriate that we devote some space to describing the nature of the majority of these programs.

Historically, the teaching of study skills has been based on factors that teachers intuit to be important for reading to learn. For example, Sandwick (1915) suggested that important factors included self-confidence; setting fixed study hours; beginning by recalling what you know; studying the passage as a whole, then going back to difficulties; studying aloud; using drill or repetition; making a synopsis and visualizing it; and knowing how and when to read rapidly. Swain (1917) argued for the importance of questioning habits, critical evaluation, using summarization, and drawing conclusions. Smith and Littlefield (1938) suggested the use of specific skills such as underlining, taking notes, and outlining. In addition, many authors stress use of other aids (index, illustrations, charts, maps, diagrams, references, questions, glossaries, and appendices) as important study skills.

In 1961, Francis P. Robinson formalized much of the then-current thought about study skills and developed a study skill technique that encouraged use of the hypothesized useful skills. The technique, known by the acronym SQ3R, is still in use today. The SQ3R technique urges students to do the following:

1. *S*urvey the material by quickly skimming the text.
2. *Q*uestion—form questions by using headings (or main ideas).
3. *R*ead the passage to answer the questions.
4. *R*ecite what is remembered.
5. *R*eview the material.

Robinson (1961) cites evidence "documenting" that each of these five techniques is helpful in study situations. Unfortunately, proper control groups were not incorporated in the supporting studies, and as a result it is difficult to have confidence in the empirical base on which this program was established. In spite of this questionable beginning, however, the SQ3R technique for studying became a major focus of how-to-study manuals for college students and teaching study skills manuals for teachers (e.g., Gray, 1963; Livesay, 1966; Moburg, 1966; Morgan & Deese, 1957). Many modifications or variations of the technique were subsequently developed (e.g., Casale & Kelly, 1980; Donlan, 1980; Moore, 1981). Notably, all authors endorsing the SQ3R technique or a variation of it tend to be vague about the actual processes that take place as the reader studies.

Although SQ3R has an intuitive appeal to many teachers, the supporters of the technique offer very little evidence to substantiate their claims that it actually helps students modify processing in an effective way. In a recent review of the literature on the technique, Johns and McNamara (1980) claimed that there is no empirical evidence that SQ3R is more effective than many other study skills in use, and the perceived potency of the method is based on opinion rather than fact. These authors pointed out that even recent evaluations of the technique are flaws methodologically and as a result are virtually uninterpretable. Understandably, Johns and McNamara (1980) called for empirical studies to evaluate this and other study skills techniques by using objective, reliable tests as the primary assessment instruments.

One problem with the application of this technique that seems particularly relevant to us as developmental and educational psychologists is that it may solely provide an acronym that conveniently represents a fully developed schema in the adult, but that would be a meaningless label to a child or less mature reader who did not have the same study schema. We have presented evidence that the young child lacks knowledge that the more mature reader has, and this lack of knowledge may cause problems for the developing reader who attempts to use the technique. For example, how are we to explain to a child that he or she must start the study process by skimming the passage when that child does not know what skimming is (Forrest-Pressley & Waller, in press)?

We sadly conclude this section by noting that virtually every college campus in North America has a remedial study skills program that is often based largely on the unproven SQ3R technique. For example, the program currently being used at one major university in Canada teaches the SQ3R technique, along with concentration control techniques, time management, and lecture note taking (MacInnis, Hodson, & MacFarlane, Note 19), many of the same skills advocated in study skills manuals of the early 1900s (e.g., Sandwick, 1915; Swain, 1917). It would appear that we have made very little progress over the past 75 years, at least as far as substantiating our teaching methods is concerned! Given the prevalence of the need for study skills interventions, research on them should have high priority. Eventually, our ideal strategy might evolve, but the groundwork must be done first. (Cook & Mayer, in Chapter 4 of this volume, also discuss study skills programs and particularly SQ3R.)

Conclusions

In this chapter we have suggested that the appropriate model for mature reading should be one that includes metacognitive factors. We think that metacognition (or executive functions) directs the flexible use of various strategies. The presented conception of reading skills is, of course, speculative, but it directs attention to areas in which future research should be concentrated. For example, does it follow that an increased knowledge base automatically increases the child's chance of choosing the most efficient strategy for any particular situation? Is it necessary that the knowledge base be explicit? Does the knowledge base have any direct effect on the monitoring system, or is the monitoring system an independent process? If the monitoring system identifies an error, what conditions increase the probability that the error will be corrected? What conditions lead to an error's being undetected or uncorrected, and what are the consequences of such failures? What conditions produce a monitoring individual rather than a nonmonitoring individual? Is it possible to train complex metacognitive skills? In this chapter, we have taken the position that metacognition is a necessary component of flexible strategy usage during reading. However, we urgently need data collected in controlled situations that allow inferences about the directions of the effects. Indeed, we stress that we do not believe that simply training knowledge will be the answer, since it appears as if it is quite possible to create mimickers (i.e., children who can mimic a verbal response but do not use the knowledge to increase performance—Forrest-Pressley & Waller, in press). Rather, we expect that training will be a complex procedure, perhaps involving the introduction of specific knowledge, practice with using different strategies, evaluation of the effectiveness of various strategies, practice at monitoring, comparison of good and poor messages, modeling of appropriate responses, and feedback on predictions of success. Research involving each of these components in a practical setting is desperately needed. The tremendous gap between research and practice is appalling, as is the lack of empirical evaluation of study techniques. Indeed, instructional research must be conducted on these problems, and should be conducted in such a fashion as to add to our knowledge of the actual processes involved (Belmont & Butterfield, 1977).

In spite of an obvious lack of progress in developing study skills programs that can be substantiated by empirical evidence, a historical overview does point to an interesting recurring notion. This notion is that at all costs, the reader must be motivated to become an "active" learner (i.e., "keeping the mind active"—Swain, 1917). This is attempted by suggesting that the reader *do* certain things that will ensure an active involvement with the material (e.g., question, recite, review, take notes, underline, summarize, visualize, monitor progress). Certainly, one problem inherent in this notion is that the child must not only know how to use these specific skills, but he or she also must know what information should be questioned, recited, reviewed, underlined, and visualized. In addition, the child must continually monitor performance and check progress against the desired goal. These skills definitely are metacognitive in nature, yet traditional study skills programs have not emphasized the metacognitive aspect of reading to learn. It is only in recent years that researchers and practitioners began to consider knowledge and monitoring as essential to reading for meaning (e.g., Baker & Brown, in press; Forrest-Pressley & Waller, in press; Yussen et al., 1982; Baker, Note 5). It is hoped that within the next several years, researchers and practitioners will begin to bridge the gap between research and practice and to develop empirically substantiated methods of teaching study skills.

Acknowledgments. We express our sincere thanks to T. Gary Waller and to R. W. Barron, without whose help much of the research discussed in this chapter could not have been possible. Much of this chapter was written while the first author was in the Department of Psychology, Dalhousie University, Halifax, Nova Scotia, Canada.

Reference Notes

1. Paris, S. G. *Metacognitive development: Children's regulation of problem-solving skills.* Paper presented at the Midwestern Psychological Association, Chicago, May 1978.
2. Flavell, J. H. Metacognition. In E. Langer (Chair), *Current perspectives on awareness and cognitive processes.* Symposium presented at the meeting of the American Psychological Association, Toronto, 1978.
3. Schneider, W. *Developmental trends in the metamemory-memory behavior relationship: An integrative review.* Unpublished manuscript, Max-Planck-Institut für Psychologische Forschung, München, West Germany, 1982.
4. Sternberg, R. J. *The development of human intelligence* (Tech. Rep. 4). Cognitive Development Series, Department of Psychology, Yale University, New Haven, CT, 1979.
5. Baker, L. *Comprehension monitoring: Identifying and coping with text confusions.* (Tech. Rep. 145). Center for the Study of Reading, University of Illinois, Urbana-Champaign, 1979.
6. Forrest-Pressley, D. L. Monitoring and knowledge of stories. Paper presented at the annual meeting of the American Educational Research Association, New York, April 1982.
7. Winograd, P., & Johnson, P. Comprehensive monitoring and the error detection paradigm. (Tech. Rep. 153). Center for the Study of Reading, University of Illinois, Urbana-Champaign, 1980.
8. Grabe, M., & Doeling, D. *Age and ability differences in purposeful reading behaviors.* Paper presented at the annual meeting of the American Educational Research Association, Los Angeles, April 1981.
9. Forrest, D. L., & Barron, R. W. *Metacognitive aspects of the development of reading skill.* Paper presented at the biennial meeting of the Society for Research in Child Development, New Orleans, March 1977.
10. Revelle, G., Karabenick, J., & Wellman, H. M. *Comprehension monitoring in preschool children.* Paper presented at the biennial meeting of the Society for Research in Child Development, Boston, 1981.
11. Pace, A. J. *The ability of young children to correct comprehension errors: An aspect of comprehension monitoring.* Paper presented at the annual meeting of the American Educational Research Association, Boston, April 1980.
12. Pace, A. J. *Monitoring comprehension monitoring: An attempt to assess students' awareness of their own comprehension.* Paper presented at the annual meeting of the American Educational Research Association, April 1981.
13. Forrest-Pressley, D. L. *Comprehension monitoring in reading.* Manuscript in preparation, Althouse College, University of Western Ontario, London, Ontario, 1982.
14. Rushton, V. P., Brainerd, C. J., & Pressley, M. Manuscript in prepration, University of Western Ontario, London, Ontario, 1982.
15. Cavanaugh, J. C. *Metamemory-strategy relationships: A new chapter for Bulfinch or our Rosetta stone?* Paper presented at the annual meeting of the American Educational Research Association, New York, March 1982.
16. Anderson, T. H., & Armbruster, B. B. *Studying* (Tech. Rep. 155). Center for the Study of Reading, University of Illinois, Urbana-Champaign, 1980.

17. Tierney, R. J., & Cunningham, J. W. *Research on teaching reading comprehension* (Tech. Rep. 187). Center for the Study of Reading, University of Illinois, Urbana-Champaign, 1980.
18. Ferrara, R., Brown, A. L., & Campione, J. C. *Children's learning and transfer of inductive reasoning rules: A study of proximal development.* Paper presented at the biennial meeting of the Society of Research in Child Development, Boston, 1981.
19. MacInnis, R., Hodson, S., & MacFarlane, P. *Coping with the load: A practical outline of effective study technique.* Study skills manual, Counselling and Psychological Services, Dalhousie University, Halifax, N.S., Canada, 1979.

References

Adams, M. J. Failures to comprehend and levels of processing in reading. In R. J. Spiro, B. C. Bruce, & W. F. Brewer (Eds.), *Theoretical issues in reading comprehension.* Hillsdale, NJ: Erlbaum, 1980.
Anderson, R. C., & Biddle, W. B. On asking people questions about what they are reading. In G. Bower (Ed.), *The psychology of learning and motivation* (Vol. 9). New York: Academic Press, 1975.
Anderson, T. H. Study strategies and adjunct aids. In R. J. Spiro, B. C. Bruce, & W. F. Brewer (Eds.), *Theoretical issues in reading comprehension.* Hillsdale, NJ: Erlbaum, 1980.
Ackerman, R. C. *Approaches to beginning reading.* New York: Wiley, 1971.
Ausubel, D. In defense of advance organizers: A reply to the critics. *Review of Educational Research,* 1978, *48,* 251–257.
Baker, L., & Anderson, R. L. Effects of inconsistent information on text processing: Evidence for comprehension monitoring. *Reading Research Quarterly,* 1982, *17,* 281–294.
Baker, L., & Brown, A. L. Metacognitive skills in reading. In D. Pearson (Ed.), *Handbook of reading research,* in press.
Barnes, B., & Clawson, E. Do advance organizers facilitate learning? Recommendations for further research based on an analysis of 32 studies. *Review of Educational Research,* 1975, *45,* 637–659.
Belmont, J. M., & Butterfield, E. C. The instructional approach to development cognitive research. In R. Kail & J. Hagen (Eds.), *Perspectives on the development of memory and cognition.* Hillsdale, NJ: Erlbaum, 1977.
Bloom, L., & Lahey, M. *Language development and language disorders.* New York: Wiley, 1978.
Borkowski, J. G., & Büchel, F. Learning and memory strategies in the mentally retarded. In M. Pressley & J. R. Levin (Eds.), *Cognitive strategy research: Psychological foundations.* New York: Springer-Verlag, 1983.
Borkowski, J. G., Reid, M. & Kurtz, B. Metacognition and retardation: Paradigmatic, theoretical and applied perspectives. In R. Sperber, C. McCauley, & P. Brooks (Eds.), *Learning and cognition in the mentally retarded.* Baltimore: University Park Press, in press.
Bransford, J., Stein, B., Shelton, T., & Owings, R. Cognition and adaptation: The

importance of learning to learn. In J. Harvery (Ed.), *Cognition, social behavior and the environment.* Hillsdale, NJ: Erlbaum, 1980.

Brown, A. L. Knowing when, where, and how to remember: A problem of metacognition. In R. Glaser (Ed.), *Advances in instructional psychology* (Vol. 1). Hillsdale, NJ: Erlbaum, 1978.

Brown, A. L. Metacognitive development and reading. In R. J. Spiro, B. C. Bruce, & W. F. Brewer (Eds.), *Theoretical issues in reading comprehension.* Hillsdale, NJ: Erlbaum, 1980.

Brown, A. L., Campione, J. C., & Day, J. Learning to learn: On training students to learn from texts. *Educational Researcher,* 1981, *10*(2), 14–21.

Brown, A. L., & DeLoache, J. S. Skills, plans, and self-regulation. In R. Siegler (Ed.), *Children's thinking: What develops?* Hillsdale, NJ: Erlbaum, 1978.

Brown, A. L., & Smiley, S. S. Rating the importance of structural units of prose passages: A problem of metacognitive development. *Child Development,* 1977, *48*, 1–8.

Brown, A. L., & Smiley, S. S. The development of strategies for studying texts. *Child Development,* 1978, *49*, 1076–1088.

Casale, U., & Kelly, B. Problem-solving approach to study skills (PASS) for students in professional schools. *Journal of Reading,* 1980, *24*, 232–238.

Cavanaugh, J. C., & Borkowski, J. G. Searching for metamemory-memory connections: A developmental study. *Developmental Psychology,* 1980, *16*, 441–453.

Cavanaugh, J. C., & Perlmutter, M. Metamemory: A critical examination. *Child Development,* 1982, *53*, 11–28.

Chall, J. The great debate: Ten years later, with a modest proposal for reading stages. In L. Resnick & P. Weaver (Eds.), *Theory and practice of early reading* (Vol. 1). Hillsdale, NJ: Erlbaum, 1979.

Chi, M. Interactive roles of knowledge and strategies in development. In S. Chapman, J. Segal, & R. Glaser (Eds.), *Thinking and learning skills: Current research and open questions* (Vol. 2). Hillsdale, NJ: Erlbaum, in press.

Clay, M. The development of morphological rules in children with different language backgrounds. *New Zealand Journal of Educational Studies,* 1974, *9*, 113–121.

Dansereau, D. F., Collins, K. W., McDonald, B. A., Holley, C. D., Garland, J., Dickhoff, G., & Evans, S. H. Development and evaluation of a learning strategy training program. *Journal of Educational Psychology,* 1979, *71*, 64–73.

DiStefano, P., Noe, M., & Valencia, S. Measurement of the effects of purpose and passage difficulty on reading flexibility. *Journal of Educational Psychology,* 1981, *73*, 602–606.

DiVesta, F. J., Hayward, K. G., & Orlando, V. P. Developmental trends in monitoring text for comprehension. *Child Development,* 1979, *50*, 97–105.

Donlan, D. Locating main ideas in history textbooks. *Journal of Reading,* 1980, *23*, 135–140.

Faw, H., & Waller, T. G. Mathemagenic behaviors and efficiency in learning prose materials: Review, critique and recommendations. *Review of Educational Research,* 1977, *46*, 391–420.

Flavell, J. H. *Cognitive development.* Englewood Cliffs, NJ: Prentice-Hall, 1977.

Flavell, J. H. Comments. In R. Siegler (Eds.), *Children's thinking: What develops?* Hillsdale, NJ: Erlbaum, 1978.

Flavell, J. H. Metacognition and cognitive monitoring: A new area of psychological inquiry. *American Psychologist,* 1979, *34*, 906–911.

Flavell, J. H. Cognitive monitoring. In W. P. Dickson (Ed.), *Children's oral communication skills.* New York: Academic Press, 1981a.

Flavell, J. H. Monitoring social cognitive enterprises: Something else that may develop in the area of social cognition. In J. H. Flavell & L. Ross (Eds.), *Social cognitive development.* New York & London: Cambridge University Press, 1981b.

Flavell, J. H., Speer, J. R., Green, F. L., & August, D. L. The development of comprehension monitoring and knowledge about communication. *Monographs of the Society for Research in Child Development,* 1981, *46*(5, Serial No. 192).

Flavell, J. H., & Wellman, H. M. Metamemory. In R. Kail & J. Hagen (Eds.), *Perspectives on the development of memory and cognition.* Hillsdale, NJ: Erlbaum, 1977.

Ford, N. Recent approaches to the study and teaching of "effective learning" in higher education. *Review of Educational Research,* 1981, *51,* 345–377.

✗ Forrest-Pressley, D. L., & Waller, T. G. *Reading, cognition and metacognition.* New York: Springer-Verlag, in press.

Frase, L. T. Maintenance and control in the acquisition of knowledge from written materials. In J. B. Carroll & R. O. Freedle (Eds.), *Language comprehension and the acquisition of knowledge.* New York: V. H. Winston, 1972.

Frase, L. T. Prose processing. In G. Bower (Eds.), *The psychology of learning and motivation* (Vol. 9). New York: Academic Press, 1975.

Frase, L. T. Purpose in reading. In J. Guthrie (Ed.), *Cognition, curriculum & comprehension.* Newark, DE: International Reading Association, 1977.

Friedman, F., & Rickards, J. P. Effect of level, review, and sequence of inserted questions on text processing. *Journal of Educational Psychology,* 1981, *73,* 427–436.

Garner, R., & Reis, R. Monitoring and resolving comprehension obstacles: An investigation of spontaneous text lookbacks among upper-grade good and poor comprehenders. *Reading Research Quarterly,* 1981, *16,* 569–582.

Gibson, E. J. Reading for some purpose. In J. F. Kavanaugh & I. G. Mattingly (Eds.), *Language by ear and by eye: The relationships between speech and reading.* Cambridge, MA: MIT Press, 1972.

Gibson, E. J., & Levin, H. *The psychology of reading.* Cambridge, MA: MIT Press, 1975.

Glover, J. A., Plake, B. S., Roberts, B., Zimmer, J. W., & Palmer, M. Distinctiveness of encoding: The effects of paraphrasing and drawing inferences on memory from prose. *Journal of Educational Psychology,* 1981, *73,* 736–744.

Gray, L. *Teaching children to read* (3rd ed.). New York: Ronald Press, 1963.

Hausfeld, S. Speeded reading and listening comprehension for easy and difficulty materials. *Journal of Educational Psychology,* 1981, *73,* 312–319.

Hiebert, E. H. Developmental patterns and interrelationships of preschool children's print awareness. *Reading Research Quarterly,* 1981, *16,* 236–260.

Huey, E. B. *The psychology and pedagogy of reading.* Cambridge, MA: MIT Press, 1968. (Originally published by MacMillan, 1908.)

Johns, J. L. First graders' concepts about print. *Reading Research Quarterly,* 1980, *15,* 529–549.

Johns, J. L., & McNamara, L. The SQ3R study technique: A forgotten research target. *Journal of Reading,* 1980, *23,* 705–708.

Johnson, C. N., & Wellman, H. M. Children's developing understanding of mental verbs: Remember, know, guess. *Child Development,* 1980, *51,* 1095–1102.

Just, M. A., & Carpenter, P. A theory of reading: From eye fixations to comprehension. *Psychological Review,* 1980, *87,* 329–354.

Kachuck, B., & Marcus, A. Thinking strategies and reading. *Reading Teacher,* 1976, *30,* 157–161.

Kavale, K., & Schreiner, R. The reading processes of above average and average readers: A comparison of the use of reasoning strategies in responding to standardized comprehension measures. *Reading Research Quarterly,* 1979, *15,* 102–128.

Kobasigawa, A., Ransom, C., & Holland, C. Children's knowledge about skimming. *Alberta Journal of Educational Research,* 1980, *26,* 169–181.

Kreutzer, M. A., Leonard, C., & Flavell, J. H. An interview study of children's knowledge about memory. *Monographs of the Society for Research in Child Development,* 1975, *40*(1, Serial No. 159).

Levin, J. R., & Pressley, M. Improving children's prose comprehension: Selected strategies that seem to succeed. In C. Santa & B. Hayes (Eds.), *Children's prose comprehension: Research and practice.* Neward, DE: International Reading Association, 1981.

Livesay, M. Helping teachers meet the objectives of a reading program. In H. A. Robinson (Ed.), *Reading: Seventy-five years of progress.* Chicago: University of Chicago Press, 1966.

Markman, E. M. Realizing that you don't understand: A preliminary investigation. *Child Development,* 1977, *48,* 986–992.

Markman, E. M. Realizing that you don't understand: Elementary school children's awareness of inconsistencies. *Child Development,* 1979, *50,* 643–665.

Markman, E. M., & Gorin, L. Children's ability to adjust their standards for evaluating comprehension. *Journal of Educational Psychology,* 1981, *73,* 320–325.

Meichenbaum, D. H., & Asarnow, J. Cognitive-behavior modification and metacognitive development: Implications for the classroom. In P. C. Kendall & S. D. Hollon (Eds.), *Cognitive-behavioral interventions: Theory, research and procedures.* New York: Academic Press, 1979.

Miller, G. A., Galanter, E., & Pribram, K. H. *Plans and structure of behavior.* New York: Holt, 1960.

Moburg, L. Helping teachers meet the needs of underachievers in reading. In H. A. Robinson (Ed.), *Reading: Seventy-five years of progress.* Chicago: University of Chicago Press, 1966.

Moore, M. C2R: Concentrate, read, remember. *Journal of Reading,* 1981, *24,* 337–339.

Morgan, C., & Deese, J. *How to study.* New York: McGraw-Hill, 1957.

Myers, M., & Paris, S. G. Children's metacognitive knowledge about reading. *Journal of Educational Psychology,* 1978, *70,* 686–690.

Olshavsky, J. E. Reading as problem solving: An investigation of strategies. *Reading Research Quarterly,* 1976/77, *12,* 654–674.

Papandropoulou, I., & Sinclair, H. What is a word? Experimental study of children's ideas on grammar. *Human Development,* 1974, *17,* 241–258.

Petros, T., & Hoving, K. The effects of review on young children's memory for prose. *Journal of Experimental Child Psychology,* 1980, *30,* 33–43.

Pressley, M. Mental imagery helps eight-year-olds remember what they read. *Journal of Educational Psychology,* 1976, *68,* 355–359.

Pressley, M. Imagery and children's learning: Putting the picture in developmental perspective. *Review of Educational Research,* 1977, *47,* 585–622.

Pressley, M., Heisel, B., McCormick, C., & Nakamura, G. Memory strategy instruction with children. In C. J. Brainerd & M. Pressley, (Eds.), *Verbal processes in children.* New York: Springer-Verlag, 1982.

Pressley, M., Levin, J. R., & Bryant, S. L. Memory strategy instruction during adolescence: When is explicit instruction needed? In M. Pressley & J. R. Levin (Eds.), *Cognitive strategy research: Psychological foundations.* New York: Springer-Verlag, 1983.

Reid, J. Learning to think about reading. *Educational Research,* 1966, *9,* 56–62.

Robinson, F. P. *Effective study* (rev. ed.) New York: Harper & Row, 1961.

Rothkopf, E. Z. Structural text features and the control of processes in learning from written material. In J. B. Carroll & R. O. Freedle (Eds.), *Language comprehension and the acquisition of knowledge.* New York: V. H. Winston, 1972.

Rothkopf, E. Z., & Billington, M. A two-factory model of the effect of goal-descriptive directions on learning from text. *Journal of Educational Psychology,* 1975, *67,* 692–704.

Ross, H. S., & Killey, J. C. The effect of questioning on retention. *Child Development,* 1977, *48,* 312–314.

Sandwick, R. *How to study and what to study.* New York: Heath, 1915.

Smith, S., & Littlefield, A. *Best methods of study: A practical guide for the student.* New York: Barnes & Noble, 1938.

Singer, H. Active comprehension: From answering to asking questions. *Reading Teacher,* 1978, *3,* 901–908.

Singer, H., & Donlan, D. Active comprehension: Problem-solving schema with question generation for comprehension of complex short stories. *Reading Research Quarterly,* 1982, *17,* 166–186.

Sternberg, R. J. The evolution of theories of intelligence. *Intelligence,* 1981, *5,* 209–230.

Swain, G. F. *How to study.* New York: McGraw-Hill, 1917.

Thorndike, E. Reading as reasoning: A study of mistakes in paragraph reading. *Journal of Educational Psychology,* 1917, *8,* 323–330.

Walker, C., & Meyer, B. Integrating information from text: An evaluation of current theories. *Review of Educational Research,* 1980, *50,* 421–437.

Wellman, H. M., & Johnson, C. N. Understanding of mental processes: A developmental study of "remember" and "forget." *Child Development,* 1979, *50,* 79–88.

Whaley, J. F. Reader's expectations for story structures. *Reading Research Quarterly,* 1981, *17,* 90–114.

Worden, P. E. Memory strategy instruction with the learning disabled. In M. Pressley & J. R. Levin (Eds.), *Cognitive strategy research: Psychological foundations.* New York: Springer-Verlag, 1983.

Yussen, S. R., & Berman, L. Memory predictions for recall and recognition in first, third, and fifth-grade children. *Developmental Psychology,* 1981, *17,* 224–229.

Yussen, S. R., Matthews, S., & Hiebert, E. H. Metacognitive aspects of reading. In W. Otto & S. White (Eds.), *Reading expository text.* New York: Academic Press, 1982.

Zimmerman, B. J., & Ringle, J. Effects of model persistence and statements of confidence on children's self-efficacy and problem solving. *Journal of Educational Psychology,* 1981, *73,* 485–493.

6. From Theory to Practice in Reading Research: Toward the Development of Better Software

Dale M. Willows, Diane M. Borwick, and Irwin S. Butkowsky

The fostering of literacy in society is undoubtedly the most basic and valued objective of formal education. Because of the centrality of learning to read in the educational process, the topic of reading instruction has been much debated. There is almost universal agreement among educators and reading researchers that reading can be taught, and that some methods of teaching reading are more effective than others; what is not agreed upon is specifically how reading should be taught. Variants on the question, What is the best method of teaching reading? have served to motivate much research on reading during the last 100 years. Approaches to addressing this question have shifted quite dramatically over the years, ranging from applied research in the classroom to theoretically oriented laboratory research on basic processes, but the underlying goal has remained essentially the same: to contribute to the improvement of reading instruction.

Despite this longstanding concern and commitment on the part of researchers, most reading instruction today is based, as it was a century ago, on the intuitions of educators. Research and theory have contributed surprisingly little to the pendulum swing of approaches to reading instruction. That is not to say that theory and research on reading have been without influence in educational practice. Allusions to current theories of reading and adoption of their terminology abound in educational literature. What has been lacking is any evidence that the evolution of reading instructional methods is toward a higher form as a result of the influence of theory and research. It is doubtful whether current methods are any more effective than those in vogue a century ago.

Since empirical investigations on reading began around 1880, reading researchers have sought to shed light on the "best method" question. Even today, after a long history without success, many are still committed to the view that eventually reading research will lead to sounder educational practice. We too are of this persuasion, but we believe future success must rest upon an understanding of the reasons for past failures. Thus, in this chapter we will attempt to elucidate some of the reasons why reading research and theory have contributed little to the improvement of reading instruction in the past.

The chapter contains four main parts. In the first, we point to a range of explanatory factors that have accounted for the failure of research to contribute to the improvement of reading instruction in the early history of research on reading. In the second part, we examine a more recent period, the last 15 years, demonstrating that recent research has not moved perceptibly closer to the attainment of practical goals. In the third section, we present the results of a review of articles of relevance to both theory and practice in reading published between 1967 and 1981 in two major journals concerned with reading research, the *Journal of Educational Psychology* and the *Reading Research Quarterly*. This review focuses on four aspects of the research: the goals of the research questions, the kinds of research designs employed, the types of variables considered, and the nature of the inferences drawn. Finally, in view of the shortcomings we have outlined in the previous section, our conclusions focus on the need for a shift of emphasis from the "hardware" of reading, the relatively stable cognitive, linguistic, and perceptual factors, to the "software," the modifiable skills and the cognitive strategies.

Historical Background of the Relation Between Theory and Practice in Reading Research

During the early period of reading research, from the 1880s until about 1910, the relation of theory and practice apparently was not an issue. That is, at that time, there was no articulation of the view that one could or should make a sharp distinction between basic and applied research. The causes and consequences of this perspective will be sketched briefly in what follows.

The first experiments related to reading formed a large and important part of early experimental psychology. Conducted in the laboratory and using normal adult subjects, these studies were primarily concerned with visual perception rather than with reading.[1] Influenced by the methods and interests of the new experimental physiological psychology of Wundt in Germany, American and European researchers performed numerous experiments on such topics as the speed of reading, eye movements and fixations, the eye-voice span in oral reading, and cues in word recognition. Cattell, for example, was very influential in this field; it was he who showed that a familiar word is perceived as a whole and not read letter by letter, as was previously believed. In laboratory experiments, Cattell (1885/1947; 1886)

---

[1] Regardless of its main focus, however, this research contributed a great deal to the field of basic processes in reading. Indeed, it has often been said that this productive early period provided far more knowledge about reading than was unearthed in the 40 or 50 years that followed.

found that adult subjects were able to identify two unconnected words, or four connected words, in the same time that it took to identify three or four unconnected letters.[2]

Like his colleagues, Cattell's chief aim in these experiments was not to investigate the reading process per se. In Cattell's case, the goal was to discover the range of individual differences in various psychological abilities; this contrasted with the Wundtian, or structuralist, aim of determining general laws of human perception. Because they were interested in finding causes or explanations, Cattell and many of his contemporaries were part of a movement that represented a major break with structuralist psychology. Boring (1950) has described this functionalist perspective as the pervasive spirit of early American psychology, a spirit that is essentially practical in nature in that there is a desire to predict, and therefore to control, the future.

To reiterate, the earliest studies of reading were concerned with, in modern terms, basic rather than applied questions. Although this research was practical in the sense that functionalism is practical, it was not directed toward improving educational practice. In fact, it is quite conceivable that the early experimental psychologists rarely considered how their work might have related to teaching. The idea that educational practice could be based on scientific research was only beginning to be considered at that time: It was around 1890 that G. Stanley Hall established the first department of pedagogy and started the journal *Pedagogical Seminary*. That the functionalists did not make a sharp distinction between basic and applied research is one criticism that was raised by their contemporaries (see Marx & Hillix, 1973).

There is further evidence that the early researchers in reading did not perceive the relation of basic research and educational practice as an issue. Huey (1908/ 1968), whose book *The Psychology and Pedagogy of Reading* has become a classic in the field, did not try to determine the practical implications of the research he summarized. Instead, his recommendations concerning the teaching of reading seem to have been based on his own intuitions or on the opinions of other educators. This is so despite Huey's strong interest in the teaching of reading and his obviously practical orientation toward research, as exemplified by his words:

> So slowly does thought find its way to the rationalization of the common things that we do in life. So rich are the possibilities for research in many lines. (p. 11)

At the same time (1880-1910) that these pioneering studies of reading were being conducted, there was another line of work just beginning that was to have a lasting effect on the field: the development of mental testing. According to Boring (1950), this movement was a natural consequence of the functionalist interest in

[2] Very often over the years, Cattell's work has been cited, inappropriately, as demonstrating support for the whole-word approach in beginning reading instruction (for discussion of this, see Samuels, 1976). (It was incorrectly assumed that the performance of highly skilled adult readers could be generalized to children learning to read.) Although in his writings Cattell did occasionally make some isolated comment about teaching, it is clear that he did not set out to improve educational practice.

individual differences, and so at first there was not the philosophical division between experimental psychologists and mental testers that later developed. Indeed, Cattell, for one, worked in both areas and was instrumental in launching the testing movement in the United States; it was he who coined the term *mental test* (Cattell, 1890). In the 20 years that followed Cattell's 1890 publication the testing movement expanded tremendously and, as educational psychology developed into a distinct field of study, testing (and in particular intelligence testing) became its primary focus. This almost-exclusive emphasis on testing was to last for decades.

The rise of the testing movement was one of two major influences in psychology that combined to produce a sharp decline in the continued scientific study of reading; the other factor was the growth of behaviorism, initiated by Watson (1913). Because behaviorism excluded mental processes from study, experimental psychologists turned away from research on reading since, as an area, it did not fall into the category of directly observable behavior.

Psychological research on reading remained in a virtual state of neglect for the next 40 or 50 years. During this time, the testing movement in educational psychology flourished and diversified, while experimental psychology was dominated by behaviorism. What little reading research there was most often concerned the assessment of reading ability through standardized tests (Gates, 1921). There was also some work on such topics as the eye-voice span (Buswell, 1920) and the legibility of print (Tinker, 1963), as well as on case studies of reading disability (Orton, 1937).

Although during the period from the 1920s to the 1960s psychologists conducted hardly any research on reading, educators and educational researchers performed a great many classroom studies of reading instruction. For the most part, the question posed in these studies was simple and direct: What is the best method of teaching reading? And the attempt to answer this question was also direct: success in reading achievement using one method in the classroom was compared with that using a different method. In general, the perspective taken by the researchers was strictly an applied or practical one; they did not base their studies on models or theories of the reading process. Of course, at that time, there was a paucity of models and theories, but the approach taken in the classroom studies did not include a consideration of the fact that such a gap existed.

The failure of the authors of the classroom studies to look at the problem from a broader and more analytical viewpoint extended to include a lack of integration with previous studies as well as with theory. The result was that most researchers were unaware that their efforts had been duplicated elsewhere. This is just one of several criticisms raised by Chall (1967), who undertook a massive review of the research on beginning reading instruction. Over the years, the best-method controversy nearly always centered on two general methods: phonics and whole word. Chall's book, *Learning to Read: The Great Debate,* was written as an attempt to resolve this controversy, but she discovered that the several decades of classroom studies had produced results that were "shockingly inconclusive" (p. 88).

In essence, the reason the classroom studies were not successful is that the question, Which method is best? is unanswerable. No method of teaching reading is composed of immutable principles that can be unequivocally and uniformly translated into practice by teachers; nor can it be expected that all pupils will respond in the same way to the same method of teaching. Indeed, it is probably misleading to talk about a particular "method" of teaching reading, if the meaning intended is that of a completely specified and systematic plan to be followed. The guidelines that constitute a method of teaching are, with few exceptions, far more general and open to individual interpretation than that. Furthermore, even purportedly similar methods (e.g., two "linguistic" approaches) may differ on many important and fundamental dimensions (Willows, Borwick, & Hayvren, 1981).

The enormous complexity of the question together with multiple attendant methodological problems rendered the classroom studies, with few exceptions (e.g., Bond & Dykstra, 1966/67), a wasted effort. Fortunately, publication of Chall's (1967) book and of the results of Bond and Dykstra's (1966/67) large-scale study created a widespread awareness of the problems associated with the classroom studies. Subsequently, there was a considerable decrease in the number of such studies being published.

In summary, an examination of the history of reading research from 1880 to 1960 reveals that very little progress was made toward improving educational practice. We have argued that in the productive early period of basic research (1880–1910), psychologists were barely aware of the possibility of tying together research and practice. Shortly afterward, basic research on reading was abandoned as experimental psychologists embraced behaviorism. At the same time, the reading research being conducted by educators either was not directed at improvement of practice (the testing movement) or was unsystematic and flawed (the classroom studies). Thus the era from 1920 to 1960 was marked by very little progress in joining basic theory and research with reading instruction.

Recent Trends in the Relation Between Theory and Practice in Reading Research

Writing in 1965, Williams commented on a notable change of direction in reading research:

> The present state of reading research differs greatly from that of 1958. Within this period there has been a renewal of interest in theoretical analysis of the basic reading process, and recent contributions by psychologists and linguistics have been of great influence in focusing interest on basic studies. (p. 147)

Since the mid 1960s, there has been a burgeoning interest in the field of reading. Growing numbers of researchers from a wide range of backgrounds (e.g., child development, perception, verbal learning, neuropsychology, cognitive science, linguistics, educational psychology, and artificial intelligence) have become active contributors to the literature of research on reading. Whereas 15 years ago there was little being written about reading other than practical advice for educators, today there are dozens of books and hundreds of articles in the field.

This influx of researchers into the field of reading was the result of a variety of factors: availability of funding for basic educational research (Holtzman, 1967; Penney, Hjelm, & Gephart, 1970); pressure on researchers to conduct socially relevant studies (Kling, 1971); a waning of the influence of the behaviorist movement, which had relegated complex human mental processes to the realm of the unresearchable (Kagan, 1967); and the rapid growth of the new field of cognitive psychology (Neisser, 1967), in which complex mental processes are of central interest. Many of the early investigators entering the field of reading in the 1960s held the view that applied research approaches to the study of reading had reached a point of diminishing returns and believed that basic research offered greater promise of answering questions about reading (Carroll, 1968). These pioneers of the movement were committed to the position that an understanding of the reading process is a *prerequisite* to the improvement of reading instruction. Gibson and Levin, for example, advanced such a position in a number of their writings, stating that "good pedagogy is based on a deep understanding of the discipline to be taught and the nature of the learning process involved" (Gibson, 1965, p. 1072), but that "the process of communicating from written materials, in spite of its ubiquity, is not well understood, either in terms of the acquisition of the skill or its characteristics in the mature reader" (Gibson & Levin, 1968, p. ix). In an address "Reading Research: What, Why and for Whom?" Levin (1966) also stated that "the prior question is *What is the process of reading* rather than *What is the optimal teaching procedure?* Definitive answers to the second wait on the first" (p. 140).

In a discussion of basic and applied research on reading, Carroll (1968) strongly promoted "basic educational research" on the assumption that it *would lead ultimately* to better educational practice. His view was that

> although results of many of the studies have no immediate application, they promise to contribute towards a new theory of the reading process that will guide the development of practical materials and procedures for the teaching of reading. (p. 274)

That many researchers investigating basic processes in reading believe that their findings have implications for or will eventually contribute to, educational practices has been quite evident from the discussion sections of published articles. Since the beginning of the recent reading research movement, speculative forays into what a given result may mean in practical terms have abounded in the journals. Only occasionally have questions been raised about whether such speculations are justified. In 1970, Levin and Williams did raise a problematic issue. They pointed out that "the relationship between understanding the nature of a complex skill and teaching that skill is not at all clear" (p. ix). A few years later, Williams (1972/ 73) was beginning to become sceptical about whether the study of basic processes in reading would lead to the solution of practical problems. As editor of the *Journal of Educational Psychology* at that time, she would have had considerable familiarity with the issues and problems associated with the field. She stated her concerns as follows:

Our focus seems to have changed in the past few years. Clearly, our ultimate goal is still the improvement of reading instruction. However, what we are really working toward at present is the development of a model of reading geared more nearly to the generation of research hypotheses. In fact, we are quickly proceeding to the point where our theoretical formulations—and empirical findings—may become too refined and sophisticated to be of great use in helping to determine instructional procedures . . . Perhaps I am being too sanguine about the progress we are likely to make in theory development or too pessimistic about how effectively our work will be translated for use in the classroom, but I do feel that we must keep at least part of our attention on the goal of how our models can be applied to instructional problems. (p. 123)

Similar cautionary words also came from the editors of the *Reading Research Quarterly,* Farr and Weintraub, in 1974. On the basis of nearly 10 years of basic research on reading, they expressed some strong concerns about the appropriateness of the approach for the resolution of educational issues. In an editorial comment, they wrote (Farr & Weintraub, 1973/74):

Psychology oriented research . . . tends to have an elegance of design and sophistication of statistical technique that far surpasses that in most other areas. It is number oriented and unquestionably superior in terms of the basic design to studies in the teaching section. Despite this—or perhaps because of it—one feels that it is sometimes flawed. Some of the studies appear to bury themselves in statistics. The numerical displays become so dazzling as to overpower the studies themselves. One wonders if the fragmented nature of much of this research is not due in part to what almost appears to be a subservience to the design. Perhaps psychologically oriented research is not the ultimate solution for the reading field either.

Maybe we haven't solved our problems or answered many questions because we have attempted to be too rigorous in applying our statistical procedures. Rigor comes in many forms, including mortis. Perhaps a fresh breath, a new view is needed. Observational studies, case reports of an intensive nature, historical research, depth interviews, Piaget-type experimentation, broadly based evaluation studies may all help us to understand the reading process more fully. If nothing else, they might permit us to view reading from a different perspective— and possibly we need that different viewpoint now. (Preface)

Despite the mounting pessimism of journal editors about the emerging trends in reading research, optimism still reigned among researchers about the potential for fruitful interactions between theory and practice in reading. In 1976, a series of three conferences was held at the University of Pittsburgh organized around the topic of theory and practice in early reading. These conferences were established on "the basic and optimistic premise . . . that basic research is relevant and helpful in education" (White, 1979, p. 287). A careful examination of the theoretical and practical papers included in the three-volume series based on the conferences (Resnick & Weaver, 1979a, 1979b, 1979c) reveals, however, that communication and mutual influence between the theoreticians and practitioners has been very limited. The questions addressed by basic researchers tend to be very circumscribed, aimed at clarifying and refining current theoretical formulations. Such questions usually bear little relevance to instructional issues. Conversely, problems investigated by applied researchers rarely arise out of current theories and models of reading. Rather, they emerge from the practical concerns surrounding reading instruction.[3] Various discussants at the Pittsburgh conferences pointed to ways in which "the marriage of research and practice in beginning reading instruction" has been a disappointing one.

Kintsch's (1979) commentary on the interaction between theory and practice in reading focuses on the need for a good model of the reading process. As the following quotation indicates, he argues for a position much like that of Gibson (1965) and Levin (1966) more than a decade earlier. Implicit is the assumption that improved reading practice will follow from better theories of the reading process.

> Applied work on reading instruction appears to flourish (although the actual practice in the classroom seems to be another matter). Basic research in reading is going equally strong, especially insofar as it concerns decoding problems. However, the interaction between the two is insufficient: Applications rely more on intuition and experience than on laboratory research, and the laboratory research frequently bypasses the issues that are most important in reading instruction.
>
> I have tried to argue that the lack of a serious theory of reading is one of the main reasons for this state of affairs. Compared to the level of specificity that is found in some of the applied work (e.g., Beck & Block; Bateman) and the precision of the experimental research (e.g., Venezky & Massaro; Perfetti & Lesgold), the poorly articulated global analyses that pass for theories in the field of reading are disappointing indeed. I do not think that we can hope for an improvement in the relation between reading research and practice, and between basic and applied research in reading, until we have a good model of the reading process. (p. 328)

In contrast to Kintsch's view, Venezky (1979) in his evaluation of the theory-practice relation expresses pessimism about the feasibility of developing comprehensive models of the reading process, as indicated in the following comment:

> In reading, there are theories and models of the processes of reading (whether in the child or the adult), theories and models of the learning process (either learning in general or the acquisition of literacy itself), and theories and models of instruction and the instructional environment. However, I tend to agree with Gibson and Levin (1975) that we probably don't know enough to build useful models of the total reading process and that we are truly chasing after the wind in doing so. (p. 273)

Moreover, Venezky considers the territory between theory and practice to be relatively inhospitable to researchers:

> Whatever might be the difficulties of building sound instructional programs, the task of finding practical implications from reading theory is exceedingly more difficult. The gap between the two is the La Brea tar pit of education and mires many well-intending people. (p. 279)

Samuels (1979) offers yet another point of view. His remarks about the interaction between theory and practice suggest that the perspectives of the different disci-

[3]That the degree of mutual influence between the basic scientists and the applied scientists conducting research on reading has been quite limited is very clear from the citations at the end of the theoretical and practical chapters. There is remarkably little overlap between the two.

plines contributing to the field are each limited to some small portion of the whole. None reflects a comprehensive picture, and hence communication between them is ineffective. Thus, he wrote:

> Having discussed a number of views regarding theories and practices in reading, I am reminded of John Godfrey Saxe's poem "The Blind Men and the Elephant." Curious about the appearance of an elephant, the six blind men decided to study the elephant by direct examination. The first touched the elephant's sturdy side and likened it to a wall. The second felt the tusk and thought the elephant resembled a spear. The third touched the squirming trunk and thought the elephant was much like a snake, while the fourth touched the elephant's knee and thought the elephant was like a tree. The fifth chanced to touch the ear, and to him, the elephant was like a fan; and the sixth, having touched the tail, thought the elephant was like a snake. Saxe concluded his poem with this thought:

> And so these men of Indostan
> Disputed loud and long,
> Each in his own opinion
> Exceeding still and strong,
> Though each was partly in the right,
> And all were in the wrong!
> The Morale:
> So oft in theologic wars
> The disputants, I ween,
> Rail on in utter ignorance
> Of what each other mean,
> And prate about an elephant
> Not one of them has seen!

> Perhaps we who study the reading process are like the blind men. Our views of the process, colored by the discipline orientations within which we work and by the procedures we use to study the process, give each of us but a limited perspective of the process, and so all our views of reading process are partly in the right and all are in the wrong. (p. 367)

Finally, Resnick (1979) in her concluding remarks touches on a whole range of issues. She points to a need to take a new approach to reading research that combines cognitive psychology, learning theory, and developmental psychology. She sums up as follows:

> We must . . . learn a great deal more about the relationship between skilled performance in reading and patterns of its acquisition. Therefore we must enlarge and extend developmental research in reading. We must also—and this is both the larger and in many respects the newer question—learn how development is modified by certain kinds of environmental events, particularly those we call instruction. A view of learning that acknowledges the learner's role in constructing his or her own knowledge and skill must be joined with an analysis of the environmental events that can foster—or hinder—such constructions. We cannot choose between a constructive learner operating in an undifferentiated environment and a passive "receptacle" of knowledge whose environment is structured to provide all needed information. We must begin to take the notion of interaction between learner and environment quite seriously, specifying features of the environment that interact with characteristics of the learner's knowledge and processes to produce transitions in cognitive competence. Finally, the new psychology of reading instruction that I envisage will be highly attentive to individual differ-

ences, seeking to explain and predict the effects of instructional environments on individuals characterized in terms of their psychological processes of learning and their cognitive performance. (p. 371)

Thus, although the explanations vary, the view that basic reading research has made little headway toward the improvement of educational practice is widely shared. There is clearly merit in the issues these authors have raised, but there is no common thread in their concerns, and the criticisms are global and not open to investigation. Our objective in this chapter is to take a more analytic view of the theory-practice problem in reading research in the hope of uncovering specific, and perhaps alterable, impediments to movement from theory into practice.

Fifteen Years of Research on Reading: Analysis of Motives, Methods, and Inferences

The past 15 years in the history of reading research have been far more productive than any previous period. The range of disciplines contributing to the literature has become very broad, with questions being raised from many different perspectives. The diversity of researchers has resulted in a proliferation of journals and edited books. Despite the large number of journals now publishing articles on reading, the literature may be divided into three general groupings: research on basic processes, basic educational/instructional research, and applied/instructional research. These groupings are reflected in the publications and professional organizations concerned with research on reading. The journals in which research of the three different types is likely to appear are shown in Table 6-1.[4]

In our attempt to understand why 15 prolific years of basic research have failed to yield a better understanding of how reading should be taught, we undertook a review of a large portion of the research that has been published since the onset of the movement beginning during the mid 1960s. We sought to detect trends in the relation between theory and practice that might account for the relatively small contribution basic research has made toward the improvement of educational practice.

Our analysis began with an informal sampling of the period extending from 1967 to 1981.[5] This preliminary overview was intended to provide us with a firsthand

---

[4]There is a domain of investigation that we have not included in our research review, that of specific learning disabilities. It is not yet clear whether specific dyslexics are qualitatively different from "poor readers," or simply represent an extreme manifestation of similar characteristics. Our exclusion of publications such as the *Journal of Learning Disabilities,* should not, however, limit the validity of our observations about the reading research literature.

[5]Although many researchers had become active in the field of reading during the late 1950s, this thrust did not become evident in the journals until about the mid 1960s. We selected the years from 1967 to 1981 because they represent the 15-year period during which the vast majority of reading research has been published. In 1967, the *Reading Research Quarterly* had just begun publication, and the *Journal of Educational Psychology* was experiencing an unprecedented period of growth. As Holtzman (1967), the new editor, put it, educational research had just "come alive." Enthusiasm for the new educational research movement and the availability of grant support swept many new contributors into the field of reading research.

Table 6-1 Some Journals Publishing Reading Research

Basic Processes in Reading	Basic Educational Research on Reading	Applied Research on Reading
Cognitive Psychology	American Educational Research Journal	Curriculum Inquiry
Discourse Processes		Elementary English
Journal of Experimental Psychology	Child Development	The Elementary School Journal
Journal of Verbal Learning and Verbal Behavior	Contemporary Educational Psychology	Journal of Reading
Memory & Cognition	Developmental Psychology	Journal of the Reading Specialist
Perception & Psychophysics	Educational Communication and Technology Journal	Psychology in the Schools
Perceptual and Motor Skills	Journal of Educational Psychology	The Reading Teacher
Quarterly Journal of Experimental Psychology	Journal of Experimental Child Psychology	Research in the Teaching of English
Visible Language	Journal of Reading Behavior	
	Journal of Research in Reading	
	Reading Research Quarterly	

sense of the history of the development of the field, as well as to assist us in deriving a set of questions that would serve as the basis for a more systematic analysis. Although we examined reading research in all three of the groupings shown in Table 6-1, our greatest efforts were placed on research in the middle category, on the journals in which one would expect to find research that has been influenced by both theoretical and practical concerns. Given our objective, we spent much less time on journals that are clearly basic research journals whose concern is with theory development (e.g., *Cognitive Psychology, Memory & Cognition, Quarterly Journal of Experimental Psychology*). Similarly, we considered only cursorily journals that are clearly intended for applied audiences focusing on issues directly related to reading instruction with little consideration of theories (e.g., *Journal of Reading, The Reading Teacher, Elementary English*).

On the basis of our preliminary work, we set out to trace the relation between theory and practice in reading research more systematically. We selected the two most prominent educational journals in which reading research is published, the *Reading Research Quarterly* and the *Journal of Educational Psychology*, and reviewed all of the studies of reading that appeared between 1967 and 1981. A total of 267 research articles on reading appeared during this 15-year period.[6] Our exami-

---

[6]The definition of "research on reading" was not entirely without ambiguity. There is one line of research literature that we considered particularly problematical in this regard—that of adult prose learning from text. We excluded this large and impressive body of research because we did not believe that it would shed much light on our question about the lack of movement from theory to practice in *reading*.

nation was guided by a number of general questions that we hoped would help in characterizing and quantifying trends in the literature. Specifically, we asked:

1. What are the goals of reading research?
2. What kinds of research designs are employed?
3. What types of factors are considered?
4. What is the nature of the inferences drawn?

Our observations and conclusions about the factors that may be hindering the theory-practice interaction in the field of reading are organized around the answers to these questions.

What Are the Goals of Reading Research?

During the behaviorist era in experimental psychology, researchers traditionally investigated rather circumscribed aspects of human behavior. Perception, memory, and learning were distinct research fields, each with its own literature, paradigms, and theoretical models. Because these elemental processes were studied outside the context of more complex behavior, a concern for practical application would have been inappropriate. Instead, scientific curiosity was deemed a goal of high intrinsic value.

In contrast, reading involves a complex set of processes that cross many traditional lines; this is clear from the range of disciplines represented in current research. Unlike its component processes, which have little meaning outside the laboratory, reading is a behavior that has great real-world significance. Because of the potential practical value of research on reading, it is possible for a researcher to have, in varying degrees, both theoretical and applied goals. Carroll (1968) has suggested that researchers' goals may reflect "a hierarchy of motives, each imperceptibly merging into the next" (p. 267), ranging from "curiosity" at one pole to "well-defined practical goals" at the other.

In our examination of the literature, we found that each of the reading-related studies published in the *Journal of Educational Psychology* and *Reading Research Quarterly* in the last 15 years could be classified according to the goals underlying the research question posed. Rather than a continuum of motives, however, there were fairly distinct types of research. The three categories that emerged ranged from theoretical to practical, representing essentially the same three groupings that appear in the journals in Table 6-1:

1. Basic research on reading directed toward understanding the basic cognitive processes involved in reading. The research designs and methodology are predicated on an essential concern with issues of internal validity. The research questions are derived from theories and models of the reading process.
2. Basic educational/instructional research on reading concerned with issues related to educational practice. This research involves the kinds of methods, experimental designs, and statistical analyses that characterize basic research: Considera-

tions of internal validity are usually given priority over external validity.[7] The questions addressed have clear long-term practical relevance, and may or may not be derived from theories and models of the reading process or reading instruction.

3. Applied/instructional research on reading, which in contrast to basic educational research, deals more immediately with practical questions. This research uses procedures, designs, and settings more typical of applied science: External validity is a guiding principle. The questions may arise out of direct educational concerns or out of theories and models of reading instruction, and the results are intended to address practical concerns.

In classifying the 267 articles on reading, we found that the vast majority of them could, with a reasonable degree of confidence, be placed in one of these categories. Table 6-2 shows the numbers of each type of article in the sample of the literature we examined. It is evident from the table that the numbers of basic studies and basic educational/instructional studies of reading have increased substantially, but the number of applied studies published in these two journals has remained essentially the same for 15 years. Also, it is clear from the table that although the two journals we reviewed published very similar numbers of research articles during the 15 years, the emphasis differed between the journals. The *Reading Research Quarterly* placed much greater emphasis on practical articles, while the *Journal of Educational Psychology* showed a clear preference for the basic process oriented articles.

Thus, in the current field of reading there appear to be three groupings of researchers, ranging from basic to applied, with a middle grouping representing educational psychologists, traditional intermediaries between theory and practice. Such a distribution of researchers might seem to support Carroll's (1968) suggestion of a continuum of motives ranging from purely theoretical to purely practical; the variations in research motives along the continuum might seem to provide a vehicle for "movement" from theory into practice (and vice versa). Our review of the details of the studies, however, indicates that there is surprisingly little movement of information across this continuum. Research questions (and researchers) seem to be closely tied to one of the three groupings in Table 6-2 and it is quite unusual for the implications of a particular line of research to be explored across the boundaries between the groupings. So, for example, relatively little basic educational/instructional research is closely connected to research on basic processes; very little applied research is an extension of basic educational/instructional research. Moreover, it is even rarer to find movement in the reverse direction. That is, applied research is hardly ever followed up by basic educational/instructional research, and it is also uncommon for basic educational/instructional research to affect the direction of basic process research.

[7]Carroll (1968) has suggested that basic and applied research can be distinguished "on a fairly objective basis . . . in terms of the nature of the work, the kinds of questions investigated, the procedures, and the like." We found this to be true in making our distinctions between basic educational/instructional research and applied/instructional research.

Table 6-2 Number of Articles Published in the *Reading Research Quarterly* (RRQ) and *Journal of Educational Psychology* (JEdP) Between 1967 and 1981, by Origin of Research Goal

Year	Journal	Origin of Research Goal			
		Basic Reading Processes	Basic Educational/Instructional Research	Applied/Instructional Research	
1966/67	RRQ	1	3	3	
1967	JEdP	1	1	2	
1967/68	RRQ	1	3	1	
1968	JEdP	2	2	1	
1968/69	RRQ	2	1	8	
1969	JEdP	5	2	1	
1969/70	RRQ	0	2	2	
1970	JEdP	2	4	0	
1970/71	RRQ	2	4	0	
1971	JEdP	4	2	0	
Total					
1966/67–1970/71	RRQ	6	13	14	33
1967–1971	JEdP	14	11	4	29
5-year total	Overall	20	24	18	62
1971/72	RRQ	0	1	1	
1972	JEdP	1	0	2	
1972/73	RRQ	2	6	1	
1973	JEdP	6	1	2	
1973/74	RRQ	2	4	7	
1974	JEdP	5	9	0	

Year	Source				
1974/75	RRQ	2	5	1	
1975	JEdP	7	6	1	
1975/76	RRP	3	2	3	
1976	JEdP	8	6	1	
Total					
1971/72–1975/76	RRQ	9	18	13	40
1972–1976	JEdP	27	22	6	55
5-year total	Overall	36	40	19	95
1976/77	RRQ	4	2	0	
1977	JEdP	9	3	1	
1977/78	RRQ	4	2	1	
1978	JEdP	6	5	1	
1978/79	RRQ	1	4	1	
1979	JEdP	3	2	0	
1979/80	RRQ	7	9	6	
1980	JEdP	6	3	3	
1980/81	RRQ	3	7	8	
1981	JEdP	3	6	0	
Total					
1976/77–1980/81	RRQ	19	24	16	59
1977–1981	JEdP	27	19	5	51
5-year total	Overall	46	43	21	110
15-year totals	RRQ	34	55	43	132
	JEdP	68	52	15	135
	Overall	102	107	58	267

Better communication between theory and practice in reading requires that there be much greater movement across the continuum of research goals. Such movement could occur if a researcher or a team of researchers were to follow up the implications of a particular problem across the "boundaries" between groupings. To do so the researchers would have to be familiar with the literature in more than one of the groupings of journals shown in Table 6-1. Occasionally a researcher or research team does perform a series of studies that extends across boundaries in order to explore the implications of their findings, but this practice is quite exceptional. In most instances, a particular line of research is pursued, if at all, only by research of the same "type." Hence, there is very little movement from theory to practice and even less from practice to theory.

Just *how* theoretical knowledge about reading should be *translated* into practical terms has rarely been addressed in the literature. Theoreticians who have made reference to this issue have usually portrayed the process as one of providing practitioners with knowledge that should help them make wiser decisions, without indicating more explicitly how the knowledge would be useful in terms of particular instructional issues. The prevailing view among basic reading researchers about the usefulness of theory to reading practice is expressed in the following statement by Posner (1979), who served as one of the discussants at the Pittsburgh conference on theory and practice of early reading:

> I have viewed theory as a lens and also as a blinder which, when worn by programmers or curriculum designers, helps them to make the many decisions necessary to develop a curriculum. (p. 340)

In essence, then, the view has been of a one-way communication with theoreticians passing their insights down to practitioners. Clearly, this conceptualization about the relation between theory and practice is not the *only* view, but it has been and continues to be the prevailing one. The failure of basic research approaches to contribute to the improvement of reading practice is due, in part, to the limitations of this view. The solution we have suggested—that of crossing boundaries—has been raised by others. To some extent, as Resnick and Beck (1976) and White (1979) have indicated, it is already happening. But our impression from the reading research literature, where the practice would be expected to be most prevalent, is that the following statement by Venezky (1977) is nearer the mark:

> An abiding appreciation of the complexities of curricular design and classroom practice is required for translating research results into improved instruction, yet . . . few experimental psychologists who work on reading have involved themselves in these areas. (p. 344)

What Types of Research Designs Are Employed?
What Kinds of Factors Are Considered?

Irrespective of the general goals of reading research, we wished to determine whether there were any discernible patterns in the types of research designs being employed and the kinds of variables being considered. We reasoned that if there were some essential similarities in the way research was being conducted and in the types of factors being investigated, these might provide some insight into the general failure of the theory-practice interaction in reading research.

The designs predominating in the literature are of three basic types: correlational designs, in which the objective is to determine what "goes with" or predicts reading achievement; Treatment $\times$ Subjects designs, in which the effects on reading performance of a variety of conditions (e.g., tasks, methods, materials) are assessed; and Treatment $\times$ Levels $\times$ Subjects designs, in which the effects of a variety of conditions (e.g., tasks, methods, materials) on individuals representing different levels of reading skill are assessed. Of these three basic types of designs, the last is by far the most frequent in the literature: It appears in more than half of the articles published in the *Reading Research Quarterly* and the *Journal of Educational Psychology* in the last 15 years.

These comparisons across levels of reading skill are either within-grade comparisons, across-grade comparisons, or some hybrid of the two. The implicit assumption in such comparisons is that the factors differentiating individuals of more and less skill may account for the skill differences. In other words, researchers using these designs are seeking not just correlates but causes of reading success and failure.

The types of factors accounting for reading skill differences vary in across-grade and within-grade studies. In both, potential causes of skill differences include, first, relatively stable individual difference factors, the "hardware" of reading; and second, relatively modifiable skill and strategy factors, the "software" of reading. Carroll (1977) has presented an analogy that quite aptly describes the respective contributions of hardware and software in the development of reading skill:

> Reading comprehension has to be considered in the light of general language comprehension and in the light of the student's general cognitive maturity. Each of these sets limits on the preceding. To make this idea a little more concrete, imagine a mechanical gadget with three vertical lever controls something like what you find on some hi-fi sets. Each lever can go up or down, or be pushed up or down. Imagine that the three levers are labeled, left to right: Reading Skills, Language Competence, and Cognitive Ability. Now according to my theory, these levers cannot work completely independently. In fact, the one on the right, Cognitive Ability, is not a lever at all, but just an indicator. You can't push it up or down, but as time goes on, it moves slowly upward. But inside our mechanical gadget things are fixed so that you can move the Language Competence lever upward, but only so high as the Cognitive Ability indicator is set. Likewise, things are fixed so that you can move the Reading Skills lever upward, but only so high as the Language Competence lever is set. (p. 13)

The suggestion that general cognitive ability "is not a lever at all, but just an indicator" is certainly open to debate, but few would dispute the more conservative position that some abilities, skills, and strategies are *more easily* modified than others. Ordinarily, as children progress through the first 5 or 6 years of school, their reading proficiency as reflected in the speed and accuracy of their decoding, the size of their recognition vocabulary, and their comprehension of text increases quite dramatically. These across-grade (age) differences in reading ability are undoubtedly attributable to the combined effects of experiential factors (e.g., instruction, practice) and biological factors (e.g., maturation). Even among children who are at the same age-grade level there are quite large differences in reading ability, but the causes of these within-grade (age) differences are not as obvious. It is likely that they are in part due to factors such as perceptual speed, rote memory, verbal comprehension, and ability to profit from experience—in other words, Spearman's (1927) general ability factor *(g)*. But in addition to these relatively stable factors, a whole range of more modifiable factors may contribute to the difference between skilled and less skilled readers. Among these will be specific reading subskills, cognitive strategies, and affective variables. In what follows, we will argue that there are often confounds in both within-grade and across-grade studies that drastically reduce the practical utility of the results, and that these confounds present a serious impediment to movement from theory into practice.

Within-Grade Reading-Skill Differences. In studies comparing children who are at the same grade or age level but who differ in reading skill, the goal is to determine the causes of these differences between skilled and less skilled readers. A standard format is followed in most of these within-grade (age) studies: Groups of individuals representing different levels of reading skill are selected, various levels of some treatment factor are administered, and then differential effects of the factor on individuals ranging in reading skill are assessed.

The subjects in these within-grade (age) studies are selected in various ways. Sometimes teachers' recommendations are used to form skilled and less skilled reading groups (e.g., Denney, 1974; Garner & Reis, 1980/81; Katz, 1977; Samuels & Anderson, 1973). Sometimes standardized reading tests are administered and "high" and "low" groups, determined by some arbitrary procedure such as a median split or the selection of extreme scorers, become the skilled and less skilled readers (for examples of variations on this very common practice see Blank, Higgins, & Bridger, 1971; Isakson & Miller, 1976; Katz & Wicklund, 1971; Kavale & Schreiner, 1979/ 80; Mason, Katz, & Wicklund, 1975; Pace & Golinkoff, 1976; Perfetti & Hogaboam, 1975; Rickards & Hatcher, 1977/78; Smith, 1967/68). In other studies, performance on some dependent measure such as speed and/or accuracy of word identification is used as a basis for dividing subjects into skilled and less skilled groups (e.g., Cohen, 1974/75; Samuels, 1967). Finally, attendance of a special class for reading and/or learning disabilities is sometimes used to select less skilled readers, while "normal" readers are defined by membership in a "normal" class (e.g., Fleisher, Jenkins, & Pany, 1979/80; Senf & Feshbach, 1970; Smiley, Oakley, Worthen, Campione, & Brown, 1977; Spring & Capps, 1974).[8]

In all of these within-grade comparisons the objective is to reveal factors that differentiate skilled and less skilled readers. Relatively few of the studies, however, are designed to assess the contributions of hardware and software. In our survey of

[8]The lack of comparability of the less skilled reader groups in the literature is very striking. In our review we found 17 different designations for less skilled readers, and many more operational definitions based on subject-selection procedures. Clearly reading researchers ought to heed the concerns that have been raised about representativeness of subject samples (see Campbell & Stanley, 1963; Farr, Weintraub, & Tone, 1976; Samuels, 1972/73).

the *Journal of Educational Psychology* and the *Reading Research Quarterly* we found that a confound of hardware and software factors is very common: In about three quarters of the studies using a within-grade design, there was no attempt to partial out general cognitive ability. Hence, when conclusions are drawn about factors that differentiate skilled and less skilled readers, those factors may well be part of the constellation of basic cognitive processes that constitute *g*.

This confound very seriously threatens the usefulness of the results for educational practice because it is impossible to specify exactly how much variance hardware—relatively stable linguistic abilities and nonlinguistic processing efficiency factors—may contribute to observed reading-skill differences.[9] It is clear, however, that a fairly high proportion of the variance in reading skill is attributable to a general ability factor. In our research, for example, we have found correlations ranging from +.5 to +.7 between Cattell's (1963) measure of fluid intelligence,[10] a nonverbal culture-fair test, and measures of reading. More than 3000 children ranging from Grade 2 to Grade 6 have been included in these studies (e.g., Butkowsky & Willows, 1980; Campbell, Note 1; Frisk & Willows, Note 2; Killey & Willows, Note 3; Willows, 1974, 1978, Note 4, Note 5; Willows & Ryan, 1981). Various other investigators have documented this relation using a range of IQ and reading measures (e.g., Durkin, 1966; Fransella & Gerver, 1965; Silberberg, Iversen, & Silberberg, 1969; Yule, 1967; Yule, Rutter, Berger, & Thompson, 1974).[11]

In terms of Carroll's (1977) analogy, our concern is that if the goal of reading researchers is to investigate the workings of the reading skill lever and discover ways of moving it upward, then it would seem important to distinguish the reading skill lever from the cognitive ability lever (or "indicator"). This is not to deny the importance of the cognitive ability lever as a causal influence in the development of reading skill; indeed, it is to argue for the central role of the cognitive ability lever. Since the setting of this lever accounts for up to 50% of the variance in the reading skill lever, it cannot be overlooked.[12] But if the ultimate goal is to learn about the reading skill lever and how it can be moved, then the research focus needs to be on

[9] Undoubtedly, many of these factors are relatively stable by school age. Whether "hardware" is primarily a result of genetic endowment (Jensen, 1969b) or of early experience (Hunt, 1961), or of both, is immaterial to the issues we are addressing here.

[10] Cattell's (1963) theory of fluid and crystallized intelligence conceptualizes fluid intelligence as being "directly physiologically determined whereas [crystallized intelligence] is a product of experientially determined investments of [fluid intelligence]" (p. 3).

[11] The idea that both "hardware" and "software" play a role in the acquisition of reading skill is certainly not original. The long history of educational research on "underachievement" is based on a similar assumption: that general intelligence sets a limit on an individual's achievement potential. Those who fail to fulfill that potential are regarded as lacking in motivation or some other modifiable factor (Thorndike, 1963).

[12] The desire of researchers to investigate factors that account for large proportions of variance may be a primary reason for the focus on hardware factors in reading research. But, surprisingly, very few of the studies we reviewed used statistical procedures to determine how much variance was accounted for by the variables under study. Analysis of variance was the primary method of data analysis, so main effects and interactions with "reading skill" represented the primary findings; few researchers employed multiple regression analysis to assess the relative importance of the factors being investigated.

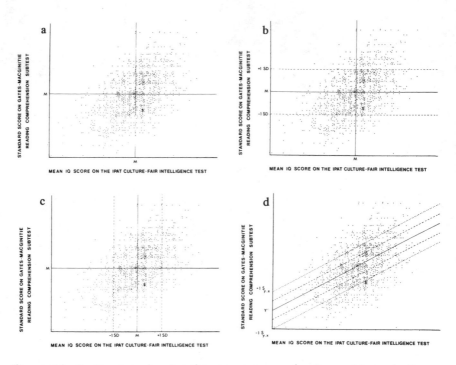

Figure 6-1. Scatterplots showing the consequences of various subject-selection procedures on skilled versus less skilled reader comparisons.

the remaining 50% of the variance in reading achievement that is not accounted for by general cognitive ability.

If reading researchers fail to take the hardware-software confound into account in making within-grade reading skill comparisons, then their conclusions might well be unjustified. The scatterplots in Figure 6-1 show the correlation for almost 1000 fifth- and sixth-grade children between Cattell's measure of fluid intelligence and a widely used reading measure.[13] In Figure 6-1a we show the consequences of performing a median split on reading comprehension without regard to general cognitive ability. It is obvious from the scatterplot that this practice, which is very common in skilled-less skilled reader comparisons, results in a highly significant hardware-software confound. That is, a sample of skilled readers will contain substantially more individuals of high intelligence than a sample of less skilled readers. As shown in Figure 6-1b, even more extreme confounds occur when the highest and lowest reading groups are compared. In studies in which the teacher's "high" and

---

[13] In many studies, a reading comprehension subtest of some standardized test is used as the basis for subject-selection, and the resultant skilled and less skilled groups are referred to as "good and poor reading comprehenders." In the reading test we have used extensively (Gates-MacGinitie), at a variety of grade levels we have found the reading comprehension subtest to account for 90–95% of the overall variance of three subtest scores (Speed and Accuracy, Vocabulary, and Comprehension). Thus, the word *comprehenders* in this case seems superfluous.

"low" reading groups are used to define the skilled and less skilled readers, the degree of confound is probably of this extreme type. Besides differing in reading proficiency, the skilled and less skilled groups will almost inevitably differ in a whole range of general cognitive ability factors. In other words, the better readers will generally also be significantly superior to the poorer readers in perceptual speed, rote memory, verbal comprehension, ability to profit from experience, and so on.

Even in research in which some concern has been demonstrated about a potential confound of general cognitive ability factors with reading skill the measures taken are often inadequate. In some studies, the researcher simply presents a mean IQ score for the less skilled reading group in order to demonstrate that they are within the "normal" range without testing the skilled readers to ensure that they are not in the "superior" range (e.g., Spring & Capps, 1974). In others, the IQ scores are limited to the "normal" range (with or without IQ tests), but no measures are taken to ensure that the reading skill groups do not differ in general cognitive ability (e.g., Kail & Marshall, 1978). As shown in Figure 6-1c, restricting the sample to the "normal" range would often be inadequate to eliminate a confound of general cognitive ability factors and specific reading skill factors. The mean IQ of the skilled reader group might still be significantly higher than that of the less skilled reader group. Sometimes researchers even administer an IQ measure, demonstrate a substantial difference between their reading ability groups, and then fail, in their analyses and interpretations, to consider the variance attributable to these general cognitive ability differences (e.g., Cohen, 1974/75; Perfetti & Hogaboam, 1975; Perfetti, Finger, & Hogaboam, 1978).

There are alternatives to the usual subject selection approaches employed in within-grade reading skill comparisons that avoid some of the problems discussed. One option, a regression approach, is shown in Figure 6-1d. It is obvious from the figure that variations in reading comprehension scores are directly related to level of general cognitive ability, but it is also clear that the scatter of scores above and below the regression line accounts for a considerable amount of variance. Individuals with similar levels of general cognitive ability differ significantly in reading achievement. According to a number of investigators (e.g., Silberberg et al., 1969; Willows, 1974; Yule, 1967), it is the factors that contribute to these variations that warrant special attention; in the figure, it is the comparisons between individuals similar in general intelligence whose reading scores are significantly above and below the regression line rather than significantly above and below the median (or mean) that should be investigated. Among the potential contributors to these variations is a range of factors that are more specific to the processing of written language: linguistic competence, specific auditory and visual perceptual abilities, and a variety of reading subskills and cognitive strategies. In comparison with the constellation of factors that constitutes basic cognitive ability, these more *reading-specific* factors individually account for relatively small proportions of the overall variance in reading skill. Moreover, they probably include both software and reading-specific hardware. That is, beyond the basic cognitive ability hardware differences between skilled and less skilled readers, there are probably additional hardware differences that determine the efficiency of processing written language.[14] Although the total variance may be less than that contributed by more general abilities, it is nevertheless the study of these reading-specific hardware and software factors that will eventually lead to understanding of the reading skill lever and how to move it upward.

We do not know of any simple solution to the hardware-software confound in within-grade skilled versus less skilled reader comparisons. Various research design and statistical options are available (e.g., ANCOVA, multiple regression, or matching procedures), but each has certain drawbacks. In view of the widespread incidence of this confound and the very substantial proportion of variance attributable to it, however, we believe that continuing to overlook it in future research may lead to theories and models of reading skill that have relevance almost exclusively to hardware and few implications for the development of software.

Across-Grade Reading Skill Differences. Hardware and software are frequently confounded in across-grade studies too. Borrowing from Carroll's (1977) analogy again, one could conceive of the cognitive ability lever as the basic hardware factor. As a child matures, the lever moves gradually upward. Consequently, in any study in which subjects of different ages are compared, differences in performance on a reading task are likely to be the result of both hardware factors (e.g., linguistic and cognitive development) and software factors, including the effects of practice and instruction. In other words, differences between younger, less skilled readers and older, more skilled readers may be due largely to factors that have been shown in developmental literature to be relatively unresponsive to training. One example of such a factor is the ability to use language to mediate behavior. This is a skill that develops sometime during the so-called 5-to-7 shift (White, 1965) and has been well documented in the developmental literature. Recently, cognitive psychologists have recognized a very similar inability of the younger child to direct his or her own thought. In questioning the appropriateness of constructing training programs for teaching young children to use strategies in reading, Brown (1980), for example, has stated that

> a cursory review of the literature concerning the ontogenesis of metacognition would suggest that the developmentally young share a fundamental problem: They are less conscious of the workings of their own mind, less facile with the introspective modes necessary to reveal their mental states, and, therefore, less able to exert conscious control of their own cognitive activity. (p. 471)

This "mediational deficiency" (Kendler, 1963) that is a characteristic of the developmentally young is but one of a wide range of dimensions on which children

---

[14] A variety of factors, including measures of linguistic ability (e.g., Isakson & Miller, 1976), perceptual recognition of orthographic structure (e.g., Massaro & Taylor, 1980), text monitoring (e.g., Garner & Reis, 1980/81), use of text structure (e.g., Taylor, 1979/80), decoding speed (e.g., Perfetti & Hogaboam, 1975), and memory (e.g., Torgesen, 1977), have been found to distinguish between skilled and less skilled readers. These measures could well be tapping reading-specific hardware, but because of the general cognitive ability confound in most of the studies the conclusion of "specificity" may not be warranted.

varying in age may differ. The problem of assessing the relative contribution of such maturational factors in a variety of behavioral differences that covary with age has long been a central concern in developmental research (see Baltes, 1968; Kessen, 1960; Schaie, 1965; Wohlwill, 1970). The problem of a hardware-software confound in across-grade reading skill comparisons is but a special case of a much more general issue in developmental research. Moreover it is only one of a whole set of research design problems that make cross-sectional developmental research difficult to interpret. Experience-maturation confounds, task difficulty confounds, and cohort confounds that have presented major methodological and conceptual problems in the field of developmental psychology also occur in the field of reading. The counsel of developmental psychologists concerning these issues, however, has not always served to guide the design and methodology in across-grade reading skill comparisons. In our review of the reading research literature we found many instances of these confounds, but because they represent "chronic" problems in developmental research, they do not require further discussion here.

The confounding of hardware and software factors in across-grade developmental studies means, however, that the relevance to teaching is questionable at best. This is particularly pertinent in those cases where a researcher may try to infer strategy differences between skilled (older) and less skilled (younger) readers. A younger child may not have the necessary cognitive ability to comprehend or use the strategies of an older reader, even when given instruction.

The Hardware and Software in Reading Skill. In an attempt to assess the validity of our concern about the hardware-software confound in most of the reading research published during the last 15 years, we examined the actual measures being related to reading skill in each study. The measures were rated as involving primarily hardware (i.e., factors that are probably directly physiologically determined and hence relatively unresponsive to training), software (i.e., factors that are experientially determined and therefore relatively modifiable), or both hardware and software in varying proportions.[15] According to our ratings of the studies in which level of reading skill was included as a factor, less than 10% involved measures that were unambiguously software, about 20% involved hardware only, and the remaining 70% of the studies employed measures that include both hardware and software components. Thus, a failure to make any distinction between hardware and software in the research designs would almost invariably result in at least some contribution to reading skill variance by hardware factors. Given the major involvement of general cognitive ability hardware factors in reading skill, in many cases no additional explanation of research outcomes may be necessary.

Both hardware and software factors are clearly important in the development of

---

[15] Clearly, our hardware-software dimension is a relative one. Factors such as perceptual speed and memory, which we would place near the hardware end on a hardware-software dimension, can both be augmented through training and practice in specific situations, but each of these factors nevertheless represents an individual difference that tends to be relatively stable and is probably physiologically determined (cf., Cattell, 1963; Eysenck, 1967; Horn, 1968; Jensen, 1969a, 1969b, 1970; Spiegel & Bryant, 1978).

reading skill, but if they are not distinguished in research designs, the potential practical value of experimental findings is greatly diminished. If the ultimate goal of basic educational research is to develop theories and models that will be *useful in guiding educational practice,* it is crucial that hardware and software be differentiated. In order to select appropriate teaching methods for different groups of children, the practitioner needs to know which individual difference factors are relatively stable, the *hardware* of reading. Because of specific strengths and weaknesses in hardware some children may benefit more from one instructional approach than another. This idea is well established in educational research in the Aptitude × Treatment interaction (ATI) literature (Cronbach & Snow, 1977; Labouvie-Vief, Levin, & Urberg, 1975; Levin, 1973). The "aptitudes" in this type of research should be based on the hardware factors that differentiate between skilled and less skilled readers, particularly, the reading-specific hardware factors. As well, in order to develop better reading instruction, the practitioner needs to know which factors are likely to be responsive to training, the *software* of learning to read. What "programs"—cognitive strategies, reading subskills, attitudes, and so on—do skilled and less skilled readers use in the process of learning to read?

The failure of reading researchers to distinguish between hardware and software aspects of learning to read has, we believe, been a major factor underlying the ineffectiveness of the basic research movement in contributing toward the improvement of reading instruction. Basic research on reading has been focused primarily on hardware. The key to improving reading instruction is, however, to design better software. Few researchers have employed appropriate methodology and research designs to determine how to develop software for reading instruction.

What Is the Nature of the Inferences Drawn?

As reflected in the high proportion of studies in which readers varying in skill are compared, a general concern in reading research is to determine the factors that contribute to the development of reading skill. Furthermore, it appears that the ultimate goal of many reading researchers is to identify *causal* factors; however, the research designs required to establish causality are just as difficult to execute in reading research as in any other area of psychology (Campbell & Stanley, 1963). Therefore, it is not surprising that a very small proportion of the studies we reviewed used a research design that would justify more than correlational conclusions. What is surprising is that a large number of researchers did discuss skilled versus less skilled reader differences as though causal inferences were warranted.

In over half of the articles we examined, researchers have pointed to the implications of their work for reading instruction, albeit sometimes "cautiously." Frequently it is demonstrated that better readers are superior to less skilled readers on measures tapping factors—such as speed of information processing or memory capacity—that may actually reflect hardware differences. Yet, then, in discussing the implications of their findings it is not unusual for the researcher to suggest the possibility of training procedures to improve performance on those measures among less skilled readers. The expectation is that such training will increase proficiency in reading; unfortunately, this assumption may not be justified. Of all the studies of reading in the *Journal of Educational Psychology* and the *Reading Research Quarterly* published during the last 15 years, fewer than 10% have dealt with factors that we judged to be clearly trainable—explicit cognitive strategies (e.g., Meyer, Brandt, & Bluth, 1980/81; Pressley, 1976; White, Pascarella, & Pflaum, 1981), certain reading subskills (e.g., Samuels, Dahl, & Archwamety, 1974; Marsh & Mineo, 1977; Williams, 1975), attributions (e.g., Butkowsky & Willows, 1980; Nicholls, 1979), and so on.[16] Many of the remaining studies could be said to demonstrate some implicit strategy differences between groups of readers, but the research designs (as discussed in the previous section) would not permit clear distinctions between hardware and software factors. Despite this, few researchers have raised the possibility that a measure under consideration might reflect an immutable individual difference—hardware—that could keep many poor readers from ever achieving average or above average levels of reading ability. Without appropriate research designs— that is, those that permit the identification of *causal* factors that are *modifiable*— inferences suggested for educational practice must remain largely speculative.

Toward the Development of Better Software

The trend 15 years ago away from applied research toward basic research as the most promising approach for answering questions about reading instruction was based on two widely held assumptions: first, that understanding the nature of the reading process is a *prerequisite* to answering questions about the most appropriate methods of reading instruction; and second, that the development of adequate theories and models of the reading process *would lead* ultimately to improvements in reading practice.

Despite a lengthy and very productive period of basic reading research, however, there is little evidence of a corresponding improvement in educational practice. This failure of theory-based research to lead to better reading instruction should not be taken as a condemnation of the approach. Without question, the quality of the reading research in the last 15 years has, in general, been vastly superior to what preceded it. Many excellent and fascinating studies have resulted from the approach and as a result the reading process is far better understood. Clearly, there is much to recommend a continued faith in the value of basic research in the field of reading.

The problem appears not to be with the approach itself; rather, it is with researchers' priorities in selecting their research questions, in designing their studies, and in choosing their measures. Their focus has been on understanding the relatively stable factors that account for a high proportion of the variance in reading skill. It is doubtful whether the development of theories and models of the hardware of the

---

[16]That the magnitude of strategy-training effects in some of the studies in the literature is relatively small probably indicates the importance of a hardware component in the ability to benefit from certain types of strategy training.

reading process alone will ever be of much use to educators. Only if reading researchers find ways of distinguishing between hardware and software factors and shift their emphasis to the development of theories and models of the software of reading will basic research approaches to the study of reading enlighten educators on the perennial best-method question. One sign of a movement in this direction is the growing interest among reading researchers in cognitive strategies (see Chapter 5, this volume). But in comparison with other types of reading research, this field still represents a minor thrust.

Reference Notes

1. Campbell, L. Boys' and girls' reactions to success and failure on math and reading tasks. Unpublished master's thesis, University of Waterloo, 1980.
2. Frisk, V. A., & Willows, D. M. The effect of cognitive tempo on the development of word recognition skills with and without context cues. Paper presented to the American Educational Research Association, San Francisco, 1979.
3. Killey, J. C., & Willows, D. M. Good-poor reader differences in detecting, pinpointing and correcting errors in orally presented sentences. Paper presented to the American Educational Research Association, Boston, 1980.
4. Willows, D. M. Reading comprehension of illustrated and non-illustrated aspects of text. Paper presented to the American Educational Research Association, San Francisco, 1979.
5. Willows, D. M. Effects of picture salience on reading comprehension of illustrated and non-illustrated aspects of text. Paper presented to the American Educational Research Association, Boston, 1980.

References

Baltes, P. B. Longitudinal and cross-sectional sequences in the study of age and generation effects. *Human Development,* 1968, *11,* 145–171.

Blank, M., Higgins, T. J., & Bridger, W. H. Stimulus complexity and intramodal reaction time in retarded readers. *Journal of Educational Psychology,* 1971, *62,* 117–122.

Bond, G. L., & Dykstra, R. The Cooperative Research Program in first-grade reading instruction. *Reading Research Quarterly,* 1966/67, *2,* 5–41.

Boring, E. G. *A history of experimental psychology* (2nd ed.). New York: Appleton-Century-Crofts, 1950.

Brown, A. Metacognitive development and reading. In R. J. Spiro, B. C. Bruce, & W. F. Brewer (eds.), *Theoretical issues in reading comprehension: Perspectives from cognitive psychology, linguistics, artificial intelligence and education.* Hillsdale, NJ: Erlbaum, 1980.

Buswell, G. T. An experimental study of the eye-voice span in reading. *Supplementary Educational Monographs,* 1920, No. 17.

Butkowsky, I. S., & Willows, D. M. Cognitive-motivational characteristics of children varying in reading ability: Evidence for learned helplessness in poor readers. *Journal of Educational Psychology*, 1980, *72*, 408–422.

Campbell, D. T., & Stanley, J. C. *Experimental and quasi-experimental designs for research*. Chicago: Rand McNally, 1963.

Carroll, J. B. Basic and applied research in education: Definitions, distinctions, and implications. *Harvard Educational Review*, 1968, *38*, 263–276.

Carroll, J. B. Developmental parameters of reading comprehension. In J. T. Guthrie (Ed.), *Cognition, curriculum, and comprehension*. Newark, DE: International Reading Association, 1977.

Cattell, J. M. On the time required for recognizing and naming letters and words, pictures and colors (1885). In A. T. Poffenberger (Ed.), *James McKeen Cattell: Man of science* (Vol. 1, *Psychological research*). Lancaster, PA: Science Press, 1947.

Cattell, J. M. The time it takes to see and name objects. *Mind*, 1886, *11*, 63–65.

Cattell, J. M. Mental tests and measurements. *Mind*, 1890, *15*, 373–380.

Cattell, R. B. Theory of fluid and crystallized intelligence: A critical experiment. *Journal of Educational Psychology*, 1963, *54*, 1–22.

Chall, J. *Learning to read: The great debate*. New York: McGraw-Hill, 1967.

Cohen, A. S. Oral reading errors of first grade children taught by a code emphasis approach. *Reading Research Quarterly*, 1974/75, *10*, 616–650.

Cronbach, L. J., & Snow, R. E. *Aptitudes and instruction methods: A handbook for research on interactions*. New York: Irvington, 1977.

Denney, D. R. Relationship of three cognitive style dimensions to elementary reading abilities. *Journal of Educational Psychology*, 1974, *66*, 702–709.

Durkin, D. *Children who read early: Two longitudinal studies*. New York: Teachers College Press, 1966.

Eysenck, H. J. Intelligence assessment: A theoretical and experimental approach. *British Journal of Educational Psychology*, 1967, *37*, 81–98.

Farr, R., & Weintraub, S. The summary: Views on a statistically significant trend. *Reading Research Quarterly*, 1973/74, *9*(3).

Farr, R., Weintraub, S., & Tone, B. (Eds.). *Improving reading research*. Newark, DE: International Reading Association, 1976.

Fleisher, L. S., Jenkins, J. R., & Pany, D. Effect on poor readers' comprehension of training in rapid decoding. *Reading Research Quarterly*, 1979/80, *15*, 30–48.

Fransella, F., & Gerver, D. Multiple regression equations for predicting reading age from chronological age and WISC verbal IQ. *British Journal of Educational Psychology*, 1965, *35*, 86–89.

Garner, R., & Reis, R. Monitoring and resolving comprehension obstacles: An investigation of spontaneous text lookbacks among upper-grade good and poor comprehenders. *Reading Research Quarterly*, 1980/81, *16*, 569–583.

Gates, A. I. An experimental and statistical study of reading and reading tests. *Journal of Educational Psychology*, 1921, *12*, 308–314.

Gibson, E. J. Learning to read. *Science*, 1965, *148*, 1066–1072.

Gibson, E. J., & Levin, H. *Communicating by language: The reading process*. Washington, DC: U.S. Government Printing Office, 1968.

Holtzman, W. H. Editorial. *Journal of Educational Psychology*, 1967, *58*, 1.

Horn, J. L. Organization of abilities and the development of intelligence. *Psychological Review*, 1968, *75*, 242–259.

Huey, E. B. *The psychology and pedagogy of reading.* Cambridge, MA: MIT Press, 1968. (Originally published by Macmillan, 1908.)

Hunt, J. McV. *Intelligence and experience.* New York: Ronald Press, 1961.

Isakson, R. L., & Miller, J. W. Sensitivity to syntactic and semantic cues in good and poor comprehenders. *Journal of Educational Psychology,* 1976, *68,* 787–792.

Jensen, A. R. Intelligence, learning ability and socioeconomic status. *Journal of Special Education,* 1969, *3,* 23–35. (a)

Jensen, A. R. How much can we boost I.Q. and scholastic achievement? *Harvard Educational Review,* 1969, *39,* 23–35. (b)

Jensen, A. R. Hierarchical theories of mental ability. In W. B. Dockrell (Ed.), *On intelligence.* Toronto: Ontario Institute for Studies in Education, 1970.

Kagan, J. On the need for relativism. *American Psychologist,* 1967, *22,* 131–142.

Kail, R. V., Jr., & Marshall, C. V. Reading skill and memory scanning. *Journal of Educational Psychology,* 1978, *70,* 808–814.

Katz, L. Reading ability and single-letter orthographic redundancy. *Journal of Educational Psychology,* 1977, *69,* 653–659.

Katz, L., & Wicklund, D. A. Word scanning rate for good and poor readers. *Journal of Educational Psychology,* 1971, *62,* 138–140.

Kavale, K., & Schreiner, R. The reading processes of above average and average readers: A comparison of the use of reasoning strategies in responding to standardized comprehension measures. *Reading Research Quarterly,* 1979/80, *15,* 102–128.

Kendler, T. S. Development of mediating responses in children. *Monographs of the Society for Research in Child Development,* 1963, *28*(2, Serial No. 86).

Kessen, W. Research design in the study of developmental problems. In P. Mussen (Ed.), *Handbook of research methods in child development.* New York: Wiley, 1960.

Kintsch, W. Concerning the marriage of research and practice in beginning reading instruction. In L. B. Resnick & P. A. Weaver (Eds.), *Theory and practice of early reading* (Vol. 1). Hillsdale, NJ: Erlbaum, 1979.

Kling, M. Background and development of the literature search: Targeted research and development program in reading. In F. B. Davis (Ed.), *The literature of research in reading with emphasis on models.* New Brunswick, NJ: Graduate School of Education, Rutgers University, 1971.

Labouvie-Vief, G., Levin, J. R., & Urberg, K. A. The relationship between selected cognitive abilities and learning: A second look. *Journal of Educational Psychology,* 1975, *67,* 558–569.

Levin, H. Reading research: What, why, and for whom? *Elementary English,* 1966, *43,* 138–147.

Levin, H., & Williams, J. P. *Basic studies on reading.* New York: Basic Books, 1970.

Levin, J. R. Inducing comprehension in poor readers: A test of a recent model. *Journal of Educational Psychology,* 1973, *65,* 19–24.

Marsh, G., & Mineo, R. J. Training preschool children to recognize phonemes in words. *Journal of Educational Psychology,* 1977, *69,* 748–753.

Marx, M. H., & Hillix, W. A. *Systems and theories in psychology* (2nd ed.). New York: McGraw-Hill, 1973.

Mason, M., Katz, L., & Wicklund, D. A. Immediate spatial order memory and item memory in sixth-grade children as a function of reading ability. *Journal of Educational Psychology,* 1975, *67,* 610–616.

Massaro, D. W., & Taylor, G. A. Reading ability and utilization of orthographic structure in reading. *Journal of Educational Psychology*, 1980, *72*, 730–742.

Meyer, B. J. F., Brandt, D. M., & Bluth, G. J. Use of top-level structure in text: Key for reading comprehension of ninth-grade students. *Reading Research Quarterly*, 1980/81, *16*, 72–103.

Neisser, U. *Cognitive psychology*. New York: Appleton-Century-Crofts, 1967.

Nicholls, J. G. Development of perception of own attainment and causal attributions for success and failure in reading. *Journal of Educational Psychology*, 1979, *71*, 94–99.

Orton, S. T. *Reading, writing and speech problems in children*. New York: Norton, 1937.

Pace, A. J., & Golinkoff, R. M. Relationship between word difficulty and access of single-word meaning by skilled and less skilled readers. *Journal of Educational Psychology*, 1976, *68*, 760–767.

Penney, M., Hjelm, H. F., & Gephart, W. J. The targeted research and development program on reading. *American Educational Research Journal*, 1970, *7*, 425–448.

Perfetti, C. A., Finger, E., & Hogaboam, T. Sources of vocalization latency differences between skilled and less skilled young readers. *Journal of Educational Psychology*, 1978, *70*, 730–739.

Perfetti, C. A., & Hogaboam, T. Relationship between single word decoding and reading comprehension skill. *Journal of Educational Psychology*, 1975, *67*, 461–469.

Posner, M. I. Applying theories and theorizing about applications. In L. B. Resnick & P. A. Weaver (Eds.), *Theory and practice of early reading* (Vol. 1). Hillsdale, NJ: Erlbaum, 1979.

Pressley, G. M. Mental imagery helps eight-year-olds remember what they read. *Journal of Educational Psychology*, 1976, *68*, 355–359.

Resnick, L. B. Toward a usable psychology of reading instruction. In L. B. Resnick & P. A. Weaver (Eds.), *Theory and practice of early reading* (Vol. 3). Hillsdale, NJ: Erlbaum, 1979.

Resnick, L. B., & Beck, I. L. Designing instruction in reading: Interaction of theory and practice. In J. T. Guthrie (Ed.), *Aspects of reading acquisition*. Baltimore, MD: Johns Hopkins Press, 1976.

Resnick, L. B., & Weaver, P. A. (Eds.) *Theory and practice of early reading* (Vol. 1). Hillsdale, NJ: Erlbaum, 1979. (a)

Resnick, L. B., & Weaver, P. A. (Eds.) *Theory and practice in early reading* (Vol. 2). Hillsdale, NJ: Erlbaum, 1979. (b)

Resnick, L. B., & Weaver, P. A. (Eds.) *Theory and practice of early reading* (Vol. 3). Hillsdale, NJ: Erlbaum, 1979. (c)

Rickards, J. P., & Hatcher, C. W. Interspersed meaningful learning questions as semantic cues for poor comprehenders. *Reading Research Quarterly*, 1977/78, *13*, 538–553.

Samuels, S. J. Attentional process in reading: The effect of pictures in the acquisition of reading responses. *Journal of Educational Psychology*, 1967, *58*, 337–342.

Samuels, S. J. Success and failure in learning to read: A critique of the research. *Reading Research Quarterly*, 1972/73, *8*, 200–235.

Samuels, S. J. Hierarchical subskills in the reading acquisition process. In J. T. Guthrie (Ed.), *Aspects of reading acquisition*. Baltimore, MD: Johns Hopkins Press, 1976.

Samuels, S. J. How the mind works when reading: Describing elephants no one has ever seen. In L. B. Resnick & P. A. Weaver (Eds.), *Theory and practice of early reading* (Vol. 1). Hillsdale, NJ: Erlbaum, 1979.

Samuels, S. J., & Anderson, R. H. Visual recognition memory, paired-associate learning and reading achievement. *Journal of Educational Psychology*, 1973, *65*, 160–167.

Samuels, S. J., Dahl, P., & Archwamety, T. Effect of hypothesis/test training on reading skill. *Journal of Educational Psychology*, 1974, *66*, 835–844.

Schaie, K. W. A general model for the study of developmental problems. *Psychological Bulletin*, 1965, *64*, 92–107.

Senf, G. M., & Feshbach, S. Development of bisensory memory in culturally deprived, dyslexic, and normal readers. *Journal of Educational Psychology*, 1970, *61*, 461–470.

Silberberg, N. E., Iversen, I. A., & Silberberg, M. C. A model for classifying children according to reading level. *Journal of Learning Disabilities*, 1969, *2*, 24–33.

Smiley, S. S., Oakley, D. D., Worthen, D., Campione, J. C., & Brown, A. L. Recall of thematically relevant material by adolescent good and poor readers as a function of written versus oral presentation. *Journal of Educational Psychology*, 1977, *69*, 381–387.

Smith, H. K. The responses of good and poor readers when asked to read for different purposes. *Reading Research Quarterly*, 1967/68, *3*, 53–83.

Spearman, C. *The abilities of man: Their nature and measurement.* New York: Macmillan, 1927.

Spiegel, M. R., & Bryant, N. D. Is speed of processing information related to intelligence and achievement? *Journal of Educational Psychology*, 1978, *70*, 904–910.

Spring, C., & Capps, C. Encoding speed, rehearsal, and probed recall of dyslexic boys. *Journal of Educational Psychology*, 1974, *66*, 780–786.

Taylor, B. M. Children's memory for expository text after reading. *Reading Research Quarterly*, 1979/80, *15*, 399–411.

Thorndike, R. L. *The concepts of over- and under-achievement.* New York: Teachers College Press, 1963.

Tinker, M. A. *Legibility of print.* Ames: Iowa State University Press, 1963.

Torgesen, J. K. Memorization processes in reading-disabled children. *Journal of Educational Psychology*, 1977, *69*, 571–578.

Venezky, R. L. Research on reading processes: A historical perspective. *American Psychologist*, 1977, *32*, 339–345.

Venezky, R. L. Harmony and cacophony from a theory-practice relationship. In L. B. Resnick & P. A. Weaver (Eds.), *Theory and practice in early reading* (Vol. 2). Hillsdale, NJ: Erlbaum, 1979.

Watson, J. B. Psychology as the behaviorist views it. *Psychological Review*, 1913, *20*, 158–177.

White, C. V.. Pascarella, E. T., & Pflaum, S. W. Effects of training in sentence construction on the comprehension of learning disabled children. *Journal of Educational Psychology*, 1981, *73*, 697–704.

White, S. H. Evidence for a hierarchical arrangement of learning processes. In L. P. Lipsitt & C. S. Spiker (Eds.), *Advances in child development and behavior* (Vol. 2). New York: Academic Press, 1965.

White, S. H. Old and new routes from theory to practice. In L. B. Resnick & P. A.

Weaver (Eds.), *Theory and practice in early reading* (Vol. 2). Hillsdale, NJ: Erlbaum, 1979.

Williams, J. P. Reading research and instruction. *Review of Educational Research, 1965, 35*, 147–153.

Williams, J. P. Learning to read: A review of theories and models. *Reading Research Quarterly, 1972/73, 8*, 121–146.

Williams, J. P. Training children to copy and discriminate letterlike forms. *Journal of Educational Psychology, 1975, 67*, 790–795.

Willows, D. M. Reading between the lines: Selective attention in good and poor readers. *Child Development, 1974, 45*, 408–415.

Willows, D. M. Individual differences in distraction by pictures in a reading situation. *Journal of Educational Psychology, 1978, 70*, 837–847.

Willows, D. M., Borwick, D., & Hayvren, M. The content of school readers. In G. E. MacKinnon & T. G. Waller (Eds.), *Reading research: Advances in theory and practice* (Vol. 2). New York: Academic Press, 1981.

Willows, D. M., & Ryan, E. B. Differential utilization of syntactic and semantic information by skilled and less skilled readers in the intermediate grades. *Journal of Educational Psychology, 1981, 73*, 607–615.

Wohlwill, J. F. The age variable in psychological research. *Psychological Review, 1970, 77*, 49–64.

Yule, W. Predicting reading ages on Neale's analysis of reading ability. *British Journal of Educational Psychology, 1967, 37*, 252–255.

Yule, W., Rutter, M., Berger, M., & Thompson, J. Over- and under-achievement in reading: Distribution in the general population. *British Journal of Educational Psychology, 1974, 44*, 1–12.

7. Strategies in Language Learning

Allan Paivio

One dictionary defines strategy as "the skillful planning and management of anything"; another as "the use of artifice or finesse in carrying out a project." Such definitions provide a general orientation for the topic of this chapter, although they encompass rather more than is useful for our purposes. Closer to home is Levin's use of the term in the context of prose-learning strategies, where he defines strategy as "any auxiliary materials or learner activities designed to enhance processing of text" (Levin, 1982). But that definition, too, is a bit off the mark because we are dealing here not with learning or memory for prose material expressed in language already familiar to the reader or listener, but rather with language learning *de novo* —the acquisition of the unfamiliar vocabulary units or syntactic structures of a first or second language. So let us say that language-learning strategy refers to the skillful planning and management of language learning as carried out by the learner or language teacher. Such strategies include the use of auxiliary materials or learner activities designed to enhance language learning. This will serve as our orienting definition, but later it will be useful to distinguish further between informal and formal strategies and settings, mnemonic and nonmnemonic strategies, and comprehension versus production as strategy goals. Following a brief explanation of these distinctions, I present a schema for classifying language-learning strategies and then go on to fill in the schema with examples of relevant strategies and an evaluation of research evidence where this is available.

Some Preliminary Distinctions

A number of researchers (e.g., D'Anglejan, 1978; Krashen, 1976) have emphasized the distinction between *informal language-learning settings*, such as the home or playground, and *formal* ones, such as the classroom. The distinction has been applied in particular to the analysis of second-language learning. Informal situations foster incidental and unconscious acquisition of linguistic skills, whereas formal situations encourage the conscious use of rules to mediate performance in the second language. Krashen (1976) describes the formal effect in terms of the development of a monitoring system that inspects and modifies the output of the unconsciously acquired system when time and other conditions permit. He provides evidence suggesting that some people are handicapped in spontaneous communication through excessive reliance on such monitoring, whereas others do not take advantage of error corrections in the formal setting because they do not consciously monitor their linguistic performance. The implications of the monitoring model will be discussed further in relevant contexts. The point to note at the moment is that monitoring is clearly a conscious strategy on the part of the language learner. By definition, such a strategy is not involved in informal language learning. Language teachers in formal settings also use conscious strategies in their teaching, and these strategies may be designed either to promote the development of conscious use of rules (the monitoring function), or unconscious linguistic habits through drills and the like. As we shall see, however, informal settings may involve unconscious language-teaching strategies in the sense that mothers and other adults speak to young children in ways that seem to be designed to promote language development.

Levin (1982) draws the distinction between *mnemonic* and *nonmnemonic* *strategies*. The former include the use of pictures or imagery instructions that involve transformations or physical recodings of linguistic material with the aim of providing direct retrieval paths back to the language. Thus, mnemonic pictures, for example, may prominently display objects or events that are not directly related to the to-be-learned linguistic units but that can function as retrieval cues for those units. Comparable nonmnemonic strategies would include pictures that simply represent, elaborate on, or provide visual interpretations of the target language without involving transformations explicitly designed to provide a link to the language material. The distinction implies that mnemonic strategies ought to be more effective than nonmnemonic ones in promoting language learning. The implication is supported by some experimental evidence, although we shall also see that nonmnemonic techniques can vary in their effectiveness as learning aids.

The third distinction is that between *comprehension* and *production* as strategy goals. Some strategies are designed to enhance learning of the meanings of units in the target language, whereas others are designed to enhance the ability to produce the language units as written or spoken responses. The former might be measured by a translation test in which a second-language word must be translated into the native language or an unfamiliar native-language word must be translated into a familiar defining synonym. Production is illustrated by the converse procedure, namely, the translation of the familiar native-language word into its translation equivalent in the second language or into the less familiar native-language synonym. One of the questions raised in the research literature is the degree to which the effect of comprehension-learning strategies transfer to production skills and vice versa.

The three distinctions are themselves logically orthogonal and we shall encounter them in different combinations in the research literature, to which we turn after a useful classification schema has been described.

Schema for Classifying Strategies

The classification scheme is based on the nature of the context associated with the target language during learning. The term *contextual learning* is often used in a special sense to refer to conceptual and syntactic contexts that are usually intra-verbal in nature. Presenting new words in sentences designed to reveal their meaning is an example of a contextual learning procedure. The term will be used in that sense in later sections, where the effects of contextual learning are compared with other procedures. The point to notice here is that the term *context* has a broader meaning and that all language learning takes place in a context of some kind. The problem is to specify the type of context involved, to treat context as a variable, and to investigate its effects.

The schema presented in Table 7-1 is essentially a classification of language-learning strategies according to their contexts, with examples of procedures corresponding to each type of context. It is a 2 X 3 schema in which the strategy is either *verbal* or *nonverbal*, and its principal aim is to emphasize *semantic, syntactic*, or *pragmatic* features of the to-be-learned language unit.

Verbal strategies include all translation and definition methods, as well as all contextual learning methods based on learning unfamiliar words in sentence contexts. Note that these involve verbal stimuli and verbal activities on the part of the learner. Nonverbal strategies include all methods in which the context associated with the unfamiliar word is nonverbal—referent objects, pictures, or mental images, as well as referent activities by a model or by the learner (e.g., acting out the actions specified by a command).

Table 7-1 Scheme for Classifying Learning Strategies According to Context, with Examples.

	Semantic	Syntactic	Pragmatic
Verbal	Synonyms Translations Definitions	Sentence contexts Grammar drill Transformations	Conversational language courses
Nonverbal	Pictures of referents Imagery (referents)	Pictures or imagery of relations, actions, objects, and qualities	Language learned in context of relevant situations and activities

The other dimension obviously derives from the three relations that signs can enter into according to semiotics. Thus, *semantic learning strategies* involve contexts intended mainly to provide clues to the meaning of a new vocabulary unit. Examples of such contexts are translation equivalents or familiar synonyms, dictionary definitions, and referent objects or their pictures. The contexts for *syntactic learning strategies* are intended to provide clues to the role of the new word in a larger linguistic context, such as its grammatical function in a sentence. These are usually verbal syntactic contexts, although a few studies have used nonverbal contexts to provide syntactic information. Finally, *pragmatic language-learning strategies* are ones in which the context provides clues to the use of the new words as communication tools. Thus, they involve activities of the learner in social and situational contexts that could be primarily verbal (e.g., second-language conversation classes that minimize the use of referent objects or pictures) or could include a substantial nonverbal component (e.g., objects to be described, manipulated, or responded to).

The discussion of pragmatic strategies highlights the fact that many language-learning strategies do not fit neatly into one of the cells of the schema, in that they may include more than one component. Nonetheless, some do belong to a single cell, and others can be analyzed in terms of their emphasis or loading on each component. Thus, the schema provides a framework for analyzing contextual variables in language-learning strategies.

The analytic schema will be used to the extent that it is informative to do so in the following discussion of research evidence. We begin with a brief review of informal learning contexts and strategies, followed by a more detailed but selective review of language-learning research involving formal settings and strategies.

Informal Contexts and Strategies

The main questions here are whether parents and other adults react to speech of young children in ways designed to promote language learning, and if they do, whether it has any effect. Systematic reinforcement of verbal behavior under different conditions would be the clearest example of such a strategy. However, the general view among students of language development is that the evidence is negative, at least in regard to reinforcement of grammatical behavior. For example, Brown, Cazden, and Bellugi (1969) found essentially no relationship between the grammatical correctness of a child's speech and parental approval or disapproval. Instead, approval or disapproval depended on whether or not the utterance corresponded to reality. The evidence on the problem is sparse, however, so strong conclusions may not be warranted at this time. In addition, aspects other than syntax may be more systematically reinforced. For example, de Villiers and de Villiers (1979) note in their review of the problem that correcting errors is bound to help the child's vocabulary learning, even if it does not help syntax or pronunciation.

Systematic reinforcement aside, parents do respond differently to children's verbal behavior than to that of adults (e.g., see reviews by de Villiers and de Villiers, 1978, 1979; or the volume of papers on the topic edited by Snow & Ferguson, 1977). Such "motherese" is characterized by brevity, repetitiveness, and completeness. Thus, parents, as well as other adults and even older children, seem to have informal instructional or modeling strategies in regard to children's language; or perhaps they just speak differently in order to be understood. The end result may be the same in either case, for much of the evidence suggests that "the corpus of speech provided by adults to children represents an input well-suited for the learning of linguistic structure and form, input carefully graded in complexity to the child's capacities and containing many teaching devices" (de Villiers & de Villiers, 1978, p. 195; alternative interpretations can be found in Snow & Ferguson, 1977).

The more important question is whether such input makes any difference to the child's learning. The review by the de Villierses (1979) indicates that one type of motherese, how often the mother expands on the child's utterances, shows no relation to linguistic development. Another, recasting the child's utterance into a different form, was found to have a selective positive effect (K. Nelson, Note 1, cited in de Villiers & de Villiers, 1979, p. 108). The frequency of partial expansion coupled with the addition of something new has also been found to correlate significantly with vocabulary (auxiliary) growth (Newport, Gleitman, & Gleitman, 1977). In reviewing the research on this important problem, however, one is struck more by the relatively small amount of research that has been published than by the results to date.

Formal Settings and Strategies

The amount of systematic research has been much greater in formal settings, including psychological experiments, language laboratories, and classrooms. This section deals briefly with reinforcement of verbal behavior, and then more fully with special language-learning techniques that have been experimentally investigated or that have features worth noting even if research evidence is presently lacking. General educational strategies, such as the highly successful total immersion approach to bilingual education (Lambert & Tucker, 1972), are also relevant and interesting, but they are beyond the scope of this chapter.

Reinforcement of Verbal Behavior

Laboratory studies of operant conditioning of verbal behavior have mostly been done with adults or older children using verbal responses already in the person's repertoire. Some systematic evidence on the learning of new linguistic responses comes from studies with retarded or autistic children with speech problems. The results have generally been positive in regard to the learning of both vocabulary and grammar (for reviews, see de Villiers & de Villiers, 1978, pp. 266–271; Harris, 1975). The studies have also revealed a transfer problem in that such children tend to lose their linguistic skills outside of the experimental setting (presumably because the controlling conditions for the acquired verbal responses are absent or weak). Nonetheless, the studies establish that systematic reinforcement can be an effective strategy for language learning.

Verbal Contextual Learning

This section deals with contextual learning in the restricted sense in which the term is ordinarily used, namely, the presentation of new vocabulary units in intra-verbal contexts that are designed to reveal the word's meaning. To illustrate with an example from Gipe (1979), the word *barbarian* might be used in the following sentences: "The barbarian kicked the dog and hit the owner in the nose. Any person who acts mean to anybody or to anything is a *barbarian*. *Barbarian* means a person who is very mean" (p. 630). This contextual approach has long been a favored strategy for second-language vocabulary learning among second-language teachers and has recently received considerable attention from researchers in the area of reading.

Sternberg, Powell, and Kaye (in press) proposed a detailed list of "armchair" criteria for evaluating contextual strategies, along with a theoretically based approach to learning from contexts. Their suggestions will be described briefly before we turn to some research evidence on the effectiveness of such strategies. Three criteria are proposed. Two of these, *internal connectedness* and *external connectedness*, refer respectively to the richness and degree of integration for the cognitive structure that is built to define a new word, and the integration between that structure and other cognitive structures (e.g., those associated with old concepts). The third criterion is the *practical ease of use* of a given method. These are useful and relatively conventional criteria in that language teachers, for example, have emphasized the importance of grouping new words according to conceptual domains or areas of interest.

Sternberg et al. base their theoretical approach on a classification and analysis of contextual cues. These include *external cues* found in the context surrounding a new word and *internal cues* that are provided by the morphemes within the word. Some of the cues draw on the learner's *competence* in that they are potentially available for use in a given context. Others are *performance cues*, which depend on the learner's ability to exercise his or her competence in a given situation. Competence and performance models are then proposed, specifying particular kinds of context cues along with the mediating variables that can affect the application of such cues in a given situation.

For example, their competence model for decoding of external contexts specifies the following types of cues: temporal, spatial, value, stative-descriptive, functional-descriptive, causal/enablement, class membership, and equivalence. Temporal cues refer to the duration or frequency of the unknown word, or to a temporal property of some known word. Spatial cues similarly specify the general or specific location of the unknown word individually, or in relation to the known word. Analogous definitions are provided for the other cues. Some of these cues are illustrated by a contextual sentence for the new word, *sol*: "At dawn, *sol* arose on the horizon and shone brightly." That *sol* refers to the sun can be inferred from temporal cues ("At dawn" and "shone"), a functional descriptive cue ("arose"), a spatial cue ("on the horizon"), and a stative-descriptive cue ("brightly").

The performance model for decoding external cues specifies such factors as variability of contexts, the importance of the new word for understanding the context in which it is embedded, the concreteness of the new word and the surrounding context, and so on. The same general approach is used for other models, such as the decoding of internal contexts.

The theory was tested by having students read passages containing varying numbers of extremely low-frequency (unfamiliar) words. Their task was to define each low-frequency word. Independent ratings of various competence and performance variables were used to predict ratings of definition goodness. The combined models accounted for 55–84% of the variance of the difficulty of words in different types of passages, indicating that the approach has some promise.

The important question, however, is whether contextual learning strategies have any advantage over other techniques. The research is sparse and the results are mostly negative, in that contextual learning has not proved to be superior to learning under free-strategy control conditions. Morgan and Foltz (1944) had seventh- and eighth-grade students study and translate French vocabulary either in a story context or without the context. Three study-test sessions were given per week over a 6-week period, as well as a final test at the end. The tests consisted of sentences to be translated into English. The results showed no significant differences between groups in the number of vocabulary items that were correctly translated during the learning exercises or in the final test. Several recent studies cited by Pressley, Levin, Kuiper, Bryant, and Michener (1982) similarly showed negative results. Gipe (1979) reported results that favored contextual learning over a control condition, but a replication attempt yielded negative results (Gipe, Note 2). Pressley, Levin, Kuiper, Bryant, and Michener (1982) also obtained negative results in an elaborate experiment that compared the effects of a number of learning strategies on the learning of unfamiliar words. The results of that study will be described in detail in a later section.

The conclusion from the research to date is that verbal contextual learning does not appear to have any advantage over simple translation practice in vocabulary learning, at least when learning is measured by translation tests. It does not necessarily follow, however, that contextual learning has no value. Such learning might be effective in developing linguistic skills that are not tapped by the translation tests typically used in the experimental studies. For example, it might be especially helpful in learning to use new words for communicational purposes. In the absence of confirmatory evidence, however, we cannot assume that contextual learning has any special advantages over other strategies.

Pictures as Contexts

We now consider the use of pictures as nonverbal contexts for vocabulary learning. The emphasis has generally been on providing referential-semantic contexts for words, although a few studies have also explored their usefulness in the learning of syntax.

A large experimental literature exists on the effects of pictures or objects as compared to words on the learning of verbal material by children and adults. Most of the studies are not relevant here because they were concerned with the learning and memory for already familiar verbal material, such as lists of words or sentences or prose passages. The most relevant studies have involved foreign-language or nonsense vocabulary to be learned by associating the words with pictures or objects, or with native-language translation equivalents. These studies have been concerned with *production skills,* in that the familiar items have served as stimuli for the unfamiliar words. There is a lack of comparable studies on the role of pictures in promoting *comprehension* skills, but some relevant data are available from a study that was mainly concerned with imagery mnemonics. That study is reviewed in the next section. We shall see that the distinction is crucial in that the effect of pictures is positive in production but not comprehension tasks.

Research on the use of pictures as stimuli in vocabulary learning goes back to the beginning of the century. Carroll's (1963) summary of that research, among others, is that "foreign words are best learned (and probably better retained) when presented in association with the objects, actions, qualities, and conditions which are their referents" (p. 1007). Although Carroll notes that many of the early studies were of limited design, it turns out that the generalization has been confirmed by more recent studies.

Kopstein and Roshal (1952) presented concrete English words or drawings of their referents to adult subjects as stimuli for Russian vocabulary. Recall was significantly higher with pictures than words as study stimuli, with the difference being greater when the subjects were also tested with pictures during recall. Wimer and Lambert (1959) studied the problem with university students using nonsense syllables as "vocabulary" units for which concrete words or objects served as stimuli. Learning was better with objects than words in terms of both trials to criterion and errors. Similar results were obtained by Deno (1968) with adults learning a Japanese vocabulary, Kellogg and Howe (1971) with children from Grades 4 to 6 learning a Spanish vocabulary, and by Webber (1978) with fourth-grade students learning Indonesian. Thus, the superiority of pictures or objects has considerable generality over subjects, age, and target language.

Two suggestive qualifications occurred in these studies. Deno found that the picture superiority occurred only when the stimulus-response pairs were grouped according to conceptual similarity but not when unrelated stimuli were presented in random order. However, the reliability of the observation is questionable, since all of the other studies obtained the picture superiority with unrelated items. The second qualification is that Kellogg and Howe obtained an interaction of sex and materials so that the picture advantage was greater for boys than girls. Looked at another way, recall was higher for boys than for girls with pictures as stimuli, whereas girls surpassed boys with words as stimuli.

The findings can be interpreted in several ways. First, the general superiority of pictures is consistent with the conceptual peg hypothesis (Paivio, 1963; 1971), according to which the effectiveness of stimuli as retrieval cues is directly related to their imagery value or picturability. A second possibility is that pictures are semantically more distinct, and so less confusable, than words. This interpretation was supported by a semantic differential measure of stimulus similarity in the Wimer and Lambert (1959) study. Of course, the conceptual peg and distinctiveness interpretations are not mutually exclusive, and both have been proposed as explanations of stimulus concreteness effects in general (Anderson, Goetz, Pichert, & Halff, 1977; Bellezza, 1983; Paivio, 1971). A final speculative but intriguing possibility in regard to the Kellogg and Howe (1971) study is that their Sex X Materials Interaction may be related to sex differences in spatial and verbal abilities (somewhat comparable interactions have been obtained in native-language memory studies—see Ernest, 1977; also relevant is Waters and Andreassen, 1983). This hypothesis, as well as the conceptual peg and distinctiveness interpretations, merits further study in the context of new vocabulary learning.

The foregoing studies involved only words as the units to be learned. Even less research has been done using more complex pictures (representing relations between objects, actions, etc.) as a strategy for learning correspondingly complex linguistic structures. This is surprising because such pictures are widely used in second-language teaching programs, such as the *Voix et images* (1958) approach to French and in books that teach languages through pictures. The pictures are intended to provide syntactic as well as semantic contexts.

Moeser and Bregman (1972, 1973) provided some experimental evidence on the problem by using miniature artificial languages. Learning was studied under conditions in which perceptual referents were provided or were absent. Thus, a series of "sentences" constructed from nonsense words according to a phrase-structure grammar would be presented either alone or accompanied by pictures related to the language in various ways. One of these was a syntax-correlated condition, in which the syntactic constraints of the language were also mirrored in the logical constraints of the pictures. For example, the 1973 experiment used "words" grouped into classes so that some words referred to rectangles of different colors, others to various nonrectangular forms, others to changes in orientation or shape of the rectangle, still others to variations in the borders of the shapes, and so on. Thus, *mir fet cas lim* is a correct sentence for which the corresponding syntax-correlated picture was a tilted red rectangle with a double-lined border, followed by a rectangle.

The results of the experiments showed that learning as measured by forced-choice sentence recognition tests was generally best under the syntax-correlated condition. The effect was particularly striking in the 1973 study, where subjects in a words-only condition were unable to learn a complex grammar even when they had seen a total of 3200 instances of correct sentences. In contrast, subjects in the syntax-correlated condition did very well. The authors concluded that semantic referents and imagery are necessary for the initial learning of syntax. Once the syntax has been so learned, the syntactic class memberships of new words could be learned in a purely verbal context.

In summary, the evidence indicates that the use of pictures as stimuli can be a highly effective strategy for learning new vocabulary units and even syntactic structures. It is interesting to note that the strategy was effective even though the pictures simply represented the linguistic units and structures, and did not include transformations or recodings that would qualify it as a mnemonic strategy in Levin's (in press) sense. We shall see in the next section, however, that strategies are even more effective when they include mnemonic elements than when they do not. We shall also see that pictures or images that simply represent the referents of new vocabulary units are ineffective in comprehension tasks.

Imagery-Based Strategies

Imagery strategies for language learning are like picture-word studies, in that new words are learned in nonverbal referential-semantic contexts. The parallel is especially close in the case of experimenter-provided or imposed imagery conditions, where pictures are used to show the referents of the to-be-learned words, usually in interaction with other items that serve a mnemonic function of some kind. Imposed imagery contrasts with subject-generated or induced imagery, where the learners must generate their own images in response to verbal instructions and native-language translation equivalents of the target vocabulary items.

The nonmnemonic-mnemonic distinction is especially relevant here. Nonmnemonic imagery simply requires the subject to image the referent when the unfamiliar word is presented, much as in the picture studies reviewed earlier. The two procedures would be fully comparable if subjects used the imaged familiar word as a cue for the unfamiliar response. Under such conditions, imaging the referents would be expected to facilitate retrieval of the unfamiliar responses just as pictures do, perhaps because images reduce interitem interference or because they function as additional retrieval cues (supplementing the familiar stimulus words), or both. Be that as it may, the few studies of the problem have required subjects to translate the unfamiliar word into its provided definition (usually in the form of a familiar synonym). This would not be expected to produce better learning than no-strategy conditions because the unfamiliar word cannot be an effective cue for image arousal until its meaning is known. We shall see that this in fact turns out to be the case.

Mnemonic imagery techniques involve auxiliary components designed to provide a link between the unfamiliar word and its meaning. Such techniques have been reviewed in detail elsewhere (Paivio & Desrochers, 1981; Pressley, Levin, & Delaney, 1982; see also Bellezza, 1983; Pressley, Levin, & Bryant, 1983). Accordingly, the present treatment will center mainly on recent studies that involve comparisons of different strategies. Two mnemonic imagery strategies are considered, namely, the keyword method and the hook method.

The keyword method has a long historical background, but systematic experimental research on its effect began with the work of Atkinson and Raugh (1975). The technique involves the use of a familiar native-language keyword and visual imagery to establish an acoustic and a semantic bridge between a foreign word (or an unfamiliar native-language word) and its meaning as represented by a familiar translation equivalent or synonym. For example, *toe* would be an appropriate keyword for the French word *couteau* (knife) because it sounds like the second syllable *teau*. The learner notes the acoustic relation and constructs an interactive image incorporating the referent of the keyword and the meaning of the word to be learned—for example, a knife cutting a toe. The target word *couteau* will subsequently serve as a reminder for the word *toe* through the acoustic link, which in turn will prompt retrieval of the image of a knife cutting a toe, yielding *knife* as the meaning of *couteau*.

The initial experiments by Atkinson and his co-workers established the superiority of the keyword technique over rote-repetition and free-strategy controls. Pressley (1977) found similarly that children using the imagery keyword technique surpassed free-strategy controls as well as a no-imagery keyword control group that simply learned the keywords. These and other studies also revealed various limitations and qualifications of the technique. For example, children up to about the second-grade level benefit from imposed imagery conditions (where pictures showing the crucial interactions are presented) but not from interactive imagery instructions, unless the stimulus items are presented as pictures (Pressley & Levin, 1978). Another relevant qualification for our purposes is that the technique reliably enhances only retrieval of the meaning of the unfamiliar word (as measured, e.g., by the subject's ability to translate the word into a native-language translation equivalent). It does not reliably facilitate retrieval of the target word as a response to, say, the familiar word as a cue, although special conditions can be devised to overcome this limitation (Pressley & Levin, 1981; see further below). In brief, the keyword technique facilitates learning of comprehension skills more than production skills.

Subsequent experiments have compared the keyword method with a variety of other strategies. Pressley, Levin, Hall, Miller, and Berry (1980) included rote-repetition, keyword-alone (i.e., excluding the imagery component), exposure to the target words and their meaning in an initial learning stage, and a keyword-plus-repetition condition. The keyword-imagery condition was superior to all the alternatives except keyword plus repetition, which produced equivalent learning.

The comparisons were extended further in a series of experiments (Levin, McCormick, Miller, Berry, & Pressley, 1982; Pressley, Levin, Kuiper, Bryant, & Michener, 1982; Pressley, Levin, & Miller, 1982), all of which showed that the keyword technique was superior to a variety of semantic and contextual learning strategies. The study by Pressley, Levin, Kuiper, Bryant, and Michener (1982) illustrates the important points, and so it will be summarized in some detail. The alternatives to the keyword technique were suggested by theoretical and empirical literature that emphasized the memory functions of depth of processing (e.g., Craik & Lockhart, 1972), the self as an organizing principle (e.g., Rogers, Kuiper, & Kirker, 1977), and contextual information (as discussed above). Accordingly, the standard keyword imagery method was compared in three experiments with a total of 10 alternative methods, including (1) keyword-sentence, in which subjects were asked to construct sentences rather than images to link the target item to its meaning; (2) keyword-image familiar, where the imaged entitites were to be ones with which the subject was personally familiar; (3) keyword-imagery self, where the subjects were to imagine themselves as part of the interactive image involving the keyword and target referents; (4) imagery of the meaning referent (a nonmnemonic imagery strategy, as described above); (5) imagery of a familiar referent; (6) self-imagery, in which the self is imaged to be interacting with the meaning referent; (7) synonym generation, where the subject was asked to think of a synonym for the target item; (8) multiple context, in which the subjects were shown the target items on cards, together with elaborate contextual information including its general and specific verbal meaning, semantically related items, a sentence using the word, and a colored line drawing of the definition referent; (9) read and copy; and (10) a no-strategy control condition.

The subjects were university undergraduates and the vocabulary items were very low-frequency English words, such as *cordite* (explosive) and *claymore* (sword).

The results are summarized in Table 7-2, where it can be seen that correct recall of definition was substantially higher for all of the keyword conditions than for all other strategies—significantly so in every case. The four keyword conditions did not differ significantly among themselves, nor did the six alternative strategies. The latter observation means that none of the semantically elaborative strategies was any more effective than the no-strategy control condition.

Two additional experiments demonstrated that the keyword method surpassed referent imagery, synonym, and no-strategy controls on a vocabulary-matching test, but was no better than or inferior to the others in free recall and recognition of the definitions of the target words presented on the study list. Thus, the authors concluded that the keyword method enhances *associative* learning (i.e., the linkage between the target and its definition) but not *response* learning (i.e., memory for the definition per se).

Summarizing the results of their own and other experiments, the authors con-

Table 7-2 Percentage of Correct Definition Recall for Different Conditions for Three Experiments

Keyword (imagery)	48.9–63.4[a]
Keyword (sentence)	55.0
Keyword (imagery familiar)	63.4
Keyword (imagery self)	47.6
Imagery of referent	23.1–33.8
Imagery of familiar referent	23.7
Self-imagery	23.7
Synonym	20.9
Read and copy	24.1
Multiple context	28.0
No-strategy control	28.9–35.3

Note. Data from "Mnemonic versus nonmnemonic vocabulary-learning strategies: Additional comparisons" by M. Pressley, J. R. Levin, N. A. Kuiper, S. L. Bryant, and S. Michener, *Journal of Educational Psychology,* 1982.
[a] Correct recall for all keyword conditions surpassed that for all other strategies.

clude that the keyword imagery strategy enhances the linkage of a new vocabulary unit with its definition and whatever else can be directly accessed by using the linkage. This occurs because the keyword readily elicits the vocabulary word, and the interactive image strengthens the keyword-definition linkage. On the other hand, the keyword method as presently formulated does *not* enhance: recall of the vocabulary target item as a response to its definition (i.e., its translation equivalent or synonym), spelling or pronunciation of the target, nor free recall of the definition. These problems might be alleviated by appropriate modifications of the technique or by supplementary procedures. For example, Pressley and Levin (1981) found that the keyword technique did facilitate recall of the target vocabulary items as responses to their definitions provided that subjects had learned the responses (though not their definitions) during a prefamiliarization stage.

The *hook technique* is another imagery-based strategy that was designed specifically to do what the standard keyword technique does not achieve, namely, enhance productive recall of new vocabulary items as responses. At the same time, it lacks the acoustic bridge provided by the keyword method. The hook technique began as a mnemonic system for recall of lists of familiar units. Like the rhyming (one-bun, two-shoe, etc.) pegword system, the hook technique uses an ordered list of concrete words as cues for the recall of new items, recall being mediated by interactive images connecting the cues to the targets. The cue list itself is constructed according to a number-consonant-word code that makes it easy to learn the cues and their numerical position. For example, the consonant sounds *t* (or *d*), *n*, *m*, *r*, *l*, *sh* (or *ch*), *k* (or *c*), *f* (or *v*), *p* (or *b*), and *s* (or *z*) are typically used to represent the numerals 1–9 and 0, respectively. The rationale is that *t* stands for 1 because it has one downstroke, *n* has two legs and *m* has three, *r* is the last consonant sound in the word for 4 in several languages, and so on. The cue words themselves are chosen so that they contain only the relevant consonant sounds—for example, *tea* (1), *N*oah (2), *emu* (3), *oar* (4). Cue words corresponding to two-digit numbers contain the two relevant consonants—for example, *toes* (10), *nun* (22), *mat* (31), *disease* (100). Once the cue list is learned, it can be used to remember new words in order simply by constructing interactive images linking cue and target word referents. Retrieval begins with numbers, so that 1 reminds the learner of tea, which in turn redintegrates the image of, say, a teapot interacting with the first item to be remembered. Experimental studies (e.g., Foth, 1973) have shown that the hook technique is effective in enhancing recall of familiar native-language items.

An adaptation of the hook technique for second-language learning (Paivio, 1978; Paivio & Desrochers, 1979) requires the learner first to learn a list of cue words in the target language, following the number-consonant-word scheme described above. For example, *thé* (tea), *noeud* (knot), *main* (hand), and *roi* (king) would serve as French cue words corresponding to serial positions 1–4. Once overlearned together with the meanings, the items can be used as mnemonic cues for new French vocabulary items by constructing interactive images of the referents of the cues and target items. Of course, the procedure differs from the use of the hook technique as a native-language mnemonic in that the target items are initially unfamiliar, so they must be accompanied by native-language definitions so that the interactive images can be constructed. This aspect is like the keyword technique, but the techniques differ in that the cue words in the hook technique do not provide any acoustic links with the target items. They simply provide image-mediated links to the meanings of the targets. Because of this limitation, Paivio (1978) reasoned that the hook technique might be most useful for mental rehearsal of foreign-language vocabulary at a late stage of practice, when the items are already somewhat familiar to the learner. That is, the learner can use the hook system to practice recalling the target items *as responses* entirely mentally, without relying on a written text, simply by starting with numbers as cues. Moreover, such rehearsal would be contextually relevant in that the cue words are themselves from the target language, and these words together with the items to be learned are used to construct interactive images that constitute a nonverbal context for productive recall.

Paivio and Desrochers (1979) tested the effectiveness of the French version of the hook technique for the learning of lists of French vocabulary items. The vocabulary lists included concrete and abstract nouns that were of high, medium, or low familiarity to the university students who served as subjects. The results showed that recall of the French nouns to number cues after one study trial was about three times higher for items learned by the hook technique than for items learned by rote repetition of the cue words and target items, thereby demonstrating the mnemonic effectiveness of the interactive images. Moreover, the hook technique was about equally effective with concrete and abstract vocabulary, and with words of different levels of familiarity. Finally, a translation test administered before the experiment and 1 day after the experiment showed that the increase in correct translation of the French vocabulary items was twice as great for the hook than for the repetition condition. Thus, the technique facilitated comprehension of the new words, as well as productive recall.

Desrochers (1980) subsequently studied the usefulness of the hook technique in the learning of French grammatical gender. The method was as described above with the addition that subjects were asked to include a male or female person in each interactive image to represent the masculine or feminine grammatical gender of the target noun. For example, if *couteau* (a masculine noun) were the first vocabulary item to be learned, one might imagine a man trying to cut through a teapot with a knife (1-*thé*-couteau). The subjects were required to recall each noun together with the appropriate definite article (*le* or *la*). The result was that hook subjects correctly recalled more French article-noun pairs than did subjects using rote rehearsal. Relative to a free-strategy control group, however, the hook technique facilitated recall only of the articles and not the French nouns.

The results from the few experiments to date suggest that the hook technique promises to be a useful strategy for enhancing the learning of foreign-language vocabulary, both in terms of production and comprehension skills. It may also be a useful aid to learning simple grammatical skills such as grammatical gender. However, its strengths and limitations in these and other domains of language learning remain to be explored more fully. The most obvious immediate need is to compare it with the keyword technique using designs that would reveal the comparative advantages and disadvantages of each strategy in simple vocabulary learning. Such research is currently under way along with an attempt to develop a more complex but workable mnemonic that incorporates the effective features of both procedures. (Readers interested in other serial mnemonics are referred to Bellezza, 1983, and Roberts, 1983.)

It will be important also to extend the research on both types of imagery-based strategies to more complex problems, such as the learning of larger linguistic units (phrases, idioms, sentences) and grammatical relations (involving, e.g., verbal and prepositional phrases), the degree to which skills learned by these techniques transfer to language use in natural communicational situations, and their effectiveness in language-learning classrooms. These and other problems, including theoretical analyses of the techniques, have been discussed more fully elsewhere (Paivio & Desrochers, 1981).

The nonverbal strategies discussed up to this point have focused mainly on the use of semantic contexts in the form of pictures or mental images. A few studies have also used pictures and images as contexts for syntactic information. We turn now to techniques that were designed especially to highlight the pragmatic aspect of language as a communication tool.

The Total Physical Response Strategy

James Asher has been the most active researcher of the language-learning strategy of "the total physical response" that was originally advocated by Harold and Dorothee Palmer in 1925 (see, e.g., Asher, Kusudo, & de la Torre, 1974). The strategy is based on the assumption that physically responding to verbal stimuli is one of the most fundamental forms of speech activity. The strategy is aimed at developing listening skills by having learners act out responses to commands. They first observe the teacher carrying out the commands and then they act out the commands themselves. A number of second-language learning experiments have shown that this strategy can be quite effective in comparison with various controls.

Asher (1966) reported five experiments with subjects of different ages. The first experiment involved college students with no prior experience with Japanese. They were required to learn a sample of Japanese language that began with simple commands to stand, walk, and so on. The complexity was increased over a 20-minute period to the point where subjects responded to such commands as "Run to the window, pick up the book, put it down on the desk, and sit on the chair." The experimental group listened to the commands on tape and after each utterance acted, with the teacher as the model. One control group simply observed the model perform; another listened to English translations of the Japanese commands but did not observe the model perform. A third control group read the English translations in a booklet after hearing the Japanese utterances.

Retention tests were given immediately after training as well as 24 hours and 2 weeks later. The experimental group was given points for carrying out the actions, and the controls were given points for writing correct English translations. The results showed that the experimental group exceeded all controls, especially on long or novel utterances and on delayed tests.

Similar results were obtained in two subsequent experiments with adults and sixth-grade children learning Russian. However, two further experiments showed no significant advantage for the total physical response condition when subjects in all conditions acted out the responses during the retention test, or when the control groups spoke (rather than wrote) the English translations. Thus, the superiority of the experimental condition seemed to be attributable to a confounding of learning and test conditions.

The results favoring the total physical response strategy were clearer in subsequent studies, which involved more complex commands. Thus, Asher (1972) observed that most grammatical features of German could be nested in the imperative form. For example, the future tense must be understood in the command "When Luke walks to the window, Marie *will* write Luke's name on the blackboard," and the past tense in "Josephine, if Abner *ran* to the blackboard . . . ." Using such commands, Asher found that an experimental group had significantly better listening comprehension scores after 32 hours of training than did college students completing either 75 or 150 hours of college instruction in German. Moreover, the experimental group showed positive transfer to reading. The results were equally impressive in another "field test" of listening skills, in which undergraduates using the total physical response strategy to learn Spanish from scratch exceeded the performance of high school and college students at different stages of classroom Spanish study. The experimental group performed at least as well as the other groups on tests of reading skill, and achieved normatively high scores on a standardized test of Spanish proficiency.

The results to date suggest that the pragmatic learning strategy of the total physical response may be more effective than some other *standard* second-language learning strategies, at least in regard to certain language skills. The experimental studies are relatively few in number, however, and most of them have involved comparisons with classroom learners whose actual study times and strategies have not been experimentally controlled. Accordingly, more research is needed under tightly controlled conditions. Finally, the strategy has not yet been compared with a variety of other strategies, including especially those based on the use of imagery. A recent memory experiment by Saltz and Nolan (1981), using a selective interference procedure, showed that "motoric imagery" is at least partly distinct from visual imagery. This means that it should be possible to compare the effectiveness of imaginal physical response strategies with ones based on interactive visual images without the motoric involvement, and all of these with the total physical response method.

The Silent Method

The silent method ("la méthode silencieuse") of foreign-language teaching was proposed by Caleb Gattagno (as described in Wehle, 1976) as part of a general approach to education in which teaching activity is subordinated to learning activity. No systematic research appears to be available on the effectiveness of the method. Nonetheless, I describe it here briefly because it is a counterintuitive and basically pragmatic strategy, which merits research evaluation.

The general procedure is as follows. The teacher remains silent throughout a language-learning session. He or she identifies the individual sounds of a language by pointing to phonetic symbols printed in colors on a large cardboard. The students pronounce the sounds, then words and phrases presented in the same way, always without any modeling by the teacher. Then the teacher uses colored sticks of different lengths to construct different spatial arrangements, which the students attempt to describe. They also describe the sequences of activities of the teacher or of a fellow student as he or she manipulates the sticks.

A more detailed description is needed to indicate why such an unusual strategy might be effective. First, the sticks used as referent objects are 10 Cuisenaire rods of different lengths and colors. The phonetic tables present each sound of a language printed in different colors. Eleven lists of words on cardboards are grouped by areas of interest, so that the first one introduces the vocabulary necessary to describe the colors and relative lengths of the sticks, along with prepositions and verbs to describe their spatial arrangements and actions with them. Other word lists are related to meals, family, means of transport, and so on.

The procedure begins with each student pronouncing the words in turn. The teacher guides and corrects by means of gestures and by using students as models. The gestures might involve, for example, rounding the lips to show the articulation for a particular sound, gesturing with the hands to indicate longer or shorter durations, tapping out a rhythm on the table, and so on. The involvement of students in the teaching process is based on the assumption that each student is good at producing some sound, and so he or she is used as a model for that sound. The same procedure is followed with respect to words and phrases.

The colored sticks are used in a similarly progressive fashion. The students first name the colors of individual sticks as the teacher touches a side. Then they name arrays of colors, then make comparisons such as "One is light green, the other is dark green." Spatial arrangements might begin with a series of "steps" constructed from sticks of different lengths, which can be described (e.g., "A small white stick is beside a red, which is beside a green"). A more complicated arrangement might be described thus: "A blue stick is lying on two upright orange sticks and a short red one is on top of the blue and under the white." Finally, an example of a described activity is "You take a green stick and you put it on two orange sticks."

In summary "the object of the teacher using the silent method is to lead the students to discover the structures of the language by themselves, by inducing them to describe the size, the form, and the number of sticks, to establish comparison, to describe the spatial and temporal relation, and also the activities applied to the sticks in the hands of the teacher or different students" (translated from Wehle, 1976, p. 18).

Benefits are claimed with respect to both the teacher and the students. The teacher thinks in terms of the student's capacities, not demonstrating his or her own skills. Students find the experience noncompetitive and enjoyable. As one student put it, "We learn in joy. We are always very relaxed and happy to be together, without feeling the obligation to compete with each other nor to satisfy the teacher." No experimental evidence is yet available on the effect of the method on learning rate, and we are left with the impression of teachers such as Wehle, who found her personal experience as a student and teacher of the method to be so positive that she strongly recommends it.

Some Theoretical and Practical Conclusions

At least two general conclusions can be drawn from the research literature. One pertains to the importance of providing relevant *nonverbal* situational, cognitive, and behavioral contexts for language learning. This conclusion emerges from all areas of research that were reviewed: the superiority of pictures over words as referents for vocabulary items; the superiority of the keyword imagery technique and, to the extent that it has been investigated thus far, the hook technique over other strategies in vocabulary learning; and the apparent effectiveness of the total physical response strategy, along with the promise of the silent method, in developing general communicative skills in a new language.

These empirical observations are consistent with all current cognitive approaches that stress the role of nonlinguistic experiential and semantic factors in language acquisition (for a summary of some of these approaches, see Paivio & Begg, 1981, chap. 10). The facts are especially compatible with a dual-coding approach that has guided my research on language and cognition (e.g., Paivio, 1971, Paivio & Desrochers, 1980). According to that approach, language and other cognitive tasks are mediated by the activity of two general symbolic systems that are specialized for dealing with verbal and nonverbal information. The systems can function independently or they can interact in the sense that one system can initiate activity in the other through their interconnections. Thus, language can activate representations of nonverbal objects and events, which may be experienced in the form of mental imagery. Conversely, nonverbal objects and events, or mental images, can be described. The developmental onset of the nonverbal system precedes that of the verbal system, which depends initially on the already established nonverbal base. These assumptions, which are only sketchily presented here, lead to a strong emphasis on the role of situational contexts and nonverbal imagery in language learning. More specifically, the theory predicts that language-learning strategies based on the use of referent objects, pictures, activities, and mental imagery would be especially effective. At the same time, it draws attention to the importance of mapping linguistic input systematically onto the nonverbal contexts.

The second general conclusion is that research has only scratched the surface of fundamental issues in this area. More factual evidence is needed on the effectiveness of different techniques in regard to different language-learning goals. Some techniques, such as the silent method, have hardly been touched by researchers. In contrast, the keyword method has been intensively studied by rigorous experimental procedures, but even so we lack information on its potential applicability to the learning of linguistic units larger than the word and to grammatical rules, how to use it effectively in the classroom setting, and the extent to which skills learned by the technique transfer to real communicational situations. The empirical gaps are even greater in the case of the other imagery or picture-based vocabulary-learning strategies. Among the pragmatic procedures, the physical response strategy has been evaluated in a few experiments but the experimental controls could be tightened. It would be interesting to compare the physical response strategy with other strategies (such as the imagery-based techniques) with respect to such specific skills as vocabulary learning. Some of these problems and others have been discussed more fully by Paivio and Desrochers (1981). Filling in the empirical gaps, with a view to achieving theoretical and practical ends, could keep all interested researchers busy for some time to come.

Reference Notes

1. Nelson, K. E. *Facilitating syntax acquisition*. Paper presented to Eastern Psychological Association, New York, April 1975.
2. Gipe, J. *Investigation of techniques for teaching new word meanings*. Paper presented at the annual meeting of the American Educational Research Association, Los Angeles, April 1981.

References

Anderson, R. C., Goetz, E. T., Pichert, J. W., & Halff, H. M. Two faces of the conceptual peg hypothesis. *Journal of Experimental Psychology: Human Learning and Memory*, 1977, *3*, 142–149.

Asher, J. J. The learning strategy of the total physical response: A review. *The Modern Language Journal*, 1966, *50*, 79–84.

Asher, J. J. Children's first language as a model for second language learning. *The Modern Language Journal*, 1972, *56*, 133–139.

Asher, J. J., Kusudo, J. A., & de la Torre, R. Learning a second language through commands: The second field test. *The Modern Language Journal*, 1974, *58*, 24–32.

Atkinson, R. C., & Raugh, M. R. An application of the mnemonic keyword method to the acquisition of a Russian vocabulary. *Journal of Experimental Psychology: Human Learning and Memory*, 1975, *104*, 126–133.

Bellezza, F. S. Mnemonic-device instruction with adults. In M. Pressley & J. R. Levin (Eds.), *Cognitive strategy research: Psychological foundations*. New York: Springer-Verlag, 1983.

Brown, R. W., Cazden, C., & Bellugi, U. The child's grammar from I to III. In J. P. Hill (Ed.), *Minnesota Symposia on Child Psychology*, Vol. II. Minneapolis: University of Minnesota Press, 1969.

Carroll, J. B. Research on teaching foreign languages. In N. L. Gage (Ed.), *Handbook of research on teaching*. Chicago: Rand McNally, 1963.

Craik, F. I. M., & Lockhart, R. S. Levels of processing: A framework for memory research. *Journal of Verbal Learning and Verbal Behavior*, 1972, *11*, 671–684.

D'Anglejan, A. Language learning in and out of classrooms. In J. Richards (Ed.), *Understanding second and foreign language learning.* Rowley, MA: Newbury House, 1978.

Deno, S. L. Effects of words and pictures as stimuli in learning language equivalents. *Journal of Educational Psychology,* 1968, *59,* 202–206.

Desrochers, A. *Effects of an imagery mnemonic on the acquisition and retention of French article-noun pairs.* Unpublished doctoral dissertation, University of Western Ontario, 1980.

de Villiers, J. G., & de Villiers, P. A. *Language acquisition.* Cambridge, MA: Harvard University Press, 1978.

de Villiers, P. A., & de Villiers, J. G. *Early language.* Cambridge, MA: Harvard University Press, 1979.

Ernest, C. H. Imagery ability and cognition: A critical review. *Journal of Mental Imagery,* 1977, *1,* 181–216.

Foth, D. L. Mnemonic technique effectiveness as a function of word abstractness and mediation instruction. *Journal of Verbal Learning and Verbal Behavior.* 1973, *12,* 239–245.

Gipe, J. Investigating techniques for teaching word meanings. *Reading Research Quarterly,* 1979, *14,* 624–644.

Harris, P. L. Development of search and object permanence during infancy. *Psychological Bulletin,* 1975, *82,* 332–344.

Kellogg, G. S., & Howe, M. J. A. Using words and pictures in foreign language learning. *Alberta Journal of Educational Research,* 1971, *17,* 87–94.

Kopstein, F. F., & Roshal, S. M. Learning foreign vocabulary from pictures vs. words. *American Psychologist,* 1954, *9,* 407–408.

Krashen, S. Formal and informal linguistic environments in language acquisition and language learning. *TESOL Quarterly,* 1976, *10,* 157–168.

Lambert, W. E., & Tucker, G. R. *Bilingual education of children: The St. Lambert experiment.* Rowley, MA: Newbury House, 1972.

Levin, J. R. Pictures as prose-learning devices. In A. Flammer & W. Kintsch (Eds.), *Text processing.* Amsterdam: North-Holland, 1982.

Levin, J. R., McCormick, C. B., Miller, G. E., Berry, J. K., & Pressley, M. Mnemonic versus nonmnemonic vocabulary-learning strategies for children. *American Educational Research Journal,* 1982, *19,* 121–136.

Moeser, S. D., & Bregman, A. S. The role of reference in the acquisition of a miniature artificial language. *Journal of Verbal Learning and Verbal Behavior,* 1972, *11,* 759–769.

Moeser, S. D., & Bregman, A. S. Imagery and language acquisition. *Journal of Verbal Learning and Verbal Behavior,* 1973, *12,* 91–98.

Morgan, C. L., & Foltz, M. C. Effect of context on learning a French vocabulary. *Journal of Educational Research,* 1944, *38,* 213–216.

Newport, E. L., Gleitman, G., & Gleitman, L. R. Mother, I'd rather do it myself: Some effects and noneffects of maternal speech style. In C. E. Snow & C. A. Ferguson (Eds.), *Talking to children.* New York & London: Cambridge University Press, 1977.

Paivio, A. Learning of adjective-noun paired-associates as a function of adjective-noun word order and noun abstractness. *Canadian Journal of Psychology,* 1963, *17,* 370–379.

Paivio, A. *Imagery and verbal processes.* New York: Holt, Rinehart & Winston, 1971. (Reprinted by Erlbaum, Hillsdale, NJ, 1979.)

Paivio, A. On exploring visual knowledge. In B. S. Randhawa & W. E. Coffman (Eds.), *Visual learning, thinking, and communication.* New York: Academic Press, 1978.

Paivio, A., & Begg, I. *The psychology of language.* Englewood Cliffs, NJ: Prentice-Hall, 1981.

Paivio, A., & Desrochers, A. Effects of an imagery mnemonic on second language recall and comprehension. *Canadian Journal of Psychology,* 1979, *33,* 17–28.

Paivio, A., & Desrochers, A. A dual-coding approach to bilingual memory. *Canadian Journal of Psychology,* 1980, *33,* 390–401.

Paivio, A., & Desrochers, A. Mnemonic techniques in second-language learning. *Journal of Educational Psychology,* 1981, *73,* 780–795.

Pressley, M. Children's use of the keyword method to learn simple Spanish vocabulary words. *Journal of Educational Psychology,* 1977, *69,* 465–472.

Pressley, M., & Levin, J. R. Developmental constraints associated with children's use of the keyword method of foreign language vocabulary learning. *Journal of Experimental Child Psychology,* 1978, *26,* 359–372.

Pressley, M., & Levin, J. R. The keyword method and recall of vocabulary words from definitions. *Journal of Experimental Psychology: Human Learning and Memory,* 1981, *7,* 72–76.

Pressley, M., Levin, J. R., & Bryant, S. L. Memory strategy instruction during adolescence: When is explicit instruction needed? In M. Pressley & J. R. Levin (Eds.), *Cognitive strategy research: Psychological foundations.* New York: Springer-Verlag, 1983.

Pressley, M., Levin, J. R., & Delaney, H. D. The mnemonic keyword method. *Review of Educational Research,* 1982, *52,* 61–91.

Pressley, M., Levin, J. R., Hall, J. W., Miller, G. E., & Berry, J. K. The keyword method and foreign word acquisition. *Journal of Experimental Psychology: Human Learning and Memory,* 1980, *6,* 163–173.

Pressley, M., Levin, J. R., Kuiper, N. A., Bryant, S. L., & Michener, S. Mnemonic versus nonmnemonic vocabulary-learning strategies: Additional comparisons. *Journal of Educational Psychology,* 1982, *74,* 693–707.

Pressley, M., Levin, J. R., & Miller, G. E. The keyword method compared to alternative vocabulary-learning strategies. *Contemporary Educational Psychology,* 1982, *7,* 50–60.

Roberts, P. Memory strategy instruction with the elderly: What *should* memory training be the training of? In M. Pressley & J. R. Levin (Eds.), *Cognitive strategy training: Psychological foundations.* New York: Springer-Verlag, 1983.

Rogers, T. B., Kuiper, N. A., & Kirker, W. S. Self-reference and the encoding of personal information. *Journal of Personality and Social Psychology,* 1977, *35,* 677–688.

Saltz, E., & Nolan, S. D. Does motoric imagery facilitate memory for sentences? A selective interference test. *Journal of Verbal Learning and Verbal Behavior,* 1981, *20,* 322–332.

Snow, C. E., & Ferguson, C. A. (Eds.). *Talking to children: Language input and acquisition.* New York & London: Cambridge University Press, 1977.

Sternberg, R. J., Powell, J. S., & Kaye, D. B. *Teaching vocabulary-building skills: A contextual approach.* In A. C. Wilkinson (Ed.), *Communicating with computers in classrooms: Prospects for applied cognitive science.* New York: Academic Press, in press.

Voix et images de France. Paris: Didier, 1958.

Waters, H. S., & Andreassen, C. Children's use of memory strategies under instruction. In M. Pressley & J. R. Levin (Eds.), *Cognitive strategy training: Psychological foundations.* New York: Springer-Verlag, 1983.

Webber, N. E. Pictures and words as stimuli in learning foreign language responses. *The Journal of Psychology,* 1978, *98,* 57–63.

Wehle, P. J'enseigne le français sans ouvrir la bouche. *Psychologie,* 1976, *78,* 17–26.

Wimer, C., & Lambert, W. E. The differential effects of word and object stimuli on the learning of paired associates. *Journal of Experimental Psychology,* 1959, *57,* 31–36.

Part III

Educational Applications
of Cognitive Strategy Research

Many promising educational applications have been derived from cognitive strategy theory and research. The three contributions of Part III discuss issues involved in applications and implementations of cognitive strategies in school settings.

Levin begins by reviewing studies in which pictorial strategies (both visual illustrations and visual imagery) have been applied to school learning contexts. Common arguments both for and against the inclusion of pictures in classroom curricula are considered. Successes and failures are analyzed in terms of picture qualities, as well as in terms of the functions that pictures can be expected to serve. Situations are described in which maximum pictorial benefits would be anticipated. In his discussion, Levin introduces what he calls the three R's of associative mnemonic strategies, which include a Recoding of the stimuli as presented, a Relating of the elements to be associated, and a systematic means of Retrieving the information to be remembered. Within this context, promising new areas of pictorial application are identified.

Pressley then considers the many materials modifications that follow from cognitive strategy research to date. Because children exhibit processing deficiencies that adults do not, it is necessary to attend more carefully to the materials presented to children. Pressley amplifies this point with three well-documented deficiencies in children: (1) Children are less able than adults to deal with poorly structured and ambiguous materials. (2) Children's inferential abilities are not as adequate as those of adults. (3) Children are not as adept as adults at using strategies when working with meaningful materials. For each of these problems, Pressley reviews potential "cures" that can be derived from the cognitive strategy literature. He also makes the case that materials interventions in this context all boil down to making materials more highly structured and more tightly tied to the concrete events of the world—a theme that is often forgotten by materials producers, even though it is included in diverse theoretical orientations in developmental and instructional psychology.

Peterson and Swing conclude this section, and this volume, by spelling out eight issues that they believe must be dealt with before classroom implementation of cognitive strategies will be successful. The issues overlap with the concerns expressed in other chapters in the two volumes on cognitive strategies (e.g., individual differences, strategy explicitness, and maintenance and generalization issues). At the same time, other issues are unique to the problem of *group*—as opposed to *individual*—administration of cognitive strategies (e.g., the interaction between teaching and learning dynamics, as well as the optimal packaging of strategies for classroom consumption). Peterson and Swing's review of the extant research literature on these issues suggests that efforts toward resolving them have barely scratched the surface. The authors nonetheless maintain some degree of optimism, noting that what has been learned thus far has been valuable in indicating the promising directions to be pursued. In their final remarks, Peterson and Swing are quick to point out that if cognitive strategies are to have implications for classroom learning, the research supporting their efficacy must be conducted within a classroom context.

8. Pictorial Strategies for School Learning: Practical Illustrations

Joel R. Levin

In this chapter I will provide examples, taken from a variety of school learning tasks, in which the potential utility of pictorial strategies has been explored. Included in the discussion are not only examples of situations in which pictures have proven helpful, but also examples of situations in which either negligible or negative effects of pictures have emerged. Along the way, appropriate task analyses will permit reasonable accounts of the various outcomes obtained to date, as well as speculations about those that might be anticipated in the future. Special attention will be given to the language arts area and, in particular, to word recognition and prose comprehension. Throughout the chapter, use will be made of the distinctions among picture functions that I have recently proposed in the context of prose comprehension (Levin, 1981b). These "functional" distinctions will prove helpful in understanding exactly what the addition of pictures to a task may and may not be expected to accomplish.

Basic Assumptions

Let us begin by laying out a trio of assumptions (and associated corollaries) underlying the position to be represented here. For convenient reference, the assumptions are also listed in Table 8-1.

Assumption 1. Pictures Can Substantially Improve Students' Learning of School Content

That pictures can substantially improve learning in school is *the* basic assumption from which all others follow. The word *substantially* is important to this as-

Table 8-1 Basic Assumptions and Corollaries

---

1. Pictures can substantially improve students' learning of school content.
   1a. Pictures should be used as school learning aids.
2. The degree of picture facilitation expected depends on the relationship between the particular learning task and the kind of pictures provided (or generated).
   2a. Pictures that are directly related to the task content and component processes will be more effective than those that are not.
   2b. Pictures that transform task content into a more meaningfully coded form will be more effective than those that do not.
3. Picture effects can be expected to vary as a function of relevant student characteristics.

---

sumption, for if the learning gains were only mild to moderate, then the subsequent advocacy corollary would not be justified. Fortunately, however, there is good reason to believe that picture effects can be large and educationally important (Levin, 1981a, 1981b, 1982; Levin & Lesgold, 1978; Pressley, Levin, & Delaney, 1982).

The caveat in this assumption inheres in the word *can*. As will be seen in Assumptions 2 and 3, whether *can* becomes *do* depends on the particular situational variables under consideration. There is no doubt, however, that given the proper eliciting conditions, pictures *do* substantially improve students' learning of school content.

Assumption 1a. Pictures Should Be Used as School Learning Aids. The advocacy corollary of Assumption 1, a controversial one, states that pictures should be used as school learning aids. Common arguments against the use of pictures in educationally relevant tasks focus on various aspects of cognitive immaturity or primitiveness. It is no secret that our society values abstract conceptual thinking, and to teach with an emphasis on the concrete or analogical is tantamount to heresy in some circles (Rohwer, Note 1). Moreover, as a second argument goes, much of the verbal information one has to process outside the classroom (in books, newspapers, and magazines, as well as via daily oral communications) is not accompanied by pictures. Thus, to rely on pictures as a classroom learning aid is really doing students a disservice. "How can such students possibly stand alone, on their own two feet, when the pictorial 'crutches' are no longer available?" the critics cry.

My own responses to these arguments are as follows. First, there exist in our society a significant number of "special" populations—such as the educable mentally retarded—for whom alternative routes to learning should be exploited. Would anybody complain if one could demonstrate respectable levels of learning in such students through the use of special techniques where, without these techniques, there would be little learning or none at all? As alternatives to learning through reading, ones that readily come to mind are learning through listening, enacting, or *looking at pictures*—as well as through various media combinations (see, e.g., Bender & Levin, 1978).

Second, there are many abstract concepts that are simply difficult to grasp, even for the highest achieving students. Physical representations, demonstrations, concrete analogies, and the like can be arranged so as to provide valuable clarifications and "Ahas!" (e.g., Mayer & Bromage, 1980; Royer & Cable, 1976; Chapter 4 in this volume). Do you *really* understand what a statistical sampling distribution is, for example? If so, how did you come to understand it?[1]

Finally, and in response to the "crutch" criticism, a potentially valuable payoff of picture use and instruction is one of enabling learners to transfer from a reliance on externally provided pictures to the skill of producing internally generated ones. Indeed, visual images, if skillfully constructed to suit the task at hand, are known to yield learning and retention returns that are anything but trivial (e.g., Levin, 1981a, 1981b; Pressley, Levin, & Delaney, 1982).

As an example that combines various aspects of the responses given in the preceding paragraphs, consider the results of a reading comprehension study that was conducted in our laboratory several years ago (Levin, 1973). In that study, we took poorly comprehending fourth-grade students who were thought to have difficulty organizing (and remembering) the contents of a prose passage. By instructing these children in the use of a self-generated visual imagery strategy that stressed organization of the passage content, we were able to increase their mean level of prose recall from 60% to 86% (i.e., better than a 40% increase). Visual imagery strategy success with the same type of poor-reading student was also recently achieved by Dillingofski (Note 2).

Assumption 2. The Degree of Picture Facilitation Expected Depends on the Relationship Between the Particular Learning Task and the Kind of Pictures Provided (or Generated)

Assumptions 2 and 3 are the flesh on the bones of Assumption 1, as will be illustrated in the examples and discussion included throughout this chapter. Thus, apart from having to consider the particular learning task to which pictures are applied (e.g., word decoding, the process of simple addition, recall of social studies facts), one must also consider the nature of the pictures themselves and their specific relationship to the to-be-learned content. Only then are questions about picture effects—and their magnitude—meaningful; for, as will be seen, large positive picture effects in one learning task can easily turn into tiny (or even negative) effects in another task. It will further become apparent that the "learning task" is being defined broadly here so as to encompass both the content to be acquired and the particular learning and assessment procedures employed. As noted previously, the "kind of pictures" refers to the specific picture-task relationship. Two corollaries are required to elaborate Assumption 2.

Assumption 2a. Pictures That Are Directly Related to the Task Content and Component Processes Will Be More Effective Than Those That Are Not.[2] Here it is

---

[1] It is interesting to note, as a historical footnote, that some of the world's greatest conceptual minds have permitted access to pictures from time to time—even (heaven forbid!) during the course of invention (see, e.g., Ghiselin, 1952).

[2] This assumption represents a pictorial manifestation of Morris, Bransford, and Franks's (1977) "transfer appropriate processing" notion, although I will not use their terminology here.

assumed that one can construct pictures to be either more or less relevant to (or consonant with) the learning task at hand. Moreover, pictures constructed to be in harmony with the task will be more facilitative than pictures that are either neutral to, or in conflict with, the task. In some cases, however, it is difficult (if not impossible) to construct pictures that provide the needed bridge of relevance to the task content *as presented* (i.e., the *nominal* task content). This gives rise to Assumption 2b.

Assumption 2b. Pictures That Transform Task Content into a More Meaningfully Coded Form Will Be More Effective Than Those That Do Not. This assumption follows from some very recent developments in the picture application literature (Levin, 1981a, 1981b, 1982; Pressley, Levin, & Delaney, 1982). The spirit of the assumption will become clear through the various examples to be included in this chapter.

Assumption 3. Picture Effects Can Be Expected to Vary as a Function of Relevant Student Characteristics

The message here is that even given task-appropriate pictures, not all students will experience comparable degrees of picture facilitation. In order for pictures to "work," they must activate certain information processing skills within the learner. If the learner does not possess these skills, negligible (or negative) effects would be expected. Recall, for example, the Levin (1973) prose-learning study where poor comprehenders improved their performance substantially by being given the suggestion to generate visual images of the passage content while they read. The imagery strategy was assumed to be effective because it provided the students with a compact framework for organizing and retrieving passage information. Success with such a strategy clearly depends, however, on a student's being able to decode and comprehend the constituent words included in the passage. Consistent with this assumption, students who were unskilled at processing individual words did *not* benefit from the visual imagery strategy. Other examples of "relevant student characteristics" will be provided in this chapter.

The three preceding assumptions constitute this chapter's orientation. What follows are several illustrations of educational applications that justify the assumptions and their corollaries. In this regard, it should be mentioned that the present assumptions incorporate—but are more inclusive than—both Levin and Lesgold's (1978) picture "ground rules" and Levin's (1981b) picture "functions" in the context of prose learning.

Practical Illustrations

Pictorial Strategies for Word Recognition

In this section, I focus on research in which the role of pictures has been investigated in relation to word recognition skills. Word recognition is divided here into its orthographic and lexigraphic aspects. With respect to orthography, we include both learning to decode new words and decoding with speed. With respect to lexigraphy, we include the learning of new vocabulary.

Pictures and Learning to Decode New Words. One certainly cannot accuse the reading journals of neglecting this topic in the last several years; and, as is apparent from Willows's (Note 3) thoughtful interpretations of the issues and problems in this area, there is no shortage of controversy either. The basic question, "Can pictures help children learn to read?" has been addressed from multiple theoretical and procedural perspectives, with predictably conflicting results. With the assistance of our previously stated assumptions, however, a case can be made *against* the use of pictures in this domain.

To make the arguments more concrete, let us put you in the beginning reader's seat. Imagine that you have to learn to read the four words *cup, cat, bat,* and *bed.* The printed symbols for these words are as shown in Figure 8-1.[3] Each word is displayed, one at a time, for a fixed brief time interval either (a) along with an appropriate pictorial representation, as in Figure 8-1 (Condition 1); or (b) with no picture (Condition 2). Following this study trial, you are tested on your ability to read the entire set of four words (but without pictures in either condition). Several alternating study and test trials are provided. Under which learning condition would you expect to learn to read more words? And why?

An armchair analysis of the task requisites would go something like this:

1. To read words, one must attend to, discriminate, and remember letter configurations.
2. Illustrations of the kind displayed in Figure 8-1 are not relevant to that process.
3. The extent to which one's study time is divided between a word and its corresponding picture is time taken away from the task-relevant behavior described in Point 1.
4. Assuming that study time is predictive of learning—and assuming that the pictures are successful attention grabbers—then might not pictures interfere with learning in this situation? That is, might not Condition 1 produce a lower level of performance than Condition 2?

Indeed, this represents the result that has been promoted (e.g., Samuels, 1970; Willows, Note 3), but also the one that has been challenged (e.g., Arlin, Scott, & Webster, 1978/79). I do not wish to venture too far into this territory here, other than to note that the countervailing opinion is considerably weakened by an inability to replicate crucial results and to provide proof positive (Arlin, 1980, pp. 556–557). Suffice it to say that there is certainly no convincing theoretical basis on which to anticipate picture *facilitation* in this task—as Arlin et al. (1978/79) would wish—and from the preceding task analysis, there is good reason to anticipate picture *interference.* The task analysis and prevailing picture interference result are

---

[3] The stimuli are re-creations of those of Singer, Samuels, and Spiroff (1973/74), as graciously related to me by Harry Singer and Jay Samuels. The specific symbols are taken from Bishop (1964). The experimental procedures to be described represent an amalgamation of the multiple variations that have appeared in the literature, but actually parallel closely those employed by Smedler (Note 4, Experiment 2).

Figure 8-1. Example of the use of pictures in a word-decoding task (after Singer et al., 1973/74).

consistent with the spirit of Assumption 2a and, as such, our first illustration is one in which a pictorial strategy would not be expected to be helpful.[4]

Exactly the same task-picture mismatch logic can be applied to a precursor of the word-reading task. This is the task of learning individual *letter sounds,* as described by Marsh and Desberg (1978). In that study, kindergarten children were given pictorial "mnemonics" that presumably would facilitate learning initial consonant sounds. The authors' use of the term *mnemonics* is quite inappropriate, however, as will now be argued. Each letter sound to be learned (e.g., /pə/ of *P*) was

[4] A study by Denburg (1976/77) is sometimes offered as evidence for picture facilitation in a word-decoding task. Apart from the floor-effect problem that was pointed out by Willows (Note 3), a differentially reactive initial sentence-reading task renders the subsequent word-decoding results completely uninterpretable. It should also be noted that a parallel attack on the picture interference problem has appeared in the mental retardation literature (see Renzaglia, Note 5, for a literature review and data). In support of an attentional hypothesis, when pictures are faded out over trials, subjects' word decoding generally improves (relative to maintaining pictures over trials).

Figure 8-2. Example of the use of pictures in a letter-sound learning task (after Marsh & Desberg, 1978).

accompanied by an illustration of either an object with the same initial sound (Experiments 1 and 2) or an action representing that sound (Experiment 2). For *P,* the object was a pumpkin (as in Figure 8-2), and the action was a boy blowing out a candle. The presence of such illustrations would certainly be expected to facilitate children's identification of unfamiliar letter sounds, and indeed that was the case. Relative to a no-picture control, both types of pictures were very helpful in enabling the children to anticipate the various letter sounds. But let us see what happened when the pictures were taken away.

As in the previous word-decoding studies, there is no direct mnemonic connection between the kind of pictures used and the kind of performance required on the criterion task. Of course, once the pumpkin picture is retrieved from memory, the sound /pə/ would likely follow. But the problem is that there is no obvious retrieval path back from the visual properties of the letter *P* to the picture of a pumpkin (see Figure 8-2). As a result, the children who rapidly acquired letter sounds in the presence of pictures were no better than control subjects in the pictures' absence. The fault, I submit, is not in the notion that pictures *could* assist in letter-sound learning, but rather in the authors' unsuccessful operationalization of pictorial mnemonics. An illustration of pictures designed to provide a direct retrieval path is given in Figure 8-3. The important point underlying the Figure 8-3 examples—and in contrast to the one in Figure 8-2—is that the relationship between each letter's visual and phonetic properties is strengthened by an easily identified picture that contains an analogous relationship. That is, the letter *M looks like* a mountain, *F looks like* a flag, and *S looks like* a snake.

Happily, recent independent empirical support has been obtained for the speculations made in the immediately preceding paragraph. In particular, Deffner and Ehri (Note 6) have found that truly mnemonic pictures (i.e., those containing a visual-phonetic correspondence) substantially improved young children's learning of letter sounds. In addition, a more complex variant of this kind of mnemonic strategy has also been successfully applied (Morris, Note 7, reported in Coleman, Note 8). See also Nicholson and Putnam (1975) for an actual set of classroom instructional materials based on this type of "mnemonic phonic" approach. A similar pictorial

Figure 8-3. Hypothetical mnemonic pictures for teaching the sounds made by the letters *M, F,* and *S.*

strategy that proved successful was devised by Lippman and Shanahan (1973) in a vocabulary-learning context, as will be described shortly.

As much as I believe in the value of pictures in a good many school learning tasks (see Assumption 1), I certainly do not subscribe to the belief that almost any pictures will be helpful in almost any situation. Rather, as will be reiterated in the examples and discussion throughout this chapter, the caveats associated with Assumptions 2 and 3 must be taken into consideration. We have just seen a couple of examples, related to word- and letter-sound decoding, in which the use of pictures clearly was not helpful—presumably as a result of there existing no theoretically explicit picture-task relationship (Assumption 2a). In the next section, an example of the individual differences caveat represented by Assumption 3 will be provided.

Pictures and Speed of Decoding. An important series of experiments on this topic has been provided by Dale Willows. The basic task presented to subjects is one of reading aloud a list of printed nouns as rapidly (but accurately) as possible. Some of the time, a picture appears above the to-be-identified word. In one study with third graders (Willows, 1978), it was found that the effect pictures have on decoding speed depends on three factors: the type of picture provided, word difficulty, and students' reading ability. If, for example, the pictures provided are unrelated to the words to be decoded (e.g., a picture of a bunch of grapes appears above the word *coat*), then students' reading speeds are uniformly reduced. Note that such a picture-word conflict can be thought of as a variant of the classic Stroop task, where a color name printed in a different color contributes to word-reading difficulty (see also Rosinski, Golinkoff, & Kukish, 1975). The relevance of Willows's finding is that it shows that children's reading can be adversely affected by picture-word conflicts. The pictures clearly distracted the children from the task at hand, which was to read the words as quickly as possible without paying any attention to the pictures. Even good readers were negatively affected by the presence of the pictures, although not as severely as poor readers. We will briefly return to the picture-word mismatch question later, in the context of prose comprehension.

The two most interesting aspects of Willows's (1978) results, for present purposes, come from what happened when relevant pictures appeared above the words to be read (e.g., a picture of a coat was above the word *coat*). First, subjects' reading times were either speeded up or slowed down, depending, respectively, on whether the words to be decoded were relatively difficult or relatively easy. Thus, as before, the pictures competed for the children's attention. In this case, however, the children could use the pictures to help them decode difficult words, whereas the pictures were unnecessary (and therefore proved costly) when decoding easy words. Second, and consistent with Assumption 3, there were reliable student differences associated with picture distractibility. In particular, the just-described facilitation-interference pattern was much more pronounced among the poorest readers. Even when IQ was statistically controlled, the correlation between standardized reading scores and susceptibility to picture influence was quite substantial ($r = -.52$). A similar negative relationship between reading ability and picture distractibility was reported in the classroom word-reading study of Samuels (1967, Experiment 2).

The practical implications of these findings are well taken:

> It is clear that a significant proportion of children with reading difficulties are less able to resist being influenced by adjunct pictures while reading than are more proficient readers. . . . Thus, although the adjunct pictures in children's early readers are surely intended as an aid to reading, it is clear from the present research that for some individuals, such pictures may seriously interfere with reading performance. (Willows, 1978, p. 846)

When viewed in conjunction with the previously discussed word-reading research, these results suggest that a fairly cogent case can be made *against* the use of pictures to facilitate the task of *learning to read.* As mentioned earlier, however, I aim not to bury pictures but to praise them, so let us move on to examine picture applications in other school learning domains. One, which also falls under the "word recognition" heading, is vocabulary learning.

Pictures and Learning New Vocabulary. The vocabulary domain is replete with new and exciting possibilities for the application of pictorial strategies. Yet some of the earlier efforts in this area have proven minimally effective at best, and unsuccessful at worst. The discussion here also provides us with an opportunity to introduce our meaningfulness transformation corollary, represented by Assumption 2b.

Essentially, three different kinds of pictorial-strategy manipulations have been attempted here, and in consonance with the distinctions I have made in a prose-learning context (Levin, 1981b), these manipulations appear to capitalize on the *representation, organization,* and *transformation* functions of pictures. With respect to vocabulary learning, pictures could be provided either to "concretize" the definitions (representation function) or to integrate the vocabulary words with their definitions. The latter process can be accomplished either at a literal level using the vocabulary words as given (organization function), or in terms of more meaningful, recoded stimuli (transformation function). According to Levin's (1981b) previous specifications, increasing amounts of picture facilitation would be expected from the three functions in the order listed.

Based on the empirical evidence available, this seems to be the case. Certainly it can be said for the transformation versus representation distinction, where several across- and within-study comparisons lend support (to be discussed shortly). Conclusions regarding the comparative potency of the organization function must remain tentative, however, inasmuch as only one vocabulary-learning study that qualifies can be identified. That study is the one by Lippman and Shanahan (1973), mentioned earlier, which will now be described.

Lippman and Shanahan (1973, Experiment 1) had third graders learn the meanings of new vocabulary words (actually nonsense syllables). Each vocabulary word appeared on a card, either by itself or in the company of a picture. As the card was presented, the experimenter read aloud the vocabulary word and provided its meaning (e.g., *quipson,* 'wood'; *volvap,* 'candy'). Several different picture variations were examined, but the one of concern here is illustrated at the left in Figure 8-4.[5] Note that the strategy in operation is one of integrating the orthographic and semantic attributes of the vocabulary words. That is, *quipson* on the left is built out of wood and *volvap* on the left is made to look like candy canes, whereas the pictures on the right are not integrated with their corresponding words. In this sense—and even though it differs somewhat from Levin's (1981b) conceptualization—the left-side strategy represents an attempt to *organize* stimulus and response characteristics. Using a study-test procedure. Lippman and Shanahan found that integrated pictures (at the left in Figure 8-4) improved the children's definition recall, relative both to a no-picture control condition and to nonintegrated pictures (at the right in Figure 8-4). It is interesting to note that pictures of the latter type were only slightly (and nonstatistically) superior to no pictures at all for enhancing children's definition recall. Thus, applying the present terminology, we conclude that in this experiment organizational pictures were considerably more effective than representational pictures.

Whereas representational and organizational pictures essentially portray the nominal content as presented, transformational pictures change the nominal content in some way. Effective transformations capitalize on what might be called the "three R's of associative mnemonic techniques." These are stimulus *Recoding,* semantic *Relating,* and systematic *Retrieving* components, each of which will now be illustrated.

---

[5] I am grateful to Marcia Lippman for providing the stimulus materials.

Figure 8-4. Example of facilitative (left) and nonfacilitative (right) pictures in a vocabulary-learning task (after Lippman & Shanahan, 1973, Experiment 1).

Suppose that your task were to recall a list of unfamiliar words—*quipson, volvap,* and the like. To make the stimuli more meaningful (and more memorable), one could recode them. For example, *quipson* could become *quips on,* or *quiz,* or *whips* (stimulus recoding). Suppose instead that your task were to associate two already meaningful stimuli, say, *cat* and *wood.* One could picture a cat on a woodpile, or a wooden cat, or a horticulturist crossing cattails and a dogwood tree to produce a "catwood" (semantic relating). Finally, suppose that your task were to associate an unfamiliar stimulus with a familiar response (e.g., to learn the definition of an unfamiliar term). To remember that *quipson* means *wood,* for example, one could recode *quipson* as *quiz* and then imagine a quizmaster asking as the jackpot question, "How much wood could a woodchuck chuck . . .?" (stimulus recoding plus semantic relating). Note that in the two associative learning examples (*cat–wood* and *quipson–wood*), the *recoding* and *relating* components are accompanied by a systematic means of *retrieving* the desired responses. In particular, when the stimulus *cat* is presented, one's memory is searched for a picture of a cat doing something, until—Aha!—a cat is seen on a woodpile, which produces the desired response, *wood.* Similarly, with the addition of one more systematic retrieval step, *quipson* reminds the learner of *quiz,* which reevokes the quiz scenario with the woodchuck question, which again produces the desired *wood.*

The three R's just discussed are the basic components of many common *mnemonic techniques* (see Bellezza, 1981; Levin, 1981a) and, accordingly, the transformation function is viewed as being mnemonic in nature. In contrast, whatever benefits accrue to the representation function are simply a result of an already meaningful stimulus's (e.g., the word *wood*) becoming more concrete (a picture of some wood). Although such increased concreteness is assumed to increase memory (e.g., Paivio, 1971), it is not "mnemonic" in the sense being used here (see also Bellezza, 1983, and Chapter 7 in this volume).

A good deal of evidence now suggests that as vocabulary-learning aids, representational (nonmnemonic) pictures are not nearly as effective—nor as consistently facilitative—as transformational (mnemonic) pictures. To be sure, some investigators have reported that simply picturing the to-be-learned definitions can improve vocabulary learning. However, the effects of such representational pictures are either small in magnitude (e.g., Bull & Wittrock, 1973; Pressley & Levin, 1978) or conditioned on specific stimulus and procedural characteristics (e.g., Deno, 1968; Kopstein & Roshal, 1954; Rusted & Coltheart, 1979; Webber, 1978). In the Bull and Wittrock (1973) study, for example, fifth graders learned the meanings of unfamiliar English vocabulary words. The facilitation resulting from either subject-generated or experimenter-provided representational pictures was minimal (mean differences of 6% and 4% correct, respectively, with the latter difference not being statistically reliable). In the Pressley and Levin (1978) study, second and sixth graders had to learn the meanings of Spanish vocabulary items, either with no pictorial assistance (e.g., given the Spanish word *carta* and its English equivalent *letter*), with representational pictures (given the word *carta* and a picture of a postal letter), or with transformational pictures (given the word *carta* and a picture of a postal letter inside a shopping *cart*). Although second graders benefited somewhat from the provision of a representational picture (a mean picture-word difference of 15% correct), the corresponding difference among sixth graders (6%) was not statistically significant. In striking contrast, the advantage associated with transformational pictures was substantial in both grades (mean differences of 48% and 39% for second and sixth graders, respectively). Moreover, compared directly with representational pictures, transformational pictures were by far more facilitative at both grade levels.

Other evidence of the overwhelming success of pictorial transformations, as applied to vocabulary learning, may be found in the reports of Ott, Blake, and Butler (1976) and Pressley, Levin, & Delaney (1982). An analysis of the component processes associated with this type of strategy has been provided by Atkinson (1975) and Levin (1981a) and includes the three R's that were introduced here. The nonfacilitative Lippman and Shanahan (1973) pictures at the right in Figure 8-4 clearly are lacking in all aspects. Consider also Figure 8-5, which was used to teach fourth graders the meaning of the word *surplus* (Levin, McCormick, Miller, Berry, & Pressley, 1982). Although the illustration certainly serves to instantiate the definition, there is no direct retrieval path back from that definition to the vocabulary word. As a result, comparatively less facilitation would be expected from this kind of illustration than from one in which a mnemonic route is made explicit through stimulus recoding (see Figure 8-6). Relative to students who received the

SURPLUS having some left over, having more than was needed

Figure 8-5. Example of a nonmnemonic illustration in a vocabulary-learning task. (After Levin et al., 1982, Experiment 2. Copyright 1982 by the American Educational Research Association, Washington, DC; reprinted by permission.)

words, their definitions, and either verbal contexts or nothing else, this is exactly the result that was obtained. The mean vocabulary recall of children shown transformational pictures (Figure 8-6) differed by at least 24% from that of children in the three other conditions. In contrast, there was no hint of representational picture (Figure 8-5) facilitation in that study. Note that Figure 8-6 is a more complex variant of the critical stimulus-response integration achieved by the examples in Figure 8-2 and those at the left in Figure 8-4.

In closing this section, I should mention that in the study described by Levin et al. (1982), the child's task was to provide a definition in response to the vocabulary word. That is, *associative* responding was required. In contrast, let us suppose that the child's task were to recall or recognize the definitions themselves (i.e., without having to associate them to vocabulary words). Although the data from such a task are not in hand, there is every good reason to expect that representational pictures of the kind in Figure 8-5 would be helpful in that situation. Based on the verbal-learning literature that shows the general superiority of pictures over words in free-recall and recognition tasks (e.g., Paivio, 1971), a similar increase would be anticipated here, with the representation-transformation distinction being relevant only if additional mnemonic links between items were provided (see also Pressley, Levin, Kuiper, Bryant, & Michener, 1982). Thus, as was indicated by Assumption 2, once again we have an illustration of how the particular task characteristics must be carefully considered before responding to the question, What effect do pictures have?[6]

---

[6] Part of the rationale underlying the preceding discussion parallels the recent intra- and interitem elaboration distinction made by Ritchey and Beal (1980).

SURPLUS (SYRUP) having some left over, having more than was needed

Figure 8-6. Example of a mnemonic illustration in a vocabulary-learning task. (After Levin et al., 1982, Experiment 2. Copyright 1982 by the American Educational Research Association, Washington, DC; reprinted by permission.)

Pictorial Strategies for Prose Learning

Much has already been written on this topic (e.g., Levin & Lesgold, 1978; Levin & Pressley, 1981; Pressley, 1977; Schallert, 1980; Levie & Lentz, Note 9) and therefore comparatively less space will be devoted to it here. More recently, Levin (1981b) has brought the "picture function" distinction to bear on the various prose-learning results obtained to date, and that distinction will be maintained in the present discussion. As a brief disclaimer at the outset, let it be understood that my purview of prose-learning "pictures" encompasses only content-depicting illustrations and visual images, and not other popular visual aids, such as graphs, charts, and time lines.

Pictures and Narrative Prose Learning. The area of children's recall of orally presented fictional narrative passages is the one that was focused on by Levin and Lesgold (1978). In their review they concluded that, contrary to earlier speculations (e.g., Samuels, 1970), there is little doubt that text-overlapping illustrations *do* facilitate children's recall of that content. The effect has been shown time and time again. More recently, pictures also improved children's recall of orally presented nonfictional passages taken from the newspaper (Levin & Berry, 1980). Other evidence suggests that pictures can assist children in "going beyond the information given"; that is, they can enable children to make inferences (Miller & Cureton, Note 10). Picture facilitation is recognized even by those who have argued against the inclusion of pictures in children's primers (e.g., Willows, Note 11). Thus, it is readily apparent that the role played by pictures in decoding and recognizing words is quite different from that in comprehending and recalling narrative text. That is not to say that the students' *reading comprehension skills* improve from the provision of text-relevant illustrations. In fact, they likely do not, for the same distractibility reasons mentioned in our earlier discussion of word decoding (see Willows, Note 11). However, in situations where word decoding is not a problem (e.g., listening tasks) or where it has become automatized (e.g., among skilled decoders), prose comprehension and recall can certainly be enhanced by the provision of relevant illustrations.[7]

Illustrations in the narrative prose domain have been primarily of the representational variety. That is, they depict in a literal fashion some, most, or all of the prose content. Improved learning is assumed to result from the increased concreteness of the resulting semantic representation. In contrast, it has been argued that subject-generated imaginal representations tend to be not as concrete nor as likely to lay down a strong memory trace on a consistent basis (Levin, 1981b). For this reason, subject-generated representational images are believed not to be as uniformly effective or potent in comparison to experimenter-provided representational illustrations. This position is supported by the available prose-learning evidence. Moreover—and consistent with Assumption 3—there clearly appears to be support for the hypothesis that the ability to benefit from a subject-generated visual imagery strategy is developmentally based, with younger children profiting less than older children and adolescents in prose-learning situations (Levin, 1981b), as well as in associative learning situations where the generation of transformational images is required (Levin, 1976; Levin & Pressley, 1978; Pressley & Levin, 1978).

Pictures and Expository Prose Learning. Narrative prose is typically very concrete and directly translatable into pictorial representations. So (with a certain degree of cognitive manipulation) is what has been called "procedural" prose, as exemplified by instructing students "how to" perform some concrete activity. Just as representational pictures facilitate students' processing of narrative passages (see the preceding section), recent evidence suggests that they also enable students to follow directions better (Stone & Glock, 1981).

Not all text is as concrete or as orderly. Indeed, the vast majority of instructional text in the areas of science and social studies is expository. Expository prose may be relatively abstract, which makes it difficult to illustrate the content in the same direct fashion as is possible for concrete narrative passages. Moreover, even if expository prose does contain concrete factual information (e.g., historical sequences, geographical data, scientific principles), such information may not lend itself to simple memory-enhancing illustrations. For these reasons, if pictures are to be applied in the expository prose domain, they would seem to require a different con-

---

[7] Pressley, Levin, and Hope (Note 12) have recently shown that the kind of pictures provided can greatly influence the kind of prose information recalled by children, especially younger ones. With text-complementary pictures, recall is enhanced; with text-contradictory pictures, it is either not enhanced or it is diminished (see also Willows, Note 13).

ceptualization from that underlying narrative prose pictures. That is, rather than providing literal *representations* of the text, the important functions of expository prose pictures consist primarily of content *interpretations* and *transformations* (Levin, 1981b). It should be noted that these last two functions are not restricted to expository prose. Rather, expository prose (especially that which is abstract and/or difficult to remember) affords a convenient genre to which these picture functions can be applied.[8]

Dillingofski (Note 2) has shown that pictorial interpretations of social studies passages (i.e., representing abstract concepts by familiar pictorial symbols) can be effective, and Levin and Pressley (1981) have described manifestations of the interpretation function in which pictures serve as analogical devices. That concrete analogies can improve students' comprehension and recall of abstract concepts and principles has been shown in the work of Bromage and Mayer (1981), Davidson (1976), Mayer and Bromage (1980), Royer and Cable (1976), and others (see Chapter 4 in this volume). Other examples of using illustrations to make scientific concepts more comprehensible may be found in the studies of Rigney and Lutz (1976) and Schallert, Goetz, and Dixon (cited by Schallert, 1980). In the Rigney and Lutz study, college students were taught how a battery works. Picture-assisted subjects outperformed verbally assisted subjects on several dependent variables; and consistent with the belief that illustrations make a difference, responses to a post-instructional questionnaire revealed that "students who took the verbal version of the lesson did not feel that it caused them to visualize how a battery works, whereas the students in the [picture] group thought that [the pictures] did help them to form mental imagery" (Rigney & Lutz, 1976, p. 308).

In the Bromage and Mayer (1981) study, college students read a passage about the operation of a 35-mm camera. Half the subjects were given verbal and pictorial analogies to help them understand the camera's underlying mechanisms, whereas the other half were provided the same procedural facts and rules, but with no mechanism analogies. The finding of most interest was that although the two groups did not differ with respect to recall of passage facts, the analogies group was superior with respect to both conceptual explanations and performance on a subsequent problem-solving task in which comprehension of camera concepts was required. Thus, both of these studies strongly suggest that concrete analogies are useful vehicles for teaching scientific concepts.

An example of the transformation function of pictures as applied to expository prose is seen in a recent series of three experiments conducted by Shriberg, Levin,

---

[8] Similarly, concrete expository prose can capitalize on the representation function (see Schallert, 1980). This also appears to be the case in an interesting picture application by Goldberg (1974). In that study, representational pictures accompanying a central task (e.g., a spelling exercise) positively affected fifth graders' incidental learning of the social studies and science content represented by the illustrations. Unfortunately, Goldberg's data cannot be interpreted unambiguously, in that no performance data related to the central task are provided. Thus, it is quite possible that picture subjects recalled more factual content only at the expense of not benefiting as much as controls from the spelling lesson—a result that might be anticipated from our earlier picture distractibility discussion.

McCormick, and Pressley (1982). The basic task was for junior high school students to remember the purported accomplishments of various individuals, as related in short passages. To help students better associate names and accomplishments, a transformational strategy was devised whereby (a) each individual's name was phonetically recoded into a concrete referent; and (b) each referent was semantically related to the corresponding accomplishment via a picture. For example, to remember that *Charlene McKune* was famous for having a counting cat, *McKune* was recoded as *raccoon* and then incorporated into a picture such as that in Figure 8-7. Relative to no-picture control subjects, picture subjects recalled substantially more name-accomplishment information. Moreover, students were able to benefit from this type of mnemonic strategy whether the pictures were illustrations provided by the experimenter or images generated by the students themselves (Experiments 1 and 2). The third experiment in the series showed that in contrast to the minimal learning gains often associated with subject-generated *representational* images (see previous section), the gains associated with subject-generated *transformational* images are of much more impressive magnitude (see also Assumption 2b).

Counting the Shriberg et al. three-experiment study, as well as subsequent research out of our laboratory (Levin, Shriberg, & Berry, in press; McCormick & Levin, Note 14; Shriberg, Note 15), we have now conducted 11 different prose-learning experiments that have yielded 11 independent demonstrations of mnemonic-picture benefits. Thus, and as I have argued elsewhere (Levin, 1981b, 1982), the application of transformational pictorial strategies to prose-learning situations seems to hold considerable promise. I have further argued that far greater benefits are likely to accrue from combining such pictorial mnemonic strategies and other commonly recommended prose-learning strategies (e.g., question asking, underlining, summarizing—see Levin & Pressley, 1981) than from applying either class of strategy by

Figure 8-7. Example of a mnemonic illustration for associating names and accomplishments. (After Shriberg et al., 1982, Experiment 1. Copyright 1982 by the American Psychological Association; reprinted by permission of the publisher and author.)

itself. This is because traditional prose-learning strategies appear to be suitable for retaining theme and/or main idea information, whereas mnemonic strategies are uniquely suited to coding and retrieving factual information contained in the text. Thus, it would not be at all surprising to discover that combining strategies that facilitate recall of the text fabric, on the one hand, with those that weave the fabric into a meaningful ensemble, on the other, would work to their mutual benefit. Combinations of pictorial transformations and other picture functions are also possible and are currently receiving attention in our laboratory. For example, the retention of abstract or complex concepts may profit from creating appropriate pictorial symbols or analogies (interpretation function), on the one hand, and combining these with pictorial mnemonics (transformation function), on the other (see Levin et al., in press). Finally, and as will be indicated in the next section, combinations of two or more pictorial mnemonic strategies (multiple pictorial transformations) can sometimes be profitably applied. What is abundantly clear is that we have just begun to scratch the surface of this important domain of picture application.

Pictorial Strategies for Other Educational Applications

Foreign-Language Learning. Our previous discussion of the role of pictures in new vocabulary learning applies here as well. Indeed, several different aspects of foreign vocabulary learning have been facilitated by the application of pictorial mnemonic techniques. In addition to the previously cited reviews that focus on Atkinson's (1975) keyword method, Paivio and Desrochers (1979) describe an alternative mnemonic technique (the hook method) that has also improved students' foreign vocabulary learning (see Chapter 7 in this volume). Interestingly, Desrochers (Note 16) has successfully applied the hook method to the task of learning the genders of foreign nouns. The point is that mnemonic pictures can certainly assist in multiple aspects of vocabulary learning, including vocabulary comprehension and appropriate contextual usage (Pressley, Levin, & Miller, 1981).

Social Studies and Science Facts. Just as pictures can facilitate students' recall of instructional text (see previous section), pictures can also facilitate students' recall of factual information that is presented in isolation. This includes both definitions of technical terms in the content areas and important associations involving people, places, events, dates, and sequences. Levin (1981a) and Pressley, Levin, & Delaney (1982) have discussed how mnemonic pictures can be used to help students acquire medical and scientific terminology, names and events, and facts about U.S. history and geography.

Consider, for example, the task of associating the names and numbers of the U.S. presidents. In a recent attempt to deal with this problem, we provided junior high school students with a complex pictorial transformation strategy, in which (a) each president's name was recoded as a concrete object, illustrated, and then related to (b) his proper number, which was recoded as another concrete object, illustrated, and placed in a special scene setting. Compared to students who were given the names, numbers, and actual pictures of the presidents (with unrestricted study time), students administered the pictorial mnemonic strategy exhibited superior recall of both presidents' names when given their numbers, and numbers when given their names (see Levin, McCormick, & Dretzke, 1981, for further details).

Additional likely candidates for pictorial mnemonic benefits include recall of the structural properties of chemicals (e.g., Pizza, Note 17), as well as of various scientific principles (e.g., Gagne & Redfield, Note 18) and taxonomic classifications. Even the everyday task of associating names and faces has been assisted by the application of pictorial mnemonics (e.g., McCarty, 1980), which would seem to have relevance for identifying famous faces in the social studies and science domains.

Arithmetic Skills. A recent study by Grunau (1978) purports to have obtained pictorial facilitation in an addition task given to kindergarten children. Upon inspection of the data, however, one finds that the pictorial facilitation can be explained in terms of simple object counting. Moreover, because a no-picture transfer task was not administered, one is reminded of the previously discussed word-reading studies, where the relationship between the pictures created and the skills to be acquired did not mesh well. Thus, there are no theoretical grounds on which to expect pictorial facilitation from Grunau's manipulations, and there is no convincing support of such facilitation in her data. (The same criticism can be leveled at the semantic relating manipulation she attempted.) As a result, the issue of facilitating the acquisition of arithmetic skills through the use of pictures appears still to be unresolved. What is clear, however, is that thoughtful analyses of picture functions need to be conducted in order to maximize one's chances of achieving success in this domain as well (see Assumption 2a).

It should be noted that mnemonic picture materials for teaching basic addition, subtraction, and multiplication facts are currently being marketed (Bornstein School of Memory Training, Note 19). Of course it is not known whether these particular mnemonics will stand up to scientific test (see Levin, 1981b). However, another important question is whether the traditional repetition methods for acquiring reflex-like associations to multiplication tables and other commonly used number facts *should be* replaced by mnemonic techniques that rely on the processes of phonetic recoding and semantic relating, as discussed here. The issue is a real one, and one that will not likely be easily resolved.[9]

Learning in Special Populations. There is ample evidence to support the claim that pictures can be of great assistance to children who typically experience learning difficulties. Included here are the educable mentally retarded, the learning disabled,

---

[9] Of course, the same latency argument could be applied to the mnemonic acquisition of information in any of the domains discussed in this chapter. Whether or not subjects' speed and nature of information processing changes from initial to terminal stages of learning is an issue that should be addressed on a domain-by-domain basis (see Levin's, 1981a, discussion of the latency question, as well as a recent study by Levin, Dretzke, McCormick, Scruggs, McGivern, & Mastropieri, in press).

and children with various other known neurological and sensory impairments. Illustrations of a variety of educationally relevant picture applications in such populations may be found in the reviews of Martin (1978), Pressley, Heisel, McCormick, and Nakamura (1982), and Taylor and Turnure (1979), as well as of Borkowski and Büchel (1983) and Worden (1983). In accordance with the recommendation repeated throughout the chapter, systematic analyses of picture-task correspondences need to be conducted within these populations as well, in order to gain insight regarding the "functional" components in operation.

Summary and Conclusions

To extract a summary of the message in this chapter, the reader would do well to take another look at the assumptions listed in Table 8-1. Most of the examples here were of pictorial-strategy successes; that is, examples in which illustrations have facilitated—sometimes substantially—students' learning of school content. There were, in addition, some notable exceptions to this optimistic picture of pictures. If one's goal is learning, comprehension, or memory per se, then there is good reason to recommend the use of pictures for those situations in which they have proven helpful. If, on the other hand, one's goal is to foster skill development per se, then one has to pay careful attention to the consequences for the target skill when the pictures are ultimately taken away. The skill of word decoding was offered as an example of how pictures "look good" when they are in view (during acquisition), but not when they are not (during transfer).

The chapter's overriding principle was that pictorial strategies are not uniformly beneficial in all learning situations for all people. Moreover, a picture is not always a picture, in the sense that it is certainly possible to construct differentially effective pictures for the same learning task. Let me comment briefly on what may appear to be an excessive amount of space devoted here to the case against pictures in my avowed case *for* pictures. This course of action was chosen for two reasons. First, I purposely elected not to retrace the same steps that have been exhaustively trod before, where pervasive positive picture effects have been documented (e.g., Higbee, 1979; Levin, 1981a, 1981b, 1982; Levin & Lesgold, 1978; Paivio, 1971; Pressley, 1977; Pressley, Levin, & Delaney, 1982; Schallert, 1980). Second, by concentrating on the negative instances, we were able to acquire a richer understanding of the probable reasons underlying various picture "breakdowns." Along the same lines, by cuing in on such breakdowns vis-à-vis the present assumptions, one should be much better equipped to devise the kind of pictures that will facilitate learning in situations where pictorial strategies have heretofore failed (see, e.g., our previous discussion of Marsh & Desberg's, 1978, letter-sound decoding study).

The preceding notions gave rise to a consideration of several picture caveats. One of these was that the success of a pictorial strategy depends on the relationship of the picture features and content to the task at hand. Pictures that are integrally related to the to-be-remembered content will be most effective. This can be either a direct one-to-one relationship (as in the case of representational pictures for prose learning) or a relationship that evolves through a recoding of the nominal content (transformational pictures). The latter type of picture is assumed—and has been found—to work its greatest magic when it comes to processing difficult-to-remember information. Thus, when considered in the company of the associative mnemonic R's of Relating and Retrieving, it may be concluded of the Recoding component that the more things change, the more one's memory for the content stays the same.

Finally, hints of individual-difference variation related to pictorial strategies were scattered throughout the chapter. In word-reading situations, the presence of illustrations may be more detrimental to the poorest readers than to the best. Similarly, in tasks requiring the generation of internal visual images, younger children do not seem to be as proficient as older children and adolescents. This finding, as well as a wealth of other learning data suggesting that children do not benefit as much from their own pictorial creations as from those created for them, indicates that there is a need for the development of pictorial school learning materials and curricula. The pictorial materials developed could stand alone, or they could be used as initial support components in systematic imagery-training programs. This, of course, brings us right back to our primary assumption (Assumption 1a), and I am doing my best to put picture preaching into practice (Levin, 1981a). Periodic assessments of the state of the strategy art—such as those in this volume—will surely help to shape the course of both theoretical and applied developments in this area.

Acknowledgments. This chapter is adapted from a paper originally prepared for the Teaching and Learning division of the National Institute of Education. Part of the work was supported by the Wisconsin Center for Education Research, which is also funded through the National Institute of Education. I wish to acknowledge the editorial suggestions of Susan Chipman, Christine McCormick, Jean Padrutt, Linda Shriberg, Marshall Smith, and Rosalind Wu. The artwork of Robert Cavey and the typing of Lynn Sowle are also gratefully acknowledged.

Reference Notes

1. Rohwer, W. D., Jr. *Imagery constructs vs. elaboration constructs.* Paper presented at the annual meeting of the American Educational Research Association, New York, April 1977.
2. Dillingofski, M. S. *The effects of imposed and induced visual imagery strategies on ninth grade difference-poor readers' literal comprehension of concrete and abstract prose.* Unpublished doctoral dissertation, University of Wisconsin, Madison, 1980.
3. Willows, D. M. *A distorted picture of "The effects of pictures on rate of learning sight words."* Unpublished manuscript, Department of Psychology, University of Waterloo, Ontario, 1979.
4. Smedler, A.-C. *The effect of pictures in three paired-associate reading experiments.* Unpublished doctoral dissertation, University of Wisconsin, Madison, 1978.

5. Renzaglia, A. M. *The effect of the number of faded steps in a fade-picture-out instructional procedure on the reading acquisition, retention and transfer of moderately and severely retarded individuals.* Unpublished doctoral dissertation, University of Wisconsin, Madison, 1978.

6. Deffner, N. D., & Ehri, L. C. *Mnemonics for phonics reconsidered.* Unpublished manuscript, Department of Education, University of California, Davis, 1982.

7. Morris, G. W. *Effects of stimulus and response imagery on learning the sounds of letters.* Unpublished master's thesis, University of Texas at El Paso, 1972.

8. Coleman, E. B. *Analysis of imagery for a reading technology.* Research proposal, 1974.

9. Levie, W. H., & Lentz, R. *The effects of text illustrations: A review of research* (DDSP Rep.). Bloomington, IN: Audio-Visual Center, Indiana University, 1982.

10. Miller, G. E., & Cureton, D. *Picture effects associated with young children's recall of inferential information.* Paper presented at the annual meeting of the International Reading Association, New Orleans, March–April 1981.

11. Willows, D. M. *Reading comprehension of illustrated and non-illustrated aspects of text.* Paper presented at the annual meeting of the American Educational Research Association, San Francisco, April 1979.

12. Pressley, M., Levin, J. R., & Hope, D. J. *Do mismatched pictures interfere with children's memory of prose?* Paper presented at the annual meeting of the American Educational Research Association, Los Angeles, April 1981.

13. Willows, D. M. *Effects of picture salience on reading comprehension of illustrated and non-illustrated text.* Paper presented at the annual meeting of the American Educational Research Association, Boston, April 1980.

14. McCormick, C. B., & Levin, J. R. *A comparison of different prose-learning variations of the mnemonic keyword method.* Unpublished manuscript, Wisconsin Center for Education Research, Madison, 1982.

15. Shriberg, L. K. *Comparison of two mnemonic encoding strategies on children's memory for abstract prose information.* Unpublished doctoral dissertation, University of Wisconsin, Madison, 1982.

16. Desrochers, A. *Effects of an imagery mnemonic on the acquisition and retention of French article-noun pairs.* Unpublished doctoral dissertation, University of Western Ontario, London, 1980.

17. Pizza, G. Personal communication, 1980.

18. Gagne, R. M., & Redfield, D. D. *Effects of learning elaboration procedures on retention of scientific principles.* Research proposal, 1979.

19. Bornstein School of Memory Training. *Instant multiplication memorizer* and *Subtraction & addition memorizer.* Advertisement, 1980.

References

Arlin, M. A response to Harry Singer. *Reading Research Quarterly,* 1980, *15,* 550–558.

Arlin, M., Scott, M., & Webster, J. The effects of pictures on rate of learning sight words: A critique of the focal attention hypothesis. *Reading Research Quarterly,* 1978/79, *14,* 645–660.

Atkinson, R. C. Mnemotechnics in second-language learning. *American Psychologist,* 1975, *30,* 821–828.

Bellezza, F. S. Mnemonic devices: Classification, characteristics, and criteria. *Review of Educational Research*, 1981, *51*, 247–275.

Bellezza, F. S. Mnemonic-device instruction with adults. In M. Pressley & J. R. Levin (Eds.), *Cognitive strategy research: Psychological foundations*. New York: Springer-Verlag, 1983.

Bender, B. G., & Levin, J. R. Pictures, imagery, and retarded children's prose learning. *Journal of Educational Psychology*, 1978, *70*, 583–588.

Bishop, C. H. Transfer effects of word and letter training in reading. *Journal of Verbal Learning and Verbal Behavior*, 1964, *3*, 215–221.

Borkowski, F. G., & Büchel, F. P. Learning and memory strategies in the mentally retarded. In M. Pressley & J. R. Levin (Eds.), *Cognitive strategy research: Psychological foundations*. New York: Springer-Verlag, 1983.

Bromage, B. K., & Mayer, R. E. Relationship between what is remembered and creative problem solving performance in science learning. *Journal of Educational Psychology*, 1981, *73*, 451–461.

Bull, B. L., & Wittrock, M. C. Imagery in the learning of verbal definitions. *The British Journal of Educational Psychology*, 1973, *43*, 289–293.

Davidson, R. E. The role of metaphor and analogy in learning. In J. R. Levin & V. L. Allen (Eds.), *Cognitive learning in children: Theories and strategies*. New York: Academic Press, 1976.

Denburg, S. D. The interaction of picture and print in reading instruction (abstracted report). *Reading Research Quarterly*, 1976/77, *12*, 176–189.

Deno, S. L. Effects of words and pictures as stimuli in learning language equivalents. *Journal of Educational Psychology*, 1968, *59*, 202–206.

Ghiselin, B. (Ed.). *The creative process*. New York: Mentor, 1952.

Goldberg, F. Effects of imagery on learning incidental material in the classroom. *Journal of Educational Psychology*, 1974, *66*, 233–237.

Grunau, R. V. E. Effects of elaborative prompt condition and developmental level on the performance of addition problems by kindergarten children. *Journal of Educational Psychology*, 1978, *70*, 422–432.

Higbee, K. L. Recent research on visual mnemonics: Historical roots and educational fruits. *Review of Educational Research*, 1979, *49*, 611–629.

Kopstein, F. F., & Roshal, S. M. Learning foreign vocabulary from pictures vs. words. *American Psychologist*, 1954, *9*, 407–408.

Levin, J. R. Inducing comprehension in poor readers: A test of a recent model. *Journal of Educational Psychology*, 1973, *65*, 19–24.

Levin, J. R. What have we learned about maximizing what children have? In J. R. Levin & V. L. Allen (Eds.), *Cognitive learning in children: Theories and strategies*. New York: Academic Press, 1976.

Levin, J. R. The mnemonic '80s: Keywords in the classroom. *Educational Psychologist*, 1981, *16*, 65–82. (a)

Levin, J. R. On functions of pictures in prose. In F. J. Pirozzolo & M. C. Wittrock (Eds.), *Neuropsychological and cognitive processes in reading*. New York: Academic Press, 1981. (b)

Levin, J. R. Pictures as prose-learning devices. In A. Flammer & W. Kintsch (Eds.), *Discourse processing*. Amsterdam: North-Holland, 1982.

Levin, J. R., & Berry, J. K. Children's learning of all the news that's fit to picture. *Educational Communication and Technology Journal*, 1980, *28*, 177–185.

Levin, J. R., & Lesgold, A. M. On pictures in prose. *Educational Communication and Technology*, 1978, *26*, 233–243.

Levin, J. R., Dretzke, B. J., McCormick, C. B., Scruggs, T. E., McGivern, J. E., & Mastropieri, M. A. Learning via mnemonic pictures: Analysis of the presidential process. *Educational Communication and Technology Journal,* in press.

Levin, J. R., McCormick, C. B., & Dretzke, B. J. A combined pictorial mnemonic strategy for ordered information. *Educational Communication and Technology Journal,* 1981, *29,* 219–225.

Levin, J. R., McCormick, C. B., Miller, G. E., Berry, J. K., & Pressley, M. Mnemonic versus nonmnemonic vocabulary-learning strategies for children. *American Educational Research Journal,* 1982, *19,* 121–136.

Levin, J. R., & Pressley, M. A test of the developmental imagery hypothesis in children's associative learning. *Journal of Educational Psychology,* 1978, *70,* 691–694.

Levin, J. R., & Pressley, M. Improving children's prose comprehension: Selected strategies that seem to succeed. In C. M. Santa & B. L. Hayes (Eds.), *Children's prose comprehension: Research and practice.* Newark, DE: International Reading Association, 1981.

Levin, J. R., Shriberg, L. K., & Berry, J. K. A concrete strategy for remembering abstract prose. *American Educational Research Journal,* in press.

Lippman, M. Z., & Shanahan, M. W. Pictorial facilitation of paired-associate learning: Implications for vocabulary training. *Journal of Educational Psychology,* 1973, *64,* 216–222.

Marsh, G., & Desberg, P. Mnemonics for phonics. *Contemporary Educational Psychology,* 1978, *3,* 57–61.

Martin, C. J. Mediational processes in the retarded: Implications for teaching reading. In N. R. Ellis (Ed.), *International review of research in mental retardation* (Vol. 9). New York: Academic Press, 1978.

Mayer, R. E., & Bromage, B. K. Different recall protocols for technical texts due to advance organizers. *Journal of Educational Psychology,* 1980, *72,* 209–225.

McCarty, D. L. Investigation of a visual imagery mnemonic device for acquiring face-name associations. *Journal of Experimental Psychology: Human Learning and Memory,* 1980, *6,* 145–155.

Morris, C. D., Bransford, J. D., & Franks, J. J. Levels of processing versus transfer appropriate processing. *Journal of Verbal Learning and Verbal Behavior,* 1977, *16,* 519–533.

Nicholson, H., & Putnam, M. *Putnik: Phonics of today* (3rd ed.). St. Paul, MN: PUTNIK, 5004 W. Turtle Lane, 1975.

Ott, C. E., Blake, R. S., & Butler, D. C. Implications of mental elaboration for the acquisition of foreign language vocabulary. *International Review of Applied Linguistics in Language Teaching,* 1976, *14,* 37–48.

Paivio, A. *Imagery and verbal processes.* New York: Holt, 1971.

Paivio, A., & Desrochers, A. Effects of an imagery mnemonic on second language recall and comprehension. *Canadian Journal of Psychology,* 1979, *33,* 17–28.

Pressley, M. Imagery and children's learning: Putting the picture in developmental perspective. *Review of Educational Research,* 1977, *47,* 585–622.

Pressley, M., Heisel, B. E., McCormick, C. B., & Nakamura, G. V. Memory strategy instruction with children. In C. J. Brainerd & M. Pressley (Eds.), *Verbal processes in children.* New York: Springer-Verlag, 1982.

Pressley, M., & Levin, J. R. Developmental constraints associated with children's use of the keyword method of foreign language vocabulary learning. *Journal of Experimental Child Psychology*, 1978, *26*, 359–372.

Pressley, M., Levin, J. R., & Delaney, H. D. The mnemonic keyword method. *Review of Educational Research*, 1982, *52*, 61–91.

Pressley, M., Levin, J. R., Kuiper, N. A., Bryant, S. L., & Michener, S. Mnemonic versus nonmnemonic vocabulary-learning strategies: Additional comparisons. *Journal of Educational Psychology*, 1982, *74*, 693–707.

Pressley, M., Levin, J. R., & Miller, G. E. How does the keyword method affect vocabulary comprehension and usage? *Reading Research Quarterly*, 1981, *16*, 213–226.

Rigney, J. W., & Lutz, K. A. Effect of graphic analogies of concepts in chemistry on learning and attitude. *Journal of Educational Psychology*, 1976, *68*, 305–311.

Ritchey, G. H., & Beal, C. R. Image detail and recall: Evidence for within-item elaboration. *Journal of Experimental Psychology: Human Learning and Memory*, 1980, *6*, 66–76.

Rosinski, R. R., Golinkoff, R. M., & Kukish, K. S. Automatic semantic processing in a picture-word interference task. *Child Development*, 1975, *46*, 247–253.

Royer, J. M., & Cable, G. W. Illustrations, analogies, and facilitative transfer in prose learning. *Journal of Educational Psychology*, 1976, *68*, 205–209.

Rusted, J., & Coltheart, M. Facilitation of children's prose recall by the presence of pictures. *Memory & Cognition*, 1979, *7*, 354–359.

Samuels, S. J. Attentional process in reading: The effect of pictures on the acquisition of reading responses. *Journal of Educational Psychology*, 1967, *6*, 337–342.

Samuels, S. J. Effects of pictures on learning to read, comprehension and attitudes. *Review of Educational Research*, 1970, *40*, 397–407.

Schallert, D. L. The role of illustrations in reading comprehension. In R. J. Spiro, B. C. Bruce, & W. F. Brewer (Eds.), *Theoretical issues in reading comprehension: Perspectives from cognitive psychology, linguistics, artificial intelligence, and education*. Hillsdale, NJ: Erlbaum, 1980.

Shriberg, L. K., Levin, J. R., McCormick, C. B., & Pressley, M. Learning about "famous" people via the keyword method. *Journal of Educational Psychology*, 1982, *74*, 238–247.

Singer, H., Samuels, S. J., & Spiroff, J. The effect of pictures and contextual conditions on learning responses to printed words. *Reading Research Quarterly*, 1973/74, *9*, 555–567.

Stone, D. E., & Glock, M. D. How do young adults read directions with and without pictures? *Journal of Educational Psychology*, 1981, *73*, 419–426.

Taylor, A. M., & Turnure, J. E. Imagery and verbal elaboration with retarded children: Effects on learning and memory. In N. R. Ellis (Ed.), *Handbook of mental deficiency, psychological theory, and research*. Hillsdale, NJ: Erlbaum, 1979.

Webber, N. E. Pictures and words as stimuli in learning foreign language responses. *The Journal of Psychology*, 1978, *98*, 57–63.

Willows, D. M. A picture is not always worth a thousand words: Pictures as distractors in reading. *Journal of Educational Psychology*, 1978, *70*, 255–262.

Worden, P. E. Memory strategy instruction with the learning disabled. In M. Pressley & J. R. Levin (Eds.), *Cognitive strategy research: Psychological foundations*. New York: Springer-Verlag, 1983.

9. Making Meaningful Materials Easier to Learn: Lessons from Cognitive Strategy Research

Michael Pressley

By this point in the volume, it should be apparent that cognitive psychologists (and more specifically, the authors contributing to this book) are bullish on the position that use of strategies can increase learning. Nonetheless, it should also be obvious that learners (especially children) do not always use cognitive strategies that they could use, and that sometimes strategy usage is difficult even when strategy usage instructions are provided. That does not mean, however, that when learners cannot or do not execute strategies, cognitive strategy researchers have nothing to offer. In fact, cognitive strategy research includes a plethora of data on how to modify materials so that they are easier to comprehend and learn. In this chapter that research will be selectively reviewed.

The principal concern in the chapter is with children's processing of meaningful materials including prose, television programs, and oral communication. The focus on these types of materials follows from my own research interests, as well as an awareness that much of cognitive psychology in recent years has been conducted in these content areas. However, readers should not assume that materials modifications recommendations based on cognitive research are limited to these domains. I hope that by explicating the relevance of cognitive research to materials development in the areas considered here, I will stimulate researchers with other substantive interests to reexamine research in their own problem areas with an eye toward materials development.

Learning Materials and Research

Well-intentioned educators and curriculum specialists have made many suggestions as to how to modify materials. One need only peruse any of a number of methods textbooks in language arts in order to generate a lengthy list of comments about how to prepare materials. Despite this large volume of suggestions, and even though publishers are constantly revising materials that are presented to children (e.g., Willows, Borwick, & Hayvren, 1981), evidence that materials modifications positively affect children's learning is scant (e.g., Levin & Pressley, 1981; Pressley, Levin, Kuiper, Bryant, & Michener, 1982). The research literature that does exist does little to inspire confidence in the wisdom of the armchair educator-analysts. For instance, many classroom tried and true vocabulary-learning techniques are no more effective than what learners do spontaneously (Levin, McCormick, Miller, Berry, & Pressley, 1982; Pressley, Levin, & Miller, 1982; Pressley, Levin, Kuiper, Bryant, & Michener, 1982). Moreover, in these same studies it has been demonstrated that techniques derived from conventional wisdom are impotent compared to alternatives based on cognitive learning approaches to vocabulary instruction. Such empirical failures reinforce the impression that many materials recommendations in the curriculum literature are probably wrong.

That would not be so bad if children's learning of meaningful materials were proceeding smoothly. For readers uninitiated into the deficiencies evidenced and problems encountered by children during meaningful learning, the examples cited in this chapter are convincing evidence that learning of meaningful materials can often run amok. More promising is that cognitive psychological research has provided some remedies for these failures. I contend that now is the time to begin research aimed at translating findings buried in the pages of scholarly journals into the materials that are presented in school, on television, and at home.

Children's Cognitive Deficiencies and Materials Modification

Why is it necessary to attend carefully to the materials presented to children and to modify those materials more than the ones prepared for adult consumption? The principal reason is that children exhibit processing deficiencies that adults do not. I will concretize this point with three well-substantiated deficiencies in children that can be alleviated through materials modification:

1. Children are less able to deal with poorly structured, illogical, and ambiguous materials than are adults.
2. Children are not as capable of going beyond the information given and deriving inferences from input.
3. Children are not as adept at using strategies when working with meaningful materials.

For each of these three deficiencies, materials compensations can be derived from the cognitive learning and development literatures. The discussion in this chapter will revolve around these three deficiencies and what can be done to "cure" them.

It must be pointed out that given the space limitations of a single chapter, it is not possible to deal exhaustively with the deficiencies taken up here. For each of the three problem areas, however, two subproblems are discussed, and each subproblem is illustrated with examples from the literature. Throughout the presentation, materials suggestions that follow from the problems and data cited are highlighted. The composite of sample evidence presented here is a portrait of compelling support for the main theme of this paper: Cognitive strategy research should be a guiding force in revamping curriculum research and the curriculum enterprise.

Children's Performance with Inadequate Materials

Structural Failures of Materials. Investigators in recent years have been able to document that meaningful materials have "conventional structure that is familiar to the general reader" (Kintsch & Greene, 1978, p. 1). Indeed, much effort has been expended on determining the specifics of those structures, with competing alternatives proposed such as story grammars (Stein & Glenn, 1979), script-based theories (Bower, Black, & Turner, 1979), and text hierarchies (Meyer, 1975). (Chapter 4 of this volume provides additional input about text structure.) In the present context discussion will be limited, however, to the case of stories. Additionally, the studies most relevant to the points we want to make were conceived within story grammar frameworks, and thus the materials considered here are limited even more. Finally, although there are differences in the story grammars that have been proposed (e.g., Mandler & Johnson, 1977; Rumelhart, 1975; Stein & Glenn, 1979), the commonalities among the models are far greater than the differences, and so it is not necessary in this brief section to differentiate the assumptions and structures of the various models.

Consider the simple two-episode story from Mandler (1978), presented here in Table 9-1. The story grammar structure underlying this story consists of a setting and an event structure, with the event structure further decomposable into episodes 1 and 2. Each episode consists of a beginning, reaction, attempt, outcome, and ending in that order. Mandler contends that many two-episode stories consist basically of a setting followed by one episode and then another episode. Most people implicitly "know" this, and hence they expect two-episode stories to have this structure. Most important for the present discussion is that story grammar advocates (including Mandler) posit that knowledge of story grammar structure guides retrieval. Thus, stories that are well structured should be congruent with the expectations and retrieval strategies of learners, and thus more memorable. Mandler tested these theoretical positions.

In Mandler's (1978) study, half of the subjects listened to the story at the top of Table 9-1, which is presented in the optimal order according to Mandler and Johnson's (1977) conception of story grammar. The rest of the subjects were presented an interleaved version of the two-episode story, presented at the bottom in Table 9-1. This version was perfectly sensible, although it violated the optimal ordering of information according to the grammar. The recall of the story by Grade 2, Grade 4, Grade 6, and college students was assessed 24 hours after the initial presentation. The structure of the stories affected recall. Although at the Grade 2 and college levels the amount correctly remembered did not differ between the two

Table 9-1 An Example of a Standard and an Interleaved Story Used by Mandler

Standard version

Setting	Once there were twins, Tom and Jennifer, who had so much trouble their parents called them the unlucky twins.
Beginning 1	One day, Jennifer's parents gave her a dollar bill to buy the turtle she wanted but on the way to the pet store she lost it.
Reaction 1	Jennifer was worried that her parents would be angry with her so she decided to search every bit of the sidewalk where she had walked.
Attempt 1	She looked in all the cracks and in the grass along the way.
Outcome 1	She finally found the dollar bill in the grass.
Ending 1	But when Jennifer got to the store, the petstore man told her that someone else had just bought the last turtle, and he didn't have any more.
Beginning 2	The same day, Tom fell off a swing and broke his leg.
Reaction 2	He wanted to run and play with the other kids.
Attempt 2	So he got the kids to pull him around in his wagon.
Outcome 2	While they were playing, Tom fell out of the wagon and broke his arm.
Ending 2	Tom's parents said he was even unluckier than Jennifer and made him stay in bed until he got well.

Interleaved version

Setting	Once there were twins, Tom and Jennifer, who had so much trouble their parents called them the unlucky twins.
Beginning 1	One day, Jennifer's parents gave her a dollar bill to buy the turtle she wanted, but on the way to the pet store she lost it.
Beginning 2	The same day, Tom fell off a swing and broke his leg.
Reaction 1	Jennifer was worried that her parents would be angry with her, so she decided to search every bit of the sidewalk where she had walked.
Reaction 2	Tom wanted to run and play with the other kids.
Attempt 1	Jennifer looked in all the cracks and in the grass along the way.
Attempt 2	Tom got the kids to pull him around in his wagon.
Outcome 1	Jennifer finally found the dollar bill in the grass.
Outcome 2	While the kids were playing, Tom fell out of the wagon and broke his arm.
Ending 1	But when Jennifer got to the store, the petstore man told her that someone had just bought the last turtle, and he didn't have any more.
Ending 2	Tom's parents said he was even unluckier than Jennifer, and made him stay in bed until he got well.

Note. Adapted from "A code in the node: The use of a story schema in retrieval," by J. M. Mandler, *Discourse Processes*, 1978, *1*, Table 1, p. 22. Copyright 1978 by Ablex Publishing Corporation. Adapted by permission.

presentations, there were differences in favor of standard story recall at the Grade 4 and Grade 6 levels. At all age levels there were more distortions with the interleaved version of the story than with the standard version.

Mandler's (1978) report of memory impairment when materials violate story grammar assumptions is not isolated. For example, with adults as subjects, Stein and Nezworski (1978) and Kintsch, Mandel, and Kozminsky (1977) also reported reduced recall of unconventionally structured stories relative to that of conventionally structured presentations. In a study by Brown and Murphy (1975), children's recall of picture sequences depended very much on whether they were presented in a logical order versus an arbitrary order, and recall of televised information is definitely decremented when stories are presented in unnatural orders (e.g., Collins, Wellman, Keniston, & Westby, 1978).

The message seems clear. Creators of meaningful materials should do all that they can to assure that stories presented to children are well structured. This seems to be all the more true when one considers that adults can fairly easily execute cognitive manipulations that improve recall of poorly structured stories, but children are not as able to do so, as illustrated by recently reported results.

Stein and Nezworski (1978) presented adult learners with one of four types of stories. In the well-formed stories condition, subjects heard stories containing the six categories included in Stein and Glenn's (1979) grammar in the order that those authors proposed as optimal. (See Table 9-2 for an illustration.) In the slightly disordered story condition, subjects were presented the same stories that well-formed story subjects heard, except that the consequence statements were placed immediately after the initiating-event statements. Randomly ordered stories (in which the sentences were presented in random order) were presented to one fourth of the subjects. In a fourth condition, subjects were presented unrelated statements.

Shortly after learning the stories, subjects were asked to recall them under one of two instructional sets. Half of the subjects were asked to recall the sentences of the stories in the exact order of presentation. The rest were instructed "to recall the text information in the form of a 'good, coherent story,'" while recalling as much of the semantic information as possible. This instruction was hypothesized to activate subjects' story grammar knowledge, and to thus induce subjects to use that schema to guide recall.

The recall levels in the four story-organization conditions ordered in the same way for each instructional set. Well-formed stories subjects recalled more propositions from the stories than did slightly disordered stories subjects, who recalled more than subjects in the randomly ordered stories condition. Recall of unrelated statements subjects was lowest of all. The most important result was that the recall of randomly ordered stories subjects was significantly enhanced by the "make-a-story" instruction, to the point of not being significantly different from the level of slightly disordered subjects, although still slightly lower. That is, the make-a-story instruction had very little impact on recall in the well-formed and slightly disordered conditions, but substantially increased recall in the randomly ordered stories condition. Mathews, Yussen, and Evans (Note 1) have succeeded in replicating with adults the main results reported by Stein and Nezworski. In another study, Yussen's re-

Table 9-2 Categories in a Simple Story According to Stein and an Example of a
Well-Formed Story

	Categories included in a simple story
1. Setting	Introduction of the protagonist; can contain information about physical, social, or temporal context in which the remainder of the story occurs.
2. Initiating event	An action, an internal event, or a natural occurrence which serves to *initiate* or to cause a response in the protagonist.
3. Internal response	An emotion, cognition, or goal of the protagonist.
4. Attempt	An overt action to obtain the protagonist's goal.
5. Consequence	An event, action, or endstate which marks the attainment or nonattainment of the protagonist's goal.
6. Reaction	An emotion, cognition, action or endstate expressing the protagonist's feelings about his goal attainment or relating the broader consequential realm of the protagonist's goal attainment.

	Example of a well-formed story
Setting	1. Once there was a big gray fish named Albert 2. who lived in a big icy pond near the edge of a forest.
Initiating event	3. One day, Albert was swimming around the pond 4. when he spotted a big juicy worm on top of the water.
Internal response	5. Albert knew how delicious worms tasted 6. and wanted to eat that one for his dinner.
Attempt	7. So he swam very close to the worm 8. and bit into him.
Consequence	9. Suddenly, Albert was pulled through the water into a boat. 10. He had been caught by a fisherman.
Reaction	11. Albert felt sad 12. and wished he had been more careful.

Note. Adapted from "The effects of organization and instructional set on story memory," by
N. L. Stein and T. Nezworski, *Discourse Processes,* 1978, *1,* Table 1, p. 182. Copyright 1978
by Ablex Publishing Corporation. Adapted by permission.

search group has extended research on the reordering strategy to much younger
subjects.

Buss, Yussen, Mathews, Miller, and Rembold (in press) were pessimistic that
children could gainfully employ the make-a-story strategy, since in other cognitive
domains children experience difficulty internally manipulating cognitive contents
that they have learned (e.g., Salatas & Flavell, 1976). The Grade 2, Grade 6, and
adult subjects in the study were aurally presented stories similar to those used by
Stein and Nezworski (1978), with half of the subjects presented well-ordered stories
and the rest receiving randomly ordered ones. Subjects were evenly divided in each

condition between those instructed to recall the stories exactly as presented and those given a make-a-story instruction, with recall following a few minutes after the initial presentation of the stories.

At the adult level Buss et al. (in press) once again replicated the Stein and Nezworski (1978) result. As expected, the children's total recall from the randomly ordered texts was not affected by the make-a-story instruction. See Mandler and DeForest (1979) for additional evidence that children have difficulty reordering story content at recall. Also, Yussen, Mathews, Buss, and Kane (1980) have been able to show that children do not even know which aspects of a story are most crucial to its structure, which logically must be known before such knowledge could be used to rearrange poorly structured prose.

Because children's learning can be affected pejoratively by nonoptimal organization, it is incumbent on producers of children's materials to generate well-structured presentations. The story grammar advocates (e.g., Mandler & Johnson, 1977; Stein & Glenn, 1979) present many potentially useful recommendations, although it must also be admitted that there are valid criticisms of the story grammars. For instance, the grammars do not accommodate all types of stories. Also, they fit some prose passages that are not really stories. In addition, some contend that story grammars focus too much on the surface structure of the stories and fail to attend to the more psychologically meaningful "deep" structure and that predictions of story grammars cannot be discriminated from the predictions of semantic theories (e.g., Black & Wilensky, 1979; Bower et al., 1979; Graesser, 1981; Johnson & Mandler, 1980). However, I tend to agree with Graesser's (1981) summary following his balanced review of the strengths and weaknesses of story grammars: "The story grammar approach has clearly uncovered and articulated some important regularities that stories possess" (p. 16). The recall evidence reviewed here documents that incorporating those regularities into children's stories makes a difference in their memory of prose. This should be more than sufficient motivation for creators of such materials to examine their fare for story-grammatical integrity.

In addition to the advances proceeding from the work within story grammar frameworks, other approaches to prose study and analysis are also yielding empirically defensible strategies for constructing prose passages that are more memorable, especially for the case of expository prose. Although it is not possible to review that evidence here, see Aulls (1975), Danner (1976), and Kieras (1978, 1980, 1981) for good examples of work in this tradition, as well as articles by Meyer (1977) and Goetz and Armbruster (1980) for more general commentary.

Illogic and Ambiguity in Meaningful Presentations. What happens when children are given incorrect, illogical, and/or ambiguous information? In recent years researchers interested in referential communication, comprehension monitoring, and reading have studied children's reactions to imperfect messages. One conclusion that emerges from such research is that young children (e.g., 4- to 10-year-olds) often accept inadequate information as perfectly good communication, with this deficiency being more pronounced the younger the child (e.g., Patterson, O'Brien, Kister, Carter, & Kotsonis, 1981; Singer & Flavell, 1981; Chapter 2 in this volume).

I will discuss two lines of research to illustrate the methods used, as well as the deficiencies observed in the children. In these illustrative studies, children were presented materials that were grossly deficient in ways that would be obvious to most adults. In each case the child participants often failed to note the inadequacies of the presentations.

Markman (1977, 1979, 1981) conducted a series of studies in which she presented to children paragraphs that contained blatantly contradictory pieces of information. Consider one such story (Markman, 1979):

> One of the things that children like to eat everywhere in the world is ice cream. Some ice cream stores sell many different flavors of ice cream, but the most popular flavors are chocolate and vanilla. Lots of different kinds of desserts can be made with ice cream. Some fancy restaurants serve a special dessert made out of ice cream called Baked Alaska. To make it they put the ice cream in a very hot oven. The ice cream in Baked Alaska melts when it gets that hot. Then they take the ice cream out of the oven and serve it right away. When they make Baked Alaska, the ice cream stays firm and does not melt. (p. 646)

The studies conducted by Markman have involved children spanning the entire range of the elementary school years. The consistent finding has been that children often fail to detect inconsistencies. Markman (1977, 1979, 1981; Markman & Gorin, 1981) argues that these failures occur because children do not adequately monitor whether they are understanding a message and whether the message makes sense. Of course, there are alternative explanations for the problems the children experience, for the Markman-type task often requires a complex information processing sequence and sophisticated world knowledge. That is, students must hold information in memory and make a decision about logicity. In order to make such a decision, it is often helpful to possess prior knowledge about the topics of the passage (e.g., what Baked Alaska looks like when it is served in a restaurant). Thus, at present it is not clear why children fail on such problems, but the evidence is overwhelming that they do.

Evidence provided by Flavell, Speer, Green, and August (1981) largely substantiates Markman's claims and demonstrates that children can fail to realize the inadequacy of a message even when confronted with very tangible hints that the message is flawed. In the Flavell et al. (1981) study children listened to tape recordings of a little girl explaining how to build block houses. The kindergarten and Grade 3 listeners were instructed to build houses just like the ones described by the speaker. The only problem was that the directions often did not contain enough information for the listener to carry out the instruction or were otherwise confusing.

For instance, at one point children were confronted with a square red block, a smaller circular yellow block, and a yellow tray. They were given the impossible instruction, "Put the red block on top of the square block." On another occasion, the children were presented with a red, a blue, and a yellow cube and the incomplete instruction, "Put the three blocks together to make a house." A number of nonverbal (e.g., puzzled facial expressions; motor expressions of confusion) and verbal signs of problem detection were monitored. In general, Grade 2 children were more likely to indicate that the instructions were inadequate than were the kindergarten children, although detection at the Grade 2 level was far from perfect. The bottom line for the present discussion was that many children proceeded to carry out these inadequate instructions as if nothing were wrong.

In an interesting follow-up study, Beal and Flavell (1982) showed that even when children were forced to realize that they did not succeed in constructing a well-matched building, they expressed the belief that the instructions presented to them had been adequate. The authors went so far as to show subjects that the instructions were indeterminate enough so that several buildings could be constructed from the instructions as given, and still the kindergarten subjects indicated that the speaker did a good job of telling them how to make a building just like the speaker's building. In reading these research reports, one is constantly reminded of the proverbial soul who did not know enough to come in out of the rain. We cannot depend on children to seek clarification when they are presented with vague, inaccurate, or inadequate input. For readers who need convincing that such failures are not tied exclusively to the laboratory situations investigated by Markman and Flavell, see Anderson, Lorch, Field, and Sanders's (1981) data on children's responses to random television sequences or Meissner's (1978) work on concept identification.

There are several recent developments that are heartening with respect to children's comprehension monitoring. Even though young children may not be able to or do not verbalize that material is inadequate, nonverbal indicators (e.g., body movement, response latency, signs of confusion) suggest that with some types of inadequate messages, even 4- to 5-year-olds monitor somewhat the inadequacies of the communications (Beal & Flavell, 1982; Patterson, Cosgrove, & O'Brien, 1980). Also, it has proven possible to train children to increase their comprehension monitoring (e.g., Cosgrove & Patterson, 1977, 1978; Flavell et al., 1981; Markman & Gorin, 1981; Patterson & Kister, 1981; Chapter 2 in this volume). Nonetheless, that meaningful materials are usually presented without such training suggests that other more direct interventions are necessary.

In the best of all possible worlds, producers of meaningful materials would always turn out unambiguous and accurate materials, and certainly that is a goal to strive for. Realistically, however, we can expect that sometimes materials and/or communications will not contain enough information or will be misleading in critical ways. One strategy that materials producers could adopt to increase the likelihood that children would detect inadequacies when they occur is consistent with many of my previous recommendations for increasing children's awareness of prose content. Meaningful presentations can be supplemented with pictures that explicitly convey the meanings that the authors intended. The results of a recent study support the position that pictorial accompaniments can aid in detecting ambiguities.

Pratt and Bates (1982) presented preschool children with 12 short passages about toys and presents given to particular children. Each message was followed by a question, with four of the questions having unambiguous answers and eight of them being ambiguous. One item was "Bobby got a red ball for Christmas, and Danny got a blue ball. Which one got the ball, Bobby or Danny?" Of course, this item's question was ambiguous. For each subject half of the items were illustrated with pictures and half were not, with appropriate counterbalancing employed in the study. Thus, the picture for the foregoing sentence showed two boys holding balls, one blue and one red.

The subjects were told that they were "playing a 'story game' and that some of the stories had 'bad' questions made up to try to trick them. If the question was a good one, they were instructed to answer it." If not, they were to say so and explain why it was not good. More ambiguities were detected when pictures accompanied the messages than when they did not. This result is consistent with outcomes obtained in a number of studies that show that comprehension of meaningful materials is increased by pictorial accompaniment (e.g., Levin & Lesgold, 1978).

Although a variety of mechanisms are probably implicated in picture-prose effects (e.g., dual coding, repetition effects; see Levin, 1981a; Levin & Lesgold, 1978), Pratt and Bates speculated that the effects obtained in their study were possibly because the presence of the pictures reduced the processing load of subjects faced with the task of evaluating the question against the sentence content. This interpretation is consistent with general models of communication that posit that success is more likely when processing load is minimized (e.g., Shatz, 1977), as well as with models of general cognitive functioning that contain the same theme (e.g., Case, 1980; LaBerge & Samuels, 1974). Other data (Patterson et al., 1981) are also consistent with the position that comprehension monitoring in children is better when the processing load is lighter rather than heavier. Regardless of the precise reason that pictures produce enhanced monitoring, the fact that they do increases confidence in the recommendation that interventions derived from cognitive research should be exploited by curriculum designers.

Going Beyond the Information Given

Inferential Failures with Simple Stories. During the 1970s researchers attempted to plot out the developing child's ability to "go beyond the information given" (Bruner, Olver, & Greenfield, 1966) and make simple inferences. Although different research paradigms and different types of materials were used in the various studies on the problem, the paradigm employed in an early study on children's inferences (Paris & Mahoney, 1974) illustrates the general method of workers in this tradition. For example, at initial presentation a subject would hear:

> The bird is inside the cage. (premise)
> The cage is under the table. (premise)
> The bird is yellow. (filler)

Then, at testing they would be presented with the following items:

> The bird is inside the cage. (true premise)
> The cage is over the table. (false premise)
> The bird is under the table. (true inference)
> The bird is on top of the table. (false inference)

The most important result of studies of this type was that at testing subjects would mistake true inferences for sentences that had actually occurred during the original presentation. This was interpreted as evidence of subjects' making spontaneous inferences during their encounters with text. One of the most important findings was that spontaneous inferencing increases with age during the grade school years (e.g., Collins et al., 1978; Omanson, Warren, & Trabasso, 1978; Paris & Upton, 1976; Schmidt, Paris, & Stober, 1979).[1]

There is a signal here for curriculum specialists. If knowing a particular piece of information is important, the materials producer should not rely heavily on the inferential capabilities of the young learner. One possible intervention is to modify the materials so that the probability of making a correct inference is increased. This approach has been taken in several laboratories, and we will now turn to examples of such materials research.

Wagner and Rohwer (1981) presented eight short paragraphs to preadolescents (Grade 5 students) and late adolescents (Grade 11 students). Subjects were presented either baseline paragraphs or augmented ones (see Table 9-3). In the baseline paragraph the most important information was contained in the third, fourth, and fifth sentences. These sentences contained premises from which inferences could be derived. The augmented version of the story also contained these premises but included two additional sentences as well as an altered final sentence. The additional sentences and alteration were intended to highlight the dimension on which the items were to be compared. Subsequent to the presentation of the stories, subjects were given a test on both premise items and possible inferences from those premises (see Table 9-3).

The recall of premise information was comparable for preadolescents and late adolescents in both augmented and baseline conditions. Thus, differences in inferences between age and/or conditions could not be due simply to differences in memory of the original premises (Trabasso & Nicholas, 1980). At the preadolescent level, the inference level of baseline subjects was lower than the inference level of subjects given the augmented paragraphs. Preadolescent subjects in the augmented condition answered the inference questions at the same level as the late adolescents. The inference level of augmented and baseline subjects did not differ among the adolescents. It was possible through materials modifications to increase inference scores of Grade 5 children to the level of late high school students. All that was required was more explicit structure in the text (see Pressley, 1982; Pressley, Levin, & Bryant, 1983).

At the same time, it must be noted that the inference test performance never exceeded 57% correct in any condition of Wagner and Rohwer's (1981) study, which suggests that even more drastic interventions might have been helpful. One that is consistent with the present theme of adding structure to materials is to move

---

[1] Unfortunately, the inference paradigm as specified here frequently did not produce unambiguously interpretable results, as Trabasso and Nicholas (1980) pointed out in their thorough critique. For example, it is difficult to determine if inferences occur during study or testing. Readers are referred to the Trabasso and Nicholas (1980) chapter for a discussion of critical problems with the paradigm. We do not concern readers further with these difficulties, because the relevant point for the present discussion is that younger children are less likely than older children and adults to know information that was only implied in text. This point does not seem to be debatable.

Table 9-3 Baseline and Augmented Paragraphs, and Premise and Inference Test Sentences Used by Wagner and Rohwer

<hr>

Paragraphs

Baseline

This story is about a boy named Bill who often played at a pond.

One day, he needed a part for his toy boat.

He searched his pockets and found a coin, nail, and ring.

The ring weighed less than the coin.

The ring sank faster than the nail.

Bill tied one of the things to his toy boat.

Augmented

This story is about a boy named Bill who often played at a pond.

One day, he needed a part for his toy boat.

He searched his pockets and found a coin, nail, and ring.

Since he needed an anchor for his boat, he decided to use the heaviest object.

To find out which one this was, Bill compared how fast the objects sank.

The ring weighed less than the coin.

The ring sank faster than the nail.

Bill tied the heaviest object to his toy boat.

Test sentences

Premise

The _____ (ring, coin, nail) was lighter than the _____ .

The _____ (ring, coin, nail) weighed more than the _____ .

The _____ (ring, coin, nail) would sink more quickly than the _____ .

The _____ (ring, coin, nail) would sink more slowly than the _____ .

Inference

The _____ (ring, coin, nail) would sink more quickly than the others.

The _____ (ring, coin, nail) would sink more slowly than the others.

<hr>

Note. Adapted from "Age differences in the elaboration of inferences from text," by M. Wagner and W. D. Rohwer, Jr., *Journal of Educational Psychology*, 1981, *73*, Table 1, p. 731. Copyright 1981 by the American Psychological Association. Adapted by permission of the author.

the "implied" information from the realm of the implied into the category of explicit information. This approach was successfully demonstrated in a recent study by Johnson and Smith (1981).

Subjects in the Johnson and Smith (1981) study read a long fictional narrative about a town with a border and a border guard. Included in the story were premise statements. For instance, one set of premises was, "You could only get into the town if you had a ticket. Since the town was so small, everyone could visit it only once a year." For subjects in the story-implicit condition, the inference "Everyone only got one ticket to town a year" was left for the reader to make. In the story-explicit condition, the "inference" was explicitly stated in the text after presentation of the inferences. On a subsequent test of the implied information, both Grade

3 and Grade 5 participants performed better in the story-explicit condition than in the story-implicit condition. Based on Johnson and Smith's (1981) findings, we would conclude that when children are the learners, explicit presentation is more likely to lead to learning of implied information than is leaving that information to inference.

Notably, Collins, Sobol, and Westby (1981) have obtained the same effect as Johnson and Smith (1981) when Grade 2 children's viewing of televised dramatic material was explicitly supplemented by inferential comments by an adult coviewer. Collins et al.'s (1981) study is a good example of how such supplements can be subtly added to materials and yet have a substantial effect on the learning of otherwise implied information. See Collins and Wiens (1983) for additional commentary.

Other materials modifications that affect children's performance are also being tested. There is some evidence that juxtaposing premise statements in text, rather than separating them, increases the likelihood that correct inferences will be made (e.g., Johnson & Smith, 1981; Walker & Meyer, 1980). Also, making premise statements high in importance in a passage increases the likelihood that correct inferences will be made about them (e.g., Goetz, 1979). Inferences are more likely in stories that are intact in a story grammar sense (e.g., Omanson et al., 1978). Finally, inferences are more likely if materials are structured so as to be compatible with world knowledge the child already possesses (e.g., Hildyard, 1979; Newcomb & Collins, 1979; Small & Butterworth, 1981).

The conclusion that emerges from all of the research discussed in this section is that inferences should be made as obvious as possible in materials presented to children if we want them to acquire the implicit information. Children are not as capable as adults at reading between the lines, and the look of competence in children's inferential behaviors can easily be influenced by materials differences. I will continue to develop this theme with reference to a historically prominent problem of inference in developmental psychology.

Inferences During Moral Judgments. In recent reviews Grueneich (1982) and Stein and Trabasso (1982) exhaustively analyzed the various components involved in children's understanding and reaction to one particular class of prose materials, namely, moral dilemma stories. Many, many suggestions were made in those articles about how prose structure might influence children's inferences about the moral levels of actors in the stories. Unfortunately, only a few of those structural issues can be taken up here. Readers are referred to Grueneich's and Stein and Trabasso's papers for stimulating discussions of additional factors affecting children's moral inferences.

Consider the following moral dilemma story, which was used by Piaget (1932) and which is typical of moral dilemmas included in moral judgment research studies:

> Once there was a little boy whose name was Henry. One day when his mother was out he tried to get some jam out of the cupboard. He climbed up on a chair and stretched out his arm. But the jam was too high up and he couldn't reach it and have any. But while he was trying to get it he knocked over a cup. The cup fell down and broke. (p. 122)

In the Piagetian studies children were required to make judgments about the actors in stories such as this one. Typically, participants were presented with two such stories and had to decide which of the two protagonists of the stories was naughtier—an inference, since the relative naughtiness of the actors was never explicitly addressed. The classic finding is that very young children (e.g., 4- and 5-year-olds) base their judgments on the consequences of the behaviors (i.e., the naughtier actor is the one who did the most damage), whereas slightly older children (e.g., 10-year-olds) base their judgments on the actors' intentions (i.e., the less well-intentioned actor was judged naughtier).

In Piaget's stories, however, information about intentions was always reported before the consequences, and thus order and content were completely confounded. This confounding prompted a number of investigations in which the order of intentions and consequences was systematically varied. The results of these studies are very consistent. Children between the ages of 4 and 7 base their evaluations on the most recently encountered information (Austin, Ruble, & Trabasso, 1977; Feldman, Klosson, Parsons, Rholes, & Ruble, 1976; Nummedal & Bass, 1976; Parsons, Ruble, Klosson, Feldman, & Rholes, 1976). The order of presentation also affects the evaluations of older children (8- to 9-year-olds), but its impact is much less pronounced than with the younger children (Feldman et al., 1976).

Investigators have explored two other ways of modifying moral stories so as to increase the likelihood that young children will use intentionality in making moral inferences. Both of these procedures are similar to ones used to increase comprehension, inference, and memory in studies discussed in other sections of this chapter. They will be illustrated through discussion of prominent examples of the two approaches.

Bearison and Isaacs (1975) tested the possibility that if the intentions of the actors were made more explicit than was the case in the Piaget stories, use of intentional information might increase. In their experiment, children 6–7 years of age were assigned to one of three conditions, presented with pairs of moral dilemmas, and given the task of deciding which of the two actors was naughtier. Control subjects were presented with stories similar in format to those used by Piaget. In the intentions-explicit condition, the intentions were specified during the presentation of the stories through the addition of statements in the stories about the actors' intentions. Intentions-asked subjects were presented with stories similar to Piaget's except that questions about actors' intentions were added at the end of the stories. Subjects in both the intentions-explicit and intentions-asked conditions were more likely than control subjects to base their naughtiness ratings on the actors' intentions than on the consequences, with the effect being more pronounced in the intentions-explicit condition. Brody and Henderson (1977) provided data that essentially replicated Bearison and Isaacs's (1975) intentions-explicit finding. Thus, what is processed from moral stories varies with the explicitness of the presentation.

It has also been proposed that more concrete modes of moral dilemma presentation would increase the likelihood of more mature judgments, a proposal consistent with data substantiating that concrete presentation of prose increases comprehension (e.g., Levin, 1976; Paivio & Begg, 1981). Chandler, Greenspan, and Barenboim

(1973) investigated the possibility with 6- to 7-year-old children. The children were presented with two moral dilemmas in either the traditional verbal format or as videotaped plays. In preparing the videotapes, care was taken to guarantee the comparability of the tapes with the stories. The information was presented in the intentions-consequences order, with stories presented in pairs and subjects asked to judge the relative naughtiness of the actors. In judging naughtiness, subjects were much more likely to use intentionality information when the stories were presented in the videotape format. In addition, in one of her experiments, Nelson (1980) obtained findings similar to those of Chandler et al. (1973) with moral judgment stories presented in pictorial and verbal formats. Unfortunately, the Nelson study must be interpreted with extreme caution, since within her experiments there were failures to replicate effects that have been very robust in other studies of moral judgment. However, see Pryor, Rholes, Ruble, and Kriss (Note 2) for additional data substantiating that more concrete presentations are more effective for changing children's evaluative inferences than are less concrete materials.

The findings in the moral judgment studies reinforce the general conclusion that the structure of materials can dramatically affect children's performance. When one wants young children to consider the intentions of actors, it behooves the creators of such materials to present the information late in the prose or to make the intentionality information maximally explicit, either through additional verbalizations or concretizations.

Children's Inefficient Execution of Strategies

Young children sometimes have difficulty carrying out sophisticated strategies, even if given very complete instruction. In response to these problems, and following general recommendations in the cognitive literature (e.g., Case, 1980), researchers are investigating methods of supplementing presentations with adjunct aids that reduce the amount of information processing necessary to carry out a strategy (consider also Waters & Andreassen's, 1983, comments on the same point). Also, researchers have found that the learning gains associated with successful execution of strategies can often be obtained simply by providing to subjects the products of strategies—the cognitive mediators. Recent studies of imagery and picture effects on prose have employed both of these tactics. The about-to-be-discussed studies are good illustrations of how both types of work can be carried out.

Inducing Imagery in Children Under 7 Years of Age. During the 1970s a number of studies focused on the effects of providing pictures as supplements to children's prose processing. In general, the pictures in the study were redundant with the content of the prose they accompanied. The results of this work were positive, as evidenced by large learning gains for the very young children (5 to 7 years of age) who served as subjects (Levin & Lesgold, 1978). Concomitant with the research on picture effects on prose learning, a number of researchers attempted to induce imagery in children during prose learning (e.g., Kulhavy & Swenson, 1975; Lesgold, McCormick, & Golinkoff, 1975; Pressley, 1976; Rasco, Tennyson, & Boutwell,

1975). In general, with children older than 8 years of age, it was possible to obtain modest gains by means of instructions to use mental imagery (Pressley, 1976, 1977). Notably, the gains were not as large as with provided pictures, and the gains were not obtained with children as young.

Guttmann, Levin, and Pressley (1977) proposed that it might be possible to obtain imagery strategy gains with 5- to 7-year-old children by providing pictures partially depicting the content of stories and suggesting to children that they imagine in their partial picture all the elements of the story. In Guttmann et al.'s Experiment 2, children in all of the conditions heard a set of 14 unrelated sentences (e.g., "At the circus we saw a clown throw his hat way up into the air"). In the complete condition the subjects were shown a picture completely depicting the objects and events of the stories. In two partial picture conditions, subjects were shown pictures of only the subjects of the sentence-stories. When presented with the simple sentence just given, dynamic partial picture subjects saw a clown in the throwing position. Static partial picture subjects saw the clown standing upright with his hands at his side. Imagery subjects were given no pictures. Subjects in the imagery, dynamic partial picture, and static partial picture conditions were all given a simple imagery instruction to pretend that they could see a picture depicting the contents of the sentences.

After presentation of all 14 sentences, subjects were asked short-answer questions. Half of the questions required recall of the objects of the two sentences and half required recall of the subjects. Memory in the two partial picture conditions and the complete condition did not differ significantly, and recall in all three of those conditions exceeded recall in the imagery condition. The authors concluded that kindergarten and Grade 1 participants could execute a prose-imagery strategy if partial pictures were provided, a feat that does not occur without the partial picture accompaniments (e.g., Guttmann et al., 1977, Experiment 1).

Pressley, Pigott, and Bryant (1982) hypothesized that it might be possible to get partial picture effects with even younger children and without giving even a hint of an imagery instruction to them! They speculated that the presence of partial pictures (in conjunction with the verbal message) might give rise to "spontaneous" interactive images that are more complex than the pictures themselves.

In Pressley, Pigott, and Bryant's (1982) Experiment 1 nursery school children heard 25 sentences, much like the concrete sentences of Guttmann et al. (1977). In the sentence-only condition, the children heard the sentences without pictorial accompaniment. There were four conditions of interest in this context, and in each of these conditions pictures were presented simultaneously with the sentences. Children in the completely matched picture condition viewed pictures depicting the entire contents of the sentences (i.e., subjects and objects and their interactions). Children in the actor-action condition saw pictures like the dynamic partial pictures of Guttmann et al., whereas children in the actor-static condition saw pictures comparable to the static partial pictures of Guttmann et al. In the object-correct condition, children were shown pictures of the objects of the sentences. Children in all conditions were given the same instructions to remember the contents of the sentences, with no strategy instructions presented in any condition.

The results of Pressley, Pigott, and Bryant (1982, Experiment 1) can be summarized succinctly. Only recall in the completely matched picture condition significantly exceeded recall in the sentence-only condition. Thus, Experiment 1 produced no evidence that less than complete pictures could produce recall increments over those obtained with unillustrated sentences. However, the partial picture types included in Experiment 1 did not exhaust the possible variations of partial pictures.

Thus, a second experiment was conducted that included two additional partial picture conditions. Unlike the actor-action, actor-static, and object-correct conditions of Experiment 1 in which children were shown *either* the subject or object referent but not both, the children in the two partial picture conditions of Pressley, Pigott, and Bryant's (1982) Experiment 2 were shown pictures of *both* the subject and object referents. Subjects in the actor-action/object-correct condition were presented with the picture of the actor engaging in the action and a separate picture of the object. Actor-static/object-correct subjects were shown a picture of the subject in a static position and the picture of the correct object. The experiment also included a completely matched picture and a sentence-only condition.

The recall levels of children in the actor-action/object-correct and actor-static/object-correct conditions were very comparable and significantly exceeded recall of children in the sentence-only condition. Although the means in the actor-action/object-correct and actor-static/object-correct conditions did not differ significantly from recall in the completely matched picture condition, there were strong trends favoring recall of completely matched picture subjects.

The results of Pressley, Pigott, and Bryant's (1982) Experiments 1 and 2 complemented each other nicely, and together allowed evaluation of alternative hypotheses about picture effects on sentence memory. Consider the results of Experiment 2: All three conditions that included pictures increased learning of the sentences. If just the data of that experiment were available, one could argue that the pictorial facilitation could have been due to simple dual coding of either the actors or the objects (or both) of the sentences. When combined with the data of Experiment 1, however, it is obvious that dual coding of neither the actors alone nor the objects alone was sufficient to promote sentence learning. One explanation seemed consistent with all of the data. When nursery school children are given depictions of subjects and objects of the sentences, they construct internal images containing the relationship specified by the verb of the sentence (see Pressley, Pigott, & Bryant, 1982, for an extended discussion, as well as comments by Digdon, Pressley, & Levin, Note 3).

Because of its potentially broad-based significance for models of children's imagery skills, work on this phenomenon is continuing at Western Ontario. For the present, however, the results of the Guttmann et al. (1977) and Pressley, Pigott, and Bryant (1982) studies suggest that materials can be supplemented to facilitate strategy execution. Work of this nature should be carried out whenever children appear not to be able to execute a strategy. From such work I would expect there to follow many practical insights, as well as theoretically valuable information concerning the boundaries of children's cognitive skills.

Providing Mediators. At the same time that I endorse designing materials so as to facilitate strategy execution, I do not dismiss the possibility of continuing to present fully developed mediators. There are mediators that have proven very effective when they are *provided* to learners, but it is not known at this time whether it will be possible to devise ways of instructing children to generate their own versions of these same mediators. Until such instruction becomes available (if it does at all), the most reasonable course seems to be to recommend that such mediators be explicitly presented. Again, the examples to illustrate this point are drawn from the imagery and pictures literature.

Despite many studies of picture and imagery effects with normal subjects (e.g., Bellezza, 1983; Pressley et al., 1983; Roberts, 1983; Chapter 7 in this volume), the literature on this topic with retarded subjects is extremely limited. What does exist offers little to support imagery generation as a prose-learning strategy that the retarded can use. However, providing pictures as prose accompaniments is helpful. A study conducted in Levin's laboratory substantiates these conclusions.

The EMR children in a study by Bender and Levin (1978) heard a concrete story and were subsequently asked short-answer questions about it. In the picture condition, subjects viewed pictures illustrating the complete content of the story. Imagery subjects were instructed to create internal images depicting the content. Control subjects received no strategy instructions. Recall of the story was greatly increased by provision of pictures, but no learning benefits resulted from the imagery intervention. Although researchers may eventually devise techniques that do produce imagery benefits for retardates learning prose, efforts to date, including partial picture conditions like the ones used in Guttmann et al.'s (1977) study (Wasserman, Note 4), have not been successful. Until successful imagery interventions are devised (if they are), I strongly recommend inclusion of complete pictures in prose presentations intended for retarded children, for the presence of such pictures can increase the prose learning of retarded children to a point close to that of normal children (Bender & Levin, 1978).

The pictures in the Bender and Levin (1978) study accurately illustrated the information exactly as presented in the prose. That is, they were representational pictures (Levin, 1981b). Levin and his colleagues have also begun to explore the role of another type of picture adjunct to prose, mnemonic pictures (see Levin, in press). With mnemonic pictures the prose material is somehow transformed in order to integrate it into a mnemonic-type representation. The resultant picture does not completely overlap the content of the prose, as will become evident in the subsequent discussion. Levin and his associates at Wisconsin have hypothesized that such pictures may be especially useful when learners are confronted with a large volume of information to learn, especially if there is conceptual overlap across prose presentations or subparts of a single presentation. In general, it has been possible to increase children's learning by providing such pictures (e.g., Levin, 1981a, 1981b; Shriberg, Levin, McCormick, & Pressley, 1982; Pressley, 1982; McCormick, Note 5). Parts of a recent study illustrate well the materials, procedures, and outcomes associated with studies of mnemonic-illustration effects on prose learning.

The eighth-grade subjects in the study by Levin, Shriberg, and Berry (in press) were presented, both visually and aurally, single paragraphs detailing the attributes of various fictional communities, as illustrated by this description of the town of Fostoria:

Fostoria has a lot to offer its people. People have *considerable wealth,* and everyone lives comfortably. Many of the townsfolk also become quite prosperous because the land has *abundant natural resources.* In addition, the town is especially well known for its *advances in technology,* for just about everything is run by computer. This progress has attracted many new residents, and statistics show *a growing population.*

The subjects studied the paragraph under an instruction to remember the places and features discussed in the passages.

The only learning aid provided to control subjects in this study was a page with the town name and its four attributes (i.e., the four points in italics in the passage) printed on it. Separate picture subjects were shown a page with each passage containing the town name and separate pictures of concrete symbols for each of the attributes of the town. For this example, a pile of money represented considerable wealth, an oil well concretized abundant natural resources, a computer terminal served as a symbol for advances in technology, and a crowd of people illustrated the growing population. Organized picture subjects saw the sample depictions for the four attributes, except that the four items were integrated into a meaningful picture (e.g., a crowd of people showing off their money as they watched a person sitting beside an oil well and working at a computer terminal).

In addition to the scene depicted in the organized picture condition, the organized keyword pictures contained a concrete referent of a keyword for the town's name (see Bellezza, 1983; Pressley et al., 1983; and Chapter 7 in this volume for discussion of the keyword method). Since *Fostoria* sounds something like *frost,* frost covered everything in the picture about Fostoria. Of course, subjects in the three picture conditions were advised of the relationships between the pictures and the prose, so that the pictures were interpretable to the learners. On the posttest, given shortly after the presentation of the to-be-learned materials, organized keyword picture subjects recalled many more attributes than did subjects in the other three conditions.

In general, experiments such as this one establish that mnemonic materials based on principles developed in the context of vocabulary learning (e.g., Chapter 7 in this volume) can be used to enhance some types of prose learning. It is not clear yet whether children would ever be able to produce such mediators for themselves, although work on this problem is proceeding in our laboratories. For the interim, the available data (Shriberg et al., 1982; McCormick, Note 5; Levin et al., in press) suggest that adjunct mnemonics can aid acquisition of "facts" from prose passages.

In general, we think that there is great potential demand for pictures designed for inclusion in prose. Recent investigations suggest many exciting possibilities, all of which induce processing of prose that would not have occurred without the pictorial accompaniments. In addition to the examples already discussed in this section, pictures have been shown to increase comprehension of prose when the text does not readily suggest schemata that children are knowledgeable about (e.g., Arnold & Brooks, 1976; Honeck, Sowry, & Voegtle, 1978; Chapter 4 in this volume)—see Levin and Pressley (1981) for a discussion. Illustrations have proven helpful for presenting technical material, especially information that is hard to express verbally (e.g., Stone & Glock, 1981). As a final example, moving pictorial accompaniments enhance learning of aspects of prose that static pictures do not and vice verse (Meringhoff, 1980). In short, many types of pictures increase cognitive gains from meaningful presentations.

General Discussion

If there is a theme that permeates discussions of children's reactions to meaningful materials, it is that these reactions can be understood only as products of a developing mind in interaction with a variably explicit world (e.g., Brown, 1978; Piaget & Inhelder, 1969). One of the biggest problems for that mind is that it often lacks knowledge that is helpful in dealing with messages that are not maximally explicit and well structured. As detailed here, it does not always know when a message is unclear or incomplete (Flavell et al., 1981; Markman, 1979). It does not always know how to restructure poorly structured messages (e.g., Buss et al., in press; Mandler & DeForest, 1979), even if it has the capacity to understand the structural deficiencies of the materials (e.g., Stevens, Note 6). It does not always know what to weigh into a decision (e.g., as with multifaceted moral judgment problems). It cannot always execute strategies that older learners can, as in the case of prose imagery (e.g., Guttmann et al., 1977).

A theme that my associates and I have reiterated is that it is possible to help the immature mind by presenting materials that are more concrete, more explicit, and more likely to trigger schemata that the child already knows (e.g., Levin, 1976, 1981a, 1981b; Levin & Pressley, 1981; Pressley, 1982; Pressley, Heisel, McCormick, & Nakamura, 1982). The assumption is that the less information processing required, the less likely that any structural or strategic factors can interfere with efficient execution (Levin, 1976). Virtually all of the recommendations given in this chapter are variants of this general prescription. The individual research efforts discussed here have resulted in increased understanding of when explicit structure and concretization is helpful or necessary and how such restructuring and illustration can be implemented. In short, what was reviewed here was a broad base of support for previous ideas about making materials for children more highly structured and more tightly tied to the concrete events of the world (e.g., Rohwer, 1973).

It might be added that many more examples could be cited of research results consistent with the position that increasing explicitness increases the likelihood of learning. For instance, basic math skills are more evident when problems are accompanied by concrete referents (e.g., Grunau, 1978) or when materials are made more explicit by eliminating vagueness (e.g., Smith & Cotten, 1980). A number of investigations have demonstrated that one method of making text more explicit and concrete, that of providing advance organizers, is especially effective in increasing comprehension of difficult and/or disorganized text (e.g., Beeson, 1981; Mayer, 1978; Royer & Cable, 1976; see also Chapter 4 in this volume). In a similar fashion, placing analogies into text increases learning (e.g., Hayes & Tierney, 1982). Interpretation of text can be increased by physical modifications that highlight the meaning of the text (e.g., italics, as in Pratt, Krane, & Kendall, 1981; and meaningful segmentation of text, as in Frase & Schwartz, 1979). The list could go on and on. Suffice to conclude that the explicitness framework developed here has general utility. I might also note that others have recently presented frameworks for understanding specific aspects of children's learning and cognition that contain elements of the explicitness proposals developed here (e.g., Brown & French, 1979; Day, 1983; Vygotsky, 1978; Waters & Andreassen, 1983).

Readers should not infer that the enthusiasm in this chapter for materials modification indicates a reduced concern for strategy training. There are, however, many occasions on which it is unrealistic to assume that youngsters will or can use strategies, at least given existing technologies for inducing those strategies. Although the quest for better strategies that can be used with younger and younger children will undoubtedly continue, I do not believe that children's learning and performance should be contingent on successes in research on strategy invention. To the extent that changes in materials can make up for deficiencies in the mind of the child, I believe that those changes should be made.

Implicit in this position is a view of curriculum and instruction that is different from the prevailing way of life in the curriculum and instruction establishment. The position taken here is that change should occur only after the experimental investigation of an intervention, with the assumption that many ideas that seem reasonable will turn out not to enhance learning (see, e.g., Levin & Pressley, 1983). As the studies cited here illustrate, experiments on curriculum aids can usually be carried out in a straightforward fashion, and I hope that such experimentation will soon become the heart of the curriculum and instruction discipline, replacing the untested corpus of theoretically and pragmatically derived recommendations that currently stock the shelves of the libraries in colleges of education.

I acknowledge in closing that it was apparent to me as I wrote this chapter that the principal position espoused here would be a controversial one. Already colleagues (including several authors in this volume) have cried out that I advocate spoon-feeding children and run the risk of making them "materials dependent." These colleagues contend that a steady diet of well-structured presentations might ultimately produce adults who are less strategic than the current generation, who presumably learned many of their cognitive tricks during interactions with less than optimally structured environments. My reply is that that may or may not be so, and that their position is not empirically defensible given extant data. First, the necessary conditions for the acquisition of cognitive strategies are not known—only some conditions that are sufficient to induce such acquisitions. Also, it seems likely that over the years people could abstract from optimal presentations the general rules about ways to enhance cognitive efficiency (e.g., after exposure to many mnemonic pictures that positively affect learning, one might be more likely to create mnemonics for oneself). There are a plethora of data indicating that children do engage in abstraction at that level of complexity. For instance, Salomon (1974, 1976, 1979a, 1979b) has documented that some cognitive operations can be internalized from watching television programs that incorporate the operations into their formats (e.g., operations such as spatial transformations and changing points of view). Also, a variety of cognitive rules can be abstracted from simple exposure to models exhibiting behaviors consistent with the rules (e.g., syntactical principles, quantitative concepts). See Rosenthal and Zimmerman (1978) for a summary of an impressive body of literature documenting this claim.

Thus, I am optimistic that the materials recommendations presented here will not have pejorative effects on children's cognitive development. To determine if this optimism has a basis in fact, studies are planned in my laboratory (as well as the laboratories of my associates) to determine if children can derive cognitive operating principles from materials constructed following some of the suggestions made here. Minimally, the experiments already conducted and reviewed here unambiguously support the position that the processing of meaningful content can be enhanced by following the suggestion to make materials presented to children more explicit than the versions that would be appropriate for adults.

Acknowledgments. The writing of this chapter was supported in part by a grant to the author from the Natural Sciences and Engineering Research Council of Canada. Much of the writing took place while the author was on leave to the University of Notre Dame, Notre Dame, Indiana, and the resources and support of Notre Dame are gratefully acknowledged.

Reference Notes

1. Mathews, S., Yussen, S., & Evans, R. *Remember that story? An investigation of the robustness and temporal course of the story schema's influence.* Unpublished manuscript, University of Wisconsin, Madison, 1982.
2. Pryor, J. B., Rholes, W. S., Ruble, D. N., & Kriss, M. *A developmental analysis of salience and discounting in social attribution.* Unpublished manuscript, University of Notre Dame, 1982.
3. Digdon, N., Pressley, M., Levin, J. R. Manuscript in preparation. London, Ontario: University of Western Ontario.
4. Wasserman, B. L. *Incomplete pictures and retarded children's oral prose learning* (Working Paper 268). Madison: Wisconsin Research and Development Center for Individualized Schooling, 1979.
5. McCormick, C. B. *The effect of mnemonic strategy variations on students' recall of potentially confusable prose passages.* Unpublished doctoral dissertation, University of Wisconsin, Madison, 1981.
6. Stevens, B. *Children's awareness of story order* (Tech. Rep. 577). Wisconsin Center for Education Research, University of Wisconsin, Madison, 1981.

References

Anderson, D. R. Lorch, E. P., Field, D. E., & Sanders, J. The effects of TV program comprehensibility on preschool children's visual attention to television. *Child Development,* 1981, *52,* 151–157.

Arnold, D. J., & Brooks, P. H. Influence of contextual organizing material on children's listening comprehension. *Journal of Educational Psychology,* 1976, *68,* 711–716.

Aulls, M. W. Expository paragraph properties that influence literal recall. *Journal of Reading Behavior,* 1975, *7,* 391–400.

Austin, V. D., Ruble, D. N., & Trabasso, T. Recall and order effects as factors in children's moral judgments. *Child Development,* 1977, *48,* 470–474.

Beal, C. R., & Flavell, J. H. Effects of increasing the salience of message ambiguities on kindergartners' evaluations of communicative success and message inadequacy. *Developmental Psychology,* 1982, *18,* 43–48.

Bearison, D. J., & Isaacs, L. Production deficiency in children's moral judgments. *Developmental Psychology,* 1975, *11,* 732–737.

Beeson, G. W. Influence of knowledge context on the learning of intellectual skills. *American Educational Research Journal,* 1981, *18,* 363–379.

Bellezza, F. S. Mnemonic-device instruction with adults. In M. Pressley & J. R. Levin (Eds.), *Cognitive strategy research: Psychological foundations.* New York: Springer-Verlag, 1983.

Bender, B. G., & Levin, J. R. Pictures, imagery, and retarded children's prose learning. *Journal of Educational Psychology,* 1978, *70,* 583–588.

Black, J. B., & Wilensky, R. An evaluation of story grammars. *Cognitive Science,* 1979, *3,* 213–230.

Bower, G. H., Black, J. B., & Turner, T. J. Scripts in memory for text. *Cognitive Psychology,* 1979, *11,* 177–220.

Brody, G. H., & Henderson, R. W. Effects of multiple model variations and rationale provision on the moral judgments and explanations of young children. *Child Development,* 1977, *48,* 1117–1120.

Brown, A. L. Knowing when, where, and how to remember: A problem of metacognition. In R. Glaser (Eds.), *Advances in instructional psychology* (Vol. 1). Hillsdale, NJ: Erlbaum, 1978.

Brown, A. L., & French, L. A. The zone of potential development: Implications for intelligence testing in the year 2000. *Intelligence,* 1979, *3,* 255–273.

Brown, A. L., & Murphy, M. D. Reconstruction of arbitrary versus logical sequences by preschool children. *Journal of Experimental Child Psychology,* 1975, *20,* 307–326.

Bruner, J. S., Olver, R. R., & Greenfield, P. M. *Studies in cognitive growth.* New York: Wiley, 1966.

Buss, R. R., Yussen, S. R., Mathews, S. R., II, Miller, G. E., & Rembold, K. L. Development of children's use of a story schema to retrieve information. *Developmental Psychology,* in press.

Case, R. The underlying mechanism of intellectual development. In J. R. Kirby & J. B. Biggs (Eds.), *Cognition, development, and instruction.* New York: Academic Press, 1980.

Chandler, M. J., Greenspan, S., & Barenboim, C. Judgments of intentionality in response to videotaped and verbally presented moral dilemmas: The medium is the message. *Child Development,* 1973, *44,* 315–320.

Collins, W. A., Sobol, B. L., & Westby, S. Effects of adult commentary on children's comprehension and inferences about a televised aggressive portrayal. *Child Development,* 1981, *52,* 158–163.

Collins, W. A., Wellman, H., Keniston, A. H., & Westby, S. D. Age-related aspects of comprehension and inference from a televised dramatic narrative. *Child Development*, 1978, *49*, 389–399.

Collins, W. A., & Wiens, M. Cognitive processes in television viewing: Description and strategic implications. In M. Pressley & J. R. Levin (Eds.), *Cognitive strategy research: Psychological foundations*. New York: Springer-Verlag, 1983.

Cosgrove, J. M., & Patterson, C. J. Plans and the development of listener skills. *Developmental Psychology*, 1977, *13*, 557–564.

Cosgrove, J. M., & Patterson, C. J. Generalization of training for children's listener skills. *Child Development*, 1978, *49*, 513–516.

Danner, F. W. Children's understanding of intersentence organization in the recall of short descriptive passages. *Journal of Educational Psychology*, 1976, *68*, 174–183.

Day, J. D. The zone of proximal development. In M. Pressley & J. R. Levin (Eds.), *Cognitive strategy research: Psychological foundations*. New York: Springer-Verlag, 1983.

Feldman, N. S., Klosson, E. C., Parsons, J. E., Rholes, W. S., & Ruble, D. N. Order of information presentation and children's moral judgments. *Child Development*, 1976, *47*, 556–559.

Flavell, J. H., Speer, J. R., Green, F. L., & August, D. L. The development of comprehension monitoring and knowledge about communication. *Monographs of the Society for Research in Child Development*, 1981, *46*(5, Serial No. 192).

Frase, L. T., & Schwartz, B. J. Typographical cues that facilitate comprehension. *Journal of Educational Psychology*, 1979, *71*, 197–206.

Goetz, E. T. Inferring from text: Some factors influencing which inferences will be made. *Discourse Processes*, 1979, *2*, 179–195.

Goetz, E. T., & Armbruster, B. B. Psychological correlates of text structure. In R. J. Spiro, B. C. Bruce, & F. Brewer (Eds.), *Theoretical issues in reading comprehension*. Hillsdale, NJ: Erlbaum, 1980.

Graesser, A. C. *Prose comprehension beyond the word*. New York: Springer-Verlag, 1981.

Grueneich, R. Issues in the developmental study of how children use intention and consequence information to make moral evaluations. *Child Development*, 1982, *53*, 29–43.

Grunau, R. V. E. Effects of elaborative prompt condition and developmental level on the performance of addition problems by kindergarten children. *Journal of Educational Psychology*, 1978, *70*, 422–432.

Guttmann, J., Levin, J. R., & Pressley, M. Pictures, partial pictures, and children's oral prose learning. *Journal of Educational Psychology*, 1977, *69*, 473–480.

Hayes, D. A., & Tierney, R. J. Developing readers' knowledge through analogy. *Reading Research Quarterly*, 1982, *17*, 256–280.

Hildyard, A. Children's productions of inferences from oral texts. *Discourse Processes*, 1979, *2*, 33–56.

Honeck, R. P., Sowry, B. M., & Voegtle, K. Proverbial understanding in a pictorial context. *Child Development*, 1978, *49*, 327–331.

Johnson, N. S., & Mandler, J. M. A tale of two structures: Underlying surface forms in stories. *Poetics*, 1980, *9*, 51–86.

Johnson, H., & Smith, L. B. Children's inferential abilities in the context of reading to understand. *Child Development*, 1981, *52*, 1216–1223.

Kieras, D. E. Good and bad structure in simple paragraphs: Effects on apparent theme, reading time, and recall. *Journal of Verbal Learning and Verbal Behavior,* 1978, *17,* 13–28.

Kieras, D. E. Initial mention as a signal to thematic content in technical passages. *Memory & Cognition,* 1980, *8,* 345–353.

Kieras, D. E. Topicalization effects in cued recall of technical prose. *Memory & Cognition,* 1981, *9,* 541–549.

Kintsch, W., & Greene, E. The role of culture-specific schemata in the comprehension and recall of stories. *Discourse Processes,* 1978, *1,* 1–13.

Kintsch, W., Mandel, T. S., & Kozminsky, E. Summarizing scrambled stories. *Memory & Cognition,* 1977, *5,* 547–552.

Kulhavy, R. W., & Swenson, I. Imagery instructions and the comprehension of text. *British Journal of Educational Psychology,* 1975, *45,* 47–51.

LaBerge, D., & Samuels, S. J. Towards a theory of automatic information processing in reading. *Cognitive Psychology,* 1974, *6,* 293–323.

Lesgold, A. M., McCormick, C., & Golinkoff, R. M. Imagery training and children's prose learning. *Journal of Educational Psychology,* 1975, *67,* 663–667.

Levin, J. R. What have we learned about maximizing what children learn? In J. R. Levin & V. L. Allen (Eds.), *Cognitive learning in children.* New York: Academic Press, 1976.

Levin, J. R. On functions of pictures in prose. In F. J. Pirozzolo & M. C. Wittrock (Eds.), *Neuropsychological and cognitive processes in reading.* New York: Academic Press, 1981a.

Levin, J. R. The mnemonic '80s: Keywords in the classroom. *Educational Psychologist,* 1981b, *16,* 65–82.

Levin, J. R. Pictures as prose-learning devices. In A. Flammer & W. Kintsch (Eds.), *Discourse processing.* Amsterdam: North-Holland, in press.

Levin, J. R., & Lesgold, A. M. On pictures in prose. *Educational Communication and Technology Journal,* 1978, *26,* 233–243.

Levin, J. R., McCormick, C. B., Miller, G. E., Berry, J. K., & Pressley, M. Mnemonic versus nonmnemonic vocabulary-learning strategies for children. *American Educational Research Journal,* 1982, *19,* 121–136.

Levin, J. R., & Pressley, M. Improving children's prose comprehension: Selected strategies that seem to succeed. In C. Santa & B. Hayes (Eds.), *Children's prose comprehension: Research and practice.* Newark, DE: International Reading Association, 1981.

Levin, J. R., & Pressley, M. Understanding mnemonic imagery effects: A dozen "obvious" outcomes. In M. L. Fleming & D. W. Hutton (Eds.), *Mental imagery and learning,* Englewood Cliffs, NJ: Educational Technology Publications, 1983.

Levin, J. R., Shriberg, L. K., & Berry, J. K. A concrete strategy for remembering abstract prose. *American Educational Research Journal,* in press.

Mandler, J. M. A code in the node: The use of a story schema in retrieval. *Discourse Processes,* 1978, *1,* 14–35.

Mandler, J. M. Categorical and schematic organization in memory. In C. R. Puff (Ed.), *Memory organization and structure.* New York: Academic Press, 1979.

Mandler, J. M., & DeForest, M. Is there more than one way to recall a story? *Child Development,* 1979, *50,* 886–889.

Mandler, J. M., & Johnson, N. S. Remembrance of things parsed: Story structure and recall. *Cognitive Psychology,* 1977, *9,* 111–151.

Markman, E. M. Realizing that you don't understand: A preliminary investigation. *Child Development,* 1977, *48,* 986–992.

Markman, E. M. Realizing that you don't understand: Elementary school children's awareness of inconsistencies. *Child Development,* 1979, *50,* 643–655.

Markman, E. M. Comprehension monitoring. In W. P. Dickson (Ed.), *Children's oral communication skills.* New York: Academic Press, 1981.

Markman, E. M., & Gorin, L. Children's ability to adjust their standards for evaluating comprehension. *Journal of Educational Psychology,* 1981, *73,* 320–325.

Mayer, R. E. Advance organizers that compensate for the organization of text. *Journal of Educational Psychology,* 1978, *70,* 880–886.

Meissner, J. A. Judgment of clue adequacy by kindergarten and second-grade children. *Developmental Psychology,* 1978, *14,* 18–23.

Meringhoff, L. K. Influence of the medium on children's story apprehension. *Journal of Educational Psychology,* 1980, *72,* 240–249.

Meyer, B. J. F. *The organization of prose and its effects on memory.* Amsterdam: North-Holland, 1975.

Meyer, B. J. F. The structure of prose: Effects on learning and memory and implications for educational practice. In R. C. Anderson, B. J. Spiro, & W. E. Montague (Eds.), *Schooling and the acquisition of knowledge.* Hillsdale, NJ: 1977.

Nelson, S. A. Factors influencing young children's use of motives and outcomes as moral criteria. *Child Development,* 1980, *51,* 823–829.

Newcomb, A. F., & Collins, W. A. Children's comprehension of family role portrayals in televised dramas: Effects of socioeconomic status, ethnicity, and age. *Developmental Psychology,* 1979, *15,* 417–423.

Nummedal, S. G., & Bass, S. C. Effects of the salience of intention and consequence on children's moral judgments. *Developmental Psychology,* 1976, *12,* 475–476.

Omanson, R. C., Warren, W. H., & Trabasso, T. Goals, inferential comprehension, and recall of stories by children. *Discourse Processes,* 1978, *1,* 337–354.

Paivio, A., & Begg, I. *Psychology of language.* Englewood Cliffs, NJ: Prentice-Hall, 1981.

Paris, S. G., & Mahoney, G. J. Cognitive integration in children's memory for sentences and pictures. *Child Development,* 1974, *45,* 633–642.

Paris, S. G., & Upton, L. R. Children's memory for inferential relationships in prose. *Child Development,* 1976, *47,* 660–668.

Parsons, J. E., Ruble, D. E., Klosson, E. C., Feldman, N. S., & Rholes, W. S. Order effects on children's moral and achievement judgments. *Developmental Psychology,* 1976, *12,* 357–358.

Patterson, C. J., Cosgrove, J. M., & O'Brien, R. G. Nonverbal indicants of comprehension and noncomprehension in children. *Developmental Psychology,* 1980, *16,* 38–48.

Patterson, C. J., & Kister, M. C. The development of listener skills for referential communication. In W. P. Dickson (Ed.), *Children's oral communication skills.* New York: Academic Press, 1981.

Patterson, C. J., O'Brien, C., Kister, M. C., Carter, D. B., & Kotsonis, M. E. Development of comprehension monitoring as a function of context. *Developmental Psychology,* 1981, *17,* 379–389.

Piaget, J. *The moral judgment of the child.* New York: Harcourt, Brace, 1932.

Piaget, J., & Inhelder, B. *The psychology of the child.* New York: Basic Books, 1969.

Pratt, M. W., & Bates, K. R. Young editors: Preschoolers' evaluation and production of ambiguous messages. *Developmental Psychology,* 1982, *18,* 30–42.

Pratt, M. W., Krane, R., & Kendall, J. R. Triggering a schema: The role of italics and intonation in the interpretation of ambiguous discourse. *American Educational Research Journal,* 1981, *18,* 303–315.

Pressley, G. M. Mental imagery helps eight-year-olds remember what they read. *Journal of Educational Psychology,* 1976, *68,* 355–359.

Pressley, M. Imagery and children's learning: Putting the picture in developmental perspective. *Review of Educational Research,* 1977, *47,* 585–622.

Pressley, M. Elaboration and memory development. *Child Development,* 1982, *53,* 296–309.

Pressley, M., Heisel, B. E., McCormick, C. G., & Nakamura, G. V. Memory strategy instruction. In C. J. Brainerd & M. Pressley (Eds.), *Verbal processes in children.* New York: Springer-Verlag, 1982.

Pressley, M., Levin, J. R., & Bryant, S. L. Memory strategy instruction during adolescence: When is explicit instruction needed? In M. Pressley & J. R. Levin (Eds.), *Cognitive strategy research: Psychological foundations.* New York: Springer-Verlag, 1983.

Pressley, M., Levin, J. R., Kuiper, N. A., Bryant, S. L., & Michener, S. Mnemonic versus nonmnemonic vocabulary-learning strategies: Additional comparisons. *Journal of Educational Psychology,* 1982, *74,* 693–707.

Pressley, M., Levin, J. R., & Miller, G. E. The keyword method compared to alternative vocabulary learning strategies. *Contemporary Educational Psychology,* 1982, *7,* 50–60.

Pressley, M., Pigott, S., & Bryant, S. L. Picture content and preschoolers' learning from sentences. *Educational Communication and Technology Journal,* 1982, *30,* 151–161.

Rasco, R. W., Tennyson, R. D., & Boutwell, R. C. Imagery instructions and drawings in learning prose. *Journal of Educational Psychology,* 1975, *67,* 188–192.

Roberts, P. Memory strategy instruction with the elderly: What *should* memory training be the training of? In M. Pressley & J. R. Levin (Eds.), *Cognitive strategy research: Psychological foundations.* New York: Springer-Verlag, 1983.

Rohwer, W. D., Jr. Elaboration and learning in childhood and adolescence. In H. W. Reese (Ed.), *Advances in child development and behavior* (Vol. 8). New York: Academic Press, 1973.

Rosenthal, T. L., & Zimmerman, B. J. *Social learning and cognition.* New York: Academic Press, 1978.

Royer, J. M., & Cable, G. W. Illustrations, analogies, and facilitative transfer in prose learning. *Journal of Educational Psychology,* 1976, *68,* 205–209.

Rumelhart, D. E. Notes on a schema for stories. In D. G. Bobrow & A. Collins (Eds.), *Representation and understanding.* New York: Academic Press, 1975.

Salatas, H., & Flavell, J. H. Retrieval of recently learned information: Development of strategies and control skills. *Child Development,* 1976, *47,* 941–948.

Salomon, G. Internalization of filmic schematic operations in interaction with learners' aptitudes. *Journal of Educational Psychology,* 1974, *66,* 499–511.

Salomon, G. Cognitive skills learning across cultures. *Journal of Communication,* 1976, *26,* 138–145.

Salomon, G. *Interaction of media, cognition, and learning.* San Francisco, CA: Jossey-Bass, 1979a.

Salomon, G. Media and symbol systems as related to cognition and learning. *Journal of Educational Psychology,* 1979b, *71,* 131–148.

Schmidt, C. R., Paris, S. G., & Stober, S. Inferential distance and children's memory for pictorial sequences. *Developmental Psychology,* 1979, *15,* 395–405.

Shatz, M. The relationship between cognitive processes and the development of communication skills. In C. B. Keasey (Ed.), *Nebraska Symposium on Motivation* (Vol. 25). Lincoln: University of Nebraska Press, 1977.

Shriberg, L. K., Levin, J. R., McCormick, C. B., & Pressley, M. Learning about "famous" people via the keyword method. *Journal of Educational Psychology,* 1982, *74,* 238–247.

Singer, J. B., & Flavell, J. H. Development of knowledge about communication: Children's evaluations of explicitly ambiguous messages. *Child Development,* 1981, *52,* 1211–1215.

Small, M. Y., & Butterworth, J. Semantic integration and the development of memory for logical inferences. *Child Development,* 1981, *52,* 732–735.

Smith, L. R., & Cotten, M. L. Effect of lesson vagueness and discontinuity on student achievement and attitudes. *Journal of Educational Psychology,* 1980, *72,* 670–675.

Stein, N. L., & Glenn, C. G. An analysis of story comprehension in elementary school children. In R. O. Freedle (Eds.), *New directions in discourse processing* (Vol. 2). Norwood, NJ: Ablex, 1979.

Stein, N. L., & Nezworski, T. The effects of organization and instructional set on story memory. *Discourse Processes,* 1978, *1,* 177–193.

Stein, N. L., & Trabasso, T. Children's understanding of stories: A basis for moral judgment and dilemma resolution. In C. J. Brainerd & M. Pressley (Eds.), *Verbal processes in children.* New York: Springer-Verlag, 1982.

Stone, D. E., & Glock, M. D. How do young adults read directions with and without pictures? *Journal of Educational Psychology,* 1981, *73,* 419–426.

Trabasso, T., & Nicholas, D. W. Memory and inferences in the comprehension of narratives. In F. Wilkening, J. Becker, & T. Trabasso (Eds.), *Information integration by children.* Hillsdale, NJ: Erlbaum, 1980.

Vygotsky, L. S. *Mind in society: The development of higher psychological processes* (M. Cole, V. John-Steiner, S. Scribner, & E. Sonberman, Eds.). Cambridge, MA: Harvard University Press, 1978.

Wagner, M., & Rohwer, W. D., Jr. Age differences in the elaboration of inferences from text. *Journal of Educational Psychology,* 1981, *73,* 728–735.

Walker, C. H., & Meyer, B. J. F. Integrating of different types of information in text. *Journal of Verbal Learning and Verbal Behavior,* 1980, *19,* 263–275.

Waters, J. S., & Andreassen, C. Children's use of memory strategies under instruction. In M. Pressley & J. R. Levin (Eds.), *Cognitive strategy research: Psychological foundations.* New York: Springer-Verlag, 1983.

Willows, D. M., Borwick, D., & Hayvren, M. The content of school readers. In T. G. Waller & G. E. MacKinnon (Eds.), *Reading research: Advances in theory and practice* (Vol. 2). New York: Academic Press, 1981.

Yussen, S. R. Mathews, S. R., II, Buss, R. R., & Kane, P. T. Developmental change in judging important and critical elements of stories. *Developmental Psychology,* 1980, *16,* 213–219.

10. Problems in Classroom Implementation of Cognitive Strategy Instruction

Penelope L. Peterson and Susan R. Swing

The purpose of this chapter is to describe problems that need to be solved before cognitive strategy instruction can be implemented effectively in classrooms. At this point, these problems are not clearly defined because few attempts have been made to train students in cognitive strategies for classroom use. Moreover, in the few studies that have been done, researchers have not attempted to identify the specific variables that are related to unsuccessful classroom implementation of cognitive strategy instruction (see Peterson & Swing, Note 1).

The questions that need to be addressed and the problems that must be solved include the following:

1. Can individually administered cognitive strategy training be adapted effectively to group situations?
2. What individual differences in students need to be considered for cognitive strategy instruction to be implemented effectively in the classroom?
3. Can students effectively use cognitive strategies during ongoing classroom learning?
4. Following cognitive strategy training, can strategy usage be maintained and generalized to other similar tasks?
5. What components must be included in strategy instruction for instruction to be effective?
6. How dependent is cognitive strategy training on adjunct materials, and how dependent should it be? *see also last chapter (summary)*
7. What cognitive strategies should be taught, and to whom?
8. How should cognitive strategy instruction be implemented in the classroom?

In the following sections we will consider each of these questions. In considering them, we will discuss problems that have emerged from the research that has attempted to implement cognitive strategy instruction in classroom or classroom-like situations. (For a review of this research, see Peterson & Swing, Note 1.) We will also discuss relevant research findings and issues that have arisen from selected laboratory studies of cognitive strategy instruction. More specifically, we will consider laboratory studies in cases where no attempt has been made to implement instruction of this type of strategy in the classroom.

Can Individually Administered Cognitive Strategy Training Be Adapted Effectively to Group Situations?

Obviously, for cognitive strategy instruction to be implemented in actual classroom situations, strategy instruction will need to be adapted to a group situation. Thus, strategy instruction that requires a lengthy one-to-one interaction between the trainer (teacher) and the student would not be feasible in a classroom situation. Possible ways in which cognitive strategy instruction could be adapted to a classroom situation include administering the training in small groups, administering the training to the class as a whole, and administering the training to individual students through the use of programmed materials or written exercise booklets.

An Affirmative Answer

Research that has attempted to take individually administered cognitive strategy training and adapt the instruction to a group situation has shown mixed results. On the one hand, three studies that compared individual versus group-administered training found that individually administered and group-administered training were equally effective. Allen (1973) found that undergraduate students who received individually administered or group-administered study counseling and relaxation training showed equal improvement in grade-point average over students in a placebo control group. Similarly, Kendall and Zupan (1981) found that third through fifth graders benefited equally from individually administered and group-administered training in verbal self-instruction and showed significantly greater improvements on a posttest than students in a control group. Kestner and Borkowski (1979) found that instruction in interrogative strategies administered to first-grade students was equally effective whether done in an individual or a group situation. In addition, most recent cognitive strategy instruction for test anxiety has been group administered and has been successful in improving academic performance. In the latter studies treatment effects seem to depend more on the type of treatment administered than on whether the instruction is group or individually administered. (See, e.g., Denney, 1980; Tryon, 1980.) In sum, this research suggests an affirmative answer to the question.

An Affirmative Answer with Qualifications

On the other hand, a more complex answer to the question is indicated by the findings from research on the keyword method (Bellezza, 1983; Pressley, Levin, & Bryant, 1983; Chapter 7 in this volume). The results of this research suggest that instruction in the keyword method has not been successfully administered in group situations so as to have facilitative effects on the vocabulary learning of high school and college students. However, students younger than high school students have been shown to benefit from group-administered keyword instruction (see Levin, Pressley, McCormick, Miller, & Shriberg, 1979; Pressley, Levin, & Delaney, 1982).

Levin, Pressley, and their colleagues are currently investigating two hypotheses for the lack of facilitative effects of group-administered keyword instruction with older students. The first is an attentional hypothesis and the second is a feedback hypothesis. A student's attention is more likely to wander in a group-administered situation than in an individual situation in which the experimenter is able to keep the student's attention on the task. Thus, perhaps older students do not benefit from group-administered instruction in the keyword method simply because they are not paying attention. A second and related issue is the problem of feedback. In the individually administered situation, the experimenter checks for the student's understanding of the keyword technique as training proceeds (see, e.g., Levin et al., 1979). In this way, the experimenter is able to check whether each student understands and is able to implement the keyword technique correctly. In the group-administered procedure as implemented by Levin et al. (1979), the experimenter calls on one or two students in the classroom to check for their understanding of the procedure. Thus, many students in the class or in the small group may not understand the procedure and may not have their lack of understanding detected by the experimenter.

These examples demonstrate that the effectiveness of group-administered strategy instruction may depend on a number of factors, including the type of strategy trained and the age level of the student. Future research should attempt to identify the training components that restrict effectiveness. For example, the keyword researcher's attentional hypothesis could be examined by observational techniques, such as coding students' apparent on-task behavior, or interviewing (see, e.g., Peterson, Swing, Braverman, & Buss, 1982).

◉ What Individual Differences in Students Need to Be Considered for Cognitive Strategy Instruction to Be Implemented Effectively in the Classroom?

Research suggests that the following four individual differences are important: the age of the student; the ability of the student, including the extent to which the student has developed preferred strategies; the student's prior knowledge; and the student's metacognitive proficiency.

Age of the Student

Age is related to effectiveness of training in at least two important ways. First, the student's age affects the extent to which the student can learn to use the strategy and the magnitude of the effects. Second, age may affect the kind and extensiveness of instruction needed to train the strategy.

There is considerable evidence that the extent to which a student can and will learn to use the strategy depends on the age of the student (see, e.g., Flavell, 1970; Bray, Justice, Ferguson, & Simon, 1977; Pressley, Heisel, McCormick, & Nakamura, 1982). For example, Robin, Armel, and O'Leary (1975) reported great difficulty in shaping and maintaining self-instructional responding by 5- and 6-year-olds:

> Even though the experimenter provided repeated modeling and continuous reinforcement, the subjects often eclipsed the verbalizations to a single word, uttered rapidly and in many cases not in coordination with the motoric response. In fact, while some subjects self-instructed correctly, they were simultaneously observed to make incorrect writing responses. (p. 185)

Similarly, Kendall, Borkowski, and Cavanaugh (1980) found that students with a mental age of 6 years could maintain an interrogative strategy for approximately 2 weeks, but could not generalize the strategy to a transfer task, whereas students with a mental age of 8 years. could both maintain and generalize the strategy.

Several studies suggest that the ability to select and effectively apply a memory strategy may depend on the age of the student (Pressley, Heisel, McCormick, & Nakamura, 1982). For example, Butterfield and Belmont (1977) found that 10-year-old subjects took more time to stabilize their initial strategy selection than 17-year-olds, and both 10- and 12-year-olds reinstated a previously effective mnemonic strategy less rapidly and less precisely than the older subjects. In commenting on the results of a study by Brown and Barclay (1976), Brown, Campione, and Murphy (1977) concluded that applying a task-relevant mnemonic strategy and monitoring its success or failure appears to involve a complex coordination of introspective and overt behavior—a coordination that is late in developing in both normal and retarded populations.

A number of studies have reported that younger students may require more extensive training in order to use a strategy. For example, Bray et al. (1977) found that whereas third-grade students required only cumulative rehearsal instructions in order to use the strategy, first graders required these instructions plus modeling of the strategy. Similarly, findings from research on the keyword method suggest that although children as young as 3 years old can learn to use the keyword method, extensive support must be provided by the experimenter in the form of providing the imagery and the keyword that is to be used to learn each vocabulary word. By the late elementary school years, students can be trained in the keyword strategy with the same kind of training that has been used for adults (i.e., generating interactive visual images from verbal materials), although some less able students may still require additional support (see Pressley, Levin, & Delaney, 1982). We will return to these findings again when we discuss the dependence of strategy instruction on adjunct materials.

One interpretation of the foregoing results is that students' ability to learn and use certain strategies and to benefit from training may depend on a student's achieving the prerequisite level of cognitive development. Thus, age-related differences in the ability to learn to use certain strategies may in fact reflect important transitions between cognitive-developmental stages, such as the transition from the preoperational level to concrete operations or from concrete operations to formal operations. For example, we would speculate that the use of certain problem-solving strategies may require students to operate at a formal operational level. The lack of positive results of teaching problem-solving strategies to younger students supports the hypothesis that perhaps these students have not reached the appropriate level of cognitive development to use the strategy effectively. Other explanations of age-related differences involve consideration of factors such as capacity limitations and prior knowledge. These are discussed elsewhere in this chapter.

Finally, there is evidence to suggest that once the younger student has learned to use the strategy, the younger student may benefit more from the strategy than the older student. This may be because the older student has already developed strategic approaches to the task. This finding is most clearly shown in the research on the keyword method in which greater gains have been shown for children who learn to use the keyword strategy than for adolescents and adults (see, e.g., Levin et al., 1979; Pressley, Levin, & Delaney, 1982).

Student Ability

Some research indicates that low-ability students benefit from strategy instruction more than high-ability students. In two laboratory studies of the effects of instruction in learner-generated questioning on prose comprehension, Andre and Anderson (1979) found that low-ability students benefited significantly more from training than did high-ability students. Similarly, in a laboratory study of training in the use of elaborative techniques to increase reading comprehension, Mayer (1980) found significant results in terms of increased performance mainly for low-ability subjects. Finally, Holley, Dansereau, McDonald, Garland, and Collins (1979) found that training in a networking strategy increased the reading comprehension of low-ability students but actually impaired the comprehension of high-ability students.

A possible explanation for these findings is that able and/or older students may have developed sophisticated and effective cognitive strategies of their own. For example, in a study by Schoenfeld (1979b) in which problem-solving strategies were taught to upper division science and mathematics undergraduates, Schoenfeld noted that the students were often reluctant to use the heuristic strategy that was being taught. This may have been due to students' reliance on problem-solving strategies that they had already developed. Furthermore, some nonsignificant findings of strategy instruction with college students may, in fact, be due to the strategy instruction's interfering with students' already developed strategies. The nonsignificant positive effects of strategy instruction for learning from teaching in two experiments by Winne and Marx (1980) may have been due to the strategy training's interfering with existing strategies (e.g., note taking) of the college students. Winne and Marx trained college students to identify lecturer behaviors and to make prescribed mental responses to the behaviors. They found that training did not have significant positive effects on student achievement. Students reported that "doing all that" (using the strategy) while engaging in note taking was too difficult. (Pressley, Heisel, McCormick, & Nakamura, 1982, comment additionally on the concerns raised in this paragraph.)

For the most part, significant Ability X Treatment interactions have been neither investigated nor found in studies of the keyword method (Pressley, Levin, & Delaney, 1982). However, in a recent laboratory study with fifth-grade children, McGivern and Levin (1983) found that the advantage of a condition in which extensive support was provided (both keyword and interactive pictures provided) was significantly greater for low-ability students than for high-ability students. This finding is consistent with conclusions from aptitude-treatment-interaction research that suggest that less able learners do better in treatments in which information processing demands are reduced by the provision of external support (Snow, 1977).

Prior Knowledge

The mere possession of a repertoire of specific strategies does not guarantee their effective use. It is generally acknowledged that without sufficient prior knowledge— defined here as general or content-related verbal information and skills (Gagne, 1980)—some strategies cannot be implemented (Baker & Brown, 1982; Borkowski, Reid, & Kurtz, in press; Gagne, 1980; Kantowski, 1977; Simon, 1980; Schoenfeld, 1979a). The relationship of prior knowledge to strategy use will be illustrated through examples involving verbal self-instruction, reading, and problem solving.

The verbalization of the steps required to perform a given task is typically a component of verbal self-instruction training (Pressley, Reynolds, Stark, & Gettinger, 1983; Reynolds & Stark, 1983). The method thus requires that the student already possess this task-specific knowledge or that he or she learn it during training along with the other aspects of the procedure. These requirements may impose too great a processing demand on the young learner. That this may indeed be the case is suggested by Friedling and O'Leary's (1979) observation that the frequency of verbal self-instruction is high when simple motor tasks are being performed, but that verbalization is absent during performance of complex cognitive or perceptual motor responses the student has not yet learned. Additional evidence pointing to the importance of content-tied knowledge in verbal self-instruction is Higa's finding (1973) that direct instruction rather than self-verbalizations was the most important component of the training procedure.

Baker and Brown (1982) mention ways that prior knowledge may interact with the use of metacognitive strategies to improve reading comprehension and recall of text. They propose that identifying important elements of the text message and allocating attention so that it is focused on these important points facilitate comprehension and recall. They also point out that without relevant prior knowledge, it may be difficult for one to eliminate trivia and identify main points. Second, they say that one reason comprehension monitoring may not be effective is that the reader may not have enough background information on a topic to know if the interpretation he or she has imposed on the text is the correct one.

A final example of the interaction of prior knowledge and strategy use is drawn from Schoenfeld's discussion "Can Heuristics Be Taught?" (1979a). In this discussion, he identifies understanding of the heuristic and existence of sufficient prior knowledge as two of three major obstacles to the effective use of heuristics. (But as demonstrated below, the two obstacles actually merge into one when the role of content knowledge in determining the specific application of a heuristic is considered.) According to Schoenfeld, "understanding the heuristic" is difficult because the heuristic itself is a rather imprecise prescription that in actuality is a family of specific strategies. As an illustration he describes Polya's heuristic (1957) —"If you cannot solve the proposed problem, try to solve first some related problems"—as consisting of three components:

1. Determine an appropriate related problem that is more accessible
2. Solve the related problem, and
3. Exploit something from the solution—perhaps the answer or the method employed. (p. 319)

An even closer examination of the heuristic and its proposed components reveals that a number of specific facts and mathematical skills are required to employ the heuristic. First, a repertoire of previously solved problems must be a part of one's knowledge base. A comparative analysis of the present and past problems is required, with the analysis in turn calling for the subprocesses of feature selection and comparison. Selection of important features would again require consultation of a content-related knowledge structure. In addition, knowledge of specific mathematical operations is required when actually solving the problems. Although this rudimentary task analysis could continue, the foregoing seems to make the point that both factual knowledge (a store of problem types and knowledge of what features of a problem are important) and specific skills (analysis, mathematical operations) are needed before the heuristic can be used effectively.

It is a truism of development that children generally possess less content knowledge and a more limited collection of subordinate skills than do older persons. However, it is not the case that prior knowledge deficits uniquely impede their capacity to use strategies (see Schoenfeld, 1979a). This problem pervades the performance of persons of all ages with the exception of those persons whose repository of knowledge and skills is so complete as to qualify them as experts in their fields.

Metacognitive Proficiency

A number of investigators point to executive control or metacognitive knowledge and strategies as other components of cognitive functioning that intervene in the effective utilization of specific strategies (Baker & Brown, 1982; Kantowski, 1981). Schoenfeld (1979a) addresses this issue quite emphatically by identifying the lack of a managerial strategy as a major obstacle to the use of heuristics. Specifically, he says: "Instruction in heuristics alone will almost always prove insufficient: Students need to be trained in a means for selecting the appropriate strategies for problem solving and for allocating their resources wisely" (p. 317). The logical appeal of this contention is considerable. Intuitively, it seems quite plausible that memory, for example, would be enhanced by (a) knowledge of one's memory processes, capacity limitations, and repertoire of strategic skills; (b) monitoring and evaluation of strategy effectiveness; and (c) organization of activities, by selecting a task-appropriate skill and adapting strategic activities to changing task demands (Brown, 1978; Butterfield & Belmont, 1977).

Most research on the connection between metacognitive proficiency and strategy use has been correlational. In a recent meta-analysis, Schneider (Note 2) concluded that metamemory and memory were modestly correlated ($r = .41$). However, he pointed out that the strength of the relationship varied with type of metamemory, form of memory task, task difficulty, and age of subject.

Several studies point more definitively to the importance of metamemorial awareness. Borkowski, Levers, and Gruenenfelder (1976) trained first graders in strategy use by having them view a short film of a child performing the strategy. While viewing the film, the trainees received explicit cuing indicating that the filmed child's strategy use was facilitating his performance. The first graders viewing the film exhibited significantly better recall on a maintenance task than control students or students who only physically manipulated the stimuli during the memory task. Similarly, Paris, Newman, and McVey (in press, cited by Schneider, Note 2) showed that feedback about the functional value of memory strategies was related to use of a more effective strategy on a memory task.

Borkowski et al. (in press) proposed that metamemory may be more closely related to successful performance on transfer tasks subsequent to strategy instruction because in this situation strategy use is less likely to be automatic. Consequently, the more deliberate assessment of the strategic requirements of the situation may be more likely to activate metamemorial knowledge. The results reported by Schneider (Note 2) corroborated this proposal. Some evidence indicative of a metamemory-memory connection was found in four of five training studies that tested generalization. (See Borkowski and Büchel, 1983, for more on this issue.)

Other evidence suggestive of the importance of metacognition has been reported in research on problem solving. Schoenfeld (1979a) observed that students in his problem-solving class were often unable to solve the assigned problems on their own but had relatively little difficulty when a heuristic was suggested. He considered such observations as indicative of students' needs for a mechanism to aid them in the selection of an appropriate heuristic. In response to this perceived need, he devised a managerial strategy and instructed his students in its use. Schoenfeld reported that students were able to learn the managerial strategy and that their ability to determine an appropriate heuristic improved during the course. These observations suggest the usefulness of the managerial strategy. Unfortunately, a formal evaluation aimed at determining the effective components of the course was not undertaken. Therefore, the improvement cannot be attributed unequivocally to the managerial strategy.

Although research has not established a causal connection between metacognitive proficiency and strategy usage, research has indicated a correlational connection. Moreover, research has systematically shown that developmentally younger learners possess less metacognitive knowledge and exhibit poorer executive control than more mature learners (Brown, 1978, Butterfield & Belmont, 1977). If it is assumed that control processes and metacognitive knowledge actually do affect effective strategy use, naive learners' deficits in these areas may limit their capacity to benefit from strategy instruction. Thus, metacognitive proficiency should be considered until research findings indicate otherwise.

Can Students Effectively Use Cognitive Strategies During Ongoing Classroom Learning?

Whether students can effectively use cognitive strategies during day-to-day classroom learning is an important question that has not been addressed by strategy instruction research. The point is that in an actual classroom situation students' cognitive processing must be done in real time. That is, students cannot slow down their cognitive processing to incorporate the use of cognitive strategies lest they be left behind by the rest of the class. In addition, there is little opportunity for an individual student to be given a prompt or cue to use a given cognitive strategy (Schoenfeld, 1979b). This might effectively eliminate the use of such strategies as would require continuous prompting in order that their use be maintained in the classroom. Furthermore, most accounts of information processing agree that there are limitations on the amount of processing that can be conducted simultaneously (Case, 1978; Dempster, 1981; Kail & Bisanz, in press). This limitation may pose problems for the use of strategies in any setting if the strategy consists of a set of processes that, independently or in combination with the specific information requirements of the task, exceed working-memory capacity.

Speed of processing may affect strategy use indirectly through its relationship to capacity—the more rapidly a particular processing task is completed, the sooner the attentional resources allocated to that task can be switched to other processing demands (Kail & Bisanz, in press; Pressley, Heisel, McCormick, & Nakamura, 1982). Processing speed may also limit (or allow) strategy use directly (independent of information load) when processing time is constrainted. Pressley and Levin (1977) found that second graders required more than 6 seconds per pair to create imaginal elaborations for word pairs that were not easily associable. When these children were allowed only 6 seconds to form an imaginal elaboration, their performance did not differ from control subjects. However, when allowed 12 seconds to implement the strategy, their learning of paired associates was significantly better than that of the control group.

Characteristics of Classrooms Pose Problems

We propose that a number of conditions characteristic of classroom learning may exacerbate the problems in strategy use created by capacity limitations and inadequate speed of processing. These conditions may produce even greater processing demands than would occur when completing the "classroom" task in a more controlled or laboratory setting. First, students must process information in the time allowed by the teacher, particularly when learning from teaching. That is, students must select and apply appropriate cognitive strategies, monitor their effectiveness, and revise their use, all while attending to the content. Second, the increasing volume of information that students encounter across days during school would further increase processing demands. Any processing episode (e.g., information integration or memory search and retrieval) would involve more time and more processing space. Thus, the need or inclination to allocate attention to basic and simultaneous processing of the information would possibly preclude or disrupt the use of strategies that actually would allow for more effective and efficient processing. Additional demands on processing capacity, such as difficulty in determining task requirements and expenditure of effort toward maintaining attention and motivation, are also more likely to occur in a classroom than in a controlled learning environment.

Results from one study suggest that strategy use when learning from teaching may be difficult even for a learner who presumably has a large working-memory capacity and a rapid processing rate. In this study, college students reported that it was impossible to engage in the strategies for learning from teaching that had been taught while monitoring the content of the lecture and taking notes (Winne & Marx, 1980).

Processing demands specific to classroom learning may serve as a major impediment to the effective use of some strategies. However, processing load associated with application of the strategy might be reduced by practice. Considerable practice with the strategy in situations that do not tax information processing capacity should eventually result in the automatization of the strategy. That is, utilization of the strategy will require minimum mental effort, thereby increasing the likelihood that it can and will be used. This point is illustrated by a study of problem solving by Kantowski (1977). During the study, she observed that strategies committed to memory (as indicated by a prior knowledge test) were easily activated for use in solutions of problems, but those not remembered were used less often even though they were available on reference sheets.

The Importance of Executive Control

Given the time constraints on processing and the large amount of information to be processed in the classroom, it appears that proficient executive control would be necessary. An appropriate strategy must be chosen, applied, and revised rapidly in order to prevent information loss. In the future, perhaps deficits in students' executive control can be eliminated through the teaching of metacognitive strategies. In addition, Case's (1978) developmental principles for planning instruction could be applied. Using his guidelines, selection of a to-be-taught strategy would be made together with a consideration of the amount of information to be learned and its familiarity and salience so that the student's processing load would be minimized.

Following Cognitive Strategy Training, Can Strategy Usage Be Maintained and Generalized to Other Similar Tasks?

Brown (1978) argued that the durability of strategy training and the generalization of strategy use to tasks other than the training task should be considered criteria against which to evaluate the successfulness of the training (e.g., Borkowski & Büchel, 1983; Pressley, et al., 1983; Roberts, 1983). Her proposal was directed toward the assessment of laboratory training studies, but it is equally appropriate for considering the value of strategy training in the classroom.

Although considerable concern has been voiced about problems of maintenance and generalization (Brown & Barclay, 1976; Brown et al., 1977; Butterfield & Belmont, 1977; Friedling & O'Leary, 1979; McLaughlin, 1976), in actuality only a few classroom studies have produced findings related to this point. These results are mixed and are thus inconclusive. Robin et al. (1975) and Burgio, Whitman, and Johnson (1980) reported that students' improvement subsequent to verbal self-instruction training was limited to the classroom task on which they were trained. Friedling and O'Leary (1979) indicated that generalization failed to occur in their study because improvement was shown only on math problems that were quite similar to the training task (copying geometric forms; conceptual grouping). But using Borkowski and Cavanaugh's (1979) conception of a transfer task as one that differs in at least one way from the training task, it can be concluded that generalization did occur, albeit to a restricted extent. Cameron and Robinson (1980) reported that students trained in verbal self-instruction on a variety of tasks, including math problems, also showed an increased tendency to self-correct when reading. In a classroom study of strategy instruction in the keyword method, Jones and Hall (1982) provided impressive evidence for maintenance and generalization of the keyword method (see also Pressley et al., 1983).

Additional evidence has been produced in laboratory studies. In a study involving training in memory span estimation, Brown et al. (1977) reported that educable mentally retarded (EMR) students failed to generalize this trained capability when task format was changed slightly. Four studies conducted by Brown and colleagues indicated that EMR students with a mean mental age (MA) of 6 years had trouble maintaining effective use of specific memory and metamnemonic strategies (Brown & Barclay, 1976; Brown & Campione, 1977; Brown, Campione, & Barclay, 1979; Brown et al., 1977). As shown in these same studies, however, older EMRs (mean MA = 8) were more likely to maintain strategy use. In addition, they generalized strategy use from picture list learning to prose passages in a study by Brown et al. (1979). Other investigators have been successful in accomplishing long-term effects and transfer to new tasks (Barclay, 1979; Borkowski et al., 1976; Engle, Nagle, & Dick, 1980; Kendall et al., 1980; Kestner & Borkowski, 1979). All of these studies attempted to enhance recall by training a specific mnemonic strategy. Retention intervals ranged from a few days to 1 year. However, the generalization tasks typically involved only limited changes in the initial training task.

Considering that most tests of maintenance and generalization have occurred in the laboratory and that findings have been inconsistent, it is difficult to predict how serious a problem duration and transfer might be for classroom strategy training. Given that classroom learning overall is more demanding in terms of the variety and amount of material that the student is expected to learn—and similarly in terms of the diversity and number of cognitive processes that must be employed —it seems that any problematic aspect of training identified in the laboratory (including maintenance and generalization) would be compounded in a classroom setting. At any rate, we would suggest that developers and implementers of class-room strategy training anticipate the occurrence of these problems and take the steps needed to reduce the probability of their happening. That is, practitioners should consider the host of variables that are thought to be related to effective strategy use across time and tasks. These variables as identified in this section and in other sections of this chapter include training variables as well as individual differences such as the age of the learner, the learner's prior knowledge, and the proficiency of his or her metacognitive knowledge and executive control.

*What Components Must Be Included in Strategy Instruction for Instruction to Be Effective?

Obviously, determining the components to be included in strategy instruction depends on the strategy to be taught. Unfortunately, research on most cognitive strategies has not systematically investigated the components of strategy instruc-tion. For illustrative purposes, however, we will discuss here several examples of strategy instruction in which some research has been done to suggest what compo-nents may be effective and what must be included in instruction.

Borkowski et al. (1976) have suggested that the following components will increase the likelihood of obtaining durable and sizable effects of strategy training: (a) consistent use of the same strategy; (b) training the strategy by using a variety of materials; and (c) provision of detailed instructions on how the strategy should be used. In addition, Kendall et al. (1980) and Kestner and Borkowski (1979) have suggested that the following components are important in strategy instruction with young and/or mentally retarded children: (d) The instruction needs to include information that the strategy will be useful; (e) the student needs to be actively involved during strategy instruction; (f) the strategy instruction must be extensive; and (g) the strategy instruction should include experimenter prompts that are gradually faded out.

Several studies have suggested what components may be necessary for effective training in self-regulation. Training should include some means of motivating the student to engage in strategy usage. For example, studies by Ballard and Glynn (1975) and Friedling and O'Leary (1979) indicated that training in self-recording and verbal self-instruction was not effective until reinforcement was introduced. Kendall (1977) has suggested that students should be motivated to engage in verbal self-instruction by having them help determine which of their behaviors are prob-lematic. Also, the students should indicate a desire to change these behaviors. Kendall also suggests that for training in verbal self-instruction to be effective, the training must include a component in which the student learns to recognize when the strategy can be effectively implemented. The ability to recognize when the strategy should be implemented is as important as teaching the strategy itself. Finally, in teaching self-regulative strategies Kendall (1981) has emphasized the importance of a positive therapist-student relationship.

Although the foregoing researchers have mentioned these components as important in training self-regulative strategies, Cameron and Robinson (1980) have indicated that research has not really determined the components of verbal self-instruction that are most important. Training in verbal self-instruction could probably be streamlined if the effective components were identified.

In contrast to the above components, which have been hypothesized to be important for training in self-regulative strategies, the components that appear to be important for effective problem-solving instruction are quite different. This research indicates that effective problem-solving instruction should include (a) training in more than one problem-solving strategy; and (b) the presentation of numerous practice examples. Anthony and Hudgins (1978) found that better problem solvers had more problem-solving strategies than poorer problem solvers. They considered, therefore, that more than one problem-solving strategy must be taught if poor problem solvers are to improve their performance. Malin (1979) and Schoenfeld (1979a) have concluded that to be a good problem solver, one needs to learn a repertoire of problem-solving strategies. The student would also have to know or be able to discover the best strategy for a given situation. This statement also points to the importance of including a wide variety of problems in the training, so that the student would have exposure to different problems that would require different problem-solving strategies. Schoenfeld (1979a) has argued that this is important because heuristics are broadly stated strategies, and they therefore do not allow for unambiguous interpretation. Thus, the learner must practice applying the heuristic strategy in a number of different contexts with a wide variety of example problems.

In sum, it appears that the components that should be included in strategy instruction very much depend on the type of strategy being trained. Obviously, the number of components required will affect the extensiveness of training and the length of training necessary for instruction to be effective. Although some researchers have investigated length of training as a variable (Weinstein, Underwood, Wicker, & Cubberly, 1979), it seems more useful to phrase this question in terms of the components of training that are required. The training time will then vary as a function of both the inclusion of given components and their extensiveness.

How Dependent Is Cognitive Strategy Training on Adjunct Materials and How Dependent Should It Be?

Although the dependence of cognitive strategy training on adjunct materials is a matter that is related to the preceding question, we will treat it separately in our discussion. For illustrative purposes, we will use here the example of the keyword method. Research findings suggest that for students younger than the fifth or sixth grade, effective implementation of the keyword strategy requires elaborate adjunct materials in the form of a provided keyword and a picture in which the keyword and the word to be learned are shown to be interacting (Pressley, Levin, & Delaney, 1982). Such materials would be expensive to produce and would be difficult for the average teacher to create on his or her own. This dependence on adjunct materials is a potential stumbling block in classroom implementation of the keyword strategy with students before the fifth or sixth grade. On the other hand, with older students it appears that such materials would be needed only for initial demonstration of the keyword method. Subsequently, students would be able to generate the keywords and images for themselves. Thus, without the need for adjunct materials, the keyword method is a potentially inexpensive strategy to implement and use in the classroom.

In contrast, verbal-self instruction is an example of a type of strategy that might be trained and implemented in the classroom with few, if any, adjunct materials. Verbal self-instruction as designed by Meichenbaum and Goodman (1971) includes the following components: (a) questions concerning the nature and demands of the task; (b) answers to the questions in the form of cognitive rehearsal; (c) appropriate directive comments that specify steps for completing the task; (d) error correction instruction; (e) coping statements; and (f) self-reinforcement. Verbal self-instructions are typically taught with minimal adjunct materials by using a sequential modeling-fading procedure in which the trainer performs the task while verbalizing aloud and then the trainee performs the task while the trainer verbalizes. As the training progresses the trainee both performs the task and verbalizes, first overtly and then covertly, following the trainer's example. No further training or support materials are required once the student has learned the self-instructional strategy.

In sum, the answer to the first part of the question—"How dependent is cognitive strategy training on adjunct materials?"—obviously depends on the strategy to be trained. On the other hand, the answer to the second part of the question—"How dependent should it be?"—seems to be that the strategy will be implemented more easily in the classroom if the strategy instruction is less dependent on adjunct materials (see Chapter 9 in this volume for a contrasting point of view).

What Cognitive Strategies Should Be Taught and To Whom?

Important practical questions that must be answered before strategy instruction can be widely implemented in the classroom are what strategies should be taught and to whom should they be taught. For example, it must be determined what strategies would be most useful for primary students, upper elementary students, junior high students, secondary students, and college students. However, many apparent inconsistencies exist. For example, although it seems that elementary school students should be taught heuristic strategies because such strategies would improve their performance on tests of higher order mathematics achievement, it is not apparent that young students have the prerequisite basic skills and prior knowledge to benefit from training in problem-solving strategies. Furthermore, research on strategy instruction in problem solving suggests that younger children do not benefit from such instruction, possibly because they have not achieved the prerequisite cognitive-developmental level required to use such a strategy.

A similar incongruity exists with the keyword method. Research suggests that the keyword method is most beneficial for enhancing the vocabulary learning of children rather than of adolescents or adults, yet children younger than those in the fifth and sixth grades also require extensive external support. This external support takes the form of adjunct materials that may be expensive and difficult to produce. In addition, group-administered instruction in the keyword method has not been shown to be effective for students older than eighth grade. Thus, based on the research now available, one might conclude that in terms of minimal expense and ease of instruction, ability to implement instruction in a group situation, and potential effectiveness of the method, strategy instruction in the keyword method should be given to students from the fifth through the eighth grades. On the other hand, if one wanted to achieve maximal effects on learning as well as to provide students with a strategy that they could use throughout their school years, one might argue for training students as young as those in the first or second grade.

Although it seems that instruction in strategies to enhance reading comprehension (such as networking and schema training) would be potentially valuable for improving elementary and secondary students' reading achievement, classroom research on reading strategy instruction has been done primarily with college students (see Peterson & Swing, Note 1). One study done with high school students by Weinstein (1978) did not show dramatic effects of strategy instruction on prose comprehension. Thus, research is needed to determine whether instruction in such strategies would be useful for elementary as well as junior high and secondary school students.

Although an easy answer to the questions posed at the beginning of this section would be that all strategies could be taught to students at any given age, we suggest that such an approach would be neither appropriate nor necessarily effective. So far, we have only a few tentative answers to these difficult, yet important, questions for classroom practice. For example, Pressley, Heisel, McCormick, and Nakamura (1982) have summarized the following cases in which memory strategy instruction would have *minimal* effects: (a) with learners who are already using the strategy; (b) with learners who are already using a more efficient strategy than the one that is being trained; (c) situations in which Age $\times$ Strategy interactions or other Aptitude $\times$ Treatment interactions exist; and (d) with learners who fail to retrieve an available mediator that was generated at encoding. These guidelines might serve as a model for the kind of guidelines that might be developed in other areas of strategy instruction.

How Should Cognitive Strategy Instruction Be Implemented in the Classroom?

We suggest that the most practical and cost-effective way to implement cognitive strategy instruction would be to teach teachers to instruct students in cognitive strategies. Unfortunately, with the exception of a few studies, teachers have never been trained to implement cognitive strategy instruction in the classroom. (For a review, see Peterson & Swing, Note 1.) In the studies of instruction in self-regulative strategies, the training has been done by either an experimenter or a therapist. Similarly, in studies of instruction in the keyword method, the training has been done by experimenters. In recent training programs designed to improve reading comprehension, the training was implemented as part of an actual course on reading comprehension and the teacher was the experimenter. (See, e.g., Glover, Zimmer, Filbeck, & Plake, 1980; Dansereau, McDonald, Collins, Garland, Holley, Diekhoff, & Evans, 1979; Snowman, Krebs, & Lockhart, 1980; Weinstein et al., 1979). In three studies that taught strategies for learning from teaching, the experimenter served as the trainer in two of the studies, and the parents gave the instruction in one study. The latter study by Corno (1980) provides some information on whether persons other than researchers or psychologists can readily administer cognitive strategy instruction. The results of Corno's study suggested that many parents had great difficulty understanding the strategy instruction, and nearly 70% of the parents actually gave up before they completed giving the instruction to their children.

Strategy instruction research has not determined (a) whether teachers could be trained to provide the desired strategy instruction, and (b) whether the instruction provided by the teachers would then have facilitative effects on students' classroom learning. On the other hand, findings from research on teacher effectiveness suggest that teachers might be effectively and easily trained to administer such instruction. Results of this research indicate that with a minimal amount of instruction it is possible to train teachers to implement certain instructional procedures in the classroom. (See, e.g., Anderson, Evertson, & Brophy, 1979; Good & Grouws, 1979; Crawford, Gage, Corno, Stayrook, Mitman, Schunk, Stallings, Baskin, Harvey, Austin, Cronin, & Newman, Note 3). In these studies, training consisted of a 30- to 50-page training manual that teachers read and followed plus one or two short meetings with the teachers. Thus, we suggest that one fruitful area for future research would be to investigate the feasibility and effectiveness of training teachers to implement strategy instruction in the classroom.

Conclusions

At the beginning of this chapter we indicated that we would discuss the questions that need to be answered before cognitive strategy instruction can be implemented in the classroom. From our analyses, we conclude that none of these questions has been answered definitively and that more research will be needed in order to obtain definitive answers. A remaining question is, "Should attempts at classroom implementation of cognitive strategy instruction await these answers?" We would reply, "Definitely not!"

There are several reasons why researchers should attempt to implement cognitive strategy instruction in classrooms. First, many of the problems discussed in this chapter can *only* be solved by research in an actual classroom setting. For example, the question whether students can use cognitive strategies in real time during an ongoing classroom learning-teaching situation must be researched in a classroom situation.

Second, continued research on cognitive strategy instruction may result in answers to these questions that hold true in the laboratory situation but do not hold true in the classroom. This may occur because many variables that are controlled in the laboratory setting vary and interact in complex ways in the classroom. These "uncontrolled" variables may cause cognitive strategy instruction to lose effectiveness when it is transferred from the laboratory to the classroom. Such may be the case for instruction in the keyword method.

Third, classroom learning may be qualitatively different from laboratory learning. Before research on cognitive strategy proceeds much further, researchers need to examine the effects of cognitive strategy on real-life measures of classroom achievement.

Finally, and perhaps most important, many students are passing through our educational system without learning the basic skills in reading and mathematics. Other students are not achieving at high levels in these areas. Strategies to enhance vocabulary learning, reading comprehension, and mathematical problem solving have potential for directly improving students' achievement in reading and mathematics. Thus, from an educational standpoint, research on classroom implementation of cognitive strategy instruction should be given high priority.

Acknowledgments. Work on this chapter was funded by the Wisconsin Center for Education Research, which is supported in part by a grant from the National Institute of Education (Grant No. NIE-G-81-009). The opinions expressed in this chapter do not necessarily reflect the position, policy, or endorsement of the National Institute of Education.

Reference Notes

1. Peterson, P. L., & Swing, S. R. *Classroom implementation of cognitive strategy instruction.* Unpublished manuscript, University of Wisconsin-Madison, July 1982.
2. Schneider, W. *Developmental trends in the metamemory-memory behavior relationship: An integrative review.* Unpublished manuscript, Stanford University, 1982.
3. Crawford, J., Gage, N. L., Corno, L., Stayrook, N., Mitman, A., Schunk, D., Stallings, J., Baskin, E., Harvey, P., Austin, D., Cronin, D., & Newman, R. *An experiment on teacher effectiveness and parent-assisted instruction in the third-grade* (3 vols.). Stanford, CA: Center for Educational Research, 1978.

References

Allen, G. Treatment of test anxiety by group administered relaxation, self administered relaxation, and study counseling. *Behavior Therapy*, 1973, *4*, 349–360.

Anderson, L., Evertson, C., & Brophy, J. An experimental study of effective teaching in first-grade reading groups. *The Elementary School Journal*, 1979, *79*, 193–223.

Andre, M. E., & Anderson, T. H. The development and evaluation of a self-questioning study technique. *Reading Research Quarterly*, 1979, *14*, 605–623.

Anthony, B., & Hudgins, B. B. Problem-solving processes of fifth-grade arithmetic pupils. *Journal of Educational Research*, 1978, *72*, 63–67.

Baker, L., & Brown, A. L. Metacognitive skills in reading. In P. D. Pearson (Ed.), *Handbook of reading research*. New York: Longman, 1982.

Ballard, K. D., & Glynn, T. Behavioral self-management in story writing with elementary school children. *Journal of Applied Behavior Analysis*, 1975, *8*, 387–398.

Barclay, C. R. The executive control of mnemonic activity. *Journal of Experimental Child Psychology*, 1979, *27*, 262–276.

Bellezza, F. S. Mnemonic-device instruction with adults. In M. Pressley & J. R. Levin (Eds.), *Cognitive strategy research: Psychological foundations*. New York: Springer-Verlag, 1983.

Borkowski, J. G., & Büchel, F. P. Learning and memory strategies in the mentally retarded. In M. Pressley & J. R. Levin (Eds.), *Cognitive strategy research: Psychological foundations*. New York: Springer-Verlag, 1983.

Borkowski, J. G., & Cavanaugh, J. C. Maintenance and generalization of skills and strategies by the retarded. In N. R. Ellis (Ed.), *Handbook of mental deficiency* (2nd ed.). Hillsdale, NJ: Erlbaum, 1979.

Borkowski, J. G., Levers, S., & Gruenenfelder, T. M. Transfer of mediational strategies in children: The role of activity and awareness during strategy acquisition. *Child Development*, 1976, *47*, 779–786.

Borkowski, J. G., Reid, M. K., & Kurtz, B. E. Metacognition and retardation: Paradigmatic, theoretical, and applied perspectives. In R. Sperber, C. McCauley, & P. Brooks (Eds.), *Learning and cognition in the mentally retarded*. Baltimore: University Park Press, in press.

Bray, N. W., Justice, E. M., Ferguson, R. P., & Simon, D. L. Developmental changes in the effects of instructions on production-deficient children. *Child Development*, 1977, *48*, 1019–1026.

Brown, A. L. Knowing when, where, and how to remember: A problem of metacognition. In R. Glaser (Ed.), *Advances in instructional psychology* (Vol. 1). Hillsdale, NJ: Erlbaum, 1978.

Brown, A. L., & Barclay, C. R. The effects of training specific mnemonics on the metamnemonic efficiency of retarded children. *Child Development*, 1976, *47*, 71–80.

Brown, A. L., & Campione, J. C. Training strategic study time apportionment in educable retarded children. *Intelligence*, 1977, *1*, 94–107.

Brown, A. L., Campione, J. C., & Barclay, C. R. Training self-checking routines for estimating test readiness: Generalization from list learning to prose recall. *Child Development*, 1979, *50*, 501–512.

Brown, A. L., Campione, J. C., & Murphy, M. D. Maintenance and generalization of trained metamnemonic awareness by educable retarded children. *Journal of Experimental Child Psychology,* 1977, *24,* 191–211.

Burgio, L. D., Whitman, T. L., & Johnson, M. R. A self-instructional package for increasing attending behavior in educable mentally retarded children. *Journal of Applied Behavior Analysis,* 1980, *13,* 443–459.

Butterfield, E. C., & Belmont, J. M. Assessing and improving the cognitive functions of mentally retarded people. In I. Bialer & M. Sternlicht (Eds.), *The psychology of mental retardation: Issues and approaches.* New York: Psychological Dimensions, 1977.

Cameron, M. I., & Robinson, V. M. Effects of cognitive training on academic and on-task behavior of hyperactive children. *Journal of Abnormal Child Psychology,* 1980, *8,* 405–419.

Case, R. A developmentally based theory and technology of instruction. *Review of Educational Research,* 1978, *48,* 439–463.

Corno, L. Individual and class level effects of parent-assisted instruction in classroom memory support strategies. *Journal of Educational Psychology,* 1980, *72,* 278–292.

Dansereau, D. F., McDonald, E. A., Collins, K. W., Garland, J., Holley, C. D., Diekhoff, G. M., & Evans, S. H. Evaluation of a learning strategy system. In H. F. O'Neil (Ed.), *Cognitive and affective learning strategies.* New York: Academic Press, 1979.

Dempster, F. N. Memory span: Sources of individual and developmental differences. *Psychological Bulletin,* 1981, *89,* 63–100.

Denney, D. R. Self-control approaches to the treatment of test anxiety. In I. G. Sarason (Ed.), *Test anxiety: Theory, research, and applications.* Hillsdale, NJ: Erlbaum, 1980.

Engle, R. W., Nagle, R. J., & Dick, M. Maintenance and generalization of a semantic rehearsal strategy in educable mentally retarded children. *Journal of Experimental Child Psychology,* 1980, *30,* 438–454.

Flavell, J. H. Developmental studies of mediated memory. In H. W. Reese & L. P. Lipsitt (Eds.), *Advances in child development and behavior* (Vol. 5). New York: Academic Press, 1970.

Friedling, C., & O'Leary, S. G. Effects of self-instructional training on second- and third-grade hyperactive children: A failure to replicate. *Journal of Applied Behavior Analysis,* 1979, *12,* 211–219.

Gagne, R. M. Learnable aspects of problem solving. *Educational Psychologist,* 1980, *15,* 84–92.

Glover, J. A., Zimmer, J. W., Filbeck, R. W., & Plake, B. S. Effects of training students to identify the semantic base of prose materials. *Journal of Applied Behavior Analysis,* 1980, *13,* 655–667.

Good, T., & Grouws, D. The Missouri mathematics effectiveness project: Experimental study in fourth-grade classrooms. *Journal of Educational Psychology,* 1979, *71,* 335–362.

Higa, W. *Self-instructional versus direct training in modifying children's impulsive behavior.* Unpublished doctoral dissertation, University of Hawaii, 1973.

Holley, C. D., Dansereau, D. F., McDonald, B. A., Garland, J. C., & Collins, K. W. Evaluation of a hierarchical mapping technique as an aid to prose processing. *Contemporary Educational Psychology,* 1979, *4,* 227–237.

Jones, B. F., & Hall, J. W. School applications of the mnemonic keyword method as a study strategy by eighth-graders. *Journal of Educational Psychology,* 1982, *74,* 230–237.

Kail, R., & Bisanz, J. Information processing and cognitive development. In H. W. Reese & L. P. Lipsitt (Eds.), *Advances in child development and behavior* (Vol. 17). New York: Academic Press, in press.

Kantowski, M. G. Problem solving. In E. Fennema (Ed.), *Mathematics education research: Implications for the 80's.* Alexandria, VA: Association for Supervision and Curriculum Development, 1981.

Kantowski, M. G. Processes involved in mathematical problem solving. *Journal for Research in Mathematics Education,* 1977, *8,* 163–180.

Kendall, C. R., Borkowski, J. G., & Cavanaugh, J. C. Metamemory and the transfer of an interrogative strategy by EMR children. *Intelligence,* 1980, *4,* 255–270.

Kendall, P. C. On the efficacious use of verbal self-instructional procedures with children. *Cognitive Therapy and Research,* 1977, *1,* 331–341.

Kendall, P. C. Cognitive-behavioral interventions with children. In B. Lahey & A. Kazdin (Eds.), *Advances in child clinical psychology* (Vol. 4). New York: Plenum Press, 1981.

Kendall, P. C., & Zupan, B. A. Individual versus group application of cognitive-behavioral self-control procedures with children. *Behavior Therapy,* 1981, *12,* 344–359.

Kestner, J., & Borkowski, J. G. Children's maintenance and generalization of an interrogative learning strategy. *Child Development,* 1979, *50,* 485–494.

Levin, J. R., Pressley, M., McCormick, C. B., Miller, G. E., & Shriberg, L. K. Assessing the classroom potential of the keyword method. *Journal of Educational Psychology,* 1979, *71,* 583–594.

Malin, J. T. Strategies in mathematical problem solving. *Journal of Educational Research,* 1979, *73,* 101–108.

Mayer, R. E. Elaboration techniques that increase the meaningfulness of technical text: An experimental test of the learning strategy hypothesis. *Journal of Educational Psychology,* 1980, *72,* 770–784.

McGivern, J. E., & Levin, J. R. The keyword method of vocabulary learning: An interaction with vocabulary knowledge. *Contemporary Educational Psychology,* 1983, *8,* 46–54.

McLaughlin, T. F. Self-control in the classroom. *Review of Educational Research,* 1976, *46,* 631–663.

Meichenbaum, D., & Goodman, J. Training impulsive children to talk to themselves: A means of developing self-control. *Journal of Abnormal Psychology,* 1971, *77,* 115–126.

Paris, S. G., Newman, R. S., & McVey, K. A. Learning the functional significance of mnemonic actions: A microgenetic study of strategy acquisition. *Journal of Experimental Child Psychology,* in press.

Peterson, P. L., Swing, S. R., Braverman, M. T., & Buss, R. Students' aptitudes and their reports of cognitive processes during direct instruction. *Journal of Educational Psychology,* 1982, *74,* 535–547.

Polya, G. *How to solve it.* New York: Doubleday, 1957.

Pressley, M. G., Heisel, B. E., McCormick, C. B., & Nakamura, G. V. Memory strategy instruction with children. In C. J. Brainerd & M. Pressley (Eds.), *Verbal processes in children.* New York: Springer-Verlag, 1982.

Pressley, M. G., & Levin, J. R. Task parameters affecting the efficacy of a visual imagery learning strategy in younger and older children. *Journal of Experimental Child Psychology,* 1977, *24,* 53–59.

Pressley, M., Levin, J. R., & Bryant, S. L. Memory strategy instruction during adolescence: When is explicit instruction needed? In M. Pressley & J. R. Levin (Eds.), *Cognitive strategy research: Psychological foundations.* New York: Springer-Verlag, 1983.

Pressley, M. G., Levin, J. R., & Delaney, H. D. The mnemonic keyword. *Review of Educational Research,* 1982, *52,* 61–91.

Pressley, M., Reynolds, W. M., Stark, K. D., & Gettinger, M. Cognitive strategy training and children's self-control. In M. Pressley & J. R. Levin (Eds.) *Cognitive strategy research: Psychological foundations.* New York: Springer-Verlag, 1983.

Reynolds, W. M., & Stark, D. D. Cognitive behavior modification: The clinical application of cognitive strategies. In M. Pressley & J. R. Levin (Eds.), *Cognitive strategy research: Psychological foundations.* New York: Springer-Verlag, 1983.

Roberts, P. Memory strategy instruction with the elderly: What *should* memory training be the training of? In M. Pressley & J. R. Levin (Eds.), *Cognitive strategy research: Psychological foundations.* New York: Springer-Verlag, 1983.

Robin, A. L., Armel, S., & O'Leary, K. D. The effects of self-instruction on writing deficiencies. *Behavior Therapy,* 1975, *6,* 178–187.

Schoenfeld, A. H. Can heuristics be taught? In J. Lockhead & J. Clement (Eds.), *Cognitive process instruction: Research on teaching thinking skills.* Philadelphia: Franklin Institute Press, 1979. (a)

Schoenfeld, A. H. Explicit heuristic training as a variable in problem-solving performance. *Journal for Research in Mathematics Education,* 1979, *10,* 173–187. (b)

Simon, H. A. Problem solving and education. In D. Tuma & F. Reif (Eds.), *Problem solving and education: Issues in teaching and research.* Hillsdale, NJ: Erlbaum, 1980.

Snow, R. E. Learning and individual differences. In L. S. Shulman (Ed.), *Review of research in education* (Vol. 4). Itasca, IL: F. E. Peacock, 1977.

Snowman, J., Krebs, E. W., & Lockhart, L. Improving recall of information from prose in high-risk students through learning strategy training. *Journal of Instructional Psychology,* 1980, *7,* 35–40.

Tryon, G. S. The measurement and treatment of test anxiety. *Review of Educational Research,* 1980, *50,* 343–372.

Weinstein, C. E. Elaboration skills as a learning strategy. In H. F. O'Neil (Ed.), *Learning strategies.* New York: Academic Press, 1978.

Weinstein, C. E., Underwood, V. L., Wicker, F. W., & Cubberly, W. E. Cognitive learning strategies: Verbal and imaginal elaboration. In H. F. O'Neil & C. D. Spielberger (Eds.), *Cognitive and affective learning strategies.* New York: Academic Press, 1979.

Winne, P. H., & Marx, R. W. Matching students' cognitive responses to teaching skills. *Journal of Educational Psychology,* 1980, *72,* 257–264.

Author Index

Page numbers set in italic type refer to pages on which complete reference information appears.

Subject Index

Page numbers set in roman type refer to *Cognitive Strategy Research: Psychological Foundation;* page numbers set in italic type refer to *Cognitive Strategy Research: Educational Applications*.

Cognitive Strategy Research
Psychological Foundations
(Companion volume to Cognitive Strategy Research: Educational Applications)

Contents